ACCLAIM FOR
Tova Mordechai's
To Play With Fire

To Play With Fire is powerfully relevant to all of us because it is the story of our lives. Tova Mordechai's life odyssey with its bizarre twists and turns—Christian artist, composer and preacher, born to an evangelist father and an Egyptian Jewish mother—amplifies the essence of our own strange journey, through darkness and light, chaos and order.
—Simon Jacobson, author of *Toward A Meaningful Life*

The spiritual struggle documented in *To Play With Fire* is an unbelievable testimonial to the triumph of a Jewish soul over unspeakable odds.
—Basha Majerczyk, Algemeiner Journal

To Play With Fire vividly describes the author's painful ordeal in her transition from Christian pietist to Jewish observer. Never does Tova Mordechai preach. Candidly, with depth and a good deal of humor, she describes the conflicts…which ultimately led to her breaking away from the shocking, repressive routine within the college. *To Play With Fire* is a superb behind-the-scenes account of this belief…. This book is highly recommended.
—Simcha Mandel, Country Yossi Magazine

The saga of a Jewish soul is always a good read, and seldom is a *neshama* as articulate as in this book. Tova's story is compelling, her prose captivating—her heart very much in evidence. *To Play With Fire* is a great book.
—Rabbi Manis Friedman, author of *Why Doesn't Anyone Blush Anymore?*

TO PLAY WITH FIRE

TO PLAY WITH FIRE
ONE WOMAN'S REMARKABLE ODYSSEY

Tova Mordechai

Dear Cherya,
Enjy the beauty of
being Jewish,

Nov. 2010

URIM PUBLICATIONS
New York · Jerusalem

DEDICATED TO MY GRANDFATHER
RAPHAEL MORDO *A"H*

AND TO MY UNCLE
CHAIM SHMUEL MORDO *A"H*

❧ INTRODUCTION ❧

ALEXANDRIA, Egypt, had once been a great metropolis and spiritual center of the Jews of the Diaspora after the destruction of Jerusalem by the Babylonians brought Jewish exiles, together with the Prophet Jeremiah, to the city. The Jewish community, although diminished in number, continued to thrive through centuries of Christian and Arab oppression, providing a haven and economic opportunities for Jewish refugees fleeing worse persecution in other lands.

At the turn of the twentieth century, Alexandria was a high-spirited, free-living city with a multi-cultural flavor. The Jews were a minority and were dispersed throughout several European communities. Although they had little to do with the Arabs, many of the Orthodox Jews were eventually swallowed up by the city's cosmopolitan lifestyle and the variety of influences available there. My mother was one of the casualties.

She had a proud lineage; her family, together with thousands of other Jewish families in 1492, had abandoned their beloved Spain forever in order to remain true to their *Judezmo* and not be baptized as the King had commanded. After generations of wandering they eventually settled on the western isles of Greece.

Since the Fourth Crusade, the western isles of Greece have been ruled by Italians. Although the Jews of these islands had been living there long before, they adopted the language of their Italian rulers. Later, they were joined by Jews who had been expelled from southern Italy in the 1500s, and thus the Jewish communities of western Greece became Italian in their outward expressions. Just like their Jewish brethren in Italy, they were forced by the authorities to live in Ghettos, to wear a Jewish Star, and were forbidden to enter professions and large-scale commerce. As a result, many of them became peddlers and particularly tinsmiths. Two hundred years ago, my family joined these Jews of Greece, choosing to settle on the islands of Zante and Corfu.

A blood libel on the island of Corfu in 1890 initiated a terrible wave of murderous anti-Jewish riots all over Greece, forcing masses of Jews to flee once again.

My grandfather, Raphael Mordo, an orphan at the age of twelve, arrived in Alexandria where he settled with his uncle's family. At that time, the family was fully observant, keeping *Shabbat*, praying three times daily, and maintaining a kosher home. But Alexandria had no *yeshivos*, and although Raphael was secularly well-educated and fluent in nine languages, his Jewish knowledge was very limited. He became a skilled typesetter in Arabic for a prestigious British-owned newspaper, but was forever being used and cheated. He never asserted himself, and despite his brilliance, never moved up in life; thus his family remained dirt poor, taking turns eating from broken soup bowls at supper.

My grandmother Antoinette had been born in Alexandria to a Rumanian Jewish immigrant who had married a daughter of the Italian-speaking deMordo family. Quite unlike her subdued husband, she was a lively, boisterous woman. In the years before her marriage, she had gone abroad to England to serve as governess for a wealthy Jewish family in Surrey. While there, she accepted free lodging from the Y.W.C.A. and attended Christian social gatherings and occasional religious meetings. Although she knew Judaism frowned upon such behavior, she reasoned that hers was based only on social motives.

Upon her return to Alexandria she married Raphael Mordo, even though he was much more religiously observant. She bore him two children, my mother and Uncle Solomon, followed by seven children who died in their infancy. Raphael vowed to fast every Monday and Thursday if a child would live, and when my Uncle Sammy was born, he fulfilled his promise.

My grandfather loved children. On *Shabbat* day, he would collect his sons and daughter around him and tell them stories from the Talmud, trying to inspire their young hearts with a love for God and the Jewish people. Each morning before dawn, he would get them out of bed to say *Shema* at the window as the sun rose. It was said of him that he never opened his mouth except to pray and to read the Psalms. Despite their desperate poverty, he chose never to forsake the God of his youth.

My grandmother had a more difficult time maintaining tradition. In order to help make ends meet, she taught English in St. Andrew's Church of Scotland's Mission School where the headmaster agreed to take in her sons with reduced tuition fees.

Notwithstanding her husband's weak protest, she enrolled them in the school, insisting that it was for purely academic reasons, and that their religious life would in no way be effected. She sent her daughter to a French speaking Jewish Community School called "Alliance."

Gradually my grandmother's Jewish life changed. Since kosher meat was so expensive, and the butcher shop such a long walk from home, she started buying the cheaper non-kosher meat. *Shabbat* observance in her home dwindled until it was virtually non-existent.

My grandparents sank deeper into despair as the Second World War broke out. Like many other families in Alexandria, they opened their home to the young servicemen from abroad who were fighting the Nazis. Among these were many clean-living Christian boys who would congregate in the house to socialize as well as to sing and pray. In an effort to return the hospitality, they invited my grandmother to visit their mission, and it wasn't long before she and her daughter Sara readily announced their acceptance of Christianity. Antoinette hardly cared what her husband would think. He in turn recited *kaddish* in the synagogue for the lost souls of his wife and daughter, but found himself at a loss as to how to restore his family back to their Jewishness.

In 1944, at the Mission Hall, my mother met my father, an artillery sergeant in the British Eighth Army. He was a sweet, born again Christian boy named James Marlow, who soon joined the crowd of young men frequenting the Mordo home. He fell in love with my mother in short order, and they became engaged. When he left North Africa with his military unit to continue fighting in Europe, James told Sara that he would send for her as soon as he could save enough money and the war would be over, and two years later he fulfilled his promise.

My mother was ecstatic; her father was panic-stricken. Even the foreign embassy tried to warn her of the potential obstacles that stood in her way because of her father's Greek nationality. If she arrived in England and James Marlow refused to marry her, she would have to return to Greece rather than Egypt and would not be able to see her family until the wartime restrictions ended. As the war in Greece continued well past 1945, there was no telling when this might take place; but nothing could persuade her to change her mind. Without the blessing of her father, she boarded the ship and set sail for England.

My grandparents made plans to move to Israel, but Antoinette died soon afterward. With the bulk of the Alexandrian Jewish community, Raphael and his youngest son, Sammy, were among the first wave of immigrants from Egypt to Israel, while in far-off Britain, his daughter was only beginning to discover just how far away she was from her home, her people—and her heritage.

Our souls have escaped as a bird from a fowler's cage.

Psalms 124:7

❧ ONE ❧

WITH four little ones running around, and less than a year between each of them, living a mile away from the road and three miles from the nearest shop, my mother inwardly vowed she did not want any more children. My father, then a farm hand and a preacher in his spare time, brought in barely enough money to feed his growing family. Both of my parents worked very hard. Many times my mother would go out into the fields when the potato pickers had long since wended their way home, trying to find a few orphaned potatoes to feed her family. The farmer kindly gave them milk free of charge, and somehow they managed to raise strong, healthy children, but those years took their toll on my mother.

My father eventually got a bookkeeping job in an engineering firm in the small town of Greenborough, continuing to preach on the side. The family moved into low-income housing which cost my father two hundred and fifty pounds sterling with a mortgage repayment of one pound per week with a thirty pound deposit. We had one room downstairs and a tiny kitchen with no hot water. A creaking, wooden spiral staircase led up to two tiny bedrooms. Baths had to be taken in the public town bath-houses and toilets were shared across a large, muddy yard by all the residents. This slum neighborhood was no friend to a Jewish lady or her family. No matter that she was fully baptized into the Christian faith— or that her husband was a pure Anglo-Saxon "man of the cloth"—or that her children were born and raised in England. She was a wog, a dirty

Jew, and the family bore the brunt of medieval anti-Semitism. England was still in ruins from the war with Germany, but the British masses continued to applaud Hitler for his fine work with the Jews.

When my mother realized five years later that she was going to have another child, she wept bitterly, protesting that she did not want to start all over again, and moreover, the neighbors were already complaining about the oversized brood. My father continually teased her and reassured her at the same time that everything was going to be wonderful. "Just one thing, Sally," he insisted, "make sure it's a boy. We will call him Andrew, and he will be the evangelist this generation is looking for."

As the months ticked by, my father's teasing increased until my mother could stand it no longer. Desperately she ran to her friend Jane Webster for advice. Jane was married to my father's preaching partner and was the only person my mother could trust with such a confidential matter.

"Jane, Jane! I don't know what to do. Jeem want a boy, but I don't know what is inside. Only God know. What weel I do?" she exclaimed anxiously in her heavy Italian accent.

Jane tried numerous times to console her friend, assuring her that "Jeem" was only teasing, but nevertheless my mother's tension mounted steadily, until the morning when she staggered to a nearby telephone to call my father at work.

"Jeem, come queekly—the baby is coming!"

Without delay, my father rushed home to take her to the hospital, and shortly afterward his dreams were shattered. The evangelist named Andrew that he had prayed for was not a boy after all, but a squawking, chubby little girl for whom no one had a name. All his hopes were dashed.

Five years earlier, when my sister had been born, my mother very much wanted to name her Tonica after her own mother, who had passed away not long before. However, my father had insisted on the name Margaret, and after a lengthy squabble, he had gotten his way.

With hopes of Andrew now gone, my mother was very firm. "This one will be Tonica," she declared, and would not move from her decision.

And so I became Tonica Marlow, a tiny bundle of Jewish life in a pastor's home; but the irony was that my father's hopes were not totally disappointed, for his Jewish daughter would one day head down the very path he had laid out for the son he could not have.

❧

It was just two months later that tragedy struck.

My mother was busy seeing to dinner and numerous other jobs around the house while my six-year-old brother David pestered her. Obviously he had been deep in thought.

"Mummy, how do you go to heaven?" he questioned. "Do you go up in an aeroplane?"

"No, my love," my mother replied. "When you are bigger, you will understand."

"But Mummy, I want to know now—please tell me," he insisted.

My mother tried as best she could to explain that when you die, only your body stays in the ground, but the "real" you—the part that makes you think, laugh and speak—goes to heaven. "Now go out and play while I feed the baby," she said mechanically, "but don't go far. Deener is almost ready."

Obediently, David sat on the front doorstep singing his favorite hymn, "Abiding in Thee" until some boys from down the street came by and invited him to go fishing with them in the canal. Forgetting my mother's warning, he accompanied them to the canal, a favorite haunt which was about a ten-minute walk from the house. The boys had no nets. Their method of fishing was to kneel down on the canal bank and try to catch fish with their hands.

About fifteen minutes later, there was a loud knocking on the door of our home.

"Missus, missus, your David's fallen into the canal," chorused a group of frightened, anxious children.

"Don't be stupid," replied my mother angrily. "He was here just a minute ago. Go away and stop your silly lies." She was well used to their cruel pranks.

"No, no, missus! It's really true—go quickly!"

Seeing their grief-stricken faces, my mother became almost hysterical. She sent my brother Philip immediately to see what had happened and confirm if it were really true, and then called to my father, who was upstairs resting on his lunch break.

"Jeem, Jeem, *queekly*!" she screamed. "Take the bike and go to the canal. See about David—they say he fall into the water!"

Things happened speedily. My brother arrived first at the canal and found the place deserted except for a man passing by with his dog.

"Mister, my brother has fallen into the water," Philip cried.

"Oh, don't be silly, son," the irritated man replied and turned to go on his way.

However, he noticed that his dog was eager to go into the water, and so he finally gave Philip the benefit of the doubt and went down to investigate. Taking a stick, he dunked it into the canal and hooked my brother out on his first attempt. Evidently, David's galoshes had filled with water and weighted him to the bottom. His friends had panicked, and instead of trying to pull him out there and then, they ran home to my mother. By the time my father arrived, his little six-year-old boy was lying on the bank of the canal, his mission in life already over.

The headmistress of David's school later told my parents that they had always called my brother "David the Comforter," for whenever any of the children cried, no matter who it was, and no matter how old, he would run and put his arms around them in consolation. Years later, whenever my parents spoke of David, they confessed that they knew they shouldn't have favored any one of their children above the others, but there had been something special about him.

My mother in particular suffered such shock over David's death that she lost her memory to a great extent, sometimes even forgetting that she had a baby. Many times, she would take me shopping in the morning, and it wasn't until my elder brother returned home from school at four-thirty in the afternoon that my presence was missed.

"Mummy, where is the baby?" Philip would inquire.

"Eeee! I forgot! Philip, my love, go around the town and look for her. Queekly, my love, before Daddy come home."

And so my brother, only eight years old himself, would trek around the neighborhood looking for the baby carriage and bring it home. On more than one occasion, the entire family would be halfway down the road in the car before anyone realized that I was not there, and sometimes my mother would even forget to feed me.

I have one distinct memory of being left in a store when I was three. It was a huge store that sold knick-knacks, and there was a big old-fashioned rocking horse near the front counter for children to play on while their mothers shopped. Nearby was a mirror which reflected the counter, and I remember looking in the mirror while I was sitting on the horse and seeing my mother talking to the cashier; but the next time I looked, she wasn't there. I climbed down and searched all around but couldn't find her, so I went back to the rocking horse and waited. Even though I was so tiny, I did not cry; I think I had just become accustomed to being left. Eventually my two older sisters came to get me, their faces announcing their annoyance at having to round me up once again.

This went on for several years until my mother gradually came back to herself, but even then the pressures of home and family were sometimes too great for her. We were often so naughty that my mother would tease us and say she was going to run away. She would put on her coat, go down to the shop at the end of the road, and stay there for a long time while we would cry for her to come home again.

By then we had moved to a better neighborhood, and were living in a nicer house, with gardens at the front and back; but it was not long before my parents faced another trial. I was four years old when my father contracted tuberculosis, and he was away in hospital and convalescent homes for the next year and a half.

My mother worked two jobs during that time to keep the family going. She was an expert dressmaker, having been trained as a teenager at a French designing school in Alexandria, which would provide all the dresses and gowns for the Queen and the ladies of the court. Now in England, she was employed by the most exclusive dress company in Greenborough. When she was not at the shop, she did handwork for a tent manufacturing company and often brought work home at night. She was very skilled, but because of her poor English was never able to progress beyond factory-level employment.

Because of my parents' strenuous schedules, I was a latchkey child from the time I was six years old. I was always the first one home in the afternoon, and used to ride my bike to the bus stop every evening to meet my mother after her work, and help her carry home her packages and shopping. Even after my father recovered and went back to his job in the engineering firm, he was rarely at home. He was always running to church or preparing his sermons, and in his spare time, he kept a garden, from which came all of our fruits and vegetables. My parents arose at five-thirty each morning and never wasted a minute. Leisure was unknown to them, nevertheless hours and hours of community service managed to fit into their schedules each week.

The truth is that I did not have much time to think about whether I was lonely or not, because there was always church.

My earliest memories are of Sunday school. Even from the time I was three, I was always fighting for a front-row seat, always trying to sing the very loudest, and constantly full—to overflowing—with boisterous zeal for Jesus, my "savior and friend." The stories, the singing, the pictures to color—I loved them all.

But who *was* this person who was my savior? As I sat back in my seat and dangled my legs contentedly beneath me, I would listen to my father telling over and over again of how this "special person" wanted to come into my heart and take away all the bad things inside and make me good, and that one day very soon he would come back to earth and take all the good boys and girls with him. The naughty, wicked people would be left behind to a horrible, lonely life, full of terror and pain. But if I accepted Jesus, he would "clean my heart from sin" and give me peace and happiness within. My father always explained that I would know Jesus had entered my heart because I would have a "warm feeling" inside.

I always wanted to be a good girl, and I would watch my father with pride. This was my Daddy telling all these boys and girls such wonderful things. How nice and clever he was! I wanted the whole world to know he was mine and that I belonged to him.

I knew what always came after that speech. I had heard him talk this way many times before. He was building up to an altar call.

"Now I want everyone to bow their heads," he would say.

"Everyone. Forget about the person sitting next to you and think about what I have just said. Remember it is Jesus' blood that can make your heart clean, and that he died to shed that blood for you, because he loves you and wants to come close to you and be your friend."

Some of the older children at the back would giggle in embarrassment. The little ones shuffled around on their seats, confused at what was happening.

My father would start to sing quietly and encourage us all to join him.

Into my heart, into my heart,
Come into my heart today.
Come in today, come in to stay,
Come into my heart!

I would screw up my eyes tightly, bury my head in my chubby little hands, and sing with the simplicity of an infant. I wanted it to happen to me; with all my heart I wanted it to happen. "Please, Jesus, please come into my heart today," I anxiously and silently pleaded, waiting for the "warm feeling" to enter me.

My father would begin to speak again. "All those boys and girls who would like to ask Jesus to come into their lives today should come to the front now," he would say gently.

I'd carefully wriggle off my seat and stand at the front of the church with numerous other children and wait for my father to put his hands on my head and pray for me. One or two tears sometimes trickled slowly down my face, and then I would return to my seat.

Five minutes later, Bible school would be over. "We are not going to have classes today. We are going to take the lovely presence of our savior home with us," my father would announce.

We would jump off our seats and run around, chasing and calling to one other. What presence? Had Daddy said something about a lovely presence? In a moment, the solemn peacefulness was all gone.

My father usually drove the children to their homes in the minibus, and I would wait with my elder brother and sisters until he returned for us. Sitting contentedly on the steps, full of the blissful peace of Sunday school, I would wonder innocently what was for dinner and if my mother had baked any cookies or cakes.

And so I grew up, enveloped by enchanting visions of a joyful heaven, waiting always for the promised "warmth" to enter me: praying, talking and living with the presence of a savior whom I believed to be my friend, and whose faithfulness I never for one moment doubted.

Early on, we were trained in the "ABC's" of spiritual growth and eagerly looked forward to attaining each stage. First we had to repent of the sin we were born with, until we were worthy of being "saved"; then we would be baptized, and our sinful hearts would be washed away; and finally we would be pure enough for Jesus' spirit to enter us and "fill" our lives permanently. This experience of "being filled" was a major milestone in one's spiritual achievement, for it meant that Jesus would never again leave the heart.

There was always a great pressure, even on children, to be "filled with the spirit," and it rested solely on the individual's power of belief. I had been up to the altar many times as a youngster, but I had no idea what being filled was supposed to feel like, and although I longed for it, I was never quite sure it had actually happened to me.

When I was eight, I once came to the altar call and knelt down; and to tell the truth, I think I must have fallen asleep, because I was still there with my head down after the others had returned to their places. My brother Philip came up and knelt down beside me, put his arm around me, and whispered softly, "Okay—now speak in tongues." "Tongues" was the unintelligible babbling that signified that a person had been filled and had received communication from above. I could not do this properly, but Philip assured me anyway that I was filled, and he joyfully went around announcing this landmark in my life to everyone in church.

From that time on, I told people I was filled, although I was never quite sure about it, and for a young child, this kind of doubt is excruciating. But for the most part, I passed my early youth in a rosy mist of belief, safe from the blandishments of the outside world, secure in the happy innocence of Jesus' friendship.

Church was the central feature of our household. There were services at least five times a week, including Bible school; often, on Saturday afternoons, my father would take us to help put the chapel in order, as there was no regular cleaning staff. We would dust the seats, sweep the floor, put fresh flowers on the windowsills, and do any other necessary tidying-up. My father gave constantly to the church, never taking a penny even for his preaching, and he taught us that it was our special privilege to do anything we could to keep the church beautiful and clean. I trusted him implicitly.

There was an enormous security in a life of such belief, in a focus on things that were truly important, and I was always tremendously proud of my father's sincerity. And yet the fear inspired by many of the Church teachings left its imprint as well.

When I was small I would often not go to the evening services. Before everyone left, I would be put to bed and left alone in the house. I went through a stage where I frequently woke up to find the whole house empty, and I was always terribly afraid. On one such night, when I was about seven, I awoke to the eerie stillness of the midnight hours. The curtains of the bedroom were not drawn, and the street lamps flickered against the ominous inky blackness of the sky. The headlights of an occasional passing car cast grotesque shapes onto the ceiling and sent a cold shiver running through me.

Cautiously, I looked into the bottom bunk to see if my sister was there. No; her bed was still neatly made. I looked over to my elder sister's bed, but she was not there either. With my heart now thumping rapidly, I jumped down from the bunk and ran to my parents' room, then into my brother's room. No one was there. Anxiously I sped to the front window and peeped out. The car was not in the drive.

By this time, our sheepdog was awake and padding around after me, feeling my terror. I scooted downstairs and looked at the clock on the mantelpiece in the living room. One-twenty. My hands fell limply to my sides and my heart sank. I couldn't even cry; I knew it was hopeless. Silently and slowly I trudged back upstairs, with Poundy close behind.

On the top landing I hugged my furry friend. I knew what had happened. Jesus had come back and taken away the whole family, but I was so bad that he had left me behind. I should have repented more. I had only myself to blame. "Poundy, there's only you and me now," I whispered. He licked my hand, his doleful eyes staring into mine. He understood. He would take care of me.

Of course Jesus hadn't come, and it was just an exceptionally long service which had kept the family out. When my parents finally came home, I was in such a state that it took my mother a long time to calm me down. To compensate, she bought me a pair of lemon colored pajamas with fairies printed on them.

"They are angels and will keep you safe," she informed me as she dressed me for bed. This was comforting, because it sounded just like one of the lines from my evening prayer: "May angels guard us while we sleep 'til morning light appears...." I believed my mother, and I learned very early on to trust in a higher power.

But the horror and fear of those moments of abandonment never left me, and only multiplied as time went on.

❧ TWO ❦

RAYMOND Webster, the international head of our church, was a constant presence in our household when I was young, and his influence on my family—particularly on my father—was profound. He lived in Greenborough for a time, and he and my father preached in the same congregation.

Webster knew my grandparents from Alexandria. He had been in the Royal Air Force during the war, serving first in Palestine, and then in Egypt, and was one of the Christian servicemen who had spent time in my grandparents' home. He had a forceful personality, and even then was beginning to flex the muscles of his spiritual authority. My father formed a very strong attachment to him.

My father too had grown up in a Christian home, but the war was a watershed in his spiritual life. He was only sixteen when he joined the army and saw unspeakable horror during the fighting, and yet his life was spared, so he became even more intensely committed to the service of God afterward. His coincidental friendship with Raymond Webster provided a natural outlet for his growing dedication. The two men were about the same age and became preaching partners, but my father somehow never achieved equal status in the relationship. He was a dedicated and excellent preacher, but he lived in the shadow of Webster's powerful image.

Jane Webster used to laugh about the early days, when her husband and my father had gone along the beach or through the market square wearing billboards that read "REPENT" or tee shirts carefully hand stitched by my mother and Jane Webster with the words "The end is nigh" and other such slogans such as "Repent or Die." One of our favorite stories was about the time they were standing on a street corner singing hymns. My father had a nice voice but Raymond Webster sang like a crow, and a woman finally stuck her head out the window of one of the houses and shouted, "I don't know who you are or what you're up to, but will you please go away! I've never heard such a noise in all my life!"

I liked Raymond Webster quite a lot when I was little, and was a bit in awe of him. He was six feet tall and heavily built, with dark, wavy hair and a deep, resonant voice. In his immaculate suits and shining shoes, he was the perfect picture of an old-fashioned upper-class Dickensian schoolmaster.

But although his presence was commanding, he was always very kind to me. I remember running up to him whenever he came up the drive, laughing as he carried me back to the house on his shoulders. After he moved to Portfield to take over a congregation there, my father would ask him to come down whenever I was sick and pray for me. It was always quietly understood that when we children were older, we would enter the ministerial training college that he opened in Portfield and dedicate our lives to God.

I think that it was particularly because of Raymond Webster's influence that my father was so hard on us as children. He really did not have a very demanding personality, and when he had time, he enjoyed running races with us in the woods or telling us stories. But if Webster ever expressed disapproval of us, or of anything we did, we would feel the backlash from my father. I did not realize until I was much older how deeply insecure my father felt next to Webster, and this insecurity often vented itself on us.

Webster's wife Jane was more of a direct challenge. "Auntie Jane" we used to call her, but I can't say the relationship entailed any of the sweet affection connoted by that title. In fact, we had quite a different nickname for her behind her back, one that was based on the English "Mr. Men" cartoon series. This quaint strip included all sorts of little stereotyped characters like "Mr. Dizzy" and "Mr. Chatterbox," and we assigned Auntie Jane a place in the ranks by naming her "Mrs. Impossible." She was continually commanding us to do things that seemed impossible on the surface, and heaven help you if you didn't do them! To call her domineering would have been euphemistic.

The Websters had adopted a lovely child named Anette after the death of their younger daughter Claire, from leukemia. Anette was my age, and she was really the only close friend I had as a youngster. My parents used to take us to visit the Websters in Portfield during school holidays, and those occasions were always special treats for me, even though they were enjoyed under the ever-vigilant eye of Anette's mother. Auntie Jane was a cleanliness fanatic, and every morning she would check our ears, neck, hair and teeth. Everything had to be spotless. The beds had to be perfectly made—and heaven help you if they were not! Manners were an absolute must, and quietness a cardinal law. We never dared make a clatter near Auntie Jane.

Once she sent Anette and me to the butcher shop in Portfield to pick up her meat order. It was half an hour's walk from the house, and we were only ten years old.

"We've come to collect the meat for Mrs. Webster," we said sweetly to the butcher.

With a doubtful smile, he looked our skinny little frames up and down and said, "You can't take the meat."

Anette, who knew her mother well, said, "We *have* to take it, sir."

Laughing heartily, the butcher went to the back and reemerged dragging a huge side of beef, the length of the entire cow and two feet wide, wrapped up inside a dripping plastic bag. He handed it over to us, muttering that we would never be able to get it home. Nevertheless, we staggered out of the shop with our charge, thoroughly determined to do just that. Many curious onlookers were amused to see us progress down the street, sometimes carrying the beef on our shoulders, other times dragging it along the ground. It took us an hour and a half to get that cow home, and we were very proud of our great accomplishment, although I dare say the meat was no longer edible.

Auntie Jane had plenty of such tricks up her sleeve to keep us trained and obedient when we were young. But she and her husband were not the only people in her family whose standards my father borrowed to measure us against.

Their eldest daughter Victoria was perfect in my father's eyes. Although she was overweight, Victoria dressed very nicely and was always neat and clean. She carried herself with confidence and had many accomplishments to her name, including being a leader of the church's youth band. She was, in fact, a model preacher's daughter. Somehow, in a quiet way, Victoria was continually being held up as the yardstick in our home, and we never seemed to measure up. My parents were living on a smaller income than the Websters, but with a larger family, and we children were always a bit unkempt at that time, more rough-and-tumble. I think we were always something of an embarrassment to my father because of this, and even though he loved us, he drove us harder because of it. The brunt of this burden seemed to fall disproportionately on my older brother Philip.

There was a boisterous strain that had come down in the family from my grandmother in Alexandria, and so we were all pranksters when we were young, but Philip seemed to have gotten a genetic concentration. He was a sweet, fun-loving boy with many talents, but he was always acting up.

He never wanted to go to church. He would fill up the bathtub while everyone else was getting ready to leave; then at the last minute he'd sit in it with all his clothes on, and my parents would have no choice but to leave him at home. I remember the times when he and another boy from the church used to run off and smoke cigars down by the train station, and my sisters were always tattling on him.

The monkey episode was one of his particularly entertaining pranks. Grace was always an important part of the meal. Everyone had to be present at the table. My father sat at the head, my mother at the opposite end, two children on each side. This particular day, the food was beautifully arrayed on the table, steaming hot, smelling delicious. We were all seated with the exception of my brother, and we waited...and waited. No sign of him. Irritably, my father called upstairs.

"All right, all right, I'm coming," Philip insisted.

With wide eyes, we hungrily surveyed the various concoctions on the table. The food was rapidly cooling off, and a skin was forming on the gravy. My mother shifted restlessly in her chair, for her hard labor was being ruined before her eyes.

One more time my father called. "Philip, come down immediately," he demanded.

"Wait," my brother replied lightly, unperturbed by the obvious anger in my father's voice.

A deep sigh.

"We'll start without him," my father finally said.

This was a grave sin. Philip was in trouble; he would probably get the belt. We bowed our heads in silence and waited for my father to begin grace. No sooner had he said the first few words than there was a gentle tapping on the window. We children opened our eyes and burst into uncontrollable laughter.

There in the window was my stuffed toy monkey, clad in football gear, its long, gangly arms knocking against the glass pane. Philip had tied a string around its neck and was dangling it from an upstairs window. The timing was perfect, but my father was far from amused. He continued with the grace, and the meal was eaten in silence. My brother never came down.

Philip was often belted for such infractions. Sometimes his nose would bleed when he was hit, and he would sit on his bed and cry. I remember standing in the doorway of his room, staring at him and feeling so sorry. "Don't worry, Ton," he would say softly, "I'm going to be okay."

Our friendly sheepdog was as much of a comfort to Philip as he was to me. For hours he would lie by his side and stroke the dog's head, saying continually, "Poundy, have you confessed? You have to confess your sins, boy!"

My parents always clucked their tongues in disgust at such remarks, but I giggled. I secretly took Philip's part because he was always looking out for me. When he was eighteen and I was ten, he bought me an accordion, and we would go together for lessons on Sunday afternoon. He paid for the lessons out of his own pocket with the money he was making as a carpenter's apprentice.

Philip also amused me to no end, for he was always coming home with little surprises—animals in particular. He would come pedalling up the drive on his bike with a conspicuous bulge under his jacket and call loudly, "Come out, Ton, and see what I've got!" At various times, we were the proud owners of a squirrel, several white mice, rabbits, a cat, and even a hedgehog (but it had fleas, and my mother demanded adamantly that we dispose of it). Most of the animals lived in the coal shed in the backyard. The kestrel stayed the longest. Philip raised it on bits of meat, and even after it had a family, it used to come back to his windowsill and take the food that he put out for it.

Philip could tell you anything you wanted to know about nature, and he was also an excellent woodworker. My mother was the one who had insisted that he learn a trade before entering the ministry, and Philip's talent blossomed in such a short time that he was able to make beautiful doors for our church and to carve exquisite pulpits. In spite of his youthful pranks, he was extremely kind and good-natured, and eventually he became a devoted minister; but unfortunately he wasn't very advanced academically. My father had never gotten over the fact that out of his two sons he had lost the smarter one. His frustration was further exacerbated by Philip's mischievousness, and he never gave him any positive feedback.

Philip suffered quite a lot from this, but he kept it all inside. He was always full of fun and laughter, and I looked up to him.

Esther was the next eldest. She was six years older than I, and was the loudest and most rambunctious of us all, bursting at the seams with life, a perfect tease. It never mattered much to her how dirty she was, as long as she enjoyed herself.

Her love for good fun and antics was not always appreciated by those around her, but her spirits were rarely dampened. She could never resist a dare, so Philip could never resist giving her one. Consequently, she tackled outrageous feats, like jumping down from the roof of the garden shed (she landed with her tongue between her teeth and had to be rushed to the hospital) and trying to pick up a huge enamel sink, which fell and broke her foot. When she fed a live frog to our chicken, she got a beating from my father for being cruel. Esther was never perturbed, however, and her raucous laughter was heard constantly—at home, at school, and sometimes even in church.

But her fun was conducted in innocent good will; there wasn't an ounce of malice in her, and she was totally unselfish. She was always eager to share, frequently giving me her sweets and mothering me even when we were older. I was about ten years old when she left home to go to the ministerial college in Portfield, and I missed her greatly.

My sister Margaret was a different story altogether. Even as a child, Margaret never liked to share, but she would tattle on us if we didn't share with her. I would always end up giving her some of my candy because I was afraid of my father. But if I asked *her* to share, she'd promise to save some for me, and in the end the candies would never materialize. She would either eat them all and say she'd forgotten, or she would insist that she was still "saving them for later."

Margaret was clean right down to her fingernails, and she was a diligent student. She studied for hours and hours, memorizing Bible passages by heart, and was always winning prizes, even for her handwriting. She was liked by everyone in our congregation and people often invited her to visit them; and except for her selfishness at home, she was really the perfect child, the closest we would come to having a Victoria Webster in our family. My father subconsciously favored her because of this, and she was never hit or severely punished. We didn't think about this much when we were little. We just accepted the fact that Margaret was treated differently.

She was in her last year in junior school while I was still in primary school and whenever I was in trouble, she had to sort it out. Once I became very sick, and she had to come to my class and take me home. When I had an accident in the playground and cut my eye, she had to accompany me to the hospital for stitches. She was annoyed at having to be the caretaker, and from the word "go," we were never close.

But there was a deeper reason for her resentment. She had been the youngest for five years and had enjoyed her role as "Daddy's girl" until I was born. I don't think she ever really accepted me, and we fought for the coveted position of "baby" until finally I gave up the struggle. Years later, I would tease her about the teddy bear that had originally belonged to Philip and had been passed along to each child in turn. When my turn came, Margaret refused to give up the bear, and it was still on her bed in the training college when she was twenty-two. "Margaret," I used to say, "you know that's my bear," and she'd snap, "No, it's not, it's mine!" She never did give it up.

And then there was me. I was a tag-along, five years younger than Margaret, and regarded as a nuisance. The others did look out for me, but they were all much closer in age and were always doing things together. I was the intruder.

My position as youngest seemed to carry all of the liabilities and none of the privileges. I was never "the baby" when it came to being coddled, but I was "the baby" whenever it was convenient for my brother and sisters—particularly if there was trouble. They would blame me in the hope that I would get away with it because I was so young.

We were not desperately poor, but nevertheless fruit was a luxury. Each piece was counted and rationed out. One day, Margaret and I arrived home from school and found a banana skin on the table. Someone apparently had taken the banana without permission. Then we heard footsteps upstairs. We knew our parents were still at work.

We called upstairs, but there was no answer. Fearlessly we ran up, only to find my brother busy in his room.

"You ate a banana! Daddy's going to be really angry with you!"

He didn't answer. I don't think he cared much; at thirteen, what does it matter to a boy to be in trouble? Philip was almost always in that state anyway.

We busied ourselves with our own "important" little jobs, and the banana was forgotten—that is, until my father returned home.

"There were five bananas in this bowl at lunchtime, and now there are only four. Own up! Who ate a banana?" he demanded.

Almost as if they had previously rehearsed, the others chorused, "It was Tonica—*she* ate the banana!"

"I didn't!" I protested. "I came in with Margaret and the skin was on the table. It was Philip." Desperately I looked to my older sister for support, but she had moved to my brother's side and refused to bear witness to my truthful statement.

I started to cry. "I didn't take the banana. I didn't, I didn't!" I wailed.

"I know how to find out," my father said. "I'll divide up another banana and everyone will have a piece." I was so upset that I refused to eat my piece, and from this, my father concluded that I was indeed the guilty one.

He took me by the hand and led me upstairs. I knew what was coming, and I was sickened in the pit of my stomach. It just wasn't fair! I felt confused and very helpless.

My father knelt down by the side of my bed and encouraged me to do the same. I refused, still insisting that I hadn't done it. He took my hand and pulled me down. "Now, if you say you are sorry, Jesus will forgive you and make your heart nice and clean, and then you will be ready to meet him when he comes again. Say these words after me." He went into a penitential prayer, which I obediently and mechanically repeated. Then we went downstairs.

No one said a word, but as I look back I realize that even at such an early age, there was some sort of indignance brewing, although I didn't understand it and worked hard to drown it out. I wanted desperately to be good and to have the "warm feeling" enter me so that I would know I had been accepted and would not be left behind after the "second coming"; and I always asked Jesus to forgive me before I went to bed at night.

Fortunately, there was one corner of our family tapestry that was free of conflict, and actually quite charming, and that was my grandmother's corner. Every second Saturday, we would drive two and a half hours to Thorpe Hill, the small village where she lived alone. My father would help keep up her allotment, the nearby portion of field she rented from a farmer to grow produce, and we would have the run of the place. These visits were always thoroughly delightful, and I looked forward to them immensely.

Thorpe Hill was a fairy-tale village, a rustic postcard come to life. It was surrounded by open land and consisted of a few small houses, a post office, a parish church, and the necessary English pub. There were no stores; the baker, milkman, and other merchants would come by periodically to sell their wares from a truck or wagon.

My grandmother's cottage was tiny and quaint and smacked of a bygone era. Although this was in the early sixties, the house still had a thatched roof, a pump for water, and a stove that fed on kindling wood. My father always chopped up a pile of wood large enough to feed both the stove and fireplace until we came again.

Thick, heavy curtains guarded the front door to keep the draft out, and the lace-covered windows also had heavier drapes that were drawn at night to keep the house warm. There was a small front room, a pantry and a kitchen which I rarely entered because it was so cold; and beyond that, a tiny winding staircase led up to the bedroom. The ceilings were beamed, and very old paintings of country scenes hung on the walls, pictures of workhorses or children with their dogs, staring down at us from the past through murky burgundy and brown tones.

The grounds were even more fascinating. A huge barrel stood near the side of the cottage to collect rainwater, and bursts of fruit bushes were clustered all over the yard. Enormous plump loganberries, gooseberries, and even rhubarb, grew there in grinning abandon, and animals of every kind, from rabbits to foxes, could often be found sniffing about among the leaves. Luscious flowers carpeted the open spaces, and the hedges surrounding the property were artfully twisted and braided into curious patterns with a craft called "Hedge-Laying" that has long been the secret possession of the English country folk. It was a child's dreamland.

It was here that my father spent hours telling me stories of his childhood and of his parents. It was his father who was the expert "Hedge-Layer" in the vicinity. When a hedge reached a great height of twenty or thirty feet, it required "laying." Some of the hedge would have to be cut away and then the farmer had to decide which piece of hedge would be laid. He would have to cut into the thick stem enough to be able to bend it over, but not enough to break it off completely; the sap still needed to travel from the root to the piece of hedge that was laid. Supporting stakes had to be knocked into the ground; thin binders, mostly from woodnut saplings, were used to bind everything together. The finished product was a work of art and most pleasing to the eye. One such hedge that my grandfather had laid was done so magnificently that it was photographed and displayed in the local Art Gallery. Many were the time that my father would stop the car to absorb the beauty of a newly-laid hedge.

My grandfather began work on the farms when he was a mere ten years old, and consequently by the time he reached manhood he was also the fastest and most skilled at hand-milking cows and thatching roofs from straw. All of these skills he passed on to my father who began his working career at age fourteen. Work began at seven each morning until five-thirty each afternoon, and until one in the afternoon on Saturdays. By the age of fifteen, my father was skilled at ploughing with a two-team of horses and spent weeks at a time, all day, every day, working in this way. He always had amazing stories to tell us about runaway horses crashing through farm gates with ploughs or wagons tipping over and hurling him into the unknown. He never ceased to be amazed about how his life on the farm had been spared from death on numerous occasions. He even had a story about a whirlwind picking him up, spinning him around with great speed and dropping him from a great height into another field almost a mile away from his home.

My father's mother passed away when I was seventeen and had already entered the ministerial training college. My grandmother was adopted at birth by a wealthy family in Cambridge after her own mother had passed away during childbirth. She received an excellent education and was always the brains of the family—a quick thinker, an excellent cook, and an extremely perceptive person. My father always mentioned how she could discern a person's character in moments and her assessments were never wrong.

My grandmother was a conservative "churchgoer," nowhere near as religious as my father became after the war. Perhaps that is why I remember her and her little cottage as a bright spot of respite in the otherwise cheerless routine of church life, a peaceful landscape in the years of adolescent turmoil that were soon to follow.

For there was little else that provided relief in the rigorous schedule of a pastor's daughter. This was my life and I accepted it.

Church.

School.

Bed.

No television, no radio, no newspapers.

Even when we went on a trip, it always had to be somewhere near a church or Christian meeting place. I remember one day sighing deeply to my father, "Daddy, why can't we have a holiday from church?"

There was no reply, just a tap of his foot and a smile. It was his way of saying, "You know the answer. Don't ask silly questions."

❧ THREE ❧

THE small gas fire in the hearth glowed as its flames softly warmed our living room. The heavy, dark green curtains were drawn, preventing the cool night air from seeping in under the French windows. My mother sat directly in front of the fire on a high, hard-backed chair, knitting furiously, her tiny frame bent over, her feet barely reaching the carpeted floor. The dog slept lazily in the corner of the room behind the armchair.

The rest of the family were out. My mother and I, both deep in thought, sat silently. The only sounds to be heard were the clicking of knitting needles, the regular tick of "Jock the Clock" on the mantelpiece, and the two pet rabbits gnawing away in their hutch outside.

I sat at the table swinging my feet beneath my chair and staring at photographs of my cousins in Israel, which we had just received from my uncle, Sammy Mordo. Sammy was one of my mother's two brothers, and he had a daughter my age who was also named Tonica. His children looked beautiful in the pictures.

Finally I broke the silence. "Mummy, why haven't I got black hair, and why isn't my skin darker?"

"Because I married Daddy, my love," my mother responded quickly without glancing up from her work.

I didn't say more but continued to stare at the photographs. The knitting needles clicked steadily, and the rabbits finally settled down for the night while my mind drifted far away to another part of the world. I was seven years old then, and very imaginative. I tried to picture what it would be like to live in a land where the sun shone and the trees were filled with pretty orange blossoms and leaves; what it would be like to be my cousin Toni and to have beautiful long black braids and dark skin.

"Tonica Mordo, Tonica Mordo," I chanted to myself. "No, that doesn't sound right. Tonica Marlow—that goes together, but not Tonica Mordo. *Tova* Mordo." Now, *that* sounded nice. Tova Mordo.

My mother had always explained to me that I was named after my grandmother, and that she had chosen "Tonica" as a more Anglicized version of Antoinette. I knew that my cousin's Hebrew name was Tova, even though she didn't use it, and this time I wanted to know something even more.

"Mummy," I said, interrupting her again, "why didn't you call me 'Tova'?"

"Well, because that's a Jewish name and we're in England now, love...and anyway..." her voice dropped, as it always did when she told me the truthful secrets of her heart. "Daddy didn't want it."

I heard this, but did not digest it, thinking instead of the stories I had heard about the cousin Grandpa had really intended my mother to marry. "...And just think, if you had married Ninetta's father like Grandpa wanted, our surname would have been Mordo like Uncle Sammy's children, and I would have been named 'Tova Mordo.' Mummy, it's such a nice name. I like the name 'Tova.' Mummy, will you call me 'Tova'?"

It was her turn not to answer.

I didn't trouble her anymore, but lost myself in a world of fantasy, and the night lingered on.

Sitting up in bed that night, eyes tightly shut, hands clasped, I recited my evening prayer aloud as I had done hundreds of times before, but this night was different. I whispered an additional request: "And please, God, make my hair go black and my skin dark during the night...Amen." With childlike simplicity, I reasoned that God could do it if He wanted to; I knew He could! I snuggled down between the sheets and slept the contented sleep of a child awaiting an exciting adventure.

When the morning light dawned, I sat bolt upright in bed and carefully examined my arms. No, they were still the same fair color. I pulled forward one of my braids for inspection; it was still light brown. However, I wasn't disappointed. I decided I would just pray again that night, and the next, and the next, until it happened; but of course it never did, and finally I gave up the request, telling myself that God mustn't want me to have dark skin and black hair, and I would never understand the reason.

I had no idea at that time why this was so important to me; but the urgency gradually subsided as other pursuits jostled their way into my young life, and after a while I forgot the incident.

Up until the age of eleven, I innocently told everyone at junior school what a "treasure" I had in my life.

"I'm richer than a millionaire," I whispered one sunny day to my best friend, Helen Cripps.

"How can you be?" was her shocked reply.

Giggling a little, I responded, "Because Jesus loves me!" I proceeded to tell her how wonderful it was to have such a good friend who helped me every day, in every way. I was very content in school and very happy with God.

Our school was a Church of England public school, and most of the children came from families who had all the basic Christian beliefs, although none were quite as devout as we were. Each morning there was an assembly of the entire student body, and we would have prayers and hymns and hear a portion from the Bible. I often volunteered to lead these assemblies, and would stand calmly in front of all the students and read stories from the New Testament, announce hymns, and say prayers. It never bothered me that we didn't have a television as everyone else did, or that I had not the faintest idea of the names of the latest pop songs or disc jockeys, or that my skirts were several inches longer than everyone else's.

In fact, the headmaster sometimes used to call me out as a model to show off the school uniform to parents of prospective students. I was always very proud of this, and in fact, I never sensed any difference at all between myself and my friends; that is, until the last day of junior school finally approached.

After months of being prepared by our teacher for life at high school, we were finally on our way—eighty little eleven year olds, very nervous and trying hard not to show it. We would not all be going to the same high school, and we anticipated this major milestone in our lives with a mixture of apprehension and eagerness. Subtly the girls began jockeying into position, each one looking for a close companion with whom she could enter this new world. It was then that a horrible realization swept over me: I was different.

Almost overnight, a strange new attitude seemed to take possession of my friends. They suddenly became much more self-conscious about their appearance and were constantly brushing their hair. The talk turned to topics from which I was shut out: the high school clubs they would get into, social activities, boyfriends. Their innocence was being shed, and mine was still intact.

In fact, I was so terribly different that no one wanted to go to high school with me. My "best friends" made all kinds of excuses for not including me in their group. I tried hard to fight back the tears that were stinging my eyes and bursting to trickle down my cheeks. What was happening? Why was I suddenly so undesirable?

I walked home alone after the last day of school and spent the entire summer holiday amusing myself in solitude. I collected pebbles from a nearby stream and varnished them, picked flowers to dry and mount, and sometimes meandered for hours through the countryside, with the dog chasing glorious nothing ahead of me. I tried hard not to dwell on the first day of high school; maybe it would not be quite so bad, I continually assured myself.

Finally the day arrived.

My sister Margaret accompanied me to school. Self-consciously, I walked along the street, feeling that every eye was secretly watching me from the houses we passed, inspecting my crisp new uniform and sparkling shoes. I was carrying a satchel for the first time and had a new pencil case filled with brand new pencils and pens. I was completely equipped; what could go wrong?

Margaret left me at the school gates. I stood nervously in the courtyard with a few hundred other pupils awaiting the bell. Girls had come from junior schools all over the town, forty from one area, fifty from another. Anxiously I looked around for a familiar face. Surely someone from my district was here. Yes! Just a few yards away, in fact, were several girls from my old class. Happily, I bounded up to them.

"Hey up!" I greeted them in my broad Greenborough accent. "It's so good to see you here. I was afraid I wouldn't know anyone."

"Oh, hello," they responded blandly, and carried on their conversation as if I didn't exist.

And then the bell rang.

"Everyone in pairs," the teacher called.

I tried to pair up with this one and that but was repeatedly pushed out of line. Finally I linked up with another "loner," and we were taken to our respective classrooms.

The name of my class was Two Alpha. We were the highest class academically and were expected to be the cream of the crop that year, our teacher informed us. Ripples of excitement ran through the classroom at the happy realization that we were the smartest eleven-year-olds in the school. But I sensed with quiet desperation that my worst fears were being realized—I did not belong with them. Silently I stared at each girl in the room, trying in agony to figure out why I was so drastically different and wondering what I could do to become part of the "gang."

That was the beginning of my "backslidden" days, as the Church calls it. I led a double life: at church I was a quiet and obedient lamb, and at school a boisterous prankster who finally made it from being a "weirdo" and an outsider to being the most popular girl in class.

The length of my skirt suddenly became an urgent issue. I found various ways to shorten it without my parents finding out. I undid my tight braids and let my hair flow freely, which was quite a sight in itself; for the Church considered it unrespectable for a woman to have her hair cut in any way, and consequently my hair hung down to an incredible length. I picked up the popular jargon, and from time to time, even used bad language. I told my parents all kinds of stories about having to stay after school to study or do a kindness for a friend, when I had really been held behind for bad behavior.

By the time I had reached my third year at high school, I had unanimously been voted the class comedienne and head prankster. I developed a knack for committing the most outrageous crimes in class and then presenting such a cool facade that it seemed as though butter wouldn't melt in my mouth.

"Me, Miss? I did that?" I would say innocently. "No, not I!" And they believed me.

Compared to American standards of mischief, my antics might have been rated as mere innocent tomfoolery. For small town England in the sixties, however, they were considered heinous. Moreover, much to the disgust of the studious girls in class, I always managed to come home with straight A's on my report card.

It may be difficult to understand how a preacher's daughter, especially one from such a devout and strict home, could become so hopelessly enmeshed in rampant mischief. The truth is that beyond the obvious injunctions against lying and stealing, we were not given much of a concrete guideline other than the admonition to "be good," and I suppose it was assumed that conscience would take care of the rest. I always sensed that my father would not approve of my activities and was careful to keep them from him, but as a young teenager, the desire to fit in with the crowd was of paramount importance to me, and there was almost nothing I wouldn't do to satisfy that need.

There was one famous caper that won me the admiration of the entire student body.

My brother had returned a few years previously from a school trip to Europe with what he considered two worthwhile souvenirs—a pair of clogs and a plastic dog feces which he had purchased at a joke shop. My parents were naturally thoroughly disgusted with the latter item, and my father confiscated it immediately. That was the end of it, or so we all thought.

Years later, during the move to our new house, the feces had turned up again, and I had hidden it away. Now it seemed that I would have a use for my booty at last. Excitedly, I tucked it into my school bag, eagerly anticipating the fun I was going to have in school the next day.

Our first class of the day was physics, and the teacher was an Indian by the name of Mr. Tynd, whom we had nicknamed "Mr. Tin." I had previously warned my friends that something might "happen" in class and that they should play along with it. A few minutes after the commencement of the lesson, when "Mr. Tin" was well into the formation of atoms and crystals, I jumped up, clasped my hand to my nose and mouth, and screeched, "Sir, sir, I feel so sick! There's such a terrible smell near my desk, I just can't concentrate!"

With dramatic innocence, I looked all around me. "Sir, it's right here! Come and see! *Oh, sir...*!" I painfully wailed. Patiently he came over to investigate. My friends and I giggled and sent each other knowing glances behind his back. The poor gentleman was distraught, and I could tell he had no idea what to do. I felt pity for him.

"Don't worry, sir," I told him. "I'll go to the caretaker and get the necessary things to clean it up." I scampered from the room and came back with a dustpan and newspaper. Expertly I "cleaned up" the mess, but instead of throwing it into the garbage bin, I was careful to return the coveted object to the safety of my pocket, ready for the next part of the plan. If I remember correctly, I think we placed it in eleven different places in the classroom, repeating the procedure each time, and of course the entire period was wasted.

In abject puzzlement, Mr. Tynd cried, "I don't understand eet. I vaz dee firzt von in zee clazz room diz morning and no dog vaz here!"

"Maybe it came in when you didn't notice, sir," I suggested reassuringly. "Crafty things dogs are, you know!"

We even got him to look under his shoes in case he had accidentally stepped in anything, and at the end of class he gave me several credit points in appreciation of my helpfulness and cooperation.

And that was only one incident. Other pranks were equally as hilarious and well varnished with whitewash, and mostly I came out of them as the "shining star" and "good girl."

I have a notion that part of this success was due to a true strain of spiritual innocence in me that was never disturbed by even the wildest of my antics. My desperate effort to belong was in no way a contradiction to my deeply embedded belief in the Church teachings and particularly in the stories of the Bible. When it came down to brass tacks, I always spoke out for what I had been taught was true, and this strength may have had some hand in saving my reputation—for I could not simply be dismissed as a worthless troublemaker.

In high school, we had a religious education class once a week, and I distinguished myself there too, although in a totally different manner. Ironically, many theologians do not have a literal belief in the Bible. During their training, they learn Hebrew and Greek in order to study the texts in their original form, and it is simply too difficult to reconcile the many contradictions between the Old and New Testaments. So although they may be Bible experts, they are not necessarily fundamental believers. We had one such teacher.

She walked into the room one day and declared, "Today we are going to learn about Jonah and the whale—but surely no one of your intelligence believes *that* story!"

Immediately, I called out, "Well, I'm sorry, Miss, but I do!" and a whole debate followed. Finally one very studious girl, the daughter of a scientist who lectured at the university in town, stood up, raised her hand, and said snobbishly, "Scientists say that a whale's jaw is too small to swallow a man whole!"

Whereupon I retaliated, "Well, it doesn't say in the Bible that it was a whale. It says a great fish!" I knew my verses inside and out.

"Oh, dear," spluttered our poor teacher, who had been totally left out of the discussion. "I can imagine you on a soapbox!" Fortunately for her, the bell rang right on cue, and she was saved the embarrassment of having to resolve the problem. She was a brilliant woman—but she did not have answers.

On another occasion, the story of the Exodus came up. The teacher explained with assurance that God had never actually parted the waters and that the Israelites had walked on marshy ground.

"But the verse says they walked on *dry* ground," I countered.

"The Bible is not meant to be taken literally," she insisted. "It was actually a very shallow body of water. That's why the Red Sea is also called the *Reed* Sea—because it was a marshland."

I had been instilled with a very literal belief in the Bible and had been taught that the Old and New Testaments were "the living and proceeding word of God," as valid this day as if God had just spoken it all. I did not give up the fight easily and was eventually thrown out of the class for asking too many questions, a trait that would stand me in good stead in later years.

But at that time, all I felt was discomfort. It seemed that everywhere I turned, I had to make myself stand out in order to make myself fit in. In an effort to keep myself in everyone's good graces, I operated simultaneously on two tracks, spreading lively mischief among my adoring fans to assure myself a social niche, while conscientiously defending the truths of my heart to ensure my friendship with Jesus.

I spent my adolescent years stewing in this schizophrenia of mixed feelings: sometimes crying from terror and begging Jesus to forgive my "sin," sometimes rebelling, kicking and struggling, and other times mocking and laughing. It would be some years before I would be able to abandon one track and live securely on the other.

ঞ FOUR ৩

IT was during these terrible teen years that my main concern at home was not how to get out of washing the dishes or cleaning up, but how to get out of going to church.

Church was four evenings a week and twice on Sunday, although I usually tried to avoid weeknight services by going to bed very early so as to be sleeping when everyone left. I loved Jesus very much, but at the same time I hated anything that alienated me from the natural social environment at school, and I sensed strongly that our lifestyle made me "different."

The church was Pentecostal, a type of Protestantism which entails belief in the literal inerrancy of the Scriptures—both Old and New Testaments—and requiring a much stronger style of dedication to God than simply attending services once a week, as most of my friends did. Pentecostals are fundamentalists who teach that when Jesus went back to heaven after his "rising," he left behind a "Pentecostal fire," or a manifestation of his spirit, as a comfort to his followers on earth, and that anyone who believed in him strongly enough could actually become "filled" with this spirit.

This doctrine differed vastly from that of the Church of England, which designated the minister as a necessary intermediary between the congregant and God. The Pentecostals believed that ministers played an important role as leaders, but when it came to actual communication with the above, any individual was capable of being "filled" and experiencing Jesus personally. (Jesus and God were viewed as being almost interchangeable.) Consequently, there was a great emphasis on an emotional—and sometimes even fanatical—personal commitment, which would enter every area of a person's life and keep him on a spiritual "high."

The church building itself was very simple. We did not possess one of the typical grand cathedral-style buildings with enormous spires, stonework and elaborate murals. Our chapel was just a plain wooden structure, once used as a Boy Scout hall, with a corrugated iron roof and a modest, hand-painted wooden sign outside reading "Mission Hall," listing the times of the services. It was believed that the beauty was in the worship itself and not in the surrounding trimmings.

A typical service would start out very mildly and build up to a revivalistic fervor. My father sat up on the platform to the left, and the band, led by my brother, on the right. The band would begin to play a chorus or hymn over and over again; then my father would stand, followed slowly by each of the musicians, and then, one by one, the entire congregation would be on its feet, clapping and singing and having a "wonderful" time. The meeting would then be opened up to anyone who had a thought, exhortation or testimony to share; and finally my father would go to the pulpit to deliver his sermon, which could last anywhere from twenty minutes to an hour and a half. When I was small, I always went to sleep at this point, resting my head on my mother's knee, but as I grew older, I was forced to sit up and listen.

After the sermon, one or two more songs would be sung and a small velvet bag would be passed around to collect the "offering"; and then the congregants were free to greet each other with a "holy kiss" and have a chat before returning home.

Such welcoming, down-to-earth, friendly churches usually attract all kinds of strange characters, and ours was no exception. From my earliest years, I grew accustomed to seeing the most "interesting" people from every band of the human spectrum, and now that I look back on it, some of them were pitiable indeed. But we were taught that

Jesus had come for the lost, the forsaken, and the misfits, and no one was turned away from our doors. As a result, it became a refuge for the downtrodden and for all sorts of emotionally undirected people who needed support.

One such couple were an Irishman named Dan and his wife Jenny, who was blind. Due to his "burning desire" to preach the gospel, Dan could never hold down a job for more than a couple of weeks because he would drive all the workers crazy; and so he sent his blind wife to work, ten miles away by train every day. At almost every prayer meeting, Dan would jump up and down, or furiously rock back and forth in his chair and speak in "tongues," the incoherent babbling that was considered by the Church a clear manifestation of being "filled with the spirit." Dan's "tongues" consisted of a constant repetition of the same few senseless syllables, which sounded roughly like "*shinder ber, shinder ber, shinder*"; and they were apparently an embarrassment to Jenny because she used to sulk and cry during the services and tell him to "shad up." One time, Dan became so possessed that he went to the front of the church and began to tear up his Bible and eat it, publicly declaring that he was "eating the word of God."

Another regular visitor to the Sunday night service was Phoebe. Phoebe was about thirty years old and mentally handicapped. She would start talking the moment she shuffled in through the doors and would then proudly go around to every member of the congregation and show off the contents of her vinyl handbag—a tube of lipstick, plastic beads, and various other treasures. She usually made her entrance during my father's sermon, and he would patiently wait while she made her rounds and then motion her to sit quietly. She would sit for a few minutes and then trundle out, clutching her handbag tightly.

Then there was Brother Bartholomew. He had been a sailor during the war and had led a very unpleasant life. He was poorly educated, poorly employed, and unhappily married, and when my father discovered him, he was a miserable alcoholic, living in a run-down mobile home. My father began to help him out, even giving him a great deal of money from his own pocket to pay the bills, and he used to bring him home every week or two for lunch. Since we were living on a tight budget ourselves, and there was never any extra food, I would often end up losing my lamb chop so that Brother Bartholomew could have it, and I would eat my lunch in the kitchen, as it was too embarrassing to sit at the table with everyone else and have only an egg.

Brother Bartholomew eventually rose to a prominent position in the Church, but in his manners and character, he remained what he had been at the start: a simple sailor.

Another surprising regular in this kaleidoscope of characters was the Church of England reverend from the congregation next door. Silently, his black-robed form would glide in through the doors, and he would take a seat in a rear pew until the service was just about over. Occasionally he would leave a note on the back table for my father: "Thanks for the peace and spiritual uplift." One could only wonder what would have happened to him if anyone in his own congregation had found out about these surreptitious visits.

There were scores more, an endless flock of hungry searchers. It used to horrify me when some of these odd people would come up to me after the service and give me a "holy kiss." All I knew was that I wanted to be normal, a regular everyday person, and although I believed in the Church teachings with all my heart, I felt at the same time that our religiousness made me somehow abnormal. To the outside world, I was just as much a misfit as any of these eccentric hopefuls who peppered our congregation.

Most of the people in church were older as well, so I really had no close friends except for the Websters' adopted daughter Anette. But they were living in Portfield by this time, so we only saw each other on occasional visits.

I was friendly with some of the girls at school, but I lived in mortal fear of having these fragile connections damaged by my father's unthinking behavior. It was bad enough that my friends could all watch television, which I was not allowed to do, and that I could never go to their homes or attend school activities, but my father's social approach simply added to the anguish. He could never understand why I was not keen to invite my friends to services. I would try hard never to take them home, because as soon as we walked through the door, my father would say in a sickly sweet voice, "Did you invite your little friend to church, dear?" or "I hope you remembered to tell your friend that Jesus loves her!" I would cringe and either hurry my friend upstairs to my bedroom or take her out into the garden to play.

The truth is that I did sometimes invite these girls to church, but I did it privately at appropriate times, and if they refused, I never bothered them. Some would not have minded coming to Sunday school, but their parents were mostly Anglican churchgoers who had no desire for anything more extreme. The pressure from my father was very embarrassing, and it only emphasized the vast ocean of difference that lay between me and everyone else at school.

Another dread of my life at this time was "open-airs," or public evangelizing. During the summer months, my father would dedicate extra time to outreach, either by open-airs or by door-knocking. Door-knocking meant that two congregants would go to each house on a given street with questionnaires designed to draw people into conversation about Jesus. This I could squirm out of pretty easily by saying I had homework which *must* be handed in the following day; but for open-airs, the entire family had to be present, and no excuse, no matter how valid, was accepted.

We would leave early for the Sunday morning service and stop on our way at the market square in town. "Out of the car," my father would order. My mother, brother and I, who were secretly none too eager for the episode, would take our time getting out, particularly if there were many people around, and my father would call to us impatiently. My sister Margaret always refused to get out. This happened every week. She never once got out of the car and never once was punished; but whenever I tried the same tactic, she would push me out, and my father would give me a quick clout around the ear and tell me off, under his breath, for causing a scene.

We formed a circle, my father standing erect and dignified, my mother with her head down, straightening her skirt and trying desperately not to appear embarrassed, and my brother reluctantly strapping on his accordion. I would stand holding my tambourine, dying from shame due to my unfashionably long dress and bonnet, which I had to wear since the Church required all women and girls to cover their hair during worship. And my activity during the open-airs certainly qualified as worship, for I was always fervently praying to God that none of my classmates should be among the very curious onlookers.

We would start to sing. Thankfully, my father did have a wonderful voice, so the sounds were not too unbearable. After a hymn or two, he would remove his hat and address all passersby who might care to stop for a moment to view the scene. Afterwards, we would sing one or two more hymns or choruses, and finally my father would invite people to church for the evening service.

The ordeal was over—that is, until the next morning, when I had to face my friends at school. "We saw you in the market square," they would chant, teasing me about my frilly bonnet which tied under the chin with ribbon.

One open-air stands out vividly in my mind. This time, the entire congregation was invited to come along with us, and that included Jenny and Dan and a few other notable personalities. To add insult to injury, my father decided that rather than evangelizing in the public square in the center of town, we would stay in our own district. When I heard this, fear gripped my heart and sent cold chills rippling through my body.

I shouted in panic, "Daddy, no one wants to hear about Jesus in this area of town. I know, because my friends live here and they told me!"

My father only smiled softly and ordered us all to get going.

The embarrassment was excruciating. Many people came to their doors to listen to us sing as we stood on the green. I felt as though a thousand eyes were piercing through me, and I tried hard to make believe I was someone else, in no way associated with these people around me. Danny, in the grip of the gospel, shook his head violently, waving his Bible in the air and muttering, "*Shinder ber, shinder ber, shinder ber.*" Jenny, clothed in a bright red coat that did not fit her properly, tapped her oversized tambourine out of rhythm; and Hubert, another staunch devotee, just stood there whistling out, "Thank you, Jesus, thank you, Jesus!" The rest of the musicians played with gusto, and some members of the congregation clapped vigorously while others danced around.

"What exactly is this?" asked one bystander. "Is it a carnival or something?"

"Oh, no, dear," was the reply. "This is our church and we came to share Jesus with you."

After my father finished his sermon, he ordered several of the members to go around and speak to those people who were standing at their doors. Of course, he did not send Danny, but nevertheless Danny felt that he couldn't resist such a wonderful opportunity to share his zeal for his redeemer. And so he went straight to the home of a girl who was in my class.

I pulled the brim of my bonnet down further over my face and continued to pretend that this was all a dream, and that it was someone else standing here on the green and not me.

This was the first of six open-airs that same evening, all equally as dramatic and horrific; but no matter what was the response from the people around, my father was never ruffled and always enjoyed going out on the street and sharing the "good news" of his savior with all. Whenever we drove through a particular street in town, he would point to one terraced house and remind us with a chuckle of the woman who had begged Raymond Webster and him to go away because of the racket they were making. He always spoke of such onlookers with a fond indulgence, and their insults never deterred him.

There is a verse in the New Testament which states that followers should be "fools for Jesus' sake," and my father took these words literally. He believed that no one should feel ashamed to appear different if it was for the sake of publicizing Jesus' name, and in spite of all the discomfort his behavior caused me personally, it is a testimony to his utter sincerity that he was totally comfortable in his role as a missionary. By now, he had attained a high position in his engineering firm, and yet he was never concerned about what his employers would think of his outside activities. In fact, he eventually managed to initiate a prayer hour once a week in the factory, where he would read a portion from the Bible to the workers and then lead them in prayer; and as it was a huge factory, this was no small accomplishment.

Because of my father's single-minded dedication to his beliefs, he was unanimously respected. To the multitudes in the many public houses around town, he was a good friend. I hardly remember a Sunday night when we didn't stop at several pubs on the way home from the evening service, waiting in the car while my father went around giving out leaflets and singing hymns. Sometimes he would go "pubbing" during the week also, since many of the people knew and loved him, and were disappointed if he didn't show up. When he returned home, the stench of cigarettes and beer would fill the house, and he would have to change quickly and hang his clothes on the porch to air out.

All of this was routine to me. But in spite of the fact that I saw this "message of love" being spread daily by my own father, and accepted so readily by all his followers, it troubled me greatly that I was not brimming over with peace and joy myself. I was constantly repenting for my "sin," but still did not feel any closer to Jesus. What could I do? I was afraid to speak to my father. He would only tell me to repent harder and maybe even to give a testimony in church. This meant getting up in front of the whole congregation and telling a story of something that Jesus had personally done for you, or describing the wonderful satisfaction you had in the knowledge that he had forgiven a sin of yours.

The entire process was becoming an enormous pressure for me, and a sickening feeling began to crawl through me, like an insidious fungus. In Bible school, I still continued to ask sincerely for forgiveness in my seat, feeling much too embarrassed now to march to the front of the church and make a public declaration. It was not that I believed less, but part of my resistance came from my own sense of privacy. If I had dealings with Jesus, I preferred to have them quietly and not in front of a hundred people.

My father always preached that Jesus came into our lives to stay, and that he would be faithful even if we neglected him. So then, I reasoned, he must have come inside me. But it bothered me that I did not feel the "peace of the book" within. Deep down inside, there was a hurting, a pain I did not yet know how to describe. Where it came from I had no idea, but it was very real and at times made me feel lonely and estranged—even from my own family.

A deep resentment began to fester inside me, toward the Church and life in general, and toward my mother in particular. Part of this disaffinity for her was typical of a young teenager, but I also sensed quietly that there was something different about her. I had long since passed the ingenuous stage when the pictures of my mother's brother had fascinated me, when I had longed for dark skin and hair like Uncle Sammy's children; all I wanted now was to blend into the crowd. Ironically, I began to feel instinctively that I was somehow like my mother, and I did not want to be associated with anything that made me different.

No one ever mentioned my mother's Jewishness, but it was understood that she had come from a separate heritage, and the topic was discreetly avoided. We children had been told in no uncertain terms that we were gentile because my father was gentile. I had heard that the Jews believed that one's identity was determined by the mother, but Raymond Webster had once firmly explained to me that the Jews had it all wrong and that matrilineal descent was a fable of the rabbis. God had established the father as the true parent, for was He not Himself the Father of Jesus? To entertain the mere notion that a person's true essence was not derived from the father was to deny Jesus' divinity, and any such idea was blasphemous.

My mother was now considered Jewish by the Church only in terms of her ethnicity. She had become a "born again" Christian long before my birth, a "completed Jewess" whose heritage was no longer in any way contradictory to her status as a good Christian. I knew that, and yet, in her physical appearance and mannerisms, she was so obviously Sephardic!—the black hair and olive skin, the quick personality, the rich Italian accent. She did not come anywhere close to fitting the blond, blue-eyed, starched Christian stereotype. There was some little germ within me that identified with my mother, even if it was in nothing more than the similarity of our facial features, and it aggravated me to no end.

In church, the references to Jews were slight and not openly caustic. Raymond Webster preached that in fact we should be kind to the Jews because we were indebted to them; if they had not rejected Jesus, the gentiles would not have been saved. But I didn't care about that; I was very irritable and sensitive then to any discussion at all of Jews or Israel.

I had no clear sense of my own identity at that young age. It's just that I would have given fortunes to be considered normal—not Christian, not Jewish, not fanatically religious in any way, but just one of the crowd. If my father suspected my feelings, he didn't tell me, and I didn't share them with anyone.

୬

When I was twelve, my father took me on one of his preaching engagements to a small town called Bloomington, in the north of England, where Raymond Webster had established a branch of the church. The town was about two hundred miles away, a quaint little place by the sea, and for that reason I was happy to accompany him. We left early Saturday morning to get there in time for the evening service.

That night, after my father finished preaching, he looked at me from across the platform. I knew the look well. It meant, "Your turn—make a contribution." Slowly, I shook my head. He was not overjoyed.

After the service, the minister in charge said to me, "How old are you?"

"Twelve," I responded.

"Good, just the right age for an idea I have. You know the story about Jairus' daughter who gets sick, and about how Jesus brings her back to life again? She was just your age, twelve years old. Well, tomorrow we will do the play at Bible school for the children, and you will play the daughter!"

"No, I won't!" I said adamantly.

"You will," he insisted.

"We'll see," I said, and he did see. I refused to join the play, and they had to choose another girl from the Bible school to perform. I could see that my father was not impressed with my conduct. I think he was beginning to wish he hadn't brought me along.

The minister had by no means given up. On Sunday afternoon, he said to me, "Tonight you are going to say a testimony and sing, young lady, and you're not going to get away with it."

"I'm not doing it," I giggled nervously, but this time I knew I had no choice. And so, during the evening service I stood up, and in an extremely emotionless voice said exactly these words: "I was saved when I was four, baptized when I was six, and filled with the holy spirit when I was eight."

It sounded impressive, exactly the kind of thing one should hear from a reverend's daughter. I was the only one who knew it was a pack of lies. Saved? Maybe. Baptized? Yes. But filled with the holy spirit? I knew in my heart that had never happened. The entire testimony was like icing on a blackened and wormy cake. I was surprised at how easy it was to fool everyone, including my own father, who gloated over such wonderful accomplishments.

"Sing," he encouraged me from the platform. I sang a hymn entitled "I Love This Family of God," but in my adolescent heart I hated them instead.

FIVE

WHEN I was thirteen, my grandfather came to visit us from Israel. He stayed for three months.

During the months he stayed in our home, I would often peek into his bedroom without him noticing and would watch him mouth silent words from a well-worn little book. He was a small and immaculate man and always stood erect when he prayed, swaying gently back and forth, a white shawl draped over his shoulders and a big black *yarmulka* on his head. I would hover in the doorway, silently drinking in the awesome wonder of this little man, while downstairs in his study, my father knelt in prayer of his own and prepared his sermon for the evening service.

A strange house, ours was. I remember that whenever I had barged into one of the rooms at home and happened upon my father kneeling in prayer, I was always embarrassed and hurried out; but there was something different about my grandfather.

No one offered to explain Grandpa's behavior to me or to tell me anything about the family history, but they all seemed to pity him. My father told me only that Grandpa was bound to ancient customs and a dead religion, and for many years afterward that was the image of Judaism that I carried in the back of my mind: a rusted relic, a bondage of useless practices.

I did not interact much with him, he conversed in Italian to my mother even though he spoke a perfect English, but I do remember that in his humble effort to befriend me, he tried to help me put covers on my schoolbooks. He also wanted to teach me French, one of the many languages he knew, but I wasn't interested. Mostly I watched him from afar, and with great absorption. Despite what my father had told me, I was intrigued by all of Grandpa's "little ways."

My mother had thoroughly cleaned the kitchen before he arrived and was extremely careful with her menus, explaining to me that Grandpa didn't eat meat and milk in the same meal; and yet at the same time she bypassed his restrictions behind his back. Once she offered him an ice cream cone from the box my father had brought home. Grandpa had just eaten chicken and asked her if the ice cream contained milk, and she said, "No," winking conspiratorially to us over his head. I think now that this was not done maliciously, but simply out of ignorance, but at the time it was completely over my head. Didn't everybody know that ice cream contained milk? And what possible difference could it make anyway?

Though it was bitterly cold, my grandfather rose every day at the crack of dawn to pray. "Papi, put on a fire," my mother kept insisting. "Papi, pray later—God will still hear you!" But he never wavered, and as far as I know, never once missed his morning appointment with his Creator while he was with us. Before every meal, he used to dip his bread in salt, put his hand on his *yarmulka*, and mutter some words in a strange tongue; and I distinctly remember holding candles for him on Saturday evening while he muttered more of these strange words, made shadows on his hands near the flames, and looked at his nails. It was very peculiar, but by now I had become accustomed to his curious antics.

One day, my father drove us all the way to Scotland, a full day's drive from Greenborough, to show Grandpa the beautiful scenery.

"Look at the heather," my father pointed out, keeping up a running tour guide's chatter. "See how it turns the mountains a deep purple, and look at the lakes over there and that gushing river—it must be full of salmon!" But Grandpa was far away in another world. It was one of those "appointment times" which were inviolable, and his eyes were firmly fixed on the yellowed pages of his little book.

"Well, I never," my father declared to no one in particular. "I bring him all this way to see the beautiful scenery, and all he does is sit there and pray!" Now that I look back, this was such a piece of irony—my father, the preacher, complaining that someone else prayed too much! But to him, Grandpa's prayers seemed a waste of time, and he was quite indignant.

I giggled at the remark. My mother shrugged her shoulders and looked out of the window as if that would rectify the situation, and we drove on. Grandpa never even noticed that we'd stopped, or if he did, he had no idea why.

When the time came for Grandpa to return to Israel, I accompanied him to the airport with my parents. As it was difficult for him to walk, my father arranged that he be taken to the plane by ambulance, and a stewardess came to the departure office with a wheelchair.

"Please hurry," she insisted. "We are already a little late."

But Grandpa would not be rushed. He spoke to my mother in Italian and beckoned for me to come to him.

"Queekly," my mother demanded. "He wants to give you a blessing," and she burst into uncontrollable sobbing.

Obediently, I stood in front of him. He put both hands on my head, closed his eyes, and wept silently while reciting the traditional Jewish blessing for girls, which asked God to direct the child in the footsteps of the Matriarchs. Then, with tears still running down his face, he quickly kissed me on each cheek and was gone.

We watched him until he was out of sight. That was the last time I saw my grandfather.

It was only many years later that I learned the reason for his visit: my Uncle Sammy, the family peacemaker, had paid for his ticket and had literally carried him onto the plane. "Are you going to die without seeing the family?" he had implored my grandfather. "You sat *shiva* for your daughter. Why don't you go and reconcile it while you still have time?"

Whether the "reconciliation" had any effect remains questionable, but perhaps the blessing did.

❧ SIX ❧

IT was time for me to change schools again and to take G.C.E. examinations, which in England are important barometers of one's academic achievement. This time I would be moving from an all girls' school to a co-ed high school. It was a time of intense and anxious conflict. On the one hand, it was a wonderful opportunity to start all over again with a new crowd of friends and win a long coveted acceptance, one that would not have to be based on the colorful reputation of a notorious prankster; but on the other hand, I really had a sincere desire to change for the better and be a good "testimony" at school, a proud model of the Church's way of life.

Maybe if I started out with long skirts and braided hair, as was expected of me at home, it wouldn't be so bad, I reasoned. People would laugh at first, and then they would get used to it. But I was afraid to appear so outmoded in public! I was fourteen, and it was becoming worse and worse to walk through life looking like a character out of an old Bible engraving.

Innocently, I decided that my father was sure to have pity on my plight and allow me to wear a short skirt to school, and then all my fears of deceit would be over. Yes, of course, that was the answer. Daddy would agree!

A couple of weeks before school opened, my parents and I traveled to Ryster, a large town about half an hour away, on the big adventure of purchasing my uniform. We entered the enormous department store and found the correct floor. A middle-aged sales assistant greeted us warmly.

"What school are you attending, dear?" she asked.

"Rawlins Grammar," I replied excitedly.

"Good, I'll show you everything you need," she responded. "Please come with me."

I followed her at a quick trot, my parents close behind.

"Now, dear, here are the skirts. Would you like a long skirt or a short one?"

My heart began to beat fast. This was the crucial moment. I smiled gently and remained silent, until my father waved his hand with impatience and said strongly, "Come along, child, tell the lady what you want. You *know* you want a long one."

Turning to the shop assistant, who wore a slightly sympathetic smile, I replied, "A long one, please."

And so I was fitted out. Everything from my underwear up was ordered at least two sizes larger than I needed, for my mother insisted I would grow into the clothes. I dressed and stood in front of the full-length mirror, studying myself. The skirt was well past my knees, the cardigan sleeves rolled back twice. The blouse collar bulged beneath the tie, and the long, thick gray socks were bagging up around my ankles. I looked like a cross between a circus clown and a poster for Oxfam (the British equivalent of the Peace Corps), which always depicted starving children in bedraggled clothing staring out mournfully at passersby.

"Oh, that's nice, my love," admired my mother. "Show Daddy!"

I went outside the dressing room and stood in front of my father. "Very smart," he commented, and the uniform was bought. I was fourteen years old, and I never did grow into my uniform.

"We've spent a lot of money on you today, my girl," my father reminded me on the way home. "Take care of those clothes!"

"Thank you," I responded somewhat pensively.

During the coming days, I spent many moments on a mental seesaw. Finally, I decided that my father was right: I did look smart.

I would wear my skirt long! Cautiously, I opened the front door of our home on the first morning of school and stepped out, feeling terribly self-conscious, the skirt flapping around against my calves. By the time I reached the end of the street, I couldn't stand it any longer. I turned the waistband over once, twice. By the end of the next block I had turned it over several more times, bringing the skirt up to about three or four inches above my knees. This resulted in a bulging waistline, which the oversized cardigan was able to accommodate satisfactorily. I continued on to the bus stop.

One girl who was already there saw me approaching and called out teasingly, "Gosh, Tonica, your skirt's long!"

Deep inside, I breathed a sigh of relief. Thank goodness I had pulled it up! If the skirt was a cause for remark at this length, I could only imagine what kind of taunts would have come my way if I had not made any "adjustment."

All of the creative energy I had previously expended on junior school pranks was now channeled into developing clever methods of shortening my skirt for the duration of school hours. One of these was to walk the three-mile distance to school, thereby saving my bus fare until I had enough money for a pair of suspenders. These I attached to my skirt, which was pulled up under my arms to such a ridiculous height that it looked rather like a ballerina's tutu. But I covered it all with the cardigan, and though it did look slightly suspect, I was satisfied enough to relax. I was becoming one of "the gang" again.

Although my quest to belong never quite abated in high school, I felt a quest of a different sort beginning inside me—a more adult appreciation of the spiritual seeds that had been planted in my childhood. The soil was stirring.

My father had begun making several trips each week to Portfield where Raymond Webster, his former preaching partner, had opened up a ministerial training college. Webster was also in the midst of building a new church, and of course my father wanted to share in the merit of helping. My brother Philip was already at the college, so it was an opportunity to visit him as well, and I often went along.

"Put your hat in the car," my father instructed me before we left early one evening. "They will have a prayer meeting for the young people tonight."

With silent reluctance I threw my beret into the back of the car, and a few minutes later we were on our way. We had traveled this road a million times before. I knew every twist, every bend by heart, and I watched the familiar landmarks spin by with listless attention, unaware that this trip would not be quite like all the others.

Thirty minutes later, we were pulling up outside the church grounds.

Raymond Webster—or Daddy Raymond, as he was affectionately known in Portfield—had risen in these few years to become the spiritual leader of a worldwide Church movement. He claimed that he had had a revelation from God in which he had been commissioned to take young people, refine their characters, and train them for the ministry, and to this end, he had established the training college. He was also respected as an apostle of God, who had the power to pave a spiritual road for his congregants, and to alter Church doctrine in accordance with the revelations he received from God. Some of these "alterations" were as drastic as the abandonment of old holidays and the institution of new ones.

Such severe changes in practice were supposed to bring us closer to heaven, ever shedding "new light" on our service, and they constituted an extreme break from conventional Protestant tradition. Whenever Daddy Raymond had a revelation, he would travel abroad preaching his new theology and spreading "the light." His followers considered themselves the most holy Christians in the world, unstintingly dedicated to the service of God and faithful to the literal letter of the New Testament, and his teachings were blindly accepted in all branches of the church.

Here in Portfield, he had created his central headquarters, and it had already developed into quite an impressive complex. There were several buildings on the campus: the dormitory and residence of the ministerial college, the Covenant House lodging for unwed and widowed mothers and abandoned children, and the new church which was now under construction. Some of these buildings had been converted from old, regal mansions, and the campus itself was green, spacious and quite lovely, although it was located in the seediest and most rundown neighborhood in Portfield.

There was singing coming from inside Covenant House as we pulled into the drive, telling me that the young people's meeting had begun.

"You can go in," my father encouraged.

"No. They have already started," I replied, somewhat relieved. "I don't want to come in late."

I followed my father to the building site. Many members of the congregation and students from the college were building the church with their own hands, working enthusiastically night and day to complete the project. The roof was not on yet, but it was progressing. I stood there feeling bored, wondering whatever in the world had possessed me to come. Now that I had satisfied my curiosity about the building, I was more than a little impatient to return home. Of course I knew we could not leave for several hours yet.

A short while later, Philip, who was then a counselor for the young people as part of his training, came out of the meeting and spotted my father and me. Eagerly, he came over to greet us.

"Come to the meeting," he urged me.

Again, I responded negatively, but my brother would not give up easily. "No, come," he nagged. "You can slip in the back. No one will see you. Come with me now. Come on! Put on your hat and come!"

I knew it was no good refusing him further. He had made up his mind. I quickly collected my beret from the car, plunked it on my head, and hurried along. As he had promised, there was a vacant seat in the back row, but I did not slip in unnoticed, for everyone turned around to view me.

I was not so well acquainted with the Portfield young people. They were a rougher city breed, and thought of me as being snobbish because I spoke properly, was the daughter of a well-known senior minister, and attended a grammar school. I smiled at them but received no response, and the moment was very awkward, to say the least.

I had been sitting there about five minutes when three girls got up to sing. One by one, they started to cry and "get in the spirit." The lady in charge of the young people—who happened to be the Websters' daughter, Victoria—encouraged everyone to kneel down by their chairs and pray to Jesus to fill them with the holy spirit.

"Really pray, from the depths of your heart," she urged us.

Several of the young people knelt down. I felt confused; I was glad I was sitting at the back, but angry that I had been forced into attending the meeting in the first place. Almost everyone was crying now. Somewhat reluctantly, and with tenuous resolve, I knelt down in my place, buried my head in my arms, and prayed to God to get me out of there soon, and by the way, to fill me with the holy spirit.

It was a double-edged sword. I really did want to serve God, and had wanted to ever since I was a very little girl. I even remembered once having said to Him in my bedtime prayer, "God, when I grow up, I want to give You all of my life. I'll work hard and I'll give You all of my money." That simplicity of devotion, although temporarily buried in the emotional morass of adolescence, had never died; and here I was, in an excellent position to truly serve God, and yet I did not feel quite right about it.

Partly I was embarrassed inside because I had already been lying for several years, on the rare occasions when I had been forced to testify, that I was "filled with the holy spirit." I still wasn't even sure what "being filled" entailed, and the uppermost thought in my prayers right then was a wish for the meeting to be over before I might have to lie again.

While I was standing outside after the meeting, Victoria Webster approached me excitedly. She was all grown up now, a spiritual leader in her own right, with a great deal of responsibility at the college. She was still as overweight and as confident as ever.

"Did you enjoy the meeting tonight? It was wonderful, wasn't it? Aren't you glad you came?" she asked me in a bubble of excitement.

"Yes, thank you," I replied politely, not daring to confront such a persuasive personality. "It was very nice."

Night had descended, and it was very good to be heading home. It would be a long time before I agreed to accompany my father to Portfield again on a Tuesday evening, although this was more out of confusion than aversion. I had been embarrassed by the experience and yet tantalized at the same time. There was a budding curiosity inside me about what spiritual fulfillment was really like. Perhaps those young people who had knelt down in Portfield and had cried and prayed in such a shameless display of emotion really did have something of worth, and I was the one who was missing out.

A good seed had been sown, and over the coming weeks, a hunger mounted within me to drink in the "new wine from heaven" and "bask in the spirit." No one would ever have guessed these feelings, except that from time to time, I would ask my father if he were going to Portfield that Tuesday. Never wishing to quench the tiniest spark of religious enthusiasm, he always readily agreed to make the journey even if he hadn't planned to go.

Gradually my young heart was hooked into the net, and I wanted to attend the meetings in Portfield every week. No one from the Greenborough congregation attended, so I could enter into the service with intensity, and not worry about being ridiculed by friends from home. A longing deep within my life to become intimately connected with my Creator was beginning to spring forth. I wanted so badly to be *truly* filled with the holy spirit that I began to pray seriously for it, and even secretly fasted several times for an entire day, telling my mother that I was not very hungry and wanted to rest in my room. I would go upstairs, close the door, and silently, sincerely beg Jesus to fill me with his spirit.

And then it happened. It was Christmas day. I was fourteen years old.

We had recently stopped keeping Christmas, Easter and other conventional holidays, because of Daddy Raymond's revelation that such festivities were of pagan origin and, as far as could be known, had nothing to do with Jesus. This was the most radical change that had occurred yet in the Church and served to further distance us from the Christian mainstream.

The dawn broke, and the Christmas sun began its ascent in the sky. The only sounds on the street were the chatter of the birds and the caroling of a few Salvation Army members who were going from house to house on the block. Many would have been appalled to see that in the pastor's home this year, there were no decorations, no tree, no trimmings. We children were not excitedly digging into stockings and pillowcases and pulling out nuts, sweets, and toys, and there was no aroma of turkey or Christmas pudding wafting out from the kitchen.

My father tried very hard to make it into a normal day. He piled us into the car along with the dog and took us for a ramble in the woods. Normally I welcomed such outings, but today I was eager to return home. I had some private, pressing prayers to offer, and no one could know about them. I was glad when the car finally pulled into the front drive, and at the first opportunity to slip away unnoticed, I was gone.

I closed the door to my room, which by now was mine alone, as both my sisters had left home, and sat tensely on my bed, begging Jesus to fill me with his spirit that day. I was fasting as well, having told my mother that I did not feel well and did not want to eat.

"Please, please, *please*, Jesus, fill me today," I implored, knowing that in order to receive such a gift from above, one had to hunger and thirst. I tried hard to arouse such a hunger and striving from the depths of my heart. At last, it was time to leave for the regular evening service, which was being held in Portfield that night, rather than in our chapel at home. I remained silent in the car for most of the journey, still inwardly beseeching Jesus to fill me.

When we arrived at the church, three of the girls from the young people's group bounded up to me, telling me that they had already been filled. I was a little jealous and also afraid. My desire to receive the holy spirit was much more than the simple need to fulfill a requirement. I knew that this "baptism of the spirit," as it was called, was a certain seal on a person's life. It was as if Jesus himself were saying, "I accept you. You are mine." I yearned more than anything else for the peace of mind that would come from the knowledge that I was accepted, and I was sorely afraid that I would not be filled. "How do I know I am worthy?" I thought.

Daddy Raymond led the service that evening, and it turned into quite a momentous occasion. About halfway through the meeting, the "spirit" came down on the people. Not wishing to interfere with the spontaneity of the event, Daddy Raymond dispensed with his usual program and beckoned to all who wished to be filled to come up to the altar. One by one, the congregants began to make their way to the front of the church. Almost all of the young people present, boys and girls alike, went forward, plus one or two of the older members of the congregation who had not already received the "baptism of the holy spirit."

I stood rooted to my place.

The music continued to play. Everyone stood and sang, and some who were at the altar were already crying, shouting and speaking in tongues.

"Go to the front," I told myself. "Go!"

But I just couldn't. I was overwhelmed with embarrassment. My father was up there on the platform—I would have to stand in front of him! Not only that, but my mother, my family, and all the congregants I had known since childhood were present, and I had been telling people since the age of eight that I was already filled! How could I bear to let them know I'd been lying? Added to that dilemma was the horrible ordeal of having to express myself emotionally in public, the thought of which distressed me to no end.

But my soul was yearning for fulfillment.

"The next time they sing this song," I told myself, "I'm going to the front!"

But the next time came and I stood in my place.

"The next time!"

But the next time came and still I could not budge.

"So *that's* it!" I informed myself. "You don't *want* to go to the front. And if you don't go, you won't be filled, and that's all!"

I started to cry. Tears were flooding like a waterfall down my face. It was not unusual to cry in church, for it meant that one was "moved" by the spirit or under some kind of conviction; and yet for me it signified abject confusion.

After about fifteen minutes, Raymond Webster stopped praying for the individuals at the altar and started to walk down the side aisle toward the back of the room. He was looking for someone—me.

He stopped at the end of my row. Silently, he walked along the pew, took my hand, and led me to the front. Quietly, he asked me, "Tonica, are you filled with the holy spirit?"

"No," I whimpered.

"Would you like to be?" he continued softly.

"Yes," I replied.

Immediately, he began to pray over me. Daddy Raymond was recognized as an apostle in the congregation, which meant that he was considered a direct disciple of Jesus; and in that capacity he had the power to transfer spirituality to another person. He now laid his hands on my head, and I knew that the spirit would finally fill me. I raised my hands, closed my eyes tightly, and started saying over and over, "Thank you, Jesus, thank you, Jesus!"

After a few minutes, he came to me again and whispered, "Just relax, Tonica. Relax." He took my arms and pressed me gently to the floor. I lay there amidst twenty other people of various ages, some already speaking in tongues, some praising Jesus, and others quiet. I continued saying "Thank you, Jesus," until a woman who was one of the counselors from the training college came and knelt down beside me.

"Tonica, just say whatever words are inside," she told me. "That's the holy spirit. Speak those unknown words within."

I had heard people speak in tongues my whole life. Every tongue was different, and sometimes I would wonder how people could be sure they were not making it all up or subconsciously copying someone else. Now here I was, lying on the floor at the front of the church, in quite a predicament. It was my turn to launch out. But how?

"Speak those words, Tonica," the woman encouraged gently.

I stopped saying "Thank you, Jesus," and formed some garbled sounds with my tongue. Heaven only knows what they were.

"That's it, that's it," she responded excitedly. "Come on, speak more!" After a few moments, I relaxed and started to murmur more and more of these peculiar sounds which had no meaning. All the time I lay there I kept thinking, "Is this really being filled? Am I really speaking in tongues?"

"It must be," I answered myself. "Don't doubt!"

I stayed on the floor until the meeting was almost over, praising Jesus and speaking in the unknown language I had discovered; and if there was a doubt in my heart, it was quickly eradicated after the service, when everyone began to crowd around me, hugging me and asking me how it felt to be filled.

"Oh, it's great," I responded, and I was happy—very happy. It really had been a wonderful meeting for me. The doubt of fourteen years had been resolved!

❧

When I arrived back at school after the holidays, my friends were eagerly discussing the presents they had received for Christmas. As they shared their excitement with one another, I remained silently content. None of them had received a gift as wonderful as mine, I thought.

The emotional high from the prayer meeting lasted for quite some time and had a noticeable effect on me, but it was hard to maintain such an intense aura in school surroundings. I still felt the normal teenage need to be part of the crowd and didn't yet have the maturity to break away completely and stand up for my beliefs.

That capacity was tested shortly when I went with the school on a camping trip to the Pennines for a week. The outing was a required part of our curriculum, but for me it became a torturous exercise in self-restraint. On the way up to the mountains, we stopped at a motorway café, and I declined all offers of cigarettes from my classmates, despite the slightly condescending looks I received. Throughout the week I did not wander outside my own circle of girlfriends, which I knew would have opened me up to contact with the boys. I was very conscious that my behavior set me apart from the group; but somehow I pulled it off.

However, upon our return to school, my friends let me know that one of the boys on the trip had noticed me and wanted to go out with me. To this day, I still don't know if the story was true or if they arranged it themselves.

"Go on, Tonica," they pleaded. "He's so nice. He's loaded with money and has a huge wardrobe of the best clothes. Go out with him!"

"No," I responded instinctively, "I don't want to." Dating was strictly prohibited by the Church—and I knew my parents would certainly never approve—but I was actually quite flattered and just as eager as any other teenage girl to go out with a boy.

"Ton, can we tell him you'll go out with him? Can we?" they badgered me continually.

"Oh, all right," I finally agreed. I tried to sound halfhearted, but beneath the surface I was very excited.

And, so, the date was arranged for Wednesday night at school. There was only one slight problem: prayer meeting was also on Wednesday night. How could I get out of it?

I waited until Wednesday evening at tea and then said to my father, "Daddy, I won't be able to go to prayer meeting tonight."

"You're *going*," he rejoined abruptly.

"No, I can't. It's sports night at school. I have to go."

"You're going to prayer meeting," he said mechanically, not even looking up from his meal.

I was desperate.

"I have to go to sports night because I'm a reserve for the relay race," I lied, "and if I don't go and someone else doesn't turn up, the whole team will be let down."

Silence.

I had played my ace card, and apparently it worked. The idea of disappointing the whole team seemed to have mellowed my father, but on the other hand he couldn't back down completely.

"You'd better pray about it, my girl," he insisted, and the matter was dropped for the rest of the meal. My mother always stayed clear of these conversations, knowing full well that her opinions would hold no sway with my father anyway. I was relieved but also a little annoyed—and more than a little sickened. I hated that line, "Pray about it." It was the ending to every situation: "Pray about it."

Of course I didn't pray about it, and went off to sports night with my heart playing leapfrog. This was my first date. What was I supposed to do? Would he kiss me? I was too embarrassed to ask my friends what to expect, or how to act, and plunged in on my own.

Richard was waiting for me in the designated spot outside the school building. We walked around the village near the school, and on one of our circuits, I did incidentally step into the gymnasium for a few minutes, but I certainly did not participate in any relay race!

Richard was sweet. I was very shy, but he looked after me nicely. We ambled around for a couple of hours, ate fish and chips out of a newspaper, and then the evening innocently came to a close. But not quite—for Richard wanted to see me again. He bought me a necklace which he delivered discreetly through one of my classmates and was continually sending me messages via my friends, asking me to meet him again. I tried to explain that it was difficult because of my father, but to no avail.

"He loves you, Ton," my friends insisted. "Go with him."

Finally, after a couple of weeks, Richard sent a message that he would meet me in one of the rooms at school that day during lunchtime, and if I didn't come, the relationship would be over.

Lunchtime arrived. My friends nagged me persistently, and my lack of resolve ate away at me. I wanted very much to go, but inside I knew I had to make a decision. Either I was going to go the way of the world, with boyfriends, discos, and all the other wordly pleasures, or I would go with Jesus; but I had to choose clearly. And so on that day, at that moment, I chose the latter.

From a classroom window, I watched Richard cross the yard, his face downcast, his heart heavy. He had been ditched. It hurt me to see him like that, and it was hard for me not to run after him and call, "Richard, Richard, wait, I'm coming," but I stayed put.

My friends were disgusted with me, but I felt I had settled a major conflict. It was only the first of many.

◆

Although I was developing a strong internal direction, the Battle of the Skirt Length had by no means come to an end. Over the months, I had become much braver about defying my father's standards, and because my parents left the house earlier than I did in the morning, and returned later in the evening, I was able to shorten my skirt properly without arousing any suspicion. On only one occasion did my father catch me, when he arrived unexpectedly to pick me up at school.

In answer to the outraged expression on his face, I insisted, "But Daddy, I've grown!" (Actually I had grown—about a quarter of an inch.) "And it really isn't worth buying a new skirt because soon I'm going to leave school altogether!"

"I'll give you money and you'll buy material," he said coldly. "Mummy will make you a new one."

True to his word, he gave me money and sent me straight to town to buy fabric. When my mother had all but finished the skirt, she made me put it on and pinlined up only a narrow edge of the hem.

"Mummy, please make it shorter," I begged. I bent over, nose almost to the floor. "See—it's *so* long!"

"Daddy will be angry at me, love," she responded sympathetically. "You must have it long."

Just then, she was called away to the kitchen to attend to a pot that was boiling over on the stove, and in those few seconds, I hitched the pins up a bit further and innocently disappeared from the room.

And so, although my skirt was still long, it wasn't freakishly long, and after a two-time turnover at the waist it was wearable again.

"I do want to do the proper thing—I really do," I repeatedly assured myself. "But it's just so hard!" I made numerous attempts to reconcile myself to wearing a proper length, even to the extent of telling my friends that I would come to school the next day with a long skirt and they shouldn't be surprised. But when the morrow arrived, my skirt was always well up past my knees.

Until one day.

The sun shone brightly. I was sprawled out on one of the benches in the yard at school enjoying the unusual heat when I started to feel somewhat uncomfortable about my legs. I suddenly felt rude and undressed. I covered my knees with my woolen blazer and lay that way through the whole of the lunch break.

The first lesson of the afternoon was chemistry, and I sat through the period on my high stool with a blazer over my legs.

"What is the matter with your legs today, Tonica?" my teacher inquired. "You've been covering them the entire period."

I smiled and remained silent. I didn't say anything to my friends, but that night I asked my mother to take down the hem of my skirt. She was very sweet and did take it down about half an inch.

"No, no, Mummy," I insisted, "I want it to go down as far as it will go."

"Goodness gracious," she exclaimed, "whatever has gotten into you?"

And so the next day, I went to school for the first time with my skirt past my knees. I felt dressed. I also felt comfortable and proud.

The boys called out from across the yard, "Have you snapped your suspenders, Ton?"

My homeroom teacher exclaimed, "What on earth are you wearing? Now we can't see your pretty legs!"

But I didn't give in. I didn't even want to anymore, and actually in the long run, I gained tremendous respect from my friends.

This was a vast breakthrough for me and gave me confidence to clear a bit of a spiritual pathway for myself. The little girl who had once promised Jesus that she would give him all of her money when she grew up had suddenly been rediscovered, and the anguish of peer pressure dissolved to a large extent inside me. I could be myself; I could be different.

I desperately wanted to serve Jesus. I remember one time being "moved by the spirit" at a convention meeting in Bloomington which was led by Daddy Raymond. In the middle of the service there was an altar call, but not the usual call for repentance; this time Webster was asking for a further commitment to the Church, a promise to submit wholly to the authority of the ministry and to stay with the congregation forever. Many people were going up to dedicate their entire lives to Jesus. Daddy Raymond went from person to person, praying and prophesying over them.

I wanted so badly to go up to the front but was hesitant. I was afraid that people would feel that at fifteen I was too young to make such an intense lifetime commitment, and that I couldn't possibly be sincere. The pressure of undertaking such an oath in public, especially when no other people my age were present, was too much for me to handle.

The next day, I was at home alone. I sat in our drawing room with my eyes tightly shut and pleaded with Jesus to take over my life.

"I don't know if you can hear me, but if you can, please take my life. All of it. I am giving it to you now. I want to dedicate my whole life to you and serve you completely. Please, *please*, if you can see me, and if you can hear me now, then please take over my life." I repeated this over and over again, stopping now and then to sing the well-known hymn, "Take My Life and Let It Be Consecrated Dear Lord To Thee." I wanted so much for someone above to hear the cry of my heart.

It was a lonely time. I really had no one with whom I could safely share my inner world. At school, I had not been rejected. I was still far too mischievous and full of fun to be excluded, but I had grasped the confidence to be outwardly different, and that isolated me to some extent.

I spent many hours walking in the woods alone with the dog or riding

Dolly, the horse my parents had bought for me a few years earlier, after a great deal of persuasion from my grandmother that there was "nothing wrong with a horse." We kept Dolly in a stable that was four minutes away by bike from the house, and the time I spent with her was an endless comfort. She was a very friendly pony and sometimes used to come right up to the French doors in the back of our house, put her two front legs on the carpet, and look about. My mother would have a fit and scream at me to "get the horse out of the house!"

Dolly passed no judgment on me, not about my skirt length, my spiritual status, or anything else, but was merely my friend; and her soft nose and moist, sympathetic eyes were a delight to a lonely teenager. In fact, she was probably my only real friend then. There were no other young people in the Greenborough congregation, and I was not close enough to my parents to share my doubts, worries and inner feelings.

Unfortunately, things would get worse before they got better.

❧ SEVEN ❧

M Y parents were going through a difficult time of their own. They were facing a major decision which I didn't fully understand. My father told me only that they were planning to move to Portfield to receive further training at the ministerial college, and that I would stay behind in Greenborough with Brother Mark and his family.

Brother Mark was an active member of the church whom my father had pulled into the "fold" several years before from the Anglican Church. Since then, his position had grown considerably, and eventually he had taken over the children and young people's program from my father. Now Raymond Webster had decided that the time had come for my father to move on, and leave the Greenborough congregation completely in Brother Mark's hands. This was the congregation my father had shepherded—and the town we had lived in—for over twenty years.

My mother was adamantly against the idea. She was in her late forties, very settled in her home and job, and comfortable with her friends. She most definitely did not want to give up everything she had worked so hard for to move into one room in a training college where the average student was about twenty to twenty-five years of age. I heard my father repeatedly quoting this verse to her: "'Except a kernel of wheat fall into the ground and die, it abideth alone.' If you won't come with me, Sally, I'll just have to go alone," he continually insisted. He had been given a commission from the spiritual master of the entire international organization, and felt it was his duty to go. He would not back down.

My mother's heart was torn. She loved her husband and didn't want to leave him, but it was too much for her to face. For months, she cried—morning, evening, and often, throughout the night. Sometimes I would wake up during the night and hear my parents in their bedroom going over the same arguments, the same lines, again and again.

I was very unhappy. The atmosphere at home was terribly unsettling. I had the feeling that my family was about to dissolve, and I didn't understand why. I wasn't close to my parents, but they were still my parents, and this was still my home; and on top of that, the idea of moving in with Brother Mark's family was unthinkable.

I hated him. He was convinced that I was thoroughly spoiled and was determined by any means possible to "knock me into shape," even to the extent of correcting my posture. He was always accusing me of slouching and would pull my shoulders back, particularly when there were other people around. He seemed to take great pains to embarrass me in public and to force me to do things that he knew made me uncomfortable.

But perhaps there was another, deeper reason why I continually clashed with this bigheaded gentleman.

One time, my father drove him home from church because his car needed repairing. I sat silently in the back seat, listening to their conversation about Israel and saving the Jews. As my father pulled into the driveway, Brother Mark commented, "You know, Brother Raymond likes to brag to outsiders that he has Jews as members of his church, but he only has Sally. Your children are not Jewish." My father replied that he knew that already.

Then Brother Mark turned to me and said, "You're no more Jewish than I am."

"I know," I replied indignantly. "Who cares, anyway?" Who was Brother Mark to decide what I was? I thought in adolescent outrage. The thought of living with this man in his house, with my parents far away, was too much for me. He was intellectually both powerful and brutal, and I was petrified of the treatment he might subject me to. I also resented the fact that my father's church was being handed over to an "upstart" with fresh ideas and new methods of saving souls, and I resolved within myself that no matter what happened, I would always do everything my father's way. Nobody—not even an over-bearing preacher—would push me around.

I thought briefly of trying to run away, but I realized that was a stupid idea because I would only be caught and brought back. I cried silent tears many nights as I stood in front of my bedroom window, looking into the black sky and pleading from the depths of my heart, "Dear God, why was I ever born? Please, can't you let me die somehow? Why did you make me?" I vowed to myself that I would never marry, for marriage was the cruelest thing on earth. You got married, you had a child, and then that child was forced to live. There was not a cell within me at that time that wanted to live.

I lost a tremendous amount of weight within the space of a few weeks. My teachers worried about me, but my parents were too caught up in their own problems to notice that anything was wrong, and my sense of isolation only deepened.

In the middle of this gloomy time, my mother received word that her brother Sammy was very sick and would have to undergo a serious operation. She used this as a welcome excuse to escape her trauma temporarily and went to Israel, where she stayed for six weeks.

While she was away, I took my final exams, left school, and got a summer job as a clerk in a publishing company. I had wanted to continue my education and become a teacher, but my father had vetoed that idea; Raymond Webster was opposed to an extensive secular education since he felt it would almost certainly conflict with religious commitment.

My parents' situation was up in the air over the summer, and no definite plans were made. With naive hopefulness, I prayed that the problem would vanish in smoke and we could go on as always.

But the bomb finally dropped. Not only that, it dropped in public, and no one prepared me for it in any way whatsoever.

Each year, the Church held an international gathering, an impressive occasion where dignitaries from all branches came together to exchange spiritual inspiration and news of progress in their respective corners of the earth. There were a great many people there, and at the end of one of the weekend services, Raymond Webster got up on the platform and announced that for the spiritual advancement of the Church as a whole, many of the ministers would be changing places. He began to run down his list. I listened absently, until suddenly I heard my parents' names.

"...and Brother Jim and Sister Sally will be moving to Southford."

Southford?

I felt a stab of alarm. Hadn't my father said they would be moving to Portfield? Portfield was only a half hour away, and at least if they went there, I would see them about twice a week. Now I would never see them, and what was going to happen to me? Why hadn't someone told me? What was this all about?

"I'm not going to Brother Mark's if my father is in Southford," I screamed silently in protest, and before I knew it I was crying.

Webster was greatly embarrassed because it was apparent that no one had given me the slightest inkling of these developments, and he sent my father over to pacify me. But my father was also discomfited; since we were not very close, he had no idea what to say to me, and the entire scene was taking place in the midst of a vast audience. It was a thoroughly shocking and awkward moment.

Daddy Raymond approached us after the meeting, his heavy face flushed from the drama of the service, his six-foot muscular frame casting its domineering shadow over us. "My wife and I have to go to Jamaica to visit the congregation there. We must go, but if your father has to move before we get back, then you had better come to Portfield to the training college for a while," he said to me. I didn't know if this was worse or better, and I was too confused to think right then.

I didn't understand at the time that this entire arrangement was much deeper than an administrative restructuring. Raymond Webster had actually told my father that he had received a revelation from God about my parents' transfer, and the move itself was only one part of this "order from above." My parents were also to sell everything they owned and donate the entire sum to the Church. Raymond Webster claimed that God was testing my father's commitment.

Many people in the Church were aware of what was happening, and for my father, it was a great public sacrifice, but he made it with absolute equanimity. His faith was simple and undivided, and he was happy to have an opportunity to declare his devotion to God.

It was only many years later that I learned the full extent of his sacrifice. He left his managerial position in the engineering firm, knowing full well that he was only a few years away from retirement, and thereby lost his pension, which was equivalent to about $75,000 at that time. He sold our semi-detached house, the car, *everything*—and gave every penny of the money to the church. He did this without a qualm, but I think he never realized the effect it had on me.

My mother was still abroad, and so my father and I packed up the entire house by ourselves. I was hardly allowed to keep anything, for my parents were constantly being criticized in the church for spoiling me too much.

My horse had to be sold.

The dog had to be taken into another home.

My books, magazines, everything in my room, had to go. I could take nothing with me except my sewing machine and a few stuffed toys, and to these I clung stubbornly, especially my teddy bear, which had been sent to me by my Jewish grandfather when I was one year old.

A rash broke out over my entire body, and I cried endlessly, but there was no one to know or even care.

My mother returned from Israel to find that her life would never be the same again, but she had no protests left to utter, and perhaps no strength to utter them.

In Southford, my parents would be put in charge of a community home which accommodated about thirty widowed and homeless people. The change was very hard on them. It was difficult enough to uproot at such a late age, but to try to fit in with young people and dormitory life made it much more stressful.

My mother did all the cooking, shopping and organizing for the home, and it is to her credit that she threw herself into the task without letting a soul know of her previous reluctance. She never held a grudge, but continually plodded on and remained a faithful helpmate to my father all through her life. I could only appreciate that in retrospect, however, for at the time my own pain was too deep. Each of us was involved in our own private suffering, and we made our adjustments in isolation.

While we were in the midst of packing, my father offered to take me along with him to Southford. I think that he was privately concerned about leaving his sixteen-year-old daughter alone in a ministerial college, but simply did not know how to express himself.

The choice was fully mine, but after some thought, I realized that it was not such a difficult one. At some point in the last few months I had crossed the line into my future. I could not say exactly where or when this change had taken place, but I knew inside that the adolescent struggle of four or more years had disintegrated and that I was in charge of my own destiny. I had always wanted to serve God; I had prayed for the opportunity to do so in a completely unobstructed fashion, and here was the key to that doorway, open quietly before me.

Somewhere, amidst the tumult and anxiety of the sudden change,

I felt an underlying ripple of excitement at the thought of beginning a whole new life with Jesus. Now I would finally be able to dedicate myself to him completely.

I had no idea that my stay in Portfield would last much longer than I had expected and that it would take me to places I had never dreamed of. I was an innocent baby leaving home.

❧ EIGHT ❦

ON a Sunday evening at the end of October in 1972, I took my beautiful chestnut hackney pony to her new owners. We stood outside in the courtyard like the most intimate of friends, Dolly rubbing her soft brown nose up and down my leg while I held her bridle loosely and caressed her neck. We had known each other for three long years, and I was going to miss her immensely. When my father had finalized the transaction with the owners, he and I walked quickly back to our half-packed house, and I felt as though I had left a part of myself behind. The dog, faithful as ever, ran to greet us, soothing the wound somewhat; but I knew I would only have him for a few more days.

The rest of the week was spent sorting through my treasures and throwing away almost everything I had saved. I knew I would not be allocated much space in the training college.

On Thursday evening, we traveled the half-hour distance to Portfield in silence, each of us wrapped up in private thoughts. As I look back, I wonder how my father must have felt. I'm sure it was hard for him to part with me, but he was as undemonstrative as always.

I drifted turbulently on the waves of a double roller coaster, half eager about my new commitment to a life of spirituality, and half apprehensive about leaving familiar surroundings and living under the Websters' roof.

My mind raced back over the past sixteen years. I remembered as a tiny child of four the way I had anxiously awaited the visits of "Uncle Raymond." I saw myself bounding up to meet him as he rounded the corner of our street, felt myself being whisked up into his arms and carried back to our house on his shoulders. He was my Uncle Raymond. I had always fought for a place on his knee and loved to go to his house whenever I was allowed. I remembered the times he had come home with my father to pray for us when we were sick.

Those memories were vivid and real, but now he was the father of a huge community, the principal of a prestigious ministerial college. We had drifted apart as I grew older, and on the rare occasions in recent years when I had entered his office in Portfield, our conversations were always abrupt and business-like. I wondered what our relationship would be like now that I was coming to live in his house.

And then there was his wife. What a fear she had always inspired in everyone around her! On more than one occasion, she had roughly grabbed my two elder sisters and banged their heads together. There was no escaping Auntie Jane's hawk-like scrutiny—be it physical or spiritual—and in fact, Anette had often confided to me that her mother "always knows when you tell a lie!" I thought of all her stringent rules of behavior, her cleanliness checks, her "impossible" demands. As a young girl, I had learned how to avoid her, but I knew those times were now rapidly drawing to a close. I wondered if she would treat me any differently now that I was older.

Last but not least, I thought of their eldest daughter Victoria. Quite a character, Victoria was; she had always strutted so proudly into the services, with her fur coat and flamboyant hat, as she took her place at the organ as bandleader. She, like her mother, was very stern, but I also recalled one pleasantly surprising occasion when she had bought me comics and chocolate at a newsstand, and then took me for a walk through the park, singing me nursery rhymes and silly songs. But that had been a blue moon ago, and we hadn't spoken for years. Would she like me and help me to adjust? Or would she hate me and make my life a misery? As head of all the single girls in the training college, it was well within her power to take either course.

We were almost there.

᷐

Holy Fellowship College was located in the midst of the shabbiest neighborhood in Portfield. General Booth, the founder of the Salvation Army, had been famous for his motto, "Go for souls, the worst first," and Raymond Webster seemed to have agreed with him wholeheartedly; for although the college itself was elegantly endowed, he had planted it in a den of squalor. Prostitutes loitered on all the street corners, drunks rolled in the gutters, deranged people muttered to themselves on the stoops, and filthy, neglected children fought and screamed at each other in the alleyways. It was for such as these that the church was a haven.

After five minutes of twisting through these leering passageways, we finally turned into Cherry Grove Place. The sudden change was startling. A tree-lined path led to a high wall, behind which rose a pala-tial stone mansion. Over the top of the wall peered a wooden notice board, reading, "The Congregation of Jesus/Holy Fellowship College."

"Well, we're here," my father declared superfluously, breaking into my faraway thoughts.

I took a deep breath, and together we walked through the gate and up the path to the entrance of the main hall. It was a beautiful build-ing, with sprawling lawns and trees in the front and a garden in the back. The front door opened onto a small porch, and from there we entered an enormous hall, which was dominated by a majestic oaken staircase.

Anette Webster came running to greet us, her green eyes twinkling and her pretty blond hair done up in a neat knot on top of her head. It was a relief to see her pleasant and familiar face.

"Where have you been?" she questioned. "We expected you much earlier. Come hurry and eat, and then I'll show you to our room. You'll be rooming with me!"

My father kissed me lightly and was gone. There were no tears, no visible emotion. It was quietly understood that this was a wonderful occasion; his youngest daughter was giving herself up to be a living sacrifice in the service of God, and it was neither the time nor the place for a display of maudlin sentiment. I would never again sleep in their home, there would be no more personal contact. No phone calls, visits or gifts. No holidays or recreation. From this moment forth, I was the property of God.

I followed Anette through the kitchen and into the dining room, glancing about me apprehensively, but feeling at the same time strangely calm. A plate of cold chips, baked beans and scrambled eggs was placed in front of me. After a long day, I had hoped for something a bit more appetizing.

"Thank you, but I'm not hungry," I lied weakly.

"You have to eat it," Anette informed me with a very intent gaze. "Rule Number One is that you eat everything that is put before you."

My elder brother and sister, who had preceded me here, had already warned me never to argue. I resisted the temptation and struggled through the unsavory meal, silently trying to absorb my new surroundings. Familiar objects I had seen a thousand times before on my youthful visits stared at me afresh with a somewhat menacing countenance, and I seemed to be seeing them for the first time. The furniture, the windows, the ceiling, all looked museum-like in their enormity, and the emptiness of the room made our voices echo. Even the linoleum on the floor squeaked coldly beneath our shoes. It was not home.

After I had downed my first meal at the training college, Anette led me up the broad, sweeping staircase to the first floor landing, and then up a much narrower staircase to the top floor, all the while giving me a running commentary on the residents of each room. Our own room was a tiny attic loft with one small window in the roof, and was simple but comfortable. I unpacked my few belongings while we chatted.

I was glad I had not been placed in the big dormitory rooms where several girls slept in bunk beds, and I shared my joy with Anette in a quiet way. I felt very shy, but deep down I knew that everything was going to be all right. Anette was seventeen, and I only six months younger, which made us the youngest students on campus, and I sensed we would have fun together.

We spent the rest of the evening sharing stories and reminiscing about the ten years of our friendship. By the time sleep finally overcame us, I knew everything I needed to know—or so I naively thought—about the training home. The boys were in the adjoining house, along with a few married couples, and the girls did not go into that building unless they were sent on an errand by the principal. Any contact with the boys could only take place in the communal rooms downstairs. The boys had all their laundry done for them, and the girls did their own. The college was kept spick-and-span, and to this end, the girls had a daily domestic duty, a daily kitchen duty, and a larger domestic task on Sunday, such as polishing the staircase or washing the floors. The boys were only required to help with the supper crew.

"The reason the boys don't have to do very much is so that they can spend time in Bible study and prepare sermons for the meetings," Anette explained. "The girls are trained to be ministers' wives. We have to know how to run a home, cook, clean, drive a vehicle, and play at least two musical instruments. That way, if we are sent out somewhere to minister, we can organize the music and help out in any other way that's needed." I learned that Daddy Raymond was beginning to think about ordaining women as ministers, although he hadn't taken that step yet; that obedience to rules was the first rule; and thrift and moderation were *de rigeur*.

I was eager to know how I would fit into the picture.

What would my domestic duties be?

Which classes would I attend?

Would I be "sent out somewhere" to minister?

I was afraid, but I didn't tell her. In the early hours of the morning, we finally drifted into an exhausted slumber.

The next day, I was taken to the church Administration Center, where Anette worked as an office junior. The Center was about a mile and a half down the road, and consisted of two enormous old buildings that housed the church shop and offices, a print shop with a darkroom, a design studio and finishing rooms.

Portfield was the headquarters for the entire international network of the Church movement. It was here in the Center that all the printing was done on the church's own presses, and from here that thousands of pieces of literature were sent out all over the world each month. Every mailing was a mammoth task, for each piece was checked, collated, folded and stapled by hand. There was always plenty of work to do, and it was all voluntary. No student or church member was ever paid for such services.

I was set to work immediately that first morning, helping with the day's mailing. A couple of hours later, the Websters' eldest daughter Victoria, who was in charge of the administration offices, sent for me. I walked into her private office, a large and well-furnished room, and stood by the door.

"Come here!" she motioned authoritatively.

I tried to put on a friendly smile and obediently walked over to her desk. Without saying a word, she grabbed hold of one of my braids and declared firmly, "This has to be tied up! There is nothing modest about hair bouncing around all over the place!"

I remained nervously silent and erect, not daring to move unless I was told. After a few moments, she seemed to soften and then put her arms around my waist and drew me onto her knee. I balanced there stiffly while she poked me lightly all over.

"What are you thinking?" she finally said. "That it's hard to be at the training college, where you have to do things like putting up your hair?"

"No," I replied coolly, not wishing to indulge her show of authority. Even then, I suppose, there must have been a germ of stubbornness in me.

This little scene seemed to be her way of welcoming me and letting me know who was boss at the same time. I was sent back downstairs to continue working on the literature, and the day progressed uneventfully. It was only later that evening, when I was on kitchen duty, that I had my official meeting with Mrs. Webster, or "Mother," as she was now known.

She came into the kitchen quietly, and we exchanged greetings. She stood there for a few minutes, watching my movements with a hard glare. As I wiped off the countertops in growing discomfort, I sensed that she was appalled by my slowness.

Suddenly she snatched the dishcloth from my hand and shouted, "Young lady, you're useless, pathetic and empty!" She then made fun of my movements and mimicked the entire dialogue we had just been through moments before.

"Hello, Sister Tonica, what are you doing?" she said matter-of-factly. "I'm wiping the side," she continued, imitating my slow, squeaky little voice; and then she grabbed hold of my arms and shook my whole body until I thought my head would surely fall off, screaming, "*Move*, child!" And as suddenly as she had appeared, she was gone.

Auntie Jane hadn't changed a bit. If anything, she had hardened.

But if I was afraid of the principal's wife and daughter, I was even more afraid of him. No welcoming words ever came from his lips. His assessment was completely silent, and if we happened to pass on the stairs or in the hall, his penetrating eyes would bore through me. Many times, I wondered what he was thinking. Did he realize it was me, Tonica Marlow, living in his house? Surely he did know, but any of his other thoughts during those first days I was never to uncover.

It took a good month for me to settle down and get into the routine of the college, and more than six months to fully adjust to community life. The atmosphere in the church itself was very different from that of the close-knit congregation I had grown up in. Accustomed to cozy services with twenty to thirty people, I found the Portfield services too big for comfort. Well over one hundred people attended the weekday services, and twice as many on Sundays, two-thirds of whom were gospel-spouting blacks, whose fervent exuberance far surpassed anything I had seen at home. I had come to prayer meetings here on visits so many times before, but now that I belonged to the college, it was entirely different. I felt lost and strange amongst all these people.

The daily routine at college began with morning prayers at five forty-five A.M. Afterwards, there was a short period of Bible study, and then breakfast. There was no uniform schedule for the major hours of the day; some people held regular nine-to-five jobs outside the college, while others stayed on campus and had domestic duty or worked in the garage or print shop. Daddy Raymond made all the decisions about what his forty-odd students did during the day, and collected everyone's paychecks. He was the spiritual mentor of us all, and his decisions were never questioned.

The evening program lasted from seven until ten and varied according to the day of the week. Tuesday nights were set aside for the young people's meeting, Wednesday nights for the general prayer meeting. There was a rotating duty roster which assigned us various tasks for the meetings; these could entail anything from giving a five-minute "thought," to driving people to and from church, for many of the congregants were elderly, and public transportation in Portfield was poor.

On the remaining nights of the week, we were either given assigned tasks on campus or we attended classes: Bible theory, history, geography, music theory and voice training. We also received on-the-job training in preaching and in counseling young people under the tutelage of ordained ministers, and we were taught to run the printing press and to play instruments. Holy Fellowship College was recognized by the government as a theological university, and Raymond

Webster had the authority to grant ordination, but his goals were much wider in scope than the simple dispensation of diplomas. His ultimate mission was to train every student to be able to go to darkest Africa, if necessary, and to start a church from scratch—everything from printing literature to preaching, to cooking for large groups. We were indeed a missionizing people!

Each evening at ten o'clock there were evening prayers, and then we were allowed to have a hot drink and a biscuit before retiring. There was very little time to breathe during the day, and I was often quite exhausted by the time I finally crawled into bed.

During the first month, I worked on the literature at the Administration Center every day from eight-thirty in the morning until five o'clock, and then again from seven to ten in the evening on every night when services were not held. My artistic abilities were soon discovered, and I was set to work in the art department, where I soon found myself responsible for bringing out a monthly full-color paper for the tiny tots. I learned how to do the color separation, and was expected to write, illustrate and color the entire paper.

One time, I remember being seriously reprimanded because I had drawn a teacher in full gown and had forgotten to paint the gown and the shoes black on the original sheet. Consequently, the drawing was printed as an outline, only with no color filled in, and thousands of these comics were sent out with the teacher appearing in ghost-like form. I thought it was quite amusing and laughed about it to one of my co-workers, but then paid for my gaffe by being verbally abused and cold-shouldered for several weeks to come. This was the Church's way of teaching responsibility.

Right from the beginning, I also taught Sunday school, at first the infants, between three and five years of age, and later the six-and-seven-year-olds. I had never before taught children, and now I was thrown into the deep end with only the impromptu guidance of the senior teacher to direct me. Unfortunately, he was also involved in a huge maintenance project in Southford, where he spent most of his

Sundays, and so the class was left almost entirely under my supervision. It was a cold-water bath in the beginning which caused me frequent panic, but I did become a teacher and kept that Sunday school job for many years.

Sundays were even more hectic than weekdays. We rose at five thirty as usual, attended morning prayers, and then prepared for Bible school. The entire day was spent in church. First there was school itself, and then the young people's meeting, which always lasted longer than scheduled because the teenagers needed to talk. Most of them came from severely disadvantaged homes, and the church was the only place where they were able to find a bit of comfort and a listening ear. Finally there were evening services, after which we had to drive all the congregants home. The day never ended before eleven-thirty.

I was also assigned to play my clarinet in the band and was immediately given responsibilities in the choir. I had always loved music and threw myself eagerly into both jobs. I began to wake up at the crack of dawn each morning so that I would have time to go down to the cellars and practice my clarinet for a full hour before morning prayers.

Aside from these official obligations, I also had a daily domestic duty along with the other single girls, and my first task was to assist in the supper crew. "Supper" in college referred to the nighttime snack we had before bed, and for the week of our assignment, the four or five people on the crew had to clean out the milk pot, wipe the tables and mop the floors in the kitchen and dining room.

Sister Martha, the principal's secretary, was in charge of the supper crews. She was a petite, dark-haired young woman with strikingly long eyelashes and blue eyes which could seem entirely innocent; but I quickly learned that I was dealing with someone who was very sweet on the outside, but very sly and cunning within. Sister Martha came from a very large, poor family, and her parents were deaf and dumb. The Websters had taken her in when she was fifteen years old, and in the seven ensuing years, she had worked her way up to being their private secretary. She waited on them hand and foot and often tried to stay in their favor by putting others down. She would delight in relating your foibles to them and then telling you the embarrassment was "for the good of your soul." I was too young and naive to understand the basis for this approach, and although I resented her personally, I accepted her authority. There was really no alternative.

The worst of the domestic duties was Sunday morning breakfast. Most people did not eat breakfast during the week, but the Sunday morning meal was almost sacred. It was served promptly at eight o'clock and included everything from a variety of eggs and sausages to tea, toast, marmalades and cereals. Our meals in general were Spartan, and by college standards, this was practically a feast. I learned to hate Sundays in very short order.

After only one month at college, my turn came around to take care of the breakfast. Anette showed me what to do the first week, and the following Sunday I was in charge of the entire project alone. I arose at five-thirty and tiptoed down to the kitchen in a fairly confident mood; but although I had cooked often at home, I rapidly learned that making breakfast for forty was immensely different from making breakfast for three. Things did not bode well for my success when the poached eggs tipped out of the pot as I was trying to drain off the water, and landed in the sink. In quick succession, my fried eggs went hard and crispy, the toast burned, and the sausages turned into charcoal sticks. I had always cooked them at home for about ten minutes, but had no idea that when deep-fried in a fryer, they take only three minutes.

The next few batches went more easily, and by eight o'clock, I had managed to load a variety of appetizing dishes into the belling, an electric warming cabinet with shelves that kept the food hot until it was served. Of course, it all had to go into the belling and be eaten, for no food, no matter how awful, was ever thrown out.

Everyone was seated in the dining room except Mother, who always had breakfast in her room. At five minutes after eight, Sister Martha sauntered into the kitchen with Mother's breakfast tray. She looked casually into the belling and stood back, aghast.

"Whatever has happened to the breakfast this morning?" she demanded.

I stood there sheepishly, explaining that there were a number of good things to eat, and that it was only the first batch that had been burnt, but Sister Martha was not sympathetic. Chortling slyly, she began loading the breakfast tray with the worst of everything. To make matters worse, Mother's tray was made of silver and her dishes of china, and although burnt toast and a charcoaled sausage do not look too conspicuous on a chipped crock plate, they look miserable next to a silver teapot on a fine china platter.

Laughing meanly, Sister Martha scurried through the door and up the main staircase. In embarrassment, I quickly ran up the back stairs to my room and relayed the whole story to Anette. We both ended up laughing hysterically, but my humor was to be very shortlived. In a matter of minutes, Sister Martha was calling up the stairs, "Sister Tonica, Mother wants you immediately in her room!"

This was my first entrance into the Websters' private chamber. I was petrified. Humbly, I knocked on the door and went in. I could tell instantly by Mother's face that she was not amused.

"Sit down," she ordered sharply.

"Where?" I trembled.

"On the bed," she replied irritably.

To this day, I am absolutely positive that I looked at the bed and did not see anything there. But when I sat down, I sat right in the middle of her breakfast tray, turning over a cup of tea which spilled all over her light pink candlewick bedspread.

By now she was furious, and her face had turned purple. Pulling my arm almost out of its socket, she grabbed me and ordered me to go downstairs and get a bowl to rinse out the bedspread. Shaking, I hurried down the dark back staircase, the enormous wet patch on my behind branding me in disgrace. When I returned with a very small and inadequate cooking bowl—which was all I could find in my frenzy—I think Mother saw stars; but suddenly an angel in the form of Sister Samantha was sent to my rescue.

Samantha had been appointed to me as a spiritual mentor at the college, something of a big sister, and by some miracle, she happened to pass by the open door at that moment.

"Mother, can't you see that the child is petrified?" she pleaded on my behalf.

I started to cry uncontrollably, trembling from head to toe. Mother sent Samantha out of the room and then sat down and lectured me on my behavior, making it quite clear how appalled she was. After the fiercest rebuke I had ever received, she sent me on my way.

The story was not quite finished, however, for when I returned home from the Administration Center the next evening, I found Mother awaiting me. Avoiding her eyes, I attempted to walk past her into the dining room.

"Oh, no, you don't," she barked, digging her nails into my shoulder and pulling me toward her. "I have a special meal for you."

Two seconds later, a plate full of the cold, burned, rubbery remains of the previous day's fiasco was pushed into my hand.

"Eat it," she demanded. "This is your meal for tonight."

With a burning face, I sat down in the small dining room, hoping that not too many people would see me. Mother pulled up a chair, sat down with folded arms, and watched me eat every morsel with the interest and glee that a child might express while watching the chimpanzees' tea party at the zoo. I had no idea until many years later how deeply the experience had burnt a scar into my heart.

Nevertheless I discovered that I was not the only victim of Mother's "training." Auntie Jane not only had personalized instructions for her charges, but she insisted that every detail be carried out exactly as she had ordered. She once banged Anette's head against the wall for not crying when she apologized for something, and there were other incidents that were quietly passed about on the unofficial college grapevine.

None of us thought openly of questioning Mother's ways. We took it for granted that she or anyone else in authority could walk up to us out of the blue and say, "Scrub the floor," or "Eat a piece of moldy bread," and we were expected to obey blindly. It was their way of reminding us from time to time who was in charge, and I had no idea that there were any other ways to teach respect for authority. Fortunately, I somehow always managed to get up after I had been flattened, sincerely believing that such experiences were all part of the refining process.

Sister Samantha, who had pulled me out of the ditch after the breakfast catastrophe, was soon to become one of the very significant authority figures in my life. Each of us at the college was assigned an older member to "shepherd" our souls, and she had been given full charge over my spiritual welfare. Since she was also the head of the art department where I worked during the day, we saw a good deal of each other, and she had plenty of opportunities to "shepherd" me—perhaps a bit too many for my comfort.

Sister Samantha was Brother Mark's niece, and the eldest of three sisters, all of whom were brilliantly talented in music and art. She was about five-foot-three, quite a bit overweight, and very temperamental. She had been accepted into the college after her engagement was broken one week before the planned wedding day. It was Brother Mark who had intervened, assuring Samantha that even though her fiancé was a straight Pentecostal boy, he was not right for her and that God had bigger plans for her life. With the hope of fulfilling this higher calling, she left her teaching job, packed her belongings, and moved to Portfield. She advanced quickly at the college, and by the time I arrived, she was already a mentor for the younger students and in charge of the art department. Eventually she was one of the first women ministers ordained by Raymond Webster.

Six months after her arrival in Portfield, her family was involved in a car accident which killed their mother and left their eccentric French father close to insanity. The other two sisters came to the college soon afterward. The middle one, Maude, had been a police cadet. She was the tallest and most intelligent of the three and was put to work running the main printing press at the Administration Center. Josephine, the youngest, was still in high school, a very wild teenager who had almost been expelled from school on more than one occasion. She was a terrible flirt, and her supervisors at college had their hands full keeping her in line. She was sent out to work as a secretary in town in the hope that the responsibility would straighten her out, but unfortunately it didn't cure her flirting.

All three girls were fun-loving but extremely sensitive and moody. Because of their forward personalities, they tended to fill the college with their presence, and it was hard to accomplish anything without bumping into one of them.

Of all three, Samantha, as the "shepherd of my soul," had the most profound effect on my life at college. She was granted full permission by Raymond Webster to "break my spirit," work on my character, and refine me in any way she saw fit until I was ready for the ultimate sacrifice of laying down my life on the "altar." She had saved me on that one memorable occasion from Mother's wrath, but her kindness did not always assume such a conventional form.

I remember one particular morning when she had balloons to blow up for the young people's meeting that evening. Obviously she didn't want to dignify such a trivial task by performing it herself, so she handed it over to me; but rather than leaving me in the corner to finish the job, she made me blow up all the balloons in front of her so that she could laugh and make fun of me as I became beet red, huffing and puffing, with my eyes bulging from lack of breath. I was terribly embarrassed and ceased trying. She insisted I was proud, blowing the whole episode completely out of proportion, and even reporting me to higher authorities for rebellious and disgusting behavior. I was severely reprimanded and punished, but I never did blow up the rest of the balloons.

On another occasion, she took the leg of a broken stool and beat me with its brass tip more than twenty times, swinging me around by one arm so that I could not get away, and yelling all the while, "This is not for what you have done, but for what you are about to do!" I protested loudly, but she continued until she had reduced me to a crumpled heap on the floor, and then strutted into her room and slammed the door.

Her method of "refining" my character took odd extremes, running the gamut from these flagrant beatings to nauseating displays of affection. Each night, she would come to our bedroom and tuck me in for the night with slobbery kisses, the number of which depended on her mood. Most often, she came in when Anette was out of the room.

Samantha's caresses wore a friendly demeanor, but they were very strong and made me extremely uncomfortable. I was afraid at these times and always became tense and stiff, and then she would tickle me while I tried to push her off without offending her. I didn't understand any of this; all I knew then was that I didn't like it. But I had no thought of questioning. I always subconsciously assumed that if I didn't understand or enjoy the practices of my superiors, it was my fault—I simply hadn't developed enough spiritually to comprehend their ways.

My sister Margaret arrived at college about four months after me. Since my father's departure from Greenborough, she had been living at Brother Mark's house and helping him out with the congregation. Daddy Raymond changed his mind about Brother Mark's assignment and decided it was time for him to move to the college and assume responsibilities there, and so Margaret came along as well. Both she and my brother Philip had very different assignments at college and dormed in different buildings, and we did not have much time to spend with each other; so although it was reassuring in one sense to know that I had family on campus, their presence was not much of a practical comfort. In any case, I had never been able to depend on Margaret for closeness, and certainly not to get me out of scrapes with any amount of eagerness.

I found out quickly that there was not much Margaret could have done to buffer me from the shock of my initiation, for she was undergoing similar trials herself. I remember one very frightening occasion, shortly after her arrival, when she came up to my room, white as a sheet. Mother had just tried to choke her for refusing to eat a pile of peanuts, and she was still rubbing her neck and struggling for breath when she appeared in the doorway. "I thought she was going to kill me," Margaret gasped. The fact that she came to me at all was proof of the trauma she had experienced, for we were not in the habit of confiding in each other.

Although such incidents left me in mortal fear of Mother—or anyone else, for that matter, whose path I might cross on an unlucky day—things were not all bad. Anette was my one true friend at college, and I don't know what I would have done without her support. She and I managed to squeeze in some fun amongst the rigors of our training, but we had to do this mostly on the sly.

Anette knew all the secret passages in the college exceptionally well since it had been her home for quite some time now, and she rapidly initiated me. We began to slip into a regular private ritual. Each Saturday afternoon after services, we would wait up in our little attic room until the college grew still. Then we would tiptoe through all the unused back passages, creak down the dark winding staircases, and arrive surreptitiously in the kitchen. One of us would stand guard while the other would scamper to the freezer, and pry out a large ice cream cake, an item which Anette had noticed was always in the freezer but which somehow never appeared on the menu. One of us would hide the cake under her flowing skirts, and we would scurry back through the same dark alleyways, giggling quietly, until we reached our bedroom. Then we would bolt the door and burst into uncontrollable laughter while we dug into our prize. Sometimes we even dared to repeat the operation during the same afternoon or in the middle of a weeknight.

I was amazed that no one ever made an announcement about the disappearance of the walking cakes, since at least once a month, Mother called the entire student body together to lecture us on the sin of extravagance and waste. So much emphasis was placed on conservation that expenditures were cut for the smallest items, and even our paper products were rationed. We sat through lecture after lecture on the importance of frugality and the necessity of eating every crumb of bread, stale or not. I remained much too innocent and naive to ask myself exactly for whom those cakes were intended, why the stock was constantly being replenished, and why, when every piece of toilet paper had to be accounted for, these missing ice cream cakes did not.

But I was enjoying my escapades far too much to be bothered with technicalities, and the only thing that concerned me was that in spite of the disagreeable food, my waistline had managed to expand.

And so the rough edges of my initiation into college life were softened with a bit of sweetness, and any bitter feelings I had were hammered to the bottom of my consciousness, where they slept for a time.

≈ NINE ≈

WHEN I had been at college about six weeks, Daddy Raymond decided it would be good for me to get an outside job and find out about people and life, for I had always been very sheltered. Of course, it was understood that my paycheck would be handed over to the church. He sent me down to the city youth employment office.

"Tell them your father is a minister," he began. "Say that he has moved to Southford and that you are studying in a minister's training college here in Portfield, and need to get a job as part of the training program."

I was so overwhelmed and flattered that he was even talking to me that I replied, "Yes, yes, yes" to everything he said and promptly forgot most of his instructions. However, I do remember his very last words: "Tell Anette to make your hair up like a lady's—and walk straight, child! Hold up your head, keep your eyes down, and move with determination. Let them know you mean business!"

The morning of the interview dawned, and Anette put up my hair with curls and twists as she had been instructed. The style was totally overdone, appropriate for someone twice my age; but although I looked and felt stupid, I didn't have the heart to tell her to take it down. I didn't have much choice in the matter.

And so, with the face and voice of a twelve-year-old, and the appearance of a thirty-five-year-old, I walked in to the employment office in town, sat down timidly at the desk, and said to the clerk, "My father is a minister...."

Silence.

I was at a loss to continue. I had gone blank.

"Yes, so what?" the clerk replied tartly.

"Um, well, um...." I stuttered, "he...he had to move away."

"Oh, so I suppose you need a job," she finished for me flatly, in the grayest of business tones. "Just one moment."

She returned in a few minutes with a bundle of cards containing information about vacant jobs. It was soon obvious that all the poor woman could see was the mound of curls in front of her.

"Now, how about being a hairdresser?" she asked.

"Oh, no," I replied emphatically, "definitely not!"

"Hummm," she murmured as she flicked through a few more cards. Her raised eyebrows indicated that she considered most of the positions highly unsuitable.

"Are you *sure* you wouldn't like to be a hairdresser? You seem to do your own hair very originally."

"I am perfectly sure I do not want to be a hairdresser," I replied.

"Well, what *do* you want to do?" she exclaimed, totally exasperated.

"I don't know," I whispered.

After another expert flick through the cards, her eyes finally fell on one which seemed to contain possibilities, however remote.

"There's this," she said hesitantly. "A vacancy at Barclays' International Bank. Would you like to try that?"

My eyes lit up. "Oh, yes, that's fine," I said excitedly.

"Good, the interview will be arranged."

True to her word, the interview was scheduled for that afternoon. I felt like a small girl in the prestigious "high-ceiling" atmosphere of the bank, and shyly followed my escort into the manager's office. The manager, a pleasant, dark-haired gentleman named Mr. Reavey, did not seem quite as distracted by my hairstyle as the employment clerk had been, and we talked at length about my education, outside interests, hobbies and abilities. He was well-satisfied and the job was mine—that is, until I suddenly remembered that there was one more wrinkle that had to be ironed out. I would have to leave early on Fridays.

About one year before I entered the college, Daddy Raymond had traveled to every group in the country and overseas to deliver his latest spiritual revelation from God: Saturday, rather than Sunday, would now be considered the seventh day of the week and a holy day, in keeping with the Church's goal of becoming the completed people of the New Testament as "New Covenant Israel." The Christians believed that it was their mission on earth to complete the aborted task of the Jews and assume their role as the *true* chosen people, and this was Daddy Raymond's rationale for reverting to the original Jewish Sabbath Day; but although his reasoning followed standard Christian doctrine, his method was quite revolutionary.

I still remembered the meeting in Greenborough when he had spoken for hours with fire and conviction, quoting from the Old Testament, "Six days you shall labor and do all your work," he had thundered from the pulpit, as he rolled up his sleeves, shed his tie, and consumed enormous quantities of soda. "Everyone who has a job that demands work on Saturday must give it up! Or better still, tell them that you will work on Sunday for the same pay as Saturday!" Thousands of people from all parts of the worldwide movement had subsequently given up their jobs.

Daddy Raymond had not actually told me before my interview that I must leave early on Fridays, and I did not know of anyone in the congregation who did so, but in my innocence, I assumed that was what I must do. After all, the traditional Jewish Sabbath began on Friday evening, and hadn't he said there should be no labor on the Sabbath?

I informed the manager that our church kept the Jewish Sabbath and asked him if it would be possible for me to leave early on Fridays.

He thought for a while, then shook his head slowly and replied, "I am sorry, but I can not make such allowances for one worker over another. No, I am really sorry, but I just can't do it. Maybe you can find a Jewish company to work for," he continued as he showed me the door. I tiptoed quietly through the banking hall and took the bus back to the training college.

The principal was anxious to hear how the interview had gone, but instead of being pleased by my story, he was horrified.

"What?" he screamed. "You turned down a good job because you wouldn't work on the Sabbath? Call him back right now. Tell him you have talked it over with your minister and that he allows you to work on Fridays and on into the Sabbath." He took me straight into his office, dialed the number, and stood right behind me, whispering, "Speak positively, child."

"Hello, this is Tonica Marlow, the girl whom you just interviewed," I said shyly to Mr. Reavey.

"Yes, what can I do for you?"

"Well, I've just spoken to my minister, and he says that it is all right for me to work on the Sabbath. Is the job still available?"

"Well, what about *Yom Kippur*? What if the situation arose when we needed you on *Yom Kippur*? Would you come to work?" questioned the manager. I think he had no idea if I was Christian or Jewish; and frankly, my own understanding of the matter was not much more extensive than his. I had heard of *Yom Kippur* from my reading of the Old Testament, but that was about all I knew.

"One moment, sir." Covering the mouthpiece, I relayed the question to Daddy Raymond.

"Yes, yes, tell him yes," the principal insisted.

"Hello, yes, I would work on *Yom Kippur*."

"Very well," replied Mr. Reavey. "The job is yours."

Arrangements were made for a starting date, and the principal sat back contentedly, like a cat with the cream. He had already discovered that I was competent and responsible and knew that I would bring in a good salary for the church. I was to find out soon enough that there were many others in the college who had received similar dispensation, for they often did not arrive home on Friday night until the evening meal was well under way. But I did not understand any of this; I was only glad that I had satisfied the principal. Sabbath, *Yom Kippur*—what did I really know about them, and what business was it of mine anyway?

None. None at all.

Or so I thought.

❧

The November air was chilly as I set out for my first day at work in the outside world. I was a little over sixteen years old. There was a small tingle of anticipation someplace amidst my bundle of nerves. It felt good to be going out and having a little freedom, and I was fairly confident—until I rang the bell outside the two imposing wooden doors of the bank. A tall Scottish ex-serviceman, officially known as "The Messenger," and affectionately called "Jock" by all, escorted me inside, where I was introduced to a few members of the staff. As I smiled politely and exchanged pleasantries with them, my ears caught snatches of their casual conversation.

"Did you see the film on television last night?"

"No, I was out with Dave."

"I've been out every night this week—haven't turned on the TV in days."

Suddenly I froze in fright. It was only three short months since I had left school. How could I have forgotten so soon? This is what life in the outside world is like: boys, television, discos, theaters and night life. It was happening again—I was *different*!

Fear of rejection swept over me, the same terrible fear I had endured all through my school years. What would they think of me? How could I appear normal? What would I say? And my clothes! At college, we were required to be extremely modest—and needless to say, my nearly-ankle-length dress and long thick hair swept into a tight neck bun aroused much wry interest in all my co-workers, who were sporting miniskirts and the other trendy styles of the early seventies.

I was taken to the chief accountant, who swiftly escorted me to the top floor to work in the bookkeeping department. I sat quietly in the corner of the office the entire morning and did whatever I was told, never daring to open my mouth except to talk about matters related to work. There was nothing else I could say, for I had not seen any movie the night before—and I certainly did not have a boyfriend!

When the coffee break came around, I walked timorously into the staff room, found an empty seat, and never lifted my head to look at anyone. I could feel the eyes of all those present focused on me, the "weird" character who had just entered the ranks.

It was the longest fifteen minutes I had spent in many a day, and when it was over, I thankfully made my way back to my corner of the department.

The day lingered on endlessly in much the same fashion, and finally my supervisor approached me and said the most beautiful words I had heard since the morning: "You can go home now!"

How good it felt to be hurrying back to the familiarity of the college! As I bounded in through the main doors, Sister Samantha was there to greet me and to ask how the day had gone.

"Oh, fine," I replied nonchalantly. "It was really nice, everyone was extremely friendly." I was afraid to reveal the truth, afraid that I would be reprimanded for not giving a good impression, and thereby limiting my chances for advancement at the bank. And so, my secret was hidden, and for a time I fell into the old familiar habit of wearing two masks; at the college, I was fast becoming the bouncy, noisy, mischievous Sister Tonica, and at work, I was the "strange, shy girl" who never said a word.

In fact, I later learned that my co-workers used to ask one another,

"Does she talk?" Finally after about six months, the chief accountant approached me confidentially and whispered, "Are you always as quiet as this?"

With a twinkle in my eye, I replied, "Oh, no, you don't know me yet!"

His hearty laugh was tinged with relief, and it wasn't long before my companions did find out who I really was. I began to relax a bit and found that I could allow my personality and sense of humor to sparkle and shine without overstepping any of my boundaries. Everyone around me relaxed too and began to tease me about having no knees and a bald head. They were convinced my hair was a wig.

I soon came to enjoy my professional life and found myself growing in the company in leaps and bounds. I was upgraded and moved to different departments to gain experience, and within two short years was brought back to the bookkeeping department as the youngest supervisor the branch had ever had.

&

The only disappointment in this burst of success was that during the winter months, when sunset in England was as early as three-thirty in the afternoon, I was unable to be back home in time for the onset of the Sabbath.

Friday evenings were a very special time in the college, something I looked forward to all week. One hour before sunset, work would cease. We would spend that time relaxing, listening to soft music, and setting up the Sabbath tables in our rooms with clean tablecloths, china cups and breakfast boxes containing sandwiches and fruit. Shortly before sunset, we would congregate in the lounge and sit quietly and calmly in order to welcome the Sabbath spirit, and as the sun descended, we would sing special spiritual songs which the students had composed. During the winter months, it saddened me each week to let that special time of peacefulness slip by, and I would wait eagerly until the days became longer and I could be home in time for the singing.

One of the hymns we sang, taken from the words of Isaiah, was especially stirring:

> *Weep not, mourn not, this is a holy day*
> *The joy of the Lord is our strength.*
> *Eat of the fat, drink of the sweet*
> *Give unto those who have nothing to eat*
> *For this is a holy day*
> *And the joy of the Lord is our strength.*

There was a multitude of such songs. The singing, praying and praising would last for about twenty minutes, and then everyone would have a cup of freshly made tea. At about six o' clock in the evening, we would sit down to the meal, the only time in the week that everyone in the college ate together. Our seating plan was arranged so we could not choose our dinner companions; but after the meal, we would have between one and two hours to relax in the lounge, and this was the only free time that was given to us to socialize with whomever we wished.

Afterward there would be a time of formal sharing called "fellowship." Interesting letters that had been received from groups around the world would be read and taped, new songs would be sung, stories told. It was a family time, relaxed and happy, and occasionally I would get to sit with my brother or sister. But the three of us spoke only of light, superficial matters, for even though we shared the same environment, our lives were radically different. This did not trouble me greatly, for I was riding high on the crest of a spiritual wave, and there was very little that could have dampened my enthusiasm at that time.

The bank was not the only place where I began to shine. At college too, I had finally learned to flow with the tide, and I set my heart to prove that I was not such a useless ragamuffin after all. Thank God, there were no more major catastrophes like the breakfast ordeal, and I threw myself into all my studies and duties with a zealous energy. I was still working in the evenings and on Sunday afternoons in the art department at the Administration Center, where my skills developed rapidly. I practiced hard on my clarinet whenever I had a spare moment and was soon playing in all the services as second clarinetist.

My natural inclination toward children blossomed as well, and soon my Sunday Bible classes were thriving. The class of six and seven year olds was constantly growing larger, and as a result, I became a favorite with the Websters' daughter, Victoria, who was in charge of the entire children's program in the church. I drew pictures for my little tots and composed new songs, which the children learned and loved; and my success there gave me the confidence to contribute in the adult services as well, where I often plucked up enough courage to sing, testify or speak in tongues for interpretation. My young heart was open to receive, and ready to give, and within those two years, which had begun with such difficulty, I became a favorite in the college.

On my eighteenth birthday, I had a very pleasant surprise—a huge cake, beautifully decorated by Sister Victoria, with roses and bows made of delicate pink icing, and a huge bundle of presents and cards. It was a thrilling experience. I felt accepted and loved and couldn't believe there could ever be a more wonderful way of life.

There was another important occurrence at that time which inspired an even deeper love in me for the path I had chosen.

My mother became seriously ill with cancer and had to be rushed to hospital for an emergency operation. We were not allowed to have too much contact with our parents, as Raymond Webster felt it interfered with our training, but naturally these were unusual circumstances. The principal waited until I got home from work that evening to tell me the operation had been successful, and he allowed Margaret and me to take the next day off to go and visit her.

Her medical situation was serious. Eight doctors had worked on her the entire night, and not one of them had held out any hope, especially in the light of the fact that my grandmother had died at the same age of the same type of cancer. My mother's strong predisposition, coupled with the advanced spread of her own illness, had virtually sealed her fate—and yet she not only recovered completely, but never had a recurrence of the disease in any form.

Everyone who knew her—my father, Raymond Webster, all the congregants—said it was a miracle from Jesus, for without his help, she would never have gotten up off the table. This awed me; but it was somehow not quite as extraordinary as the other seemingly trivial incident that arose from the crisis. My mother gave no reason, but she told everyone that from then on she wished to be called "Sarah" rather than "Sally." And Sarah she became.

I was seeing God perform miracles right within my own family. I felt more and more strongly each day that my only business in life was to serve Him, and my one wish was that others could share in the joy I felt in that service. I was deliriously happy.

⊰ TEN ⊱

IN the course of those prosperous days, my sister Margaret approached me in the dining room one night during the evening meal, looking unusually excited. She and I rarely saw each other at college—in fact, our different duties and schedules contrived, if anything, to keep us apart. I worked with the children, Margaret with the teenagers; I spent all of Sunday in church, while she was in the kitchen; we both had outside jobs during the week and lived in different buildings. In spite of this, we did manage to stay in some sort of perfunctory contact, and this evening she seemed to be bursting with a secret of some significance.

"Do you know what day it was today?" she asked with a smile and a tease.

What was she talking about? I thought for a moment. It was a regular weekday!

My puzzled expression seemed to delight her. "It was *Yom Kippur*," she whispered.

"How do *you* know that?" I asked.

She explained that while she was at work that morning, she had seen all the Jews going into the synagogue across the street. She had thought there was a war or that something terrible had happened to the Jews, and that the rabbi had called an emergency meeting to discuss the situation. During her lunch break, she had decided to follow suit and go inside to see what was happening, purely out of curiosity. After a few inquiries, she learned that it was *Yom Kippur.* "Thank you very much," she had said politely, and then slid out as unobtrusively as she had entered. She returned to her office, ate lunch, and continued her workday in a completely normal fashion.

I was flabbergasted. A synagogue? Where was it? I had no idea that Portfield even housed a synagogue. And my sister, with her light brown hair and fair complexion—how had she *dared* to enter? I was completely convinced, ever since seeing the photographs of my cousins in Israel, that all Jews had dark skin and black hair!

"But Margaret, didn't they look at you and say you were a gentile?"

"Oh, no," she said with a laugh. "There were even Jews there with blond hair."

How brazen of Margaret to march into a synagogue, I thought. Daddy Raymond did have a special crew of students whose task it was to missionize amongst Jews, but these were an elite few, and it was unheard of for anyone else in college to enter a synagogue. Yet, somehow, the idea was tantalizing.

Seeing that I was curious, Margaret encouraged me to go and look for myself, if only to have an interesting experience. "No one will bother you," she promised. "There were crowds of people inside."

My sister went on her way. I went to my room, but for some reason my heart felt strangely heavy. I knew that *Yom Kippur* was the biblical day of atonement, and all I could think of was that all the Jews had been in synagogue and I hadn't. I had absolutely no idea why I was troubled by these stupid thoughts, and I tried to push them out of my head. But it took three whole days to break through the heaviness and strange depressive feelings.

Margaret's story stayed in the back of my mind for quite some time afterward. I was very curious to see what a synagogue was like and how the Jews observed the Sabbath. I really don't know what I expected to find that was any better than what we already had, and it annoyed me that I even had a desire to go, for I knew that as Christians, we had already perfected the worship of the Bible.

❧

The Church had taught us time and again that we were "New Covenant Israel"; that after the Jews rejected Jesus, the covenant of true service to God had been passed to the gentiles, who would now become the real Israelites that God had intended in the Bible. However, as Christians, we had come "under grace," meaning that we had been absolved by Jesus from keeping the 613 commandments enumerated in the Old Testament, and could now be saved only by believing in him.

In spite of this state of "grace," Daddy Raymond did often incorporate Jewish practices and customs into his doctrine, especially as he abandoned the pagan holidays. He felt that these would bring us closer and closer to our true mission as "New Covenant Israel," but he established his own guidelines for their observance. Passover, for example, was observed with Jesus as the Paschal lamb, and indeed we were taught that the entire Sabbath, which was now observed on the original Jewish day, drew its holiness from Jesus' spirit alone.

And yet somehow none of this did anything to squelch my mushrooming curiosity about the synagogue. Perhaps I would not find anything "better" there, but I wondered how the Old Testament Jews observed the Sabbath, what sort of belief there could be that did not center around Jesus. I knew that Orthodox Jewish customs were considered "dead tradition" and "bondage," as my father had told me; but I reasoned that it could not do me any harm to have one little peek, and in spite of the fact that I was a gentile, I felt that my mother's Jewish ancestry gave me license for the visit.

The following Saturday morning, I was up bright and early in order to attend the synagogue. I was confident that I would not be missed; fortunately, our own service on Saturday did not begin until twelve o'clock. The morning was considered a time of private devotion, during which students could be found in a variety of places—the library, chapel, or studying quietly in their own rooms—and I assured myself with crafty logic that anyone who noticed my absence would assume I was in one of the other places.

After trying in vain to persuade Anette to come with me, I set off alone, clad in the only church clothes I had: a dark-brown floor length skirt, brown high-necked sweater and dark-brown matching head-scarf. I was a little nervous, but felt excited to be going alone to a new place for the first time in my life. I was hoping to experience that special attention that newcomers always got in the church—warm smiles, friendly guidance through the songs and procedures, and after the service, a cordial welcome by all. However, my naive security was to be shortlived.

I entered the synagogue and went straight through the nearest open doorway. Obviously this was the chapel, so I tiptoed quietly to an empty pew at the back of the room and sat down. There were a number of people already in the midst of prayer, and it did not occur to me at first glance that they were all men.

An elderly gentleman turned around toward the back and caught a glimpse of me. He then seemed to go into an apoplectic fit and stood there jerking his arm toward the doorway. I was so bewildered I did not know what to do.

Finally he managed to gasp out in a whisper, "I'm sorry, but you can't stay here! You have to leave."

I was confused. My sister had promised me that no one had bothered her. I stood up quietly and left. The gentleman followed me out. He wanted to make sure I was safely out onto the street, but in the lobby, I innocently asked, "You mean...I can't stay *at all*?" Perhaps Christians were not even allowed into the building!

With a deep sigh, he resigned himself, "Okay, the women go upstairs." He pointed emphatically several times to the upper level and returned to his prayers. With my heart beating heavily, I walked slowly up the plush carpeted stairs to the chamber above. Row upon row of empty pews greeted me, and I realized with consternation that there were names inscribed on each one. "Oh, no," I thought. "There's no place to sit—all these seats are owned! I have to get out of here!"

A handful of very fashionably dressed ladies dotted the room, and it dawned on me that this was a separate section for women. My heart was beating rapidly now; I had no idea what to do. I smiled timidly at the ladies, but they rewarded me with ice-cold glares. At the last second, I pulled myself together and decided to stay for a while.

As no one seemed intent on coming over to greet me, I took a book from a pile on the window ledge and warily sat down in a seat, hoping and praying that its owner would not turn up that week. I tried to make believe I knew what was going on. At first I concentrated on looking only straight ahead, standing up when everyone else stood, and sitting when they sat, but I couldn't help glancing off to the sides. The interior of the room was lavishly furnished, with trimmings of gold and velvet in every corner and crystal fixtures hanging from the ceiling. It was obviously a wealthy synagogue.

Slowly, I dared to glance at one person, and then another, and if occasionally someone caught my eye, I would smile, only to receive a cold, stern stare in response. I suddenly became conscious of my appearance—the strange handmade clothes, the dowdy headscarf, the light brown hair. At college we were deliberately discouraged from dressing or behaving in consonance with the times, for only abstinence from the lures of the material world could truly lead one to God. But now amongst these elegantly accoutered women, I felt horrendously out of place, a gentile who could be spotted a mile away.

I noticed that each of the women had that gorgeous dark hair that I had coveted so badly as a little girl, and that beautiful, even-textured olive skin. Not only was I a gentile, but I was ugly! I wished desperately that the floor would open up and swallow me. I so much wanted to leave, but was afraid to move.

I sat through the rest of the morning, hoping at least to gain something from the service, but the only parts I was able to understand were the prayer for the queen and the royal family, read aloud by the rabbi in perfect English, and the social announcements made at the very end. Finally people began to move about to chat with one another before leaving. Cold, austere glances were shot in my direction. I collected my long skirt about me and swept down the stairs and out the door, Cinderella leaving the ball in rags. What a relief it was to be out of there! As I hurried back to the college, I vowed I would never go back again. No wonder my mother had left the religion of her youth!

It was with renewed zeal that I threw myself into my chosen life. How happy I was to serve my king and friend! I loved Jesus dearly. Continually, I sang his praises, my heart leaping and skipping for joy. All I wanted was to know him better, to become closer to him, and to serve him more fully. He was my savior. I wanted to tell the whole world what he had done for me, how he had set me free from sin and bondage.

҆

Daddy Raymond had a new revelation: sanctification. "Full salvation," the Methodist John Wesley had called it, a new heart. The principal preached his new message with fire and fervor, igniting our hearts with a hunger and greater love to know Jesus "that little bit more." Up until this time, we had always believed that Jesus had cleansed our hearts at the time of our baptism, which most of us had undergone at a very young age; but now we were learning that we could receive a brand new heart, a higher and deeper experience of communion and bliss. The principal exhorted us to make a vow never to sin again and to seal it with the body and blood of the new covenant.

"I can hear the spirit say, 'Come up higher!'" he urged us over and over again.

It was a serious time in our lives. Many people were reluctant to take such an extreme vow, and others were embarrassed to admit that there didn't seem to be anything awesome about the vow at all. Were we not already supposed to be free of sin from the time of our baptism? Hadn't the baptismal waters, which represented Jesus' blood, washed it away already, cleansing us perfectly?

I had no such doubts. I looked at the principal with awe. He had done it! He had vowed never to sin again. His level of holiness enticed me to strive higher. I was jealous of his righteousness. I too wanted to bask in the heavenly breezes on those spiritual mountaintops.

Within the college, Sister Victoria spoke kindly and compassionately to us all, saying that it was understandable that little sins had lately crept into our lives—a white lie or a small theft, such as a book or garment that was never returned to its owner. She tried to help pave the way for our "return."

"To avoid embarrassment," she said, "I will put a box out in the main hallway, and anyone who has something belonging to someone else will put it in the box. By the same token, if you see something belonging to you, you will be free to claim it immediately."

"I'll be the first one to put things into the box," she declared proudly.

"And I'll be the second," her father proclaimed.

And so they did. The box overflowed with articles and remained stuffed for quite a time. Now people were much more ready to take upon themselves the commitment never to sin again, not even the tiniest sin.

A few days later, a national convention was held in Southford, where my parents were now living. My father was up on the platform, and although I was glad to see them both, the convention was unusually intense and there was little time to chat.

Daddy Raymond preached for about five hours, telling us that evil spirits had entered our hearts, and promising us complete renewal if we would only take the vow never to sin again. "I will take away your stony heart and give you a new heart," he cried, quoting from the

Prophets as he thrust his fist at the heavens in sweat-soaked ardor, his black eyes gleaming feverishly.

I had previously made up my mind that if there was an altar call after this service, I would go out and make the commitment. There was, and I went forward; but I was one of only twenty people from a congregation of four to five hundred who did so—a congregation of Christians who had been saved, baptized and filled with the holy spirit. People were afraid. It was a frightening undertaking. Could one really promise that he would never sin again, not even the slightest sin? If he failed, what would happen?

That doubt crossed my mind, but I was not perturbed. Was not Jesus all-powerful? If our belief was strong enough, wouldn't he prevent us from sin? I wanted to progress in my spiritual growth, and I felt this was the next step. The organ played softly. I waited with my eyes closed for the principal to come and gently touch my arm and give me communion, the piece of unleavened bread and cup of wine which was believed by the Protestants to represent Jesus' body and blood.

I made my vow, and he held out a large piece of unleavened bread, saying, "This is his body, Tonica, broken for you."

I broke off a small piece of bread and held it until everyone else had also received, and then, at the principal's command, we all ate the bread together.

Next came the wine. "This is Jesus' blood, Toni," he said lovingly, "shed for you."

I took a sip, and as the wine coursed through me, I felt my life being lifted onto a higher plane. I was sanctified. It had happened to me. I was so happy! I shouted and jumped and praised my savior. I was never, ever going to sin again.

It was obvious that I had changed. My face radiated a light as it never had before. I was alive with happiness.

The next night we were back in Portfield, and there was a regular prayer meeting in church. The principal asked me to testify about my experience. I told the story of my sanctification and of the inspirational fire that had branded my soul since that holy moment. I spoke with great passion, and that night almost everyone in our congregation took the vow never to sin again. The meeting built to a frenzied pitch, and many congregants went about in the aisles, dancing in the spirit until the early hours of the morning.

After the Southford Sanctification, the college dining room was filled with the happy voices of a unified community. We were all on a spiritual high and did our best to help each other maintain it. Even the cook laughed about how she no longer had to lock away the food.

The little "thoughts" that I gave over in church grew into meaningful sermonettes with dramatic results, and I found that when I sang I was able to fully relax, get "into the spirit," and really pour out feeling from the depths of my being.

A sense of glowing aspiration suffused me, and I wanted to share goodness with everyone—everyone in the world. As I walked to and from work, I was constantly on the lookout for a needy person to whom I could lend a hand: an old woman who needed help crossing the road, a child crying, someone struggling with heavy bags. Whenever I was in the midst of such an act, I thought of the way my father always handled such situations. He would quickly offer a hand and then say gently, "Do you know that Jesus loves you? God loves you, and He sent His son to save you." The remembrance was inspiring, and yet although I was not brave enough myself to speak directly of Jesus to absolute strangers, I still felt confident that my behavior had been a good testimony. It was obvious from my dress that I was religious, and so God's name had been glorified by my action. It made me feel good and inspired me to do more kindness.

At the bank, my colleagues were continually trying to test me by poking me and making advances, all of which I ignored, and indeed these trials just served to strengthen and deepen my tie with my savior. During my lunch breaks, I would hurry a short distance away to

Portfield Castle, a beautiful mansion in the neighborhood, surrounded by a sprawling green park, and there I would find a quiet corner on the grounds to pray. I loved this time of communion so much that I never even wasted a minute to eat. I prayed fervently and quietly for the city, for each of my co-workers, my old school friends, my unsaved relatives—including the Jewish ones—and anyone else I could think of, but most of all for the revival that we all believed was soon to come.

How we longed for another sweep of Pentecostal fire to spread throughout our land, as it had done in times gone by! I imagined my workmates falling to their knees in repentance and accepting Jesus as their savior. I really believed it could and would happen; there was not a doubt in my mind.

The principal also began to encourage us to undertake longer fasts, in addition to the usual day-long fast that began on Thursday evening and lasted until the onset of the Sabbath. I started slowly at first, three days, five days, then seven or eight days at a time. We drank a little water, but that was all, and of course, we worked as usual. I was careful not to let anyone at the bank find out. It was a private time in my life, a period of semi-seclusion, of inner strengthening and purification. I grew to enjoy the extra time not spent at meals as a further opportunity to pray and study God's word.

However, I was still young, only about twenty years old now, and I was a little impatient about the rate of my spiritual growth. I wanted to be as spiritually strong and rich as Daddy Raymond. How deeply I had grown to love and respect him! We had become so close; I ate up every word that came from his lips and ran to do his bidding with pleasure. He was proud of his little girl, and I basked in the special attention he always gave me.

I had even accomplished the unimaginable: I had become close to Mother as well, and fully admired her. There was just no one in the whole congregation who could prophesy like her. Her words would strike fear and awe into the hearts of her listeners and cause them to search deep within themselves for hidden weaknesses and dark corners.

Their daughter Victoria had become my best friend. We shared secrets and talked at length of spiritual matters. She would sit me on her knee and hug me, and would give me especially hard Bible studies to inspire me and spur me on. She seemed so close to God, so pure and righteous, a wonderful model of Jesus' love. I wanted to be like her, but I was so impatient! It just couldn't happen fast enough for me.

Sister Victoria confided in me that early one morning, after she had slept through her alarm, a dark-skinned young man had appeared in her room. He was wearing a long brown robe and his face was scarred, but nevertheless there was a beauty radiating from him, the likes of which she had never seen before. He bent over her and said softly, "It's time to get up now." Immediately she sat up but he was gone. Dearest Jesus—she had seen him!

I also wanted to see Jesus, to be in closest communion with him *now.* I would do anything to sense him, to see him real and physical before me, to literally touch him. I prayed for a vision of him—not to strengthen my belief in him, because I already knew he was real—but simply because I felt that if I were to see him, it would signify that I was pure and righteous, that I had reached that high level of spirituality I so longed for.

"Dear God, please help me, sanctify me more, purify me yet further," was my constant cry to heaven.

It was this deep inner yearning for righteousness that led me to look over our wall. I had never had much interest in the activities there, which were too far removed—as I thought then—from a proper service to God.

For beyond the wall was a Catholic nunnery.

I began to watch the nuns silently gliding around their courtyard, dressed in black from head to toe, and found myself looking at them afresh. They seemed so holy; maybe they were a step closer to God than I was. I began to envy their serenity and quiet simplicity, their apparent contentment with so little.

I looked in my closet at the multitude of clothes and possessions piled up there. Actually, it was a meager collection, but in comparison to the nuns' standard, it seemed quite varied, so I decided to see how much I could do without. My bank clothes, I could not discard. As it was, my outfits were completely out of tune with contemporary fashion, and at the very least, I needed a variety; if I kept only one outfit for work, no matter how immaculate it was, my co-workers would all show up with pegs on their noses. I had to maintain a minimum standard of personal care, and appear as normal as possible for the sake of being a good testimony.

But my church clothes were different. I decided to pack away all of these except for two outfits, one to wash and one to wear, but I promised myself that I would take extra care to make sure that each garment was always freshly laundered and neatly ironed.

Then I set out to do away with all my little keepsakes and ornaments. Everything was packed in boxes and hidden away in the remotest corner of my closet shelf. I did not confide in anyone of my undertaking; and although it must have been quite obvious to those who knew me well that things in the room had disappeared, they did not know the reason for this sudden change. This was a personal matter between Jesus and myself, and it felt good. I felt very much lighter, as though a heavy burden had been lifted off my back. It was now so easy to decide what to wear for church that I could concentrate instead on preparing my soul for the service, and I no longer had to waste any emotional energy on the accumulation of material items. My constant prayer never changed: that I should merit to see Jesus face to face and to commune intimately with him. My enthusiasm was unmeasured.

I credited the nuns to a great extent for inspiring me to a new level of abstinence, and as I continued to observe them, I found their lifestyle appealing in another way as well. They had chosen to seclude themselves completely in God's service and would never marry. To me, this seemed ideal.

There were good boys in the college whom I knew wanted to marry me and whom the principal considered suitable candidates. Some of these young men had been interested in me from the time I had come to the college, a mere child of sixteen. Although, in general, Daddy Raymond was against marriage for those whose lives he felt could be better spent in full dedication to the church, he did make individual assessments, and in fact, he had even chosen a wife for my brother Philip. Apparently he felt that marriage would in no way diminish the enthusiasm and commitment I had thus far demonstrated in my service to God. Many times, he would say to me quietly, "How about such-and-such a boy, Toni? He's a nice boy for you."

Whereupon I would always reply instantly, "The answer is *no!*"

He would laugh, but he never gave up trying.

There had been a time when I quite liked the idea of being a minister's wife and going off to darkest Africa or India, or some other distant land to win souls; but now my heart was set on a path of total dedication to Jesus. I wanted to stay only with him all my life, just as the nuns over the wall did. They suffered no distractions or conflicts, no other aspirations, even of the most natural kind; and I too wanted to pay my vow of chastity and consecrate my youth, my life—everything I had—to my king and friend.

But that special place of sanctity seemed ever to elude me. I could not find words for this "thing" that seemed to be missing—and as hard as I tried, I could not find the key to the door.

Then one day, Sister Alberta, the head of the convent over the wall, came to ask for some assistance. The nuns ran a day nursery for Italian children in the neighborhood, and many of their old wooden toys were badly in need of repair. They knew that we had a woodwork shop and wondered if we could send over a carpenter to fix a few things.

My brother Philip, the master woodworker on campus, was chosen, but as there were only women in the nunnery, he was too embarrassed to go alone and asked me to accompany him. I was very excited at the opportunity to observe the nuns up-close, and they were every bit as sweet as I had imagined, especially Sister Alberta. While my brother worked, they took me into their kitchen and gave me iced peppermint water, and we chatted amiably about life in the college and in the convent. They all came to the unanimous conclusion that my life at the college was more stringent, but I was not convinced. I saw their solitude as a further opportunity for dedication to God and had a sudden great yearning to become one of them.

I had never understood the real differences between the Catholics and the Protestants. I knew that we prayed only to Jesus while they prayed to the Virgin Mary and several saints as well, which explained the presence of so many statues and figurines in the nunnery. I had no idea that Protestants considered this a form of idol worship and were therefore adamantly opposed to the Catholics' entire doctrine. All I could see in my innocence was that the Catholic nuns were married to Jesus, and that if I went with them, I too could truly marry him.

I became obsessed with a hunger and longing for more and more spirituality and was convinced that I would find it with the nuns. I began to sneak over the wall for a few minutes whenever I could manage it without being missed at home, and even once attended their mass. On Saturday mornings, I would walk to the only Catholic cathedral in town that I knew of and stand in silence, trying to drink in some kind of holiness. There were no services on Saturday, of course, but the cathedral was open to anyone who wished to come and pray quietly or sit in solitude, and I always hoped that perhaps Sister Alberta would show up.

In the space of a few months, she had become my closest confidante, and I trusted her even more than Victoria. Whenever we spoke, I would sit on the edge of my seat, hungrily anticipating the spiritual treasures I was sure she had to offer. It seemed as though I was constantly hungering and constantly waiting, while the diamonds were forever just beyond my grasp. I kept hoping that next time—perhaps next time—I would discover the secret of closeness to God.

Then one day, Daddy Raymond and his wife caught me on one of my escapades and summoned me immediately into their room. In consternation, I confessed, "I like them—I even want to go and be with them!"

As soon as the words had left my mouth, Mother turned a deep crimson with rage and pushed me so hard that she sent me hurtling across the room. Through gritted teeth, she screamed, "How dare you speak such blasphemous words, child! If you want to go into the world, go! But it will be over my dead body that you go *there*!"

The discussion ended with a command from the principal that I kneel down right there in the room and ask Jesus for forgiveness. I really did not understand why I needed to repent since I had not purposely strayed from the fold. I was only looking for a final rich pasture to lie down in, some sort of satisfying inner nourishment; but nevertheless I trusted Daddy Raymond, and I knelt down. Together we prayed, and my prayer was very sincere. But I had become attached to the nuns, and that was not the end of my communication over the wall.

ა

I couldn't forget Sister Alberta so easily. A strong bond had formed between us. I knew I should break it, but somehow the thought left me with a vague and lonely emptiness. I loved her; she was a strong and commanding woman in a position of great authority, and yet she still had a childlike twinkle of mischief in her eye.

My feeling for Sister Alberta clouded the doubts that I instinctively felt about the Catholics and caused tremendous internal conflict inside me. It is very difficult to explain this in practical terms.

All I can say is that I maintained contact with the nuns for two years, and during that time, my initial awe of them was slowly poisoned by other awarenesses. The physical trappings of their life were powerfully attractive to me—the solemnity of the black habits, the majesty of the priest's embroidered garments, the cavernous echoes of the mass rising to the spires of the cathedral. The outward show of humility seemed so much deeper than what I had, the formality of the worship so holy. And yet it *was* only an outward show. I sensed a darkness beneath the spiritual glamor, a deep and sucking darkness. I don't know how I felt this; it just seemed as though I had highly responsive spiritual sensors, and I could feel alarming chills running up and down them.

Added to these misgivings were the mysterious visits that the city priest often made to the convent at two or three o'clock in the morning. In fact, he came several times a week, and although I was too innocent to understand the purpose of these nocturnal interviews, they seemed to increase the sense of uneasiness and melancholy that I felt. The nuns were so sweet, so warm, so holy—but what if they had no buried treasure to offer me at all? What if they would not lead me to the path to God? The thought was terrifying, and I clung to the nuns in a desperate hope.

I would often sit at my bedroom window, watching and waiting for a glimpse of them, sometimes even allowing myself to be late for our own prayer meetings in the hope of seeing one of them for just a moment. I still found occasion from time to time to steal away and wait beside their gate for a chance to wave or say a quick "hello"; and one day, when Sister Alberta greeted me, she informed me that she was planning to go back to Italy and take a higher position in the church.

"Pack your belongings, and I will take you with me," she promised. "Be here at five o'clock in the morning!"

I smiled excitedly and ran back to the college, but despite the prospect of a fairy-tale-come-true, my heart was not smiling. I lay awake that night for hours—but not from indecision, because I knew already that I could not go. In the depths of my heart I realized now that they were no closer to God than I was. I cannot say how I knew this so certainly, but I felt it within myself. The nuns had held out a beckoning scepter of holiness, and I knew that if I followed it, I would find nothing at the other end.

It was with heaviness of heart that I stood at my bedroom window that morning and watched Sister Alberta leave the gates. Before entering the awaiting car that would take her to the airport, she took one last glance at my window. I had let her down, disappointed her, and I would miss her terribly.

Something inside me changed at that moment. I turned back to my own environment, to the familiar halls of the college, but the spiritual diamonds I had sought over the wall seemed to be even more elusive here at home. Only a few months before, I had walked on clouds of ecstasy, zealous for my savior, but now he had moved even further away from me. There was a murky undertow of dissatisfaction in my soul, and I did not know what to do.

I became sullen. The sparkle within my heart slowly dwindled away, the candle of enthusiasm sputtered and died.

❧ ELEVEN ❧

MY work at the bank had become more and more demanding, and I began to stay overtime to complete the extra work, often not returning to the college until nine-thirty or ten o'clock at night and missing the evening service. I was glad in a way about this because it meant I did not have the pressure of "performing" at the services when my heart was so sick inside; but it became increasingly difficult to rekindle a small flicker of light for the children at Sunday school. I found myself praying, "Oh, God, please don't let my own failures and shortcomings hinder these little lives or discourage their young and open hearts. Help me, please, help me to get through this day and show the children Your love." And I did somehow summon the ability to bring myself around for those few hours each week and teach the children as though I were the happiest person on earth.

Almost every Sunday, Sister Victoria appeared at the back of my classroom. One day I asked her why she came.

"I've sensed for a while that you've been down," she responded quietly. "But the children are the real test. If you do well with them, then you're really all right. I know you'll eventually pull yourself around." I hoped she was right, but it was taking an awfully long time.

My life seemed to sink to the very abyss of despair. What had gone wrong? Why did I suddenly feel so empty? How could everything have changed so quickly? "Oh, God, couldn't You see that my heart was sincere?" I cried. "All I wanted was to become closer to You!"

I walked home from work late each evening, tired, alone, and more often than not, in tears. Sometimes I would scratch a few words in my diary.

Oh, God, my life is a living hell. How can I go on? How can I tell people anymore that Jesus is peace, joy and happiness? My heart is dead. I vowed I would never sin again, and look at me now!

Sister Victoria tried to help me in her own way. She would talk to me, counsel me, and try to offer encouragement, but her efforts hardly availed.

"I feel like I am in a cage," I told her, "trapped and locked up."

"But why?" she would ask with feigned largesse. "The front door isn't locked. If you want to leave, leave."

"How *can* I?" I always argued. "All of my life I have learned that outside of Jesus is despair, hate, loneliness and death. It just doesn't make sense to leave, and anyway, don't you understand? I don't *want* to leave! There has to be a solution. Somehow, somewhere, I am lacking in my commitment or service to Jesus, and I have to find out what is wrong!"

I was alone in my misery. I tried hard to snap myself out of the depression, but it only went from bad to worse.

Little things began to bother me. On the nights that I was late at work, I would phone up the college and ask that my dinner be put aside, and almost every night when I arrived home, no one had remembered and all the food was gone. We were forbidden to take food from the pantry, so I always went hungry. I was still putting in time in the art department and found it difficult to work for so many hours straight without a decent meal. Sometimes I felt faint.

I could not buy anything substantial to eat on my meager allowance, and when I asked the cook to put aside some food for me as a favor, she refused, saying she would end up having to do the same for everyone.

On a few occasions, I tried approaching the person whom I had spoken to on the phone to find out what had happened, but I would only get a laugh and an admonition: "Oh, well, it's good for you to go without dinner sometimes—it will work on your carnal nature."

At first I took these words seriously, even though they were laced with sarcasm, but then it dawned on me that I was no longer supposed to have a carnal nature. Isn't that what we had been told at the Southford Sanctification? Hadn't everyone received a "new heart"? Such verbal slaps began to seem like what they were—empty excuses. But I was too submissive to complain.

Another annoyance was the dormitory situation. I was no longer in the cozy attic with Anette and had already been moved twice. We did not have a say in who our roommates were. Mother made most of these decisions, and you could stay in a room anywhere from a few months to a few years.

At this point, I was rooming with three other girls: Mary, a schoolteacher, Angela, a guttersnipe—neither of whom I particularly liked—and Maude, the middle sister of the famous campus trio. Maude had been appointed the "minister" in charge of the room, responsible for looking after our morale and making sure we got along with each other.

Maude was irritated by the fact that I was different from the other girls because I would not undress in front of them. I preferred to cover myself and dress discreetly when others were present, or to go into the bathroom, a practice which she considered an abnormal display of pride. Every night, she would take me into the showers and make me dress and undress in front of her, and even watch me take showers. All of this I did for the glory of God, submitting in the blind hope of being accepted by this people whom I so desired to follow.

Sister Maude also considered it her duty every night to deliver me a juicy, affectionate, and very emotional goodnight kiss, much in the fashion of her older sister Samantha. The moment she left her bed and started toward mine, my stomach would tighten, and as she puckered her lips and made sloppy sounds, I would turn my head away and pull up the covers. She was determined to break me, however, and night after night she came, and night after night my stomach knotted, my head turned, and the covers came up; until one day, after a number of weeks, she finally gave up and stormed around the room, speaking in tongues and rebuking the spirits that bound my life.

There was one thing she was right about, though; there did seem to be spirits binding my life. No matter how hard I tried to rid myself of these demonic chains, they clung to me, and my depression lingered on for an entire year, drawing an endless stream of pain and humiliation in its wake.

I desperately needed a winter coat. Winters in Portfield were bitterly cold, but a coat was a very expensive item, and on the small allowance we were given, it was virtually impossible to dream of purchasing one.

Sister Maude had reported my "proud behavior" in our room to Sister Victoria, who decided she had just the cure: a secondhand coat she had found that had been donated to the church. I took one look at the coat and was frantic.

"But I'm a supervisor at the bank," I wailed in protest. "I have one of the best-paying jobs for women in the whole company! It's awful! It's not a good testimony. I'm not wearing it," I declared firmly.

Sister Victoria took no notice of my anguish. She pulled me into her mother's office and made me try on the coat. It was bright red and double-breasted, with imitation fur around the neck and along the bottom edge. The coat came out at the waist and then fell straight down. It was the most old-fashioned, awful garment I had ever put on, even worse than the handmade outfits we wore in the college.

"It fits you perfectly," Sister Victoria announced with finality. "You'll wear it! You're not getting another one." It was well within her power to provide me with a new coat if she felt I needed it, but she seemed intent on "refining" my character instead.

I burst into tears.

"But you don't understand," I cried. "The girls at the bank come in real fur coats and dress in the height of fashion. I'm going to look ridiculous in this!"

"It's good for your pride," she responded sternly. "You're wearing it. And I have a black fur hat to match that you will wear as well!"

The temperature was below freezing, and I had no choice but to wear that wretched coat and ugly hat. My co-workers lifted their heads that morning to observe the spectacle walking down the elegant, marble-floored banking hall. My face, flushed with embarrassment, matched the coat's color perfectly, but no one said a word. I think they had grown to feel sorry for me.

All my disappointments seemed to have a sequel with an even worse sting, for Sister Victoria made it her business to come and visit me one day at the bank, making her grand entrance in a beautiful full-length fur coat. The message was clear: Victoria was letting me know that she had worked on her pride long enough not to be affected by luxury, just as her parents were not affected by their china and silver and the other sumptuous furnishings in their room. But I had not yet reached that stage and must still work on myself. The coat was an open put-down, and I could say nothing.

Years later, when I was an authority figure myself in the church, I would laugh about the episode to my dear friend Anette and tell her, "I must still be proud despite all those months when I wore that horrible thing, because I still go red with embarrassment when I even *think* about it—and I would never dream of wearing it even now!" We would always have a good chuckle over it, but the fact remained that the coat never did anything at all to squash my pride.

Every morning, all the way to the bank, I would say to God in my heart, "If You would only let me go back to the beginning and choose whether I wanted to come into this world or not, I would tell You a million times over, 'No, no, no!' Oh, God, can't You somehow wipe me off the face of the earth, cause everyone to forget that I ever existed, and take me away? Let me disappear for eternity!"

I repeated the prayer day after day, week after week. Every night I left work deciding that I would not go back to the college. I simply couldn't face any more shame, any more deprivation. But every night, my feet took me home. They knew no other way.

Ironically enough, a melancholy state, rather than drawing comfort from others in the college, worked adversely against a person. For it always happened that when one was "out of the spirit," he was immediately out of favor with everyone, especially the senior ministers. Depression was considered a spiritually dangerous condition, and the understanding was that others would be contaminated by it, so they all stayed away.

A smothering gloom descended over my life. Sister Victoria had tried her best with me for a while, but when she saw that my sadness had only become worse, she abandoned me altogether and in fact hardly ever looked at me anymore. The principal kept his distance for a time, and Mother wanted to have me expelled.

Apparently, the only thing that saved me was a commendation from Sister Loretta, the woman who was in charge of all the domestic work at the college. I had been given the daily duty of cleaning the public bathrooms in the lobby, the dirtiest ones on the entire campus. I won't go into the ugly details of what I found there each morning, or of the passionate hatred this job inspired in me, but by the time I left for work, those bathrooms were always fit for a queen. I hung up curtains and made frilly light shades, put up pictures, polished the tiles, and constantly disinfected every corner. In order to motivate myself, I always pretended that those bathrooms were mine and that I was preparing them for my own guests.

Sister Loretta reported my efforts to the Websters, telling them of the enormous energy I poured into my morning job, and of the excellent results, and so it seems I was given another chance.

Another thing that worked in my favor during that difficult period was that I came out on top in all of my Bible theory and practical exams at the end of the year. Incidentally, this was a disappointment to the spiritual stalwarts in my group, for they could not understand the discrepancy between my academic excellence and my seemingly abysmal spiritual state. My life just didn't seem to be measuring up to my ideals. (I have no doubt that they were also a bit jealous.)

Sister Samantha was again given the task of "shepherding my soul" and pulling me out of my depression. But this time she failed. Whenever she looked at me, I would stare straight into her eyes with a blank, dead expression, and her hugs did not move me. My heart remained like stone.

"Talk about 'deep as the ocean,'" Daddy Raymond would gently tease, in an attempt to soften me, and once again make contact with his "little girl." He didn't want to lose me, especially as I was bringing in one of the highest salaries of any student in the college. I wasn't astute enough to perceive this at the time; all I knew was that I just couldn't arouse that former joy, no matter how hard I tried. Every morning when I opened my eyes, I cursed the moment, cursed the day I was born, and cursed the womb that bore me and brought me into such misery.

At work, no one knew of my struggles. I tried to behave as normally as possible, to be friendly, outgoing and warm; until one day I could contain my agony no longer. I was working as a first cashier at the time. The banking hall was quiet and empty, and as I sat at my bench, thoughts of my life seeped involuntarily into my head. It felt as though a blanket of loneliness enveloped me, and I couldn't hold back the tears that started trickling down my cheeks. Quickly I wiped them away.

A customer entered the hall and awaited service at my window. I turned away and hurriedly tried to pull myself together, but it was no use—the tears just spilled down so thick and fast that I couldn't even take a moment to find another cashier to help the man. I left him there tapping his keys on the counter and ran to the ladies' room, where I locked myself in and let the tears gush out.

I cried for about three hours. I felt all alone in the world, and I was afraid.

One of my co-workers eventually came and knocked on the door. She was a very kind person, a Salvation Army girl to whom I could relate somewhat because we shared religious backgrounds. She tried to comfort me.

"Come home with me, Tonica," she pleaded. "I get like this sometimes and my husband always helps me. Please come home with me, just for a few hours. It'll do you a world of good."

But I couldn't. I was too afraid to go into unfamiliar territory, and I was also embarrassed to admit that I didn't have any money for the bus fare to her house.

The chief accountant finally came looking for me, but by then I had collected myself. The crying had released my tension, although it had not solved my despair. I never told a soul at college what had happened.

ॐ

Just at that time, Daddy Raymond had another revelation, which seemed to be the answer to my troubles. I was ready for any solution—anything that would set my life straight again and bring me back into the warmth of acceptance.

The revelation centered around deliverance from evil spirits. More than a few years had passed since the Southford Sanctification, when many of us had received "new hearts"—hearts which were supposed to remain eternally clean—but something had happened to our original fire; it did not seem so strong or inspiring anymore. Daddy Raymond explained to us with convincing logic that although our hearts were still clean, malevolent spirits had entered our lives over the years: spirits of rejection, lying, unbelief, hatred, and a million and one other things. He reminded us of the New Testament tale of the Gadarene Demoniac, a man who was completely demented and evil, and so wild that he had to be tied down with chains. Jesus had cast out every single bad spirit from his life, and each spirit had entered a pig. All the pigs then stampeded over the edge of a cliff and were drowned in the waters below, and the Gadarene was saved. Daddy Raymond told us the story I n depth, spurring each of us on to cast out our own evil spirits, and to resume a life of holiness.

One Sunday afternoon, not long after this revelation, I went to Sister Victoria for counseling. I was in a pit of despondency, and I just couldn't stand it anymore. Daddy Raymond's message of deliverance was still fresh, and she suggested that it might work for me. I readily agreed. Victoria brought in another minister, and the two of them prayed fervently for me. The session lasted about six hours, and they supposedly cast out of me over one hundred evil spirits. We were all emotionally and physically exhausted at the end, and Victoria hugged me and smiled. It felt so wonderful to be loved and comforted again!

I felt oddly at peace; but it seems to me now that my contentment had much more to do with being smiled at for the first time in almost a year than it did with the banishment of my evil spirits.

The Feast of Tabernacles was fast approaching: one of the Jewish holidays that the principal had adopted to enable us to fulfill our role as "New Covenant Israel." It was to be a major international gathering, and arrangements were being made to house the multitude of guests who were coming from other cities in England and abroad. Mother took me aside and told me that she had decided to entrust me with the job of hosting the Norwegian brethren. This was a big responsibility as special attention was always given to overseas guests. I was flattered and relieved at this sign of recognition.

And so I hosted my little contingent. Graciously I served them, steered them around to the various meetings, and helped them at every opportunity to feel as comfortable as possible. The best part of it all was that they actually liked me! We had a wonderful week, going on long walks and enjoying picnics on the grounds, discussing Jesus, praying and laughing together.

My stint as hostess was completely successful; I had helped spread the light of God to our foreign brethren, and in the process had relit the dying ember in my own heart. I felt myself being lifted out of the Valley of Weeping, and I began the climb to the mountaintops that Daddy Raymond had always described for us in his sermons, waiting expectantly for the heavenly breezes to touch me again.

One Friday night, after the Sabbath dinner, we gathered for fellowship in the lounge. Daddy Raymond announced that the atmosphere in the college seemed quite dry of late and that people were not sharing the talents that Jesus had given them. He had always encouraged us to write songs or put verses of the Bible to music, or make any kind of presentation that would help spread enthusiasm for his teachings. But lately, he told us, our creativity seemed to have a dull edge.

"We're going to go around the room one by one," he declared, "and anybody who has got a new song has to sing it." When it came my turn, I was prepared. I had written a song when my depression began to lift, taken from the words of Isaiah:

> *He is a hiding place to me from the wind,*
> *A covert from the raging storms,*
> *He is as rivers of water in dry places*
> *And as the shadow of a great rock in a weary land,*
> *Hamoshea, Hamoshea,*
> *Yeshua Hamoshea, my friend.*

I wept as I sang, for the power of experience was behind the words, and everyone wept along with me. There was a consuming presence in the room, an emotional aura of holiness.

The song spread like wildfire among all the branches of the Church and remained a worldwide hit for years to come. But best of all, I had found a place once more among my people, and I was overjoyed. I had truly returned to the fold.

❧ TWELVE ❦

I RETURNED to work brighter but with a strange feeling that I had finished my mission at the bank. Somehow I felt that I wouldn't be there too much longer; and sure enough, about a month later, Daddy Raymond began teasing me that I had no idea what was in store for me.

I felt a prickle of excitement—my intuition had been correct! I told the principal I had guessed his secret and that he might as well tell me, but he wanted me to guess first. I was smart enough to hold my tongue, for I didn't want to give him any new ideas, should mine prove to be wrong, but he persisted. After a couple of days, I gave in and played out my hand.

"Sister Samantha is moving away," I began, "and you're going to take me to do her job." Sister Samantha was in charge of the art department and designed all the literature, and until now I had been her assistant. "And you're going to ask me to stop working at the bank too," I finished smugly, pleased with myself for having figured out the whole puzzle. He wiggled his ears and said nothing more until the announcement was made officially in front of the entire congregation. My hunches had been exactly right.

A thrill of delight ran through me, for this meant that not only had my abilities been recognized, but Daddy Raymond trusted me enough to put me in charge of an entire department. And this was no small department—it was the headquarters for the dissemination of Church literature that went out all over the world.

And so the next day at the bank, I went up to the chief accountant and told him I was leaving.

"I'll take you off the counter," he replied quickly, for he knew that I hated working there. "I'll put you wherever you want. Just tell me where you want to go."

"No, no, it's not quite like that, Mr. Goddard. I don't really have a choice in the matter. Everything is all right," I assured him, "but I must leave."

"Oh, all right," he said disbelievingly. "I'll get you an appointment with the manager."

Later that morning, Mr. Reavey called me into his office and tried to persuade me to stay.

"Sir, I gave my life to God, and now I want to make a full dedication," I explained to him. "This is a wonderful opportunity for me to go into full-time service."

Mr. Reavey was disappointed, but somewhat sympathetic. Many of the bank employees were Catholic, and I think he had the idea that I was going to become a nun. "You are right," he sighed. "For four and a half years you came out and saw how the other half lives, and I don't blame you for going back. The best of luck to you, Tonica. We'll miss you immensely." He thanked me for all my hard work and dedication at the bank and promised that they would give me the job back immediately any time I wanted it.

I had given a month's notice, and during that time, my co-workers tried to convince me that I was making a mistake. They were furious with me for giving up such a promising career and berated me for running away from the "real world." I tried to help them understand, but it was almost impossible.

I did have a few small qualms about the discomfort of giving up a familiar routine, but for the most part, I was very contented. I was satisfied that I had been a good "testimony" at the bank; I had earned the respect of all my co-workers, not only for doing my work well, but for being a shining example of the lifestyle of a believer. Many years later, I learned during a random conversation that one of the employees remembered me as having been "serene."

I did not know exactly what my new mission was, but I knew that it was time to move on. It was a long month. I was eager to begin my new life, although of course more than a little nervous.

ॐ

My first day in the office was December thirteenth. I was twenty years old.

Sister Samantha had been called out as an evangelist and had moved to Bloomington to take up the pulpit there. This was a double advancement for me, for her absence not only left me in full charge of the art department, but it was also an acknowledgment that I no longer needed a shepherd to straighten out my soul. I could take care of myself.

Sister Victoria was the manager of the entire Administration Center, and she came up to the art department several times that day to give me work. It seemed so natural to be in charge, and I slipped on the mantle with less anxiety than I had expected. I was familiar with the department and had acquired good skills over the past four years. I knew what to do.

But there were other adjustments to make, for I soon learned that life in the office was totally different from life "on the outside." Once I happened to make mention to Daddy Raymond of "my time," referring to the private lunch hour and coffee break that most employees were entitled to during the workday. He was stunned.

"What are you talking about—'my time'? Your time is not your own, child," he bellowed. "You're in this business twenty-four hours a day, and the sooner you realize it the better off you'll be!"

I laughed. I was happy to have a standard to live up to, and felt relieved to be needed. I felt that I was accomplishing something, and indeed our department seemed to be humming with continual activity.

We were so busy that many times we would work all through the night, catnapping here and there for a few minutes, and continuing on until the next morning. I learned to shoulder full responsibility and to work with the team, and pretty soon, I was invigorating the office with fresh ideas. Everyone was amazed at the way "little Sister Tonica" was able to cope with the pressures and demands of the job.

It was also just lovely to be able to sing hymns whenever the mood struck me during the day, and not be bothered by sniggers or sneers or be told bluntly to shut up. I was back in the comfort of a religious shelter, and my heart was free to commune with my savior and dearest friend.

It was only a few months later that I reached my zenith in the college, the day every student yearns for—the time of spiritual maturity when a ministry is recognized within a person's life. In the middle of a Sabbath service, the principal beckoned to me from the platform. I walked forward, having no idea what he wanted. He told me to bow my head and placed his hands on me. The chapel waited in silent anticipation; it was so still you could have heard a pin drop.

Daddy Raymond said solemnly, "May the spirit of a prophet dwell deep within the heart of this woman, and may she arise in the spirit of David her ancestor and take her place among my people Israel." He prayed over me with deep emotion for several minutes, but I remember these words only, for I was dumbfounded. It was the last thing in the world I had expected—to be ordained so soon, and as a *prophetess!*

The Church believed that Jesus had left behind five gifts of the ministry, the highest being that of an apostle, followed by the descending levels of prophet, evangelist, pastor and teacher. Apostles and prophets were considered the very foundation of the Church, possessing the power to actually steer others along a spiritual continuum. Daddy

Raymond, a recognized apostle, had the perception to recognize these ministerial gifts in another person and to grant the appropriate ordination. The fact that he had perceived prophecy in me was absolutely astounding.

After the service, everyone came to congratulate me, and the other ministers welcomed me among them. I was ecstatic.

Riding high on a cloud of euphoria, I found the confidence to preach in a way that surprised everyone around me. For my preaching practical, I chose a verse that was particularly ruthless: "If the righteous scarcely be saved, then what of the wicked and the ungodly?" I was barely twenty-one years old, a novice challenging two hundred and fifty people—most of them at least twice my age—to assess their own commitment, and in no uncertain terms! My father was amazed that his baby girl had chosen so dynamic a rebuke, and he was enormously proud of me. The sermon was a great success, and it was only the beginning, for I was on my way to fulfilling the dream my father had long harbored for his son, "the evangelist." That son had turned into a woman of unexpected strength with a few surprises up her sleeve.

All of the students were on a constant rotation of duties in the services, and one day, it came my turn to deliver a short thought during morning prayers. To this day, I am not sure where I summoned the audacity to stand up in front of the entire college and tell them that they were all liars.

"We complain all the time that we're tired," I lashed out with the strength of perfect conviction. There wasn't a fiber in my being that did not believe every word I uttered. "But we're not tired. We have plenty of energy to do other things that we want to do, so why don't we have energy for Jesus?"

"We took a vow that we're never going to sin again, but we're all lying—because we say we're *tired*!"

Even the principal was shocked. Perhaps he began to sense that his "little girl" was not so little. Neither of us could foresee the far-reaching influence I would soon have on the campus and beyond.

On my twenty-first birthday, "The Messenger" from the bank came to church and brought me presents and cards from my friends there. It was lovely to see him and to hear all the news of my former co-workers. He decided to stay for the service, even though he was a devout Catholic who had almost entered the priesthood himself, and came away quite impressed, and thoroughly touched, by the warmth and good-heartedness of the people in the congregation. He went back to work the next day and told everyone, including the management, of the fantastic experience he had had at "Ton's church"; but unfortunately he was pressured by his own priests to refrain from attending any more of our services, and that was the last time we saw him.

In any case, Daddy Raymond was happy with me. It was obvious I had been a good testimony at the bank, and the cherry on top of the cake was the phone call I received from Mr. Goddard, the chief accountant. He was looking for a cleaning lady for the bank and wanted to know if any of the church ladies might be interested. After doing some investigating, I made a recommendation to him, and he took the woman purely on my word, without asking for further references. As it was a bank, where the security was naturally of the highest standard, Daddy Raymond was totally amazed at the level of trust my former employees had shown in me. In fact, for quite a while it just seemed as though I could do nothing wrong. I was favored and cherished—but the old fingers of doubt had wormed their way into my heart again.

Hadn't I been horribly out of favor only a few months before? I could still remember clearly how it had felt to be a college outcast, to be avoided by ninety-five percent of the students, and treated as though I had some terrible disease. Almost overnight, that had changed, but I couldn't allow myself to forget it so easily. I looked with pity at the ones and twos in the college who were also "out of the spirit," and therefore totally isolated. Even though I was basking in the sheer delight of being honored and accepted after my own long exile, I couldn't permit myself a total indulgence when others around me were suffering the same ostracism. Something about the whole system bothered me, but at this point, I did not dwell on the matter for too long. I had other, more pressing things on my mind.

 formes

For some time I had been bothered by an inner feeling that I had never sufficiently challenged my belief in God or my relationship with Him. A plan had been germinating in my mind for quite a while, but it was a serious and risky undertaking, and no one in the college, as far as I knew, had ever done it; but I had come to a point where there was no alternative. I decided that I would push my dedication to the limit and live by faith.

This meant that I would give back my weekly allowance to the church and keep no money at all. I would pray to God for whatever I needed, whether it be a tube of toothpaste, bar of soap, or article of clothing, and trust that He would hear my prayer and supply it for me.

Up until now, the only God I knew was the One who could enable a person to have a spiritual "high" or to babble in tongues. Those were powerful and gratifying experiences, but I was growing accustomed to them. A person couldn't stay on a "high" twenty-four hours a day, although the Church seemed to expect just that, and what was supposed to happen when it was over? Wasn't there anything else? I was growing, both personally and spiritually, and I wanted more.

There *must* be more. How could I possibly "outgrow" God? Wasn't He infinite?

Occasionally, when I would hint at these doubts to the principal, he would tell me that there was a "spirit of unbelief" in me, and that if I really believed completely, I would feel satisfied. I could not challenge him directly, but I was beginning to feel that this response was unfair. It wasn't my fault. How could anyone say that I hadn't tried hard enough, that I hadn't truly "believed"? I had believed with all my heart since I was a child, despite my adolescent conflicts; I had been repenting since I was two years old! I felt there must be another answer, and if I could not get it from my superiors in the college, I would have to test it myself.

All my life, I had voiced a belief in God and had lived according to that *voice*, but not necessarily according to the belief I needed to prove conclusively that God really existed and that He really did hear *my* prayers. We had always been taught that sometimes God said "no" to our requests, but wasn't it possible that circumstances were responsible for those results, and that it wasn't God after all? I needed to know that He was a personal God who could provide for my every need, who could free me from dependence on any human being, a God with whom I could have a direct relationship. I felt I would do anything to find Him—fast for a month, wear sackcloth, dig ditches, beat myself—*anything* to know that He was really there, and I knew that if I was sincere, He wouldn't let me down.

It took me several months to come to the decision to go out on faith. I was afraid to take up the challenge. I felt that if I tried and failed, I would go out of my mind, for I knew no other way of life. All I had in the world was my belief in God. What would be left to me if that were taken away? Hadn't Sister Victoria told me a dozen times that I would *never* survive out in the world, that my life would totally disintegrate and I would die of loneliness?

It was not just the decision itself that was complicated and unclear, but the whole idea of living by faith. Those who had done it in the past walked a very fine line between being considered true spirituals who were capable of existing on a higher plane, and being considered "cracks," psychologically maladjusted people whose view of faith was distorted.

Going out on faith, in its purest sense, was something we associated with the old-fashioned Christians of a bygone era. As a youngster, I had heard many miraculous stories of missionaries who had gone to India or Africa and had survived on faith, and we believed those tales. But to undertake such a lifestyle in this day and age was not quite so simple. Those who had tried to do it in our congregation in Greenborough had always seemed a little eccentric.

I remembered a story Brother Mark had once told, during one of his sermons, of a certain person he knew who had taken up the challenge. This man told Brother Mark continually that the Lord was providing for his family in the most generous way, and that every week he would find large packages of food on his doorstep. Brother Mark ended by telling us, in a more than slightly derogatory tone, that it was *he* who had put the food there because he did not want to see this man and his whole family starve to death.

There were even wilder stories of people who testified in church that not only were they living totally by faith, but that God was guiding their every footstep. My brother Philip had actually seen such a testimony. A man had stood up in front of the entire congregation and claimed that he had woken up that morning and asked the Lord, "What should I wear today?"

And the Lord said, "Wear one blue sock and one green sock."

And so he did, and then he said to the Lord, "What shall I do today, Lord?"

And the Lord said, "Go outside of the house and turn right."

And so he went outside and turned right, and he walked a little way down the pavement and said to the Lord, "Where shall I go now?"

And the Lord said, "Follow the blue van."

Such a testimony could go on for half an hour, and of course this was an extreme and silly case of a simpleton who really "believed." But such stories bothered me a little, and I wondered if I was on my way to becoming such a weirdo.

On the other hand, there were similar stories we had heard of my grandmother, and we certainly would not have associated her with anybody as misguided as the man with the blue van. My mother rarely spoke of her life in Alexandria, and even then she would only speak of the time *after* she and her mother had converted to Christianity. My grandfather had sat *shiva* for them and refused to give them any money, but my mother claimed that Jesus had provided for them instead, and food would often be left on their doorstep. One famous story of hers was of the time they opened the door and found a big tin of marmalade sitting there. They were delighted at the idea of having such a delicacy with their bread that day, but when they opened the can, it was filled with even more substantial food—pork sausages and meat. The Alexandrian missionaries had convinced my grandmother that she was giving up her old way of life for a much better one, and here was proof of it right on her doorstep. Jesus had not forgotten her family and would provide them with everything they needed to survive.

I believed these stories, and indeed we were all proud of my grandmother's faith. In our minds, she could not possibly have fit into the crazy or "disarranged" category.

And so for a long, long time I turned the idea over in my head without reaching a final decision, and I was careful to tell no one of my thoughts. Then one day, during morning devotions, Sister Victoria started to read us passages out of a book. The story was a true account of a group of German women who had lived totally by faith and of their tremendous accomplishments in the service of God. The book was amusing and inspiring, and I took this as a sign from heaven that it was my turn to demonstrate the same faith. So I finally took the plunge and set out to prove God to myself, and He never let me down.

For two full years, I gave back every penny of my allowance to the church, and not a soul knew of it. I cannot explain the joy I felt when I prayed to God for a box of tissues or a tube of toothpaste, and within a few days, found the item I had requested on my bed. I cannot tell you how it happened, or how various people had simply had a "feeling" that they would like to leave me a little gift. But I do know that I always received *exactly* what I asked for.

Once I prayed four days for a new slip to replace my old one, which had become threadbare and ragged. On the fifth day, Sister Samantha came to visit from her parish in Bloomington with a present for me—a slip. On another occasion, the cleaning lady at the bank, who had gotten her job on my recommendation, received a bonus and sent me ten pounds. This was equivalent to nearly twenty American dollars and seemed a fortune to me. I felt like a millionaire, and the money lasted quite a long time.

Other items came in a variety of ways; sometimes from a friend of my parents who would bring me little treats after services, sometimes from one of the church ladies who sold Avon products, and occasionally had a jar of powder or bottle of shampoo for me. During the entire two years I never lacked for a single thing that I really needed.

My faith was strengthened. There was a God in the world who was alive and real and who heard my prayers, and what's more, I could relate to Him! My joy knew no bounds.

When I look back at this period now, I think it was the greatest blessing God could have given me then—a way to reach Him on the only terms that were available to me. If I had been satisfied with tongues, I would never have sought more. I sincerely desired to know Him and He allowed me to do so through the only channels I could activate.

I decided to capitalize on the momentum of this wonderful experience and establish my own fast in order to purify myself and walk ever closer to the God I had newly discovered. I stopped eating luxury items like chocolate and cake and even cut down on unnecessary food. I never took a second helping at meals, never ate dessert, and drank only water.

Fasting was a common practice at college. Aside from the regular Friday fast, it was a voluntary act and took a number of creative forms. My brother would sometimes do a bread-and-water fast for weeks at a time, and occasionally a sleep fast, where he would work continually, day and night, for about three days straight. He also once took on vegetarianism for about a year. Other people did silence fasts and would not speak for a week or more. It was a natural expectation of us to work on our carnal natures and refine our characters, but no one really stopped to ponder the fact that we all supposedly had been "clean" and "holy" since the sanctification experience at Southford, and that we were no longer supposed to have active carnal natures. Any doubts that anyone may have entertained were never voiced, for to question Daddy Raymond was to question God Himself.

The few misgivings that I did have remained locked in the deep recesses of my mind. I knew that the doctrines of the Church were holy and that I must continually work on myself to achieve them; any shortcoming was mine alone. I strove painstakingly to be worthy of my God, for He had shown Himself to me, and I knew now that He was real.

ぬ THIRTEEN ✧

I BEGAN to notice a radical change in my sister Margaret. We had not become any closer during our years together at college. Perhaps she had never forgiven me for being born in the first place and stealing her role as baby, for that teddy bear that rightfully belonged to me was still on her bed. We did not confide in one another or share the ups and downs of real sisterhood; yet she was still my sister, and even from a distance, it was not hard to tell that something about her was different. She had become excited and giggly, very unlike her usual prim self.

I confided my observations to Anette. "Watch Margaret," I said to her. "She's acting really silly."

A few days later, Anette came back to me and confirmed my findings. We tried to guess the reason behind such strange behavior, but couldn't come up with anything concrete. Later that evening, it suddenly dawned on me that there could only be one explanation: Margaret must be getting engaged!

I couldn't contain my joy. After all, she was my sister. I ran to look for her and found her working in the kitchen.

"Hey, Margaret," I burst out, "are you getting married?"

"Shut up!" she screamed furiously. Grabbing my arm roughly, she pushed me into one of the storerooms and slammed the door.

Eyes steaming with anger, she demanded, "Who told you?"

"No one told me. I noticed you were really different, all bubbly and excited, and I guessed myself."

"Listen," she said in a serious whisper, "on Friday, I'm leaving. I'm going to get married to Max. We've rented a house here in town. *Don't dare say a word to anyone.* We've spoken to the principal and he's given us his blessing." She gripped my arm even tighter, and continued through clenched teeth, "I'm warning you, don't dare say a single word to anyone. Do you hear me? I don't want this to get messed up. Tomorrow night at evening devotions, the principal is going to make an official announcement. Now I've told you. Don't say I never tell you anything." She pushed me out of the storeroom and continued with her work as though nothing had happened.

I tried to collect myself and to walk back calmly to my room. Margaret's turbulent anxiety and her startling revelation had left me numb. I lay in bed, trying to put two and two together.

Margaret had met Max years ago while we were still in Greenborough. I knew they really liked each other, but when they came to the training college, the principal had split them up. He did not approve of the match, feeling very strongly that Margaret should marry someone else, and to that end he kept her in Portfield and sent Max out of town. He had promised them that if they still wanted to marry after a three-year separation, he would consider it. It was now almost four years later, and although it was apparent from Margaret's anguish that he still did not agree, they were going ahead anyway. In fact, I found out later that Daddy Raymond never did give them his blessing.

I realized that Margaret had been so rough with me because she did not want the news to leak out before the principal made the announcement. It was bad enough that she and Max were defying his wishes, but to allow such a shocking development to seep out through unofficial channels would have been tantamount to slapping him in the face.

I didn't know what to think. It was so sudden and so strange.

Margaret had been the perfect child, the model preacher's daughter; and here she was involved in an act of outright rebellion. I lay in a daze for a while, trying to sort it out, until finally sleep overtook me.

The next night, the announcement was made. There was a deathly stillness in the chapel. Usually, when a wedding was announced, there were cheers and whistles, dances and songs, but instead everyone sat in silence, totally stunned, for it was more than a little obvious that Daddy Raymond did not approve. Afterwards, one or two of the older congregants went up to Margaret and wished her well.

I went up to her room after the service. Everything was boxed and packed, ready to go. She gave me nothing, I gave her nothing. We had not a word to say to each other. The next day she was off to meet Max at his parents' home, and three weeks later my father married them in Greenborough.

The marriage was a direct blow to Raymond Webster's authority, and the effect it had on the Church was shattering. Several people from the college traveled to Greenborough for the wedding, thereby missing our regular Sabbath service, and that act automatically drew a dividing line between the "outsiders" and the "insiders"—those who consented to the marriage and those who didn't. This issue, of course, had very little to do with the marriage, and everything to do with the flagrant risk of flouting the principal's leadership.

I was caught in the middle. On the one hand, even though we were not close, Margaret was my sister, and I knew that my father himself planned to marry them. But I was bound by my allegiance to the Church, and fearful that if I disobeyed Daddy Raymond I would not only be out on the street without a thing to my name, but also adrift in the world without a shell of meaning in my life to cling to.

I did not go to the wedding.

On the Saturday night after the ceremony, my father came walking up to me suddenly in the college kitchen and said sternly, "Your sister is outside. Go and see her." I knew the principal wouldn't approve, but I was afraid of my father too.

I went outside to the street where Margaret was sitting in the car with Max. She looked very happy, but was obviously quite tense, and her attempt to put on a show of normalcy was forced. We made our usual small talk, I admired her rings, and then they went. My brother Philip refused to see her.

My father had taken an extremely difficult stand when he performed the marriage, for as a result, he sealed his own split from his long-time war friend, Raymond Webster. Together they had built up the entire organization. My father had toiled unstintingly, giving every ounce of his strength, holding back nothing for the sake of the Church, and now in an instant he was out. It was a shaky time for everyone in the entire Church community. My father had been the gentle shepherd of us all, unanimously beloved.

He was not officially dismissed, for to oust someone from such a high position—and especially someone who was so universally respected—would have been a disgrace for Raymond Webster as well. But neither could Webster tolerate this threat to his ascendancy, so he sent my father to a new parish in the south of England. The move was ostensibly nothing more than a typical church transfer and was covered over with a smear of honey, but the aura surrounding it was unwholesome. For a while, some members of the church were not even aware of what had happened, and they were always coming up to ask me where my father was, and why he never came to visit Portfield anymore. I did not fully understand the situation myself then, and these encounters were always awkward.

Many of the "outsiders" who had taken sides in the dispute subsequently left the Church altogether, including Brother Mark. Some had ideas of their own about religion and wanted to take off in new directions, free of the confining submission to a single authority, and the rift provided them with the opportunity they had been seeking. It took quite some time for the Church to recover from the political maelstrom that the marriage had left in its wake.

There wasn't a person in the entire community, however, who was as deeply effected by the split as I was. To me it was devastating. My father had told me all my life that the Church was truth, and now he was gone.

I was twenty-two years old and grown-up, but still naive and very sheltered. I knew I had to decide between allegiance to my father and allegiance to the Church, and that the choice of one would preclude connection with the other. But the choice had already been made. I had built a life in the Church and had become a minister. There was no security, no meaning for me anywhere else.

Daddy Raymond took me aside and reminded me of the covenant that I and many other congregants had taken years ago, a vow that we would remain obedient to the authority of the Church for the duration of our lives. He instructed me to write a letter to my father, telling him that I could no longer communicate with him because I'd taken a covenant with the Church, and my father had broken that covenant. I obeyed; there was no thought in my mind then of contradiction, nothing that would damage my standing in the college.

Daddy Raymond dictated the entire letter to me, and when I was finished he said, "Now, you understand that I haven't told you any of this, don't you? These are your own thoughts and feelings."

Yes, I told him, I understood.

ॐ

I had never realized until then what a deep security I had felt in my status as "Brother Jim's daughter." I pictured myself as a little child, trustingly holding my father's hand, allowing him to lead and teach me. As I grew, we walked together arm in arm; but now he had become worn out and tired, and he had to sit down and rest. He couldn't go on anymore. I had to continue alone and reach the end of the road myself.

I thought of my sister Margaret, who had estranged herself from the Church through her marriage.

I thought of my elder sister Esther, who had left the college many years before to go to Israel. Her departure had been clouded in secrecy, and no one had told me the truth about it.

And now my father was gone. He would preach for the remainder of his life, but never again in our church. I had never been very close to him, but the pain of a formal separation was great. Now I wasn't anybody's daughter, but simply "Sister Tonica."

Those who had secretly been jealous of my previous status were happy. "Now you're just like one of us," they told me.

I couldn't allow myself to be deterred or to see any connection, any underlying threads, between the events that had separated my family from the Church. I'd gone too far now.

Upon hearing of my situation, dozens of church members from up and down the country and abroad sent friendly letters, little presents and pick-me-up gifts. Even Philip began to visit me occasionally in my room to have tea and chat, something we hadn't done in years. It was encouraging to be surrounded by people who cared so much for me, and I felt blessed in the ability to decide for myself—finally—that this people and this way of life were truly right for me.

∂ FOURTEEN ∞

AFTER the break with my parents, Daddy Raymond and his wife tried hard to become closer to me and to fill the parental role. They moved me into a room right next to theirs, and close to their daughter's, which I considered an honor, even though I was sharing with an old woman named April whom I didn't like much at all. The Websters had instructed her to be warm and motherly toward me, but instead she was stubborn and stern, and she had infuriating little habits that rubbed me the wrong way, such as sitting me on her knee and cuddling me. But I told no one and tried to make the best of the situation.

I was quite lonely, though, because most of my work was done in solitude, and I found myself spending more and more time with Daddy Raymond and his wife. They constantly made me feel that my life was in trouble and that I needed them. They told me I was lonely, rejected, neglected, full of heartache and pain—but that they could raise me out of the pit. If I yielded, if I submitted, if I humbled myself, I could blend in with this people of love who were out to conquer the world with their mission of peace and hope.

I spent hours talking to them, making them tea, emptying their rubbish bin and cleaning their room. I felt privileged to be so favored and would do anything in order to be close to them. But I had no idea what kind of problem this would cause for me.

My special status with the Websters aroused strong feelings of jealousy in their daughter Victoria. She began to sulk and pout like a little girl, even though she was in her mid-thirties. She wanted her parents for *herself*. I thought this odd; every one of us in the college had had to forsake father, mother, brother, sister, in order to follow Jesus, and in fact, that was exactly what he demanded of us in the New Testament. Why was she behaving like this? After all, she was Sister Victoria! Hundreds of people throughout the world looked to her for inspiration and guidance, and it was her job to set an example. Why couldn't *she* find the strength to forsake her father and mother for Jesus?

I was confused but couldn't say anything. No one ever differed with Sister Victoria and triumphed, and so I simply retreated. My heart was set on finding a place in the good graces of everyone who mattered at college, and I decided I would no longer interfere in her private relationship with her parents. I stopped going in to the principal and his wife so often, and immediately afterward, Sister Victoria became my best friend again and openly shared her feelings with me.

Daddy Raymond was slightly embarrassed at his daughter's behavior and tried to make it up to me whenever he could, but I was willing to overlook it, for I wanted to be close to Victoria and gain inspiration from her. We shared many confidences and often talked about how special we were in that we—with the exception of my brother—were the only real "lifers" around the place.

Great plans were in store for the addition of a new wing to one of the main dormitory buildings. The principal and his wife were going to move there and have a complete flat instead of the one room they had lived in previously, which was just like everyone else's. The flat was planned to be totally self-sufficient, with a stove, sinks, refrigerator, freezer, private bathroom, and many other amenities. Of course, Sister Victoria was going to move with them to the new building, for she was never very far away, and they took me and a new roommate along as well.

The principal's abode slowly became the new center of the college. The flat was luxury itself, and those who were close to the Websters enjoyed it, while others were more than a little jealous of its bodily comforts. Many of the students' rooms were old and cramped, with uncomfortable beds and cracking linoleum floors. Somehow this didn't bother me too much. It seemed to me that the principal and his wife had reached the ultimate stage. They had made a full dedication to God, and now they could have their luxuries because it didn't mean anything to them. That's what I told myself, and it seemed right— even though I knew that my parents were now homeless as a result of their split from the church and were living in a mobile home in Cornwall that had been given to them by a friend.

But all of that belonged to another world.

My new roommate, Lily, was a West Indian girl, two years younger than I. I had met her years ago when my father had taken me to the young people's meeting in Portfield, and her strong, yet sweet, personality had left an impression on me. She worked full-time in the bookbinding department at the Administration Center, so I was able to enjoy her company during the day too, and I felt lucky to have her as a roommate. We had a lovely new room as well, and so for a while things were extremely pleasant.

Life was full, productive and happy. We had just opened a Bible shop on the premises of the Administration Center, something the principal had dreamt of for several years. I had many ideas for marketable fancy goods with scriptural verses inscribed on them, and he encouraged me to put my concepts into operation. I soon found myself immersed in a world of creativity.

All the skills I had learned in art classes at junior school were finally put to use. I designed and screen-printed tablecloths with matching napkins, headscarves with matching lace-trimmed handkerchiefs, and dresses with verses embroidered on the pockets. I bought an electric poker and inscribed verses onto all kinds of wooden items, such as egg-cups, salt and pepper shakers and napkin rings. I pressed flowers, designed cards and bookmarks, and made decorative candles, all with beautiful gift-wrapping and an assortment of "love labels." The list of possibilities seemed never ending. Sister Victoria came up with the idea that all the fancy goods should go under the signature name of "Sharon Rose," because Jesus had been known as the "Rose of Sharon."

The Bible shop at Portfield began to flourish, and more people were brought in from other parts of the country to help with production, as it was too much for me to keep up with the demands alone. There was talk of opening more shops up and down the country.

I had my hands full, to say the least, for of course the shop work was in addition to my full-time graphics job at the Administration Center and Bible school on Sundays. I was so happy and so satisfied with my accomplishments that the difficult hours seemed a small price to pay.

❧

I was in the office one day when I received a surprising phone call from Mother. What did she want with me?

"Tonica, is that you?" came her cordial, but somewhat grating, voice.

"Yes, Mother, how are you?" I replied politely.

"Ton, I'm going away for a few weeks, but I want you to do me a favor. When you go into the flat to tidy up and make the principal coffee in the mornings, take someone with you. Never go in alone."

"Oh, okay," I chirped. "I'll take Lily with me."

I was a tiny bit puzzled about the request but pushed my curiosity aside. I had done well in the college because I had learned to mind my own business, having finally come to terms with the adage I had heard numerous times: "Yours is not to reason why, yours is just to do or die." And so I did whatever I was told and asked no questions.

Mother was gone for about five weeks. She was doing a tour of all the community homes throughout the country, inspecting them for cleanliness, management, costs, and the like. It was a job that was tailor-made for her.

On a Thursday night at about ten-thirty, four weeks after Mother's departure, I wearily climbed the steps to my room, thinking of all the things I still had to do before I could go to bed. Evening prayers had just finished, and the building was quiet and dark. Lost in my thoughts, I was almost on the top flight when the sound of the principal's voice made me jump.

"Come on in and make me a coffee, Toni," he called from inside his room, in a voice most lonely and pathetic. "I haven't seen you in ages. I've missed you."

It was true. I'd hardly been in to see him since Mother had left.

"Okay," I replied hesitantly, "I'll put the kettle on now, and I'll be back in a minute to make the coffee."

I ran upstairs to our room, hoping that Lily would be there, but she had already left for her bread-baking duty and would probably be in the kitchen all night. I waited a few moments, uncertain as to what I should do, and then the principal called up the stairs, "Are you coming, gal?"

It was the first time I had disobeyed Mother outright. I was afraid, but decided it was all right for me to go into the room because the principal himself had asked me to make the coffee, and I had never disobeyed *him*, either. I had no idea why Mother had requested that I not go into the flat alone, but I felt I had no choice.

I walked into a steam-filled room. The kettle had obviously come to a boil a while ago. The principal was reclining in his chair, and all the time that I was making the coffee, my back was toward him. After about two minutes he called to me.

"Come here," he said in a soft but authoritative voice.

I walked over to him trustingly.

"Sit down," he continued.

"Where?" I inquired, for no other chair was nearby.

"Here," he said, pointing to the arm of his chair.

I sat down, and he drew me close to his chest and gave me a kiss on the cheek. This did not seem so unusual; many of the women in the college stopped by Daddy Raymond's room each morning to give him a kiss on their way to work. His eyes were aflame now with something that I did not understand, but I trusted him. I was so naive that I had no idea what was happening. I simply felt that I was a little girl, and that he was my new Daddy after my own had forsaken me.

"Thank you for loving me," I said with the simplicity of a child. I so desperately wanted things to return to normal, but the principal didn't seem to hear what I said, and his arm tightened around me. There was something wrong with these kisses; they were not ordinary fatherly kisses, and his eyes were becoming red with intensity. Before I knew it, his left hand had expertly found its way up my legs beneath my skirt and petticoats.

I was confused and began to panic. When I saw that he had no intention of releasing me, I grabbed his wrist and pushed it away.

Instantly he jumped up, pulled me across to the other side of the room, and told me to kneel down next to him beside the couch. I knelt down. He prayed to Jesus to forgive us—a short prayer, matter-of-fact, but without feeling. I stood up, totally dazed.

"Don't tell anyone of this," he commanded.

"I promise," I replied, and made my way out of the room in a stupor. The heavy wooden doors once again swung shut, leaving behind the only witness—the untouched cup of coffee on the draining board.

I stumbled into the bathroom, shaking from head to foot, my face ashen. I sat there for a while waiting for my heart to stop racing, and after several minutes finally found the strength to get to my feet and go into the bedroom and lie down. Lily had come back from the kitchen to get something. She took one look at me and knew I was not myself.

"Are you all right?" she asked. "What happened?"

"I'm fine," I replied, almost in a whisper. I was still so shaken I couldn't speak properly. "Nothing happened. I'm all right."

She was obviously not convinced, but did not press the issue.

"I'm going back to the main building now—I'm going to sleep there so that I don't have to come home on the streets in the dark," she informed me. "Are you sure you'll be all right?"

"Yes, thank you, it's okay," I replied thinly. I turned to smile at her, and my eyes lit on the photograph the principal and his wife had given to every student—a head-and-shoulders portrait of themselves. A blue shiver ran down my spine. I waited for the door to close behind Lily, placed the photograph face downward, and locked the bedroom door.

I lay on my bed for hours in a vaporous limbo, unable to think. I couldn't *let* myself think. I was deeply hurt and terribly confused, and still not quite sure what had happened. I was convinced it was merely a slight slip on Daddy Raymond's part, an odd quirk that had surfaced for an instant; it had never happened before, and would never happen again. I would never tell anyone. He could trust me. It was a secret that I would keep for him forever.

Needless to say, I did not go into the flat again until after Mother's return. Whenever she was around, the principal behaved like a little boy covering up a naughty secret. He was adamant that the door always be left wide open, and if anyone tried to close it, he would immediately call, "No, leave it open—let Mother see how we do it when she is gone."

I was slightly withdrawn around Mother and felt a little guilty inside, for she trusted me without question, and from her side, it was understood that I had not been inside the flat alone. Outwardly, however, I remained calm, and the only change was an internal one that I imposed upon myself. I had always been modest before, both in dress and in demeanor, but somehow I thought the incident might have been my fault, and from then on, I guarded myself even more rigidly.

Shortly afterward, there was another shocking development, and again I was at a loss to understand the meaning of it or to make any connection between the events.

The young people from the neighborhood who came to prayer meetings each had a special "auntie," someone in the church who looked after their spiritual welfare. It was mostly the girls who took advantage of this arrangement, attaching themselves to the auntie of their choice, and for many years, my "niece" had been Alice, a sweet young girl from a rough-and-tumble family who had come under my wing at the tender age of fourteen. We had enjoyed a close relationship for four years. I think I was the only stable presence in Alice's life, and she loved me very much. But now she was growing up, and her affection began to take on a different and uncomfortable form.

It was customary in the Church to kiss and hug in "holy" greeting, a practice which had been taken from the New Testament, but Alice began to lean on me passionately and to kiss me strongly. There were times when I felt sickened in the pit of my stomach. I would freeze into an icy stiffness and try to draw myself away from her, but she would not let go, and her feeling for me only intensified. I had no idea at all what sort of attachment this could be and searched my heart to discover what I had done wrong that could arouse such passion in a young girl. But when I looked around and quietly observed the other "auntie/niece" relationships, I realized with astonishment that mine seemed quite tame by comparison.

There was unrest in the depths of my life again; the old festering worms of doubt had poked their way up to the surface once more. Urgently I squashed them down.

I could not even explain to myself why I felt so nauseated, but I believed the problem was with me. The people in the Church understood the ultimate good of God; they were holy people, and if I did not yet feel comfortable with their ways, I had much more work to do on myself. It didn't matter that I was already an ordained minister; it didn't matter that I was already leading others in the spirit. There was still another level of sanctity that was eluding me, and I believed that if I attained that level, I would not be living with this constant sense of malaise. I knew it would take time to get there, but I told myself I would pray to God for answers—for He *must* have answers.

It was only two weeks later that the principal and his daughter drove me up to Bloomington, the small town where Sister Samantha—formerly the "shepherd of my soul"—now shepherded an entire parish. We were going to take a look at the premises of the new Bible shop that would soon open there. Victoria had been assigned to help me set up, and for a further two months, I would remain in Bloomington on my own to get the shop on its feet. It was with a great sense of relief that I made the trip, for it gave me a welcome break from the embarrassing dilemma of dealing with Alice.

It happened that there was a moment when the principal and I found ourselves alone in the lounge of the newly acquired building. It was the first time we had come into close contact since that night in his room. He opened his mouth to speak, but no words came out.

A wave of submissive joy broke over me. "It's all right," I assured him openheartedly. "I feel both privileged and happy to keep the secret, for I trust myself never to tell anyone." At that moment I saw myself as the fortunate trustee of a profound confidence, almost like an ordinary citizen holding the formula for the atom bomb. I did not think about the bomb itself, only of the magnificent trust placed in me by someone much wiser and stronger, someone who had the power to guide my life and whose favor I craved desperately.

There was no time for Daddy Raymond to respond, for someone else had entered the room. We never touched this subject again.

❧

There was so much work to do at home over the next few weeks, before setting out in preparation for the Bloomington shop, that I scarcely had time to think, and that was a great blessing. Fancy goods had to be produced in quantity, books had to be ordered, a new cash register purchased, bookshelves built, and a thousand and one menial tasks completed. I tried to prepare as much artwork as I could in advance and to write lesson plans for the woman who would be taking over my Bible school classes while I was away. There were dozens of children's letters to be answered, many good-byes to be said, and I was frantically busy until the very last second.

Finally we were on our way. The small Bloomington congregation, under the ministry of Sister Samantha, was bubbling with excitement when we arrived, proud that their little corner of the globe had been chosen for such an important mission. Eager hands were everywhere, helping us to unload our precious wares. I was also very excited. This was my first real "solo" mission, and I was anxious for it to be a success in every way.

I lived in the church community house along with eight other people. The house was comfortable, with a large lounge, a chapel, a nice-sized kitchen and eating area, and five simple, but tastefully decorated, bedrooms. I was made very welcome, and the young girls in the home who worked in the nearby factories were eager to take the shop merchandise in to work for their friends to see and buy. Having grown up in a small, close-knit community, it was not hard to adjust, and before long I was settled into a busy routine.

Most of my time was spent in the store, and I soon realized this task involved more challenges than I had estimated. First of all, the temperature was piercingly cold. Bloomington is way up in the north of England, and very pleasant in summer; but now the winter wind was bitter and stinging. It rained almost every day, which not only deterred people from leaving the comfort of their cozy fireplaces to visit the shop, but it made the books curl on the shelves and the shop windows steam up, obscuring the beautiful displays that I had so carefully arranged.

Other little trials surfaced. I found that I was much too naive and trusting when it came to inventory, for small items began to disappear rapidly without trace. I was also handicapped by my inability to understand the local dialect. The young people in the congregation had great fun trying to teach me the "in" jargon, and by the end of my stay, I had made definite progress. There were two stigmas, however, that I was never able to overcome: one, I was a foreigner, and two, I was a "snob," for in northern England, anyone who lives south of the River Tyne, as I did, is instantly a snob. How everyone loved to hear my accent just so they could have a good laugh!

Letters of encouragement constantly streamed in from my friends at the training college, and in return I sent humorous accounts of the week's labor for them to read during Friday night fellowship. It was my first experience managing a church project "on the outside," and I not only enjoyed being off the leash a bit but also liked the business end very much and found that my training at the bank came in handy. My letters to the college were bursting with pride.

The people in the congregation were sweet and companionable— from the community house residents to the outspoken, rough-and-ready Bloomington citizens. Especially endearing were two old ladies who had been attending the church for years, ever since I had visited the town with my father in my early teens. Gertrude and Phyllis were the only two remaining congregants from that time, two sweet souls who lived in the nearby old-age home and faithfully attended every service. I had always had a soft spot for old people and was instantly inspired by their simplicity and childlike faith.

Amidst the muddle of local personalities was a widow named Gillian, who particularly interested me, as her husband had been a Jew. They had started a second-hand clothing store which generated a booming trade, and she had carried it on after his passing.

Once a month she would travel four hundred miles to London with her two grown children in a huge truck and pick up used clothing from modeling centers. Such fashions were rarely seen in the north, where village life had always been grueling and unadorned, and everyone flocked to "Gillian's" to see the latest styles.

I immediately took a liking to Gillian's outgoing daughter Paula, a former model who was now divorced. I loved to hear the stories she would tell of the way her enterprising father had made money when he was alive, such as by selling homemade shampoo that he had concocted in the bathtub. Paula was an open, honest girl, and we had a lot of fun together, but for some reason our growing friendship bothered Sister Samantha, and she did her utmost to discourage it.

Sister Samantha and I had gotten along fairly well during my stay. She was a senior minister now, and even though we treated each other as equals, she felt it her duty to make mention of the difference between Paula and me. The church treated Paula as a Jew because of her paternal lineage, and as a converted Jew, she was a feather in their cap, a lost lamb whom they had brought back to the "fold." Samantha seemed intent on making it equally clear to me that Paula was as Jewish as I was gentile.

"You know," she reminded me, "Gillian's children are Jews because their father was Jewish. It's only the Jews themselves who say you are a Jew, but you're really not."

"I know," I answered defensively. "But we can still be friends, can't we?" I *had* been vaguely interested in Paula' s Jewish heritage, but I understood the difference and didn't see why the relationship was undesirable. Paula was a church member, wasn't she? What difference did it make whose father was Jewish?

All too soon, it was time for someone from the training college to come up to Bloomington and take over the shop on a permanent basis, and Sister Holly was chosen. She was a nurse by profession and had never worked in a business, and she was given only one week to learn. Needless to say, she was a trifle nervous. I felt sorry for her, as I did for anyone in a situation that was beyond their control, and I tried desperately to cover up for Holly's many mistakes; but I was worried for her. I knew that if she failed, the principal would not be pleased with her, and that was never a pleasant spot to be in.

I tried repeatedly to explain the management procedures to her in a slow and careful way, but somehow she always got them messed up. At the end of the day, the books never balanced, and many more small items had disappeared off the shelves. Poor Sister Holly! She was in tears when I finally pulled out of the driveway the following Sunday morning. Why couldn't they have chosen someone with more of a business inclination? I knew in my heart that such questions were fruitless. Ours was not to reason why....

It was the longest drive I had ever made alone in one sitting, and I was relieved to turn onto familiar city roads and find my way back to the college grounds. Lily was not home when I arrived, but the young people had just come from prayer meeting, and as soon as they heard that I was back, they flocked to my room. After unpacking the last of my belongings, I sank into my favorite chair and sipped tea while the chattering teenagers filled me in on the latest college news. I was a little relieved to see that Alice was not in the group, and asked about her.

"Auntie, she left 'cos she fort yer wernt comin' back. Auntie, we told 'er yer were, but she dint believe us," they informed me.

"I'll go and visit her during the week," I assured them, and kept my promise. When I found Alice arm-in-arm with her new boyfriend, I was overjoyed, but of course I had to show a bit of outward grief, for Alice had been "lost from the fold."

At about three-thirty, on the afternoon of my return, there came a knock at the door. It was Brother Bartholomew, the principal's understudy.

"Welcome back," he said pleasantly. "I thought you could preach the sermon tonight."

My mouth dropped open in shock. I was exhausted, having just driven over three hundred miles without a break, but didn't dare refuse, especially in front of all my little fans. "Okay," I returned with a smile.

The young people ran off excitedly to tell everyone. They loved my sermons, and tonight I knew I couldn't disappoint them. I chose as my theme the story of the prostitute who kissed Jesus' feet, washed them with her tears, and anointed them with precious ointments after the religious Jews had not even offered him water for his hands. It was the best sermon I ever preached in all my time at the college—alive, inspirational, full of emotion. I looked around as I spoke at the two hundred familiar faces in the chapel and knew that they were the ones who had drawn it out of me.

It had done me a world of good to go away, but it was wonderful to be home again.

❧ FIFTEEN ❧

THE next morning returned me to the drawing board. There was of course plenty of work to do and no time for a vacation of any kind.

The Passover season was fast approaching. We had begun keeping Passover about four years earlier, shortly following Daddy Raymond's revelation, when he explained to us that Jesus himself had observed the holiday and therefore we would too. The pagan holidays had all been long discarded, and the absorption of another Jewish festival was a further step along the road to perfecting our ultimate status as "New Covenant Israel." Daddy Raymond had many books about Jews on the shelves in his office. He knew quite a bit about them, including a number of Hebrew terms, and he had even adopted the *menorah* as the symbol for the church logo, which hung outside the building and which appeared on all our stationery and literature. He had also begun to assign Hebrew names to chosen people in the college. He saw himself as the Moses of his generation, appointed to bring a new Israel into the Promised Land, and no one in the community doubted that he was being led by the "holy spirit."

Passover meant a tremendous amount of work in every department. It was one of two events during the year which served as international gatherings, and special services and programs were arranged for the whole week. It was my job to design the song sheet, program, and any tickets for the customary outing or film. The principal considered fellowship a constructive experience and felt that an outing provided a valuable opportunity for his flock to spend time together outside of church surroundings, and so he made sure that a trip was always arranged to a nearby castle, wildlife park, or some place of historic interest. One evening during this special week was also set aside for a religious film, which we rented and played on the premises.

The choir had special functions for this spectacular festival, the most important of which was to give a master performance of the Passover story and the *Hallel*. There were always endless streams of rehearsals for the choir and the musicians in the band.

The period of preparation was very intense and highly spiritual. All of the students in the college would fast for an entire week beforehand to prepare their souls. The night before the festival was an important occasion of its own—the night of the Last Supper. A special meal was served in the evening, and afterward we would have a foot-washing service, followed by communion, which was a renewal of our vow never to sin again and to remain loyal to the Church for life.

The foot-washing ceremony came from the New Testament story of Jesus washing the feet of his disciples before the Last Supper. It was considered an act of humility and extremely holy. Everyone in the congregation would take off his shoes, socks and stockings. Several bowls and towels would be provided, and whoever wished to participate in the ceremony would take a bowl, fill it with water, and place it in front of his chosen partner. Usually the washer prayed and cried over the other person's feet as he placed them in the bowl of water, carefully washing and then drying them. This act would be repeated several times with other "chosen" people.

The actual night of Passover was the night of the crucifixion, according to Daddy Raymond, and he taught us that Jesus was considered the Paschal lamb. He insisted that the rituals be observed in a very literal way, and to that end, had several live lambs brought in, encouraging us to watch the killing. The sheep were then roasted whole over an open fire, skinned and eviscerated. Many people would become quite emotional during the ritual, crying and speaking in tongues as they remembered their many sins. Since the Church believed that the Bible was the "living and proceeding word of God," it followed that our sins were just as responsible for Jesus' death as those of anyone in past generations, and the feeling of remorse evoked by the killing of the "Paschal lamb" generated a wave of melancholy in the room.

This year, the meal was planned for eleven-thirty on Passover night, and the chapel was turned into a dining room. Long tables were set up and beautifully laid out with expertly folded napkins, candles and name cards, and the story of Passover was told in lavishly colored posters that adorned all the walls. This year I had designed most of the decorations myself.

The day before the Passover feast, the principal kept guard over the chapel, hovering over the "spirit" of the room with the protectiveness of a hen hovering over her chicks. No one was allowed in unless he had a special function there, and those who worked inside were especially selected. They performed their tasks in great solemnity, never speaking above a whisper. In the early evening, the choir gathered to rehearse, and then the chapel doors were kept closed for a few hours in order to preserve the sublime "presence" which had been ripening there throughout the day.

It was eleven-thirty. The chapel doors had been reopened, and all of the students, dressed in fine suits and specially made gowns, were seated at their places, silently waiting.

My heart thumped with nervousness. I had been dreading this moment all year, for it was my voice that was to burst forth in song and break the magic spell, hopefully leading everyone upward and closer to God.

Sister Victoria left her seat and walked toward the platform. The choir and musicians took their cue and followed suit. Our procession was very orderly and very solemn, and it was some time before we were all in formation. No one had spoken a single word since we had entered the chapel at least half an hour earlier, and anticipation filled the air. The organist began playing the introduction, and I stepped forward to the edge of the platform.

"Why is this night different?" I asked the tenor in song. "What is the meaning of it all?" The melody took my voice soaring high up the scale in a slow, moving, and very powerful crescendo.

The tenor responded that this was the night we remembered all the bitterness and bondage of our former lives of sin. The tension was broken now, and the Passover story was sung out with pathos and humor, in rich harmony, ending on a victorious note as the Egyptians were drowned in the sea—and our sins along with them.

When the drama was ended, we returned to our places, and the lambs were brought in. The men took turns in carving the freshly roasted meat and distributing it to the tables along with portions of unleavened bread. We were allowed to eat as much as we liked, and hungrily devoured platefuls, although many people tried hard to remind themselves that this was supposed to be a "spiritual" meal. Our usual fare was so meager in comparison to this extravagant feast, and we were so accustomed to fasting that only a fine line of restraint kept the evening from turning into an orgy.

The meal lasted until about three o'clock in the morning, and then the choir sang excerpts from the Psalms of the *Hallel*. The final event of the ceremonial evening was the principal's reading of the "goat poem" found at the end of the Jewish *Hagaddah* book. No one understood this poem, and I knew that many people secretly thought it stupid, but of course no verbal opinions were ever offered.

Finally, we greeted one another with the verse "Next year in Jerusalem," hoping to find ourselves soon in the messianic city so beautifully described in the Book of Revelations of the Apostle John.

The most serious fear I had during the evening, surpassing even the anxiety of having to open the program, was the feeling that I might break out into giggles at any moment. Deep within me, lodged some place among my "worms of doubt," was a feeling of scorn and ridicule, an intuitive notion that the entire ceremony was a ridiculous joke. This feeling was a constant source of embarrassment to me. Why could I not root myself in the rituals? On numerous occasions, I had confessed this fear to the principal or to Sister Victoria, begging them to help me rid myself of this gnawing impulse, and they had prayed with me. The principal would place his hands on my head and shake me violently in order to demonstrate power and authority over the "demons" in my soul and to command them to leave my life. I always believed they were gone, but then over the course of time I would realize with disappointment that those wretched feelings had sprung up again like a stubborn fungus.

"Oh, God, why can't *all* of me believe?" I would cry. "*Help me!*" I would fast and pray to purge myself of these diabolical leeches and try to push them out of my mind, until finally I told myself that it must be a test from God and that I would constantly need to do battle within. "I'll do more, I'll crowd out the worries. I'll serve God anyway," I promised myself.

For a while, it seemed that God was trying to help me over my obstacles, for very soon afterward He sent me an inspirational boost. Nicky Cruz came to town.

Posters were pasted up on walls and telephone poles throughout the city, and the Christian community came alive with excitement. Nicky Cruz was a hero in our world. Every one of us had read the well-known story by Dave Wilkerson, *The Cross and the Switchblade*, the autobiographical tale in which God had called to him to leave his small rural home town in Pennsylvania during the sixties and go to preach the gospel in New York. The New Yorkers had all laughed at this artless country fellow, but nevertheless he had persevered, reaching all the way into the innermost recesses of the drug dens and street gangs, and had finally converted the leader of the worst gang in the city—a Puerto Rican named Nicky Cruz.

Nicky had written his own fascinating story in the book, *Run Baby Run*, and now he was here in Portfield. Of course, the whole congregation was eager to hear his testimony.

Before we left, Sister Victoria instructed me to try and get permission to interview Nicky for our college paper. I was the editor of *Tiqvah*, our young people's magazine, and she thought that was a good enough pretext for an introduction.

The affair was held in the largest auditorium in town, and there wasn't an empty seat in the place. By an incredible coincidence, I happened to find myself seated about two rows away from Nicky's wife, a petite and beautiful woman.

Nicky spoke for about two hours, giving a lively and moving account of his life. Afterwards, there was an enormous altar call, and several hundred people went forward to give their lives to Jesus and to receive Nicky's blessing and prayer.

Immediately after the service, his wife stood up, intending to leave discreetly. Daddy Raymond swung around and glared at me, wordlessly indicating that I should follow her, and suddenly my legs turned to jelly. A second commanding look followed, and although I was awestruck, I somehow managed to summon up the gumption to trot after her. I stammered out that I attended one of the two theological colleges in town and gave her a few details about the work we were doing. Then I drew in my breath and blurted out that we would like to see her husband.

I think she was a bit peeved at first, and slightly cautious, but finally she agreed to allow us to interview Nicky and to take a few photographs. I made an appointment with her at the hotel where they were staying.

Sister Victoria, of course, conducted the interview, and Brother Timothy, our photographer, took many pictures. He stayed up all that night to develop his film, and we returned the pictures to Nicky's hotel before his departure the following day. Nicky was so impressed, both with the photos and with our warm attention, that he initiated a friendship. Soon afterward he sent me a beautiful card in his own handwriting that read: "Toni, always remember Jesus loves you. Love, Nicky Cruz." I was thoroughly elated and treasured that card, keeping it tucked safely in the cover of my Bible.

The month seemed to be on a sensational roll, for shortly after Passover, a well-known Christian film called "The Hiding Place" came to town. Theater-going normally was frowned upon, but Daddy Raymond was out of town, and Brother Bartholomew, in his role as understudy, had decided the film was acceptable and had given us permission to see it. I was excited; we were actually going to the "flicks," something I had never been allowed to do before. I took along my favorite chocolate bar.

"The Hiding Place" was a respected film in Christian circles. It told the true story of a Dutch watchmaker called Father Ten Boom who had risked his life to hide Jews in his shop in Holland during the Second World War. The entire topic was a blank book to me, and I sat eagerly on the edge of my seat. The reels began to turn....

The first scene took us into the quaint home of the very old gentile watchmaker, who was living with his wife and two daughters above his shop. The setting is very cozy and warm—and yet, outside in the street, a German soldier patrols, his boots beating rhythmically against the cobblestones. A "customer" calls and exchanges hushed words with the watchmaker about ration cards and identification papers. Their conversation rapidly switches to watches as the S.S. man enters the shop.

The scene then changes to show line after line of Jews in the street, awaiting the fixture of the bright yellow star to their clothing. Father Ten Boom, in sympathy with the oppressed people, joins the line in an attempt to identify with their humiliation, but seconds later he is booted out of line by one of the Jews. He moves a few yards down and tries again, but again he is rebuffed. With a heavy heart he returns home.

Later, in his humble second-floor dwelling, Ten Boom watches over a precious bundle of life, a Jewish baby just a few weeks old who has been rescued from Nazi clutches. A gentile farmer visits, and Father Ten Boom begs him to take the child to his farm and nurture it. The farmer vehemently refuses and hurries away.

The persecution in Holland becomes worse, and now it is not just a baby in Ten Boom's home, but one Jew, and then two, three, four. A false partition is built into the wall, with an entrance through a small cupboard. The word gets around quickly that a gentile is hiding Jews, and soon there are ten fugitives squashed away behind the hidden wall. At times, during the day, they are allowed to go out, but many practice drills enable them to get back to their hiding place in only a minute. Over and over again, the Jews are shown crawling in and out of that tiny hole, their faces full of terror.

Father Ten Boom is finally tracked down, and most of the Jews manage to escape over the rooftops, but no information is given about their fate. The Ten Booms are sent to the concentration camps, and their shop and house are closed down. The father and the elder daughter, we are told, did not survive, but the younger daughter was finally released years later, and it was she who told the story.

The film was meant to focus on Father Ten Boom as a true Christian, a man who is unable to stand by while others are persecuted. But at the same time, it had portrayed the Jews as cowardly sheep who displayed no interest at all in their Judaism, and showed no concern other than shedding their identity and getting out alive.

Somehow I felt nauseated. I forgot that I had finally been to see a movie; I forgot about the uneaten chocolate bar melting in my palm. All I could think of was the Jews in the wall.

On the way home, my friends talked of the film and of how much they had liked it. I was silent.

My roommate, Lily, turned to me. "Would you like to see the film again, Toni? It was great, wasn't it?"

"I feel upset about it for some reason," I replied. "I wouldn't like to see it again."

Her face did not hide her surprise.

I continued coldly, "If it was a film on black slave labor, how would *you* feel?"

"But it was a film on Jews, and you're not Jewish," she said exasperatedly. "Why are you taking it so personally? It was just a film."

As we turned into the college drive, she looked at me again. It was obvious I was still preoccupied with the film. "Stop worrying," she persisted. "Oh, you're ridiculous, you are!"

I didn't have a reply and could only stare blankly ahead. I knew she was right. I *wasn't* Jewish, so why did it bother me?

It was weeks before the inner hurting ceased and the memories of those Jews, clambering in and out of a hole in a wall like frightened animals, faded away. The words of my roommate, however, never did: "You're ridiculous, you are! It was a film on Jews, and you're not Jewish!"

At the time, the obvious gap in her logic escaped me completely: What difference did it make whether the people in the wall were Jewish or Irish or Chinese? The film was meant to illustrate the principle of Christian love. Shouldn't Lily—shouldn't *everyone*—have felt as sympathetic as I did toward the persecuted fugitives, no matter what nationality they were?

One day, when I was passing through a bookshop in town, on an errand for the college, my eye fell on a paperback entitled *The Holocaust*. It was not expensive, and I had a little money left from my allowance that week, so I decided to buy it and find out for myself what had happened to the Jews during the Second World War.

It was late when we got to bed that night. Lily and I were now sharing our room with Josephine, the youngest of the three talented sisters in the college. With just our reading lamps on, the three of us settled down for the night, and in a few minutes, the room changed magically from a busy hive of industry to a peaceful slumber house. I snuggled down between the sheets and cautiously pulled out the paperback from under my pillow.

"What are you reading?" Josephine asked.

I hesitated a moment before replying. Josephine was not a very mature person, and I didn't want her spreading my reading habits all over the campus. Finally I told her.

"Where did you get that from?" she pestered.

"I bought it," I said indignantly. "Can't I buy a book if I want to?" She said no more.

I stayed up reading well into the night, unable to put the book down, oblivious of the time. I was totally stunned by the horror of the account. The truth of the Christian responsibility in the slaughter of the Jews did not register with me on this first reading—or perhaps it did, but I wasn't ready to accept it. I replaced the book on my shelf and went about my life as usual, but the Jews were still there in the back of my mind. They were always there.

It dawned on me one day with alarming reality that I actually knew one of those people who had gone through the inferno described in the book. In order to escape the party that Josephine always held for the church teenagers in our room on Sunday afternoons, I used to visit two elderly ladies in the neighborhood, one of whom was a Jewish Holocaust survivor named Mrs. Cohen. She had been a partisan in Poland during the war and had survived in the woods by eating bark off the trees. I had always been vaguely aware of her background, but suddenly it took on an entirely new meaning.

Mrs. Cohen was traditional but not observant. She had been befriended by one of the ladies at the church who frequently tried to strike up an exchange with the women in the local synagogue; and in fact, the church was so eager for a Jewish convert that the administration had even taken great pains to see that she was well cared for after she had an operation. She never attended our services, but she did come to the college occasionally to have tea, and that's how I had met her. I began to visit her regularly. Mrs. Cohen was a difficult old lady, to say the least. She loved my "golden hands" and always had a list of jobs a mile long for me to do when I came.

"Don't forget," she used to say, "be sure you come to me first, before you go over to visit Marjorie Simmons. That apartment is a disgusting filth hole, and I don't want you bringing any of her fleas into *my* house!" I listened to her endless instructions and admonitions with whatever fortitude I could muster, but often I didn't have quite enough patience. She certainly did not present me with a shining example of Jewry, but there was something about her that always made me want to go back again.

One day, while we were sitting in her living room, the conversation turned to marriage.

"There are plenty of nice boys for you in the church, dear," she pressed, naming several. "What's wrong with them?"

I looked at her steadily and replied, "I'm not going to marry any of them. And if I ever do get married, I'm going to marry a Jew."

Mrs. Cohen all but shot out of her armchair. She stared at me with bulging eyes.

"Yes, it's true," I said calmly. "You'll see."

"But how are you going to do *that*?" she managed to croak. It was obvious that there were no Jewish boys in the church, and the idea of my leaving the church was unthinkable.

"I don't know. But you'll see," I repeated.

And I didn't know. I didn't even know where I had gotten such a harebrained notion, and I think my words surprised me even more than they did Mrs. Cohen. The odd paradox was that in spite of my nebulous interest in the Jews—or perhaps because of it—I found myself very frustrated by the whole topic and became very defensive.

❧

My brother Philip had become a maintenance manager in the Polytechnic University in town. He loved the job, for it provided him with an unpressured outlet for the handwork that he so excelled in, as well as the opportunity to do outreach work among the students.

He called me aside one evening and told me that God had spoken to him that day and told him to legally change his first name to a Jewish name and his last name to Mordo, my mother's maiden name. This way he would be able to go to the Jewish functions at the Polytechnic disguised as a Jew and do his missionizing with greater facility.

Philip was one of the few people in the college whom Daddy Raymond recognized as having a "call" to the Jews, and he had been given a special assignment to recruit them. He was one of the task force who visited the synagogue regularly, and in fact it was he who had first invited Mrs. Cohen to have tea at the college. Philip was very enthusiastic about his mission at the Polytechnic, and as there were many female Jewish students there as well, he wanted to take me along as his partner. He begged me to change my name also and was furious when I refused.

"I'll pay for the legal paper work," he pleaded. "Just do it!"

But I wouldn't hear of it. "Look," I reasoned, "God spoke to you and so you changed your name, and if God wants me to change my name, He'll speak to me too!"

"*I'm* speaking to you," yelled my brother, who had also been called out as a prophet. "This is God speaking to you!"

"I'm sorry, Philip," I said quietly, "but I just don't have the same feeling toward Jews as you do. I'm not interested. If you feel it's your call to go to the Jews, go, but my call is at the office with the literature."

He didn't argue with me further, but I knew he was quite upset. I *was* interested in Jews and in Israel, to a deeper extent than I realized myself, and it might have been for this very reason that I did not care to get any further involved at this point.

Philip went ahead and had his name changed to Nathaniel and his wife's name to Yohannah. He then signed up to attend the Jewish functions at the Polytechnic. He was very proud of himself, especially since the Jews in the school believed him; but there also seemed to be some sort of personal satisfaction for him in that he finally had a Jewish name, and he liked it. I decided not to aggravate him and dutifully called him Nathaniel, although my parents never accepted the name.

This somewhat halfhearted attempt to shelve the issue of the Jews soon backfired on me, for I learned that my Uncle Sammy was coming to England.

❧ SIXTEEN ❦

UNCLE Sammy was my mother's youngest brother. At age eighteen, he had emigrated to Israel in 1948 from Alexandria and was part of the first wave of *aliyah* from Egypt. He was taken to Ashdod Yaakov Absorption Center where he stayed for six months, met his future wife and moved to Kibbutz Bror Chayal. His older brother, Solomon, was in the Greek Army at the time and would make *aliyah* at a later date. My grandfather joined him after the passing of my grandmother in Egypt.

In spite of my misgivings, I could not contain my excitement about his visit. Finally, after all these years, we were going to meet someone from the photographs! I thought of many questions to ask him about Israel and his way of life. I knew, however, that it would be a tense time, for since my sister's wedding I had not seen my family or had any contact with them.

Daddy Raymond knew my mother's brothers, having spent many hours in my grandparents' home in Alexandria during the war. In fact, he would often stop off and visit Uncle Sammy when he went to Israel and used to comment on my Aunt Maria's prowess as a cook. He would not have refused to allow my uncle to visit, but even though Sammy was not religious, he was very wary of allowing our Jewish relatives to have contact with us. He called my brother and me into his office and told us, "Your uncle is coming from Israel to be the great peacemaker in the family. You had better be careful!"

He was not too worried about my brother, but he hovered over me like a protective bear. I wasn't certain about the reason for this, for up to then I had never openly expressed any interest in the Jews.

On the day Uncle Sammy was due to arrive, Daddy Raymond took me to one side and said, "He just might offer you a ticket to Israel, and you should be prepared." I knew that he meant "prepared to refuse."

Five minutes later, there was a knock on my door.

"He's here!" my brother exclaimed, and we ran downstairs to greet Uncle Sammy in the main foyer.

I felt an instinctive yearning, a sudden pull to be truly connected to someone in my family. I ran to him and threw my arms around him. He was *my* uncle, my *Jewish* uncle!

He wept.

Fifteen minutes later, we were walking down the front drive of the college, and my uncle said, almost as though he had been given his cue, "Toni, what are you doing here in this place, living behind high walls and wearing dark clothes? If I send you a ticket for Israel, will you come? You are a young, beautiful girl. Give yourself a chance to see what life is about. You will live with me in my home like one of my own daughters. I will provide for all of your needs. The Jews will accept you in Israel because your mother is Jewish."

I smiled gratefully and hastily gave my prepared answer. "I have given my life to God, and it is no longer mine to do with as I please. If God wishes for me to come to Israel, in His way, at His time, He will make it possible."

I was pleased, however, at his concern, and I grew to love him very quickly. Sammy was about forty-five years of age, medium height and muscular with a strong backbone and a big heart. His warmth and consideration shone in his every action—and best of all, he was part of me, he belonged to my roots. I felt even closer to him than I did to my parents.

I spent as much time alone with him as possible, and we talked a great deal. He mostly told me about everyday life in Israel, particularly in Kiryat Shemonah. He was very proud of the fact that his army boots and uniform stood at attention by his front door ready for any emergency call. I was intrigued that he had a secret code and would listen for it even over the radio!

One day I was showing him through the Sharon Rose Bible Shop and boasting "modestly" of all the products I had designed. He flipped open a "love card" attached to one of the items and stood transfixed.

"This script," he mused. "It looks so familiar. I know I've seen this handwriting somewhere before. Now, where could that have been?"

I shivered. The handwriting was mine. I had thought it would be a personal touch if the labels carried a "human" flourish rather than a plain typeset message. And suddenly I knew, beyond a shadow of a doubt, where Uncle Sammy had seen my handwriting. "My parents showed you the letter I wrote to them, didn't they? The one saying I would stay in the church," I prompted.

"Ah, so that's it! Yes, Toni, they did," he answered softly. "I can't tell you they weren't hurt by your decision. Are you sure you made the right choice?" I felt a twinge of guilt to hear his words, but it passed quickly. I assured him that I had not a qualm in the world about my decision.

Uncle Sammy's voice seemed to hint that it wasn't just a question of the break with my parents that was problematic, but my choice to stay in such a place. There was an undertone in his attitude that suggested he was somewhat disturbed by the environment of the college, but he never said anything specific about it. I thought it might be my imagination; I couldn't imagine why in the world he would have anything against the Christians, especially in light of the fact that he had come to England partially to repay a debt of gratitude to them.

Sammy had intended to go to Scotland to visit Mr. Troop, the Salvation Army headmaster who had given his mother a job in the mission school in Alexandria, and had educated him and his brother with a very generous scholarship. He credited Mr. Troop with his eventual success as an accountant and wanted to thank him while he still had the chance, but unfortunately he learned that the headmaster had died three years earlier.

His gratitude was free of any religious association, but unfortunately I soon found that this detachment extended to his own heritage as well. There were so many things that I wanted to know about Judaism, and I peppered him with questions that I had never voiced to anyone before, but his answer was invariably the same.

"Toni, I don't know. I'm not religious," he would always say, insisting repeatedly on his disbelief in God—and yet he proceeded to tell us story after story about the many miracles that had happened in his home town of Kiryat Shemonah, which was on the Lebanese border, and, therefore, a prime target of Arab terrorism. It was plain that in spite of his lack of religion, he had a strong sense of Jewish identity and love for the land of Israel. He proudly told me how he had moved out from the Kibbutz in 1955 when Aunt Maria was pregnant with their second child and they had chosen to live in the north in a village called Chalsa, now known as Kiryat Shemonah. There were only a few families living there then, in a couple of rickety cabins and a few tin huts. His first job had been to pave a road from Chalsa to Metulla. Later he had worked in an ice-making factory and then moved on to work for Tnuva as a bookkeeper. He went back to school in the evenings and finally became a certified accountant and opened his own business. No one was more proud than Uncle Sammy that he lived on Herzl Street, the first real street built in Kiryat Shemonah. He had bought one of the first houses available and vowed he would never leave, ever. Even though in later years, he had the finances to buy a magnificent villa, he always held true to this deep sentiment and pride. One of his close friends from Kibbutz Bror Chayal became the first mayor of Kiryat Shemonah, and uncle Sammy spent hours each week volunteering at City Hall and helping to improve living conditions and security for all the residents.

It was not until years later that I learned that each time a ketusha rocket fell, day or night, Uncle Sammy would take his car and go to the scene and offer assistance.

It was obvious he loved nature, history, and education in general. "Never," he said sternly, "would I allow my children to miss school, but in 1964, I heard on the BBC Radio Broadcasting that there was a huge snow in Safed. Toni, do you know what I did?" he chuckled, "I paid a friend to lend me his car for a few hours, I went to my children's school, took them out and we drove to Safed to see the snow and enjoy it for the first time in Israel!" He loved the north of the country and had especially settled there to accommodate my grandfather's memories of the mountains, valleys and luscious green fields of Greece.

Uncle Sammy was so proud to tell me that even though Israel was a small country, nevertheless, you could find every climate on earth within its borders. He had taken his children to explore the deserts of Eilat as well as the forests and valleys of the north. After the Six Day War in 1967, he had rented a bus and encouraged all of his neighbors and friends to go to Jerusalem and see all the holy places that had been previously closed and off limits to Jews.

He did so much to boost the morale of all the people in Kiryat Shemonah. Always he encouraged them to keep on living and showed them through example how to overcome their fears. It was obvious to me that Uncle Sammy was a born leader with a sharp brilliant mind, and yet he was so sensitive. He knew how to feel the wind, listen to the song of a bird, and absorb the beauty in a tiny pebble that another would so readily cast aside.

Almost apologetically, he explained to me that his eldest daughter, Naomi, married with two small children and living in Kiryat Shemonah, had decided to move to a less traumatic place in Israel and raise her family. "You have to understand, Toni," he said, "We can be in the communal bomb shelters for days, sometimes up to two weeks at a time. Naomi is tired of dragging her children out of bed in pajamas and running to shelters." What he did not share with me was that Naomi's home had been totalled by a ketusha rocket just a short time before, and she and her husband and children had been miraculously saved. He obviously did not want to frighten me, after all he still hoped to accomplish his goal of luring me away from the fetters of the church to a new life in Israel.

With great excitement, he told me that Naomi had moved to Kiryat Yam whilst he was visiting us in England, and that he was greatly looking forward to affixing a *mezuzah* on the outside of her front door. "This is a Sephardic custom for the father to do this. The *mezuzah* shows that a Jew lives in the house and not an Arab," he told me, and I begged him to explain to me what exactly a *mezuzah* was. With a twinkle in his eye, he told me that my grandfather was so religious that he had a *mezuzah* on every doorpost in his entire house, and that if he had gone out for a walk and bent down to tie his shoelaces, then when he arrived back home he would not kiss the *mezuzah* immediately, but first enter the house, wash his hands in the ritual manner, and then go back out and kiss the *mezuzah* and enter again!

We took long strolls through the dank and gloomy back streets of the slum area surrounding the college, and yet I never noticed the squalor, for my uncle and I were walking a few thousand miles away, in the land of the Bible. I saw the Sea of Galilee, calm and serene, welcoming the sun for another day; I tasted the delicious fruits that grew in abundance in the Holy Land; I meandered along the streets of the Old City in Jerusalem. I visited dozens of places, from *kibbutzim*, turkey factories, and fish-breeding ponds, to numerous sites of historical interest; and over and over again, my uncle pleaded, "Toni, come to Israel. What is the harm in your having a holiday? I promise you that if, after one day, you tell me that you don't like it and that you want to go back to England, I will put you straight back on the plane."

I remained silent.

"Don't ever forget that the Jewish people accept you as a Jew," he continued hopefully. However, I would not be swayed from my position. I told him that the call on my life meant more to me than what I perceived as "carnal desires" and wordly pleasures. Besides, I firmly believed that the Jews had got it all wrong and that according to God and the Holy Bible, I was a gentile.

My uncle looked at me seriously for a long time. Finally he said, "Toni, I wish I had your faith and could believe in something as strongly as you believe in what you are doing."

We never touched the subject again, but right before he left, he told me I could ask him for anything I wanted from Israel and he would do his best to send it to me. "I want you to at least own something from Israel." This was such an intriguing offer, and I felt that I really would like to have something from the land he had so beautifully described. The only remotely Jewish things that I owned were two small velvet cloth covers that my mother had brought me as souvenirs from her trip to Israel many years ago. They had Hebrew letters embroidered on them which I did not understand, and one contained a pocket with partitions that divided it into three separate sleeves. The covers were pretty but very curious, and I had no idea what they were meant for, so I used one as a slip cover for the back of my chair and the other as a pajama bag.

I set my mind now to figure out what kind of treasure I could possibly want from the Land of Israel, and suddenly the answer was clear.

"A *mezuzah* for the door of my room," I said simply to Uncle Sammy. It seemed a strange idea to have a *mezuzah* in the college dormitory, but for some reason that was exactly what I wanted. He promised that as soon as he returned home he would buy one for me, and he kept his word.

❧

"You have a package from your uncle," one of the students informed me. Excitedly I took it to my room and opened it. It was a simple wooden case. My uncle had very sensibly left the back panel slightly open so that I could see the roll of parchment inside, handwritten by a scribe. I fingered the scroll carefully and longed to unroll it, but dared not spoil the seal. Hurriedly I read the letter and found exact instructions on how to put the *mezuzah* up on the doorpost.

That night, after evening prayers, at about ten-thirty, I ran down to the cellars and dug up a hammer and some small nails, and then very carefully read the instructions again. I didn't want to do anything wrong. With a few cautious bangs, I had my *mezuzah* affixed to the doorpost. I jumped down from my stool and stood back to admire it. How beautiful it looked! After a quick look around to make sure that no one was watching, I instinctively kissed it.

My impulsive joy soon gave way to worry. "Maybe I should have asked before I put it up," I thought. "After all, it's not my property. I can't just go banging nails into someone else's house." I decided to take it down and ask the principal, without letting him know that I had already had it up. "Surely he will give me permission," I told myself, "and then everything will have been done in an orderly fashion."

I carefully pulled out the nails and ran straight to his office.

"Today I received a present from my Uncle Sammy in Israel," I said. "See—a *mezuzah*!"

Full of excitement, I showed him my treasure. He reached out and took the *mezuzah*, fingering it as though it were a chunk of moldy cheese. "Tonica," he said sadly, and again, "Tonica."

"Oh, please let me put it up," I begged.

"Look at it," he continued. "What is nice about it? It is so ugly. Really, Sister Tonica, it's only superstition. The Jews have it for good luck. We don't believe in that kind of rubbish." He handed the *mezuzah* back to me without another word.

I felt a sudden rush of indignation. "I don't care what you say, I still like it," I retorted, and hurried back to my room, scolding myself for not leaving it up in the first place, even though I knew that would have gotten me into even more trouble. Probably the *mezuzah* would have been confiscated altogether.

Ironically, Daddy Raymond's rebuff served only to stoke the flames of my embryonic interest in the Jews, and I realized that the only task at hand was to avoid being discovered.

❧

It was shortly after my uncle's return to Israel that I decided to pay a second visit to the synagogue. It was about five years since I had first gone, and I was curious once again. I was also determined not to stick out like a sore thumb, so I sewed myself an outfit that could have passed as "fashionable" and kept it just for the synagogue.

However, I found this second visit no more enjoyable than the first; in fact, I was petrified, and in spite of my new clothing, I was still thoroughly convinced that everyone was staring at me, wondering who this ugly gentile monster could possibly be. I wasn't keen to go back very quickly afterward, but about one month later, when the unpleasant memory had worn off, I decided to venture in a third time, and then a fourth.

Finally, one of the women approached me and tried to show me the correct place in the prayer book.

"Thank you," I said without thinking, "but I'm not Jewish."

I blushed and felt as though a dagger had pierced my heart. Why did I feel I had lied? Oh, I was so confused!

I became attached to the synagogue in spite of all the discomfort I felt and began to attend as regularly as I could. Saturday mornings in the college were still set aside for private devotional time, so chances were good that I would not be missed. I would get to the synagogue early enough so that I could see the rabbi take the Torah scroll out of the ark and say *Shema Yisrael*. I loved this part of the service, for all I had to do in order to participate was to repeat what the rabbi said! It wasn't long before I began to feel a bit more relaxed—that is, until one day when many more people than usual attended, for there was some sort of celebration going on.

After the service, everyone in the congregation was invited to a *"kiddush"* downstairs. The lady who had so kindly showed me the place in the prayer book came over and invited me to come along. I thanked her and followed after her, but as we were walking out to the stairwell, I noticed one woman staring hard at me. I smiled, but she glared back sternly with a cat-like beam that went straight through me. I turned away in embarrassment, excused myself to the first woman, and fled.

When I arrived at the college, I stood in front of the mirror in my room and scrutinized myself—my handmade clothes, my untidy eyebrows (we were forbidden to pluck them), and my face bare of make-up.

"It's true, I'm an ugly gentile," I said to myself. I was so mortified I wanted to cry. I wondered with an illogical burst of bitterness why my mother had married my father. I was so angry at her! If only she'd married somebody Jewish, I could have been so beautiful!

Oh, why did I even want to go to that place?

The print shop was growing, and it was decided that the next piece of equipment we needed was a gold-blocking machine. We could then do more elaborate business cards, letterheads and party invitations, as well as other types of fancy design. Daddy Raymond remembered that a few years ago at a printing exhibition he had seen such a machine, operated by a "little old Jew" with a black cap, beard and long sidelocks. He had inquired about the machine at the time, but was given such an evasive answer that he'd decided not to pursue it. The principal's secretary now set out to track down the "little old Jew." After several days, she succeeded, and an appointment was made.

Daddy Raymond took along his daughter Anette, another design artist, and me. Anette and the other artist would learn how to operate the machine while I wrote down all the technical details and any other interesting information that I could gather at the plant.

The journey to East London was well over one hundred miles, so we made an early start. I sat back and enjoyed the luxury of the plush seats in the principal's private Jaguar.

Daddy Raymond instructed me all along the way on how I should act, and what I should say, for he had decided that the transaction would go more smoothly if the Jewish owners saw that "one of theirs" was amongst us. Of course, he also wanted to initiate a more friendly contact with them in the hope of doing some eventual missionizing.

"You are the Jew. Don't forget to use the Hebrew name, Tova," he told me, choosing the name which my mother had once told me was a Hebrew version of Tonica.

I knew exactly what he meant. I was the Jew today because it was convenient, but tomorrow I'd better not forget that I was a gentile. In fact, when he'd begun assigning Hebrew names to some of the students, he had pointedly withheld one from me. Perhaps he was afraid that Uncle Sammy's visit had made too much of an impression on me and was trying to offset any possible Jewish leanings. In any case, I knew exactly where he stood on this issue, and that today I would only be "playing" Jew. I wore my nicest clothes, for my visits to the synagogue had firmly implanted in my mind the idea that all Jews wore beautiful clothes.

My mind raced ahead. I had never seen real Orthodox Jews before; even in the synagogue, many of the congregants had not been fully observant. The nearest I had come was meeting my grandfather, but he didn't have sidelocks or wear a black coat. I was enormously excited.

The minutes ticked into hours. Soon we were turning off the motorway and had our noses buried in the A-to-Z street directory of London. We were nearer to the plant than we had thought.

"It's here, it's here!"

Anette exclaimed.

We pulled into a narrow drive, and sure enough, the first person to emerge from the shop was a little old man with a huge *yarmulka* on his head, just as Daddy Raymond had described. The atmosphere in the factory was alive with activity. Long-bearded, black-coated men were rushing about all over the place.

"You must excuse us," the elderly gentleman said apologetically. "We have a wedding to get to this afternoon."

How strange, I thought. A wedding on a weekday, and in the afternoon...somehow I didn't like that idea. Everyone knew that weddings took place on Saturday mornings.

The principal introduced me. "This is Tova—she's Jewish, you know."

Two beady black eyes looked at me disbelievingly. I smiled gently and said, "My mother is Jewish," and no further mention was made of the fact.

We were taken into a small room where the gold-blocking machine was stored, and I busied myself with all the interesting mechanical details. After the business deal was completed, Daddy Raymond said he would take us out to eat before turning back. This was one of the great fringe benefits of going on an errand with the principal; he always stopped at a restaurant before going home, and his companions enjoyed the bonus of a delicious meal. Daddy Raymond also happened to have a special penchant for kosher food, and one of the Jews from the shop offered to direct us to the nearest kosher restaurant since he was heading in that direction himself. He drove ahead, and we followed in our car.

The restaurant was small and packed with Orthodox men—*all* men. Each one gave us a quick glance as we entered, for we were so obviously the only gentiles in the place. It seemed like ages before we were served, and even then it was in a very abrupt manner, so different from the formality and grace of other British restaurants. I felt terribly self-conscious and out of place.

I looked at the principal and said, "Do they think we are dogs or something?"

He seemed unperturbed by the service and didn't answer.

I ate very little and did not enjoy the food at all, but was afraid to show my true feelings to Daddy Raymond, as he had wanted so much to give us a "treat." But I couldn't get out of the restaurant quickly enough and begged him to forego dessert and buy some fruit instead at a nearby stand. He agreed, and we left.

I felt deeply hurt and was withdrawn on the ride home. Inside I was screaming at those people: "I am a Jew, I am a Jew, recognize me, accept me, I belong to you!" But I knew I was really a gentile and that I had no reason at all to feel so indignant.

I turned to the principal and said, "Thank you very much for the nice thought, but please don't take me anywhere like that again." He made no reply.

It was a cruel world. Why couldn't I understand it? And why couldn't I just be a normal person? Why did I so much want to be identified with those cold people? What was wrong with my *own* people? I agonized so much over these thoughts that I made myself sick.

I hated those stupid Jews anyway. I would make myself forget all about them.

ও SEVENTEEN ৩

I WAS beginning to feel that I wanted to do more with my life again—learn more or take on some sort of new project. There was a hollowness inside me that I just couldn't seem to fill. The fact that I was already designing all of the church literature, filling three shops with original handmade goods, working with the children and young people, preaching, singing, dancing and learning to play musical instruments, just didn't seem to fill that hole.

I decided to learn Hebrew. I couldn't understand what had prompted such an interest, especially after my sour experience in the Jewish restaurant, but there it was. Daddy Raymond had only recently refused me permission to put up my *mezuzah*, but I thought I might get him to agree to my new plan on the premise that I could then write Hebrew songs and use them to missionize amongst the Jewish people. I did love to sing—and yet I knew this was just a pretext. The truth was that I simply wanted to learn Hebrew and couldn't think of a sensible reason why.

I had heard of the famous language correspondence course called Linguaphone and wrote off immediately for details. I knew it would be expensive, but I wasn't prepared for the actual figures. When the large brown envelope finally came, I skimmed through the glossy catalogue which listed several reasons why I should learn the language of my choice—and *now*. I searched for the price: seventy pounds!

My heart sank. My allowance was four pounds ninety pence per week—equivalent to about eight dollars—out of which came tithe collections, all gifts and expenses, toiletries and clothing. At the very most, I knew I could only save one pound fifty pence per week, and probably not more than a pound. It would take me over a year to save seventy pounds! I would just have to forget all about it.

The months wound on. Linguaphone faithfully continued to send me correspondence. The kit had now risen to the grand price of ninety-six pounds; I would *never* be able to afford it. I tried to dismiss my disappointment by telling myself that I wouldn't have been able to learn Hebrew anyway; practically speaking, I just did not have the time.

Then one day, a surprise "special offer" package came from the company. They were having a "two for the price of one" sale. This was something I just couldn't miss—a complete Linguaphone kit for only forty-eight pounds! Somehow I had to do it, but I needed a collaborator. I went around asking if anyone else wanted to learn a language, and finally, Sister Victoria, who had been struggling with Danish for some time, agreed. She felt a strong connection with the people of that land and decided it was a good investment for her.

There was only one snag now. I had to get permission from Daddy Raymond. We were not allowed to do anything even remotely extra-curricular without explicit permission.

"Come in," came his distant voice. I entered his office but remained by the door.

"Yes, Sister Tonica, what can I do for you?"

"I wanted to ask your permission to learn Hebrew," I said quickly, in as innocent a tone as I could muster.

He was silent for a while. Obviously the answer was no, but diplomacy was preventing him from rushing in with a reply. We seemed to be growing fields apart.

"Why do you want to learn Hebrew?" he finally asked.

"Because I think it's a good thing. We would be able to learn songs in Hebrew and sing them to the Jewish people," I responded.

"But for you, Tonica," he said, "I don't think it is a step in the right direction. No. I don't think I can allow it," he concluded.

"Here we go again!" I burst out. "Whatever I want to do, it's always no. All of my life, no, no, no! I've never been allowed to do anything, and tell me, what is the harm in it? There are far worse things I could want to do!" I was surprised at my own vehemence.

This time his silence was even longer.

"All right, you can do it," he said at last, "but on one condition. When you have finished learning, you must teach everybody. You will not be the only one here to know Hebrew. Do you understand?"

"Yes," I replied. "Thank you."

I hurried out. I knew he was not happy about the request, but he had been cornered by my surprisingly urgent logic, and was fully aware of it. I wasted no time and that day sent off for both kits. The brochure said we could have them on ten days' approval and pay at monthly intervals. I knew it would take more than the money I had, and that I would have to find extra work somehow, but I was determined to do it.

Like an excited little girl, I awaited the postman daily, and then one morning while I was at the office, I received a phone call from one of the kitchen staff, "Tonica, there is a huge parcel here for you," she said. "See if you can come home at lunchtime."

I needed no encouragement and immediately readjusted my entire week's schedule to allow myself time to go home briefly that afternoon. It was only one hour that I had to find, but it was an extra hour into the night. Every minute of our time had to be accounted for; any extra activity that you tried to squeeze in always had to be deducted from sleeping time, which was already sadly lacking, but on this occasion, there was no doubt as to which was the more important thing.

I ran almost the entire mile and a half back to the college, charged into the hallway, collected my enormous parcel, and breathlessly sped to my room. I had shared my secret with Mary, the other design artist who worked part-time with me. She happened to meet me in the upstairs corridor and wanted to see the package too. Together we undid the wrappings. It was such a breath of fresh air just to get something *new*, something from outside the college that had nothing to do with church routine—and something that might open up a new horizon for me and fill the "empty space."

I took out one of the tapes right away and put it into the tape recorder. My heart plummeted to the bottom of my shoes as a gentleman's voice came booming over the speaker in a racing and completely unintelligible gibberish.

"Oh, Mary," I exclaimed, "I'll *never* be able to understand that! What have I done?"

"Well, you can send it back," Mary said encouragingly. "Don't worry!" And she was gone.

Send it back? What an outrageous thought! I decided right then that I was going to keep it?and what's more, learn it, even if it killed me!

I painstakingly read all the instructions and played the tape over and over again during the course of the next few months. Hour after hour into the night, I sat curled up on the floor next to my bed trying desperately to make sense of this alien tongue. Sometimes I would be so tired I would drift off and wake up at three or four o'clock in the morning with a stiff neck and frozen limbs, the strange shapes of the *aleph-beis* still staring at me tauntingly from the floor. I told myself repeatedly that I must be crazy, but I pressed on.

A few months later, it so happened that a man named Mr. Solnick, who owned a chain of launderettes, was opening up new premises just a few yards away from the Administration Center. He knew that we had a printing press and called in to have leaflets printed for advertisement purposes and to find out if anyone wanted the job of posting them. There were ten thousand leaflets, and he was willing to pay one pound for every hundred posted.

I wanted very much to take the job so that I could pay off the Linguaphone. I knew I would have to devise a very inventive strategy in order to find the extra time without missing any of my church duties or making myself conspicuously absent, but it was worth the effort, and I came up with a plan. I was able to put in eight hours of overtime in the art department by missing dinner eight times, thus giving myself an entire free day.

My "posting" day turned out to be windy, drizzly, and bitterly cold. A thousand leaflets beat rhythmically against my side while the shoulder strap of my bag cut into my skin. One hundred, two hundred, three hundred. This was taking longer than I had expected, and my feet were starting to get sore.

"But I've only earned three pounds so far," I told myself. "I must do more." I needed at least fifteen pounds to complete the payments on my Hebrew course, and so I carried on. It was the first time in my life I had ever walked far enough to develop blisters on my feet, but I was so determined that even when I began to feel them pop, I kept on going.

By the time I had posted a thousand leaflets, it was already well into the afternoon and rain was pouring down. Dripping from head to toe, I hobbled back to the Administration Center to collect the next batch, but first I ran my feet under cold tap water to try and ease the pain. Now I was really sure I was crazy, but I had no intention at this point of reversing that diagnosis.

By some miracle, I contrived to get permission to use one of the church vans for three and a half hours, and I thanked God for that because I never would have made it otherwise.

Finally there were no more houses left on the map. I had posted one thousand six hundred and twenty-seven leaflets and felt as though I'd climbed a mountain. But my troubles were not over. Daddy Raymond called me in the next day and asked me what right I thought I had to use up time for such an escapade.

"It was *my* time," I retorted defensively.

"What do you mean, *your* time?" he flung back. Oh, that line sounded so familiar! "There's no such thing as your time. You're on God's time! You're in this business twenty-four hours a day, young lady, and don't forget it. Haven't I told you that already?"

I walked away half-smirking. I didn't care. My Hebrew course was all mine. Nothing could diminish the joy of my success.

I had gone to Sabbath services at the synagogue once or twice during this time. One of the ladies had taken pity on me and had dared to befriend me to a certain degree. One Sabbath, she confided that the next afternoon a big wedding would be held in the synagogue. All uninvited guests would have a place in the balcony, and I was welcome to join them if I wanted to see what a Jewish wedding was like. I thanked her profusely.

At the Administration Center, I was pretty much my own boss by now, and I knew that I could escape for a short time during the Sunday afternoon break without arousing too much suspicion. Sunday was always the most hectic day of the week in the college, with people running to different duties in all directions, and although it was a risk, I was hopeful that no one would notice.

That night, I looked despairingly at my wardrobe. It was hard enough not to have anything decent to wear to the synagogue on Saturdays, and I certainly did not have anything for a wedding! I finally chose an outfit that I thought would be suitable, but I was in for quite a surprise.

I had become somewhat confident about attending the synagogue over the months, but I was unprepared for what I saw when I turned the corner the next day. A few yards ahead of me in front of the synagogue building, a chauffeur was opening the door of a silver Rolls Royce, and the woman who had glared at me a few months earlier stepped out onto the pavement. She was wearing a pale blue silk chiffon trouser suit that was nearly transparent. She shimmered with gold and diamonds from head to foot, and her glass slippers must have been at least four inches high. She was warmly welcomed by all, and no sooner had she paraded inside than another Rolls Royce pulled up—and another, and another. I stood in my tracks, totally stunned.

"I can't go in," I decided. "I'll just walk right back to the college." I stood there for a few more faltering minutes, and then my curiosity won out. Keeping my eyes down, I quickly scooted up the bright red carpeted stairs. Six or seven other people were in the balcony, and I was relieved to see they were not lavishly dressed.

Timidly, I peered over the railing, and the sight that met my eyes left me breathless. Never before had I seen such a display of wealth. The furs and feathers were mind-boggling, and each hat was a production number. Luxuriant bouquets of flowers were twined around every pole, and the train of bridesmaids was a feast for the eyes. The Royal Ascot races seemed mild by comparison, and in fact I'd never even seen the royal family turn out like this! I felt that I'd entered some other dimension of existence, that it wasn't the real world anymore.

I remembered how shocked I had been when I'd first begun visiting the homes of the neighborhood children. Daddy Raymond wanted us to follow up on all the young people who came to Bible school on Sundays, and we would go in pairs to their homes to see what we could do for them. The conditions in the tenements were unspeakable—children dressed in rags sitting on bare floorboards, with only a dysfunctional parent in sight, just as one might see in photos in a newspaper article about child abuse. But I had not been half so stunned by the poor as I now was by the rich.

Where had all this wealth been hiding? I found myself cringing, hoping that I could somehow contract myself into invisibility so that no one would see me in my own version of "rags."

The ceremony itself was quick and not nearly as memorable as the trimmings. People began heading for the doors afterward in order to drive to the reception hall. I soon began to wish I had followed my earlier inclination to slip out, for I was crushed in the throng of guests at the foot of the stairs. I kept my eyes fixed firmly on the floor, feeling my face flush bright red, both from the heat of the day and the dreadful embarrassment of the moment.

Half an hour later, my sense of humor had returned, and I laughed at my own audacity as I walked home.

ॐ

The wedding experience did not deter me, and I still felt drawn to the synagogue. I began to go to Sabbath services more and more regularly, and developed an entire strategy that would allow me to do this without interfering with my church duties. As a minister, I had to be in my seat on the platform fifteen minutes before the Saturday service, and fortunately it did not begin until twelve o'clock. I began leaving all my books under my seat on the platform so that I could run straight from the synagogue into church and not waste any time going back to my room.

I used to pray to God during morning devotions, begging Him not to let Daddy Raymond put my name on the roster for any part in the service, even a small duty like singing a song or giving a "thought"; for in that case, I knew I should spend the morning preparing rather than gallivanting off to the synagogue, and my conscience wouldn't allow it. The simple irony of my rationale was beyond my scope at this point.

The synagogue fascinated me. I loved to watch the rabbi in his hat and robes as he took the Torah scrolls out of the ark and sang *Shema Yisrael*. This was the part I could repeat afterward, the part that gave me such a wonderful feeling of participation. He would then place the scrolls on the podium, or "*bimah*," as I later learned it was called, and one by one, the men would be called up to say a blessing as the rabbi read from the parchment.

I would watch the old men scolding the young boys for their noisy behavior, and sometimes the women's chatter would annoy me as well.

"Oh, be quiet, lady," I would think in exasperation. "I want to listen! I know I don't understand, but I still want to hear."

All too soon, the reading would be over. The scroll would be lifted high in the air, and we would stand in respect.

Now it was time for the second reading, the *Haftorah*. I wished they wouldn't read it so quickly and always wondered what they were saying. The rabbi would then come to the *bimah* and lead the singing, and the Torah would be placed back in the ark. How the little boys loved to kiss the scroll as the rabbi walked by! I wished I could kiss it too. The rabbi always stood before the open ark for just a few seconds, holding the scroll protectively before he put it away. And then the doors were closed and the curtains drawn. I loved this scene and couldn't drink in enough of it.

I managed to get away with my little scheme for almost two years, but my luck could not hold forever.

Every extra penny I had during this time was scraped together to create some decent clothing for the services. I had sewn one particularly stylish outfit which I knew was not appropriate by church standards, and on the Sabbath morning when I first wore it, the service ran late and I had no time to change before going to the chapel. I had a choice: either to risk being late to church and invite an inquiry as to my whereabouts, or risk one session of public embarrassment. I chose the latter.

I will never forget the gasps as I marched to the platform in my tailored black ankle-length dress, pale pink stockings and black high-heeled shoes. Tucked into the collar of the dress was a tiny pink brooch, and my black hat was balanced in a chic manner on top of my head. Oh, what a tumult there was! I took my seat and smiled warmly at everyone, as though everything were perfectly ordinary. Sister Victoria was aghast. What had happened to the extremely pious Sister Tonica?

Needless to say, Victoria was dispatched immediately to deal with my "deviance." The most serious result of the episode was that she forced me to discard the pink stockings altogether, but I was adamant about keeping the shoes and the hat. The incident, however, was only the prelude to disaster.

One morning in synagogue, the rabbi got up to give a speech at the end of the service, which he rarely did. I was excited, for I always loved to hear his speeches, but nervous as well because I would have to rush like mad to get back to church in time.

It was eleven thirty-five. Oh, hurry, Rabbi, I thought, you have ten minutes to speak and then I have to leave. Maybe I can stretch it to fifteen....

I sat on the edge of my seat, drinking in every word. I was an ordained minister with a thorough knowledge of the Bible, and it was amazing to me that although the Jews knew the same stories, their versions were so different. Was Isaac really nearly forty years old when he was bound on the altar? We had always been told he was a little child. Other interesting tidbits followed. Where had the rabbi gotten all this information from? It certainly wasn't in the text!

Oh, no—it was ten minutes to twelve already. I'd have to sneak out. I called a silent "*Good Shabbos*" to everyone and slipped out the door. Once outside, I held onto my hat and ran as fast as I could.

"Faster, you idiot!" I berated myself. "You should have left earlier. How many times have you gotten yourself into this fix?" My side was hurting terribly and I was completely out of breath, but I kept running. It was now five minutes to twelve, and I knew I would be late.

I dashed up the steps to the church doors and stopped for two seconds to catch my breath. The worst had happened—the principal was there, and everyone was in place.

I collected myself, walked erectly down the length of the chapel, and took my seat on the platform, trying not to pant too loudly. I casually put my hand to my face in a discreet effort to cover its redness and to wipe away the perspiration. The pianist began to play. I moved along mechanically with the service, but my heart was far away, in a synagogue with a rabbi and a Torah scroll.

Immediately after the service, Daddy Raymond called me aside and demanded to know where I had been. I was afraid to lie to him because that was a grievous sin, so I admitted the truth, but I tried to make it sound as though my "outing" had been an isolated incident, prompted by nothing more than casual curiosity.

Daddy Raymond was outraged. He banned me instantly from going to the synagogue again and from having any further contact with Jews. I was heartbroken, but I knew it would be disastrous to show this openly.

That night, I wept my heart out into my pillow, and it was several days before I could bring myself around.

The alarm clock buzzed away at five-thirty one morning. I hurriedly showered and dressed and ran to morning devotions. By seven-thirty, my mind was already busy with plans for the day, and never did I dream what was coming my way.

The customary practice for all the students was to call in at the principal's flat each day to say good morning to him and Mother on the way to their various duties. This morning, he requested that I remain behind, for he had something to tell me. I sat on their couch and waited until the last few stragglers had filtered out.

Finally Daddy Raymond said, "Sister Tonica, I want you to go back upstairs and kneel down and seriously think of God. Then I want you to think of your own family, and one by one, mention each person by name and reject them. I want you to reject your whole ancestry. I feel your spiritual growth is being hindered. You are a gentile. The Bible says you are a gentile, and God says you are a gentile. I want you to tell this to yourself. Every day say to yourself three times, 'I am a gentile, I am a gentile, I am a gentile.' It must be the first thing you say in the morning and the very last thing on your mind at night."

I was a little bewildered, but had complete trust in whatever the

My grandparents Antoinette and Raphael De Mordo with Uncle Solomon and my mother, in Alexandria.

My mother's family in Alexandria. From left: my mother, grandparents, Uncle Solomon and Uncle Sammy.

My family outside our house in Greenborough. From left: Margaret, my mother, me, my father, Esther and Philip.

My grandfather's inscription in one of his *machzorim* from Greece.

My grandfather and cousins in Kiryat Shemonah, Israel, 1962.

My father in Belgium during World War II.

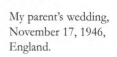

My parent's wedding, November 17, 1946, England.

My parent's engagement in Alexandria, autumn 1943.

My parents in Southford, 1972.

My grandfather Raphael's visit to my family.
From left: my mother, father, grandfather, Margaret, me, Philip and Esther.

My family at a cousin's wedding, spring 1962. From left: my father, Esther,
Philip, me (age 7), my mother, grandmother (father's mother) and Margaret.

My sister Margaret and
me (standing) at the
theological college.

Me in a park with Aunt Jacqueline
during her visit, 1976.

Me in the art department in the
Church Administration Center.

principal told me. "Yes, Father," I answered, and ran upstairs to fulfill his request. I knew I had been a little down lately, especially since the synagogue catastrophe, but I had done my best to keep it in check and was surprised that he had noticed.

Dutifully, I repeated to myself, "I am a gentile, I am a gentile, I am a gentile," and continued to do so each day for several months. There was a certain relief in this because I had never been able to shake the feeling that there was something dreadfully wrong with me. My conflicts stewed continuously inside of me, and I was so tired of feeling alienated, both inside and outside my world, that I was happy to have a diagnosis. Perhaps the problem did center around my inability to identify myself as a gentile, and if I could just get rid of this awful thought, I would stop feeling "wrong"—I would belong!

But the more I tried to convince myself that I was a gentile, the more my ancestry came back to haunt me. By the strangest coincidence, all of the little old ladies in the church who had known my parents since the early years in Greenborough began to notice me and to say, "Here comes Sarah's daughter. Oh, aren't you getting to look exactly like your mother, dear! There she is—little Sarah."

Many of them suddenly started to call me "Tova." I had never officially been given a Hebrew name and had no idea where they had come up with this particular one, or what had possessed them to start using it just at this time. Perhaps my mother had secretly discussed the name with one or another of these women in years gone by, as she had been quite close to some of them in Greenborough; or perhaps they were convinced of my likeness to my mother, and since she had given herself a Hebrew name after her miraculous operation, they felt I should have one too. Daddy Raymond had given Hebrew names to many of the students, and there didn't seem anything unusual on the surface about this.

I never did discover the reason for this bizarre development, but the name soon caught on in the college, and everyone began to call me "Tova." I would always look behind me in anxiety whenever this happened in case the principal might be close by. I was afraid that if he overheard, he would think that I had chosen a Hebrew name for myself in deliberate defiance of his command that I consider myself a gentile. I knew he would be furious, and I wished these well-meaning congregants would stop using the name, even though, deep down, I liked it for some reason. Perhaps it was a subconscious sequel to the time when I had begged my mother as a child to call me "Tova."

In any case, this was not to be a long-lived dilemma.

The Feast of Tabernacles was the second yearly event, besides Passover, which served as an international gathering for the church, and we had huge audiences for the services. The first one had just begun, and the principal was reading the program aloud. The final words were in Hebrew, in imitation of the Jewish custom: "*Leshanah Tova* to all." I had been delayed in transporting some of the elderly congregants to the service, and I walked into the chapel just as he was pronouncing these words. Everyone began to laugh, for the timing had produced an excellent play on words. "Here is Tova!" they chanted. "What?" the principal called out, somewhat perturbed. "Who's calling you Tova?" His voice became suddenly angry. "You're *not* Tova—*not* good. You have to have a name change! You're not to be called Tova anymore!"

I smiled my sweet, undaunted smile and unabashedly took my seat on the platform. But the principal had spoken!

A few days later, Sister Victoria came up to me and said that while she was praying for me that morning, my new name had come to her. I should be called "Joy."

"Ugh, that's a stupid name," I responded indignantly. "That's not a name, it's a feeling. I will not be called Joy." What a foul name! I associated it instinctively with another Joy I had known, the dirty and ill-mannered daughter of a weird friend of my father's, and I did not want any part of it.

But Victoria was shocked at my open resistance and she persisted, telling me several times over the course of the next few days that she had had a strong feeling during her prayers about my name. She claimed that it would give me a spiritual boost and encourage me to rise to a new level. I began to fear that this must be coming from God.

"All right," I said finally, "I accept."

And so the announcement was made in church, and I became Sister Joy. I learned to tolerate it slowly, but the name was no reflection at all of the state of my inner being.

I had tried to convince myself that I was a gentile.

I had discarded my Hebrew name; I wasn't Tova.

I wasn't Sister Tonica any longer.

But I didn't feel like Sister Joy either.

Who was I?

✆ EIGHTEEN ⊷

THERE was a terrible emptiness in me despite my continuous hard work in the college, and it showed in my subdued demeanor. Sister Victoria told me that there was unforgiveness in my heart, and that this was the reason for the evil spirits of doubt and unbelief that were still rampant in my life. She insisted I take time out and consciously think of all the painful things that had ever happened to me and all the people who had ever hurt me, and forgive them out loud.

And so I did.

"I forgive my mother for leaving me outside shops all day, I forgive my father for falsely accusing me of stealing a banana...." All the injustices I had ever suffered surged up from the depths of my being, and I was very sincere about my prayer, but the hollowness in the pit of my stomach remained. I was too afraid to dwell on it, but sometimes it was hard to ignore.

I was scheduled to preach the main sermon in the Sunday evening service. Taking my study books down from the shelves, I felt that I had already grasped everything there was to know about Christianity. God was right within the palm of my hand. I could reach out and touch Him and understand Him and comprehend His wonder. We were friends, walking arm in arm through life, and I knew that this feeling was supposed to be the pinnacle of achievement in the Church. But the concept of walking "arm in arm" with God bothered me now, for my mind was busy with dangerous ideas that begged attention.

I wondered, "How big is my God that I can conceive Him? Who is He, if little me can comprehend Him? How come there is still such a penetrating hunger and dissatisfaction in the deepest well of my life? Maybe there is no God? What if I have only been brainwashed my whole life about 'hell fire' and 'eternal damnation' and now I am afraid not to believe it all?"

I had no answers. I did my best to push these intrusive thoughts out of my head and went to work on my sermon for the evening service. I preached fervently that night of Jesus' love and of how he had the power to bring satisfaction to our souls and to heal our lives. It wasn't a lie; I knew he did. It was just *I* who had a slight problem, that's all.

As always, it was next to impossible to escape censure from fellow congregants if one was doing anything less than dancing with joy on the tabletops. Once, in the middle of a service, a visiting black female preacher from Kingston, Jamaica, heaving with the "gospel spirit," stood up, pointed a finger at me, and bellowed, "Sister, there's a spirit of unbelief in your heart! Reject it, right now!" When I did not respond, she boomed reproachfully, "*You want it—keep it! You want it— keep it!*" and repeated those words several times in a foghorn voice until she was hushed.

I felt horribly embarrassed, but at the same time I accepted such rebuke as part of the trial I was going through. This was my weakness, and if I did have a "spirit of unbelief" in my heart, I would simply have to conquer it.

I *would* conquer it.

૭

Daddy Raymond came up with a "new light." He had been reading a book, the dynamic true account of the life of an evangelist during the Second World War, and he gave it over to Sister Victoria so that she could read a chapter or two aloud to us every Friday night at fellowship. The author told an encouraging tale of his methods of communication with God, concentrating on the effectiveness of prostration. He would frequently fast and lie face down on the floor, empty his mind of all thoughts, and try to contact God through quiet meditation. After a few weeks, when we were well into the book, Daddy Raymond declared that on the following Sunday afternoon, he was going to prostrate on the floor of the chapel from two until five o'clock, and anyone who cared to join him would be most welcome. A ripple of mixed murmurings ran through the lounge.

Daddy Raymond would often invite us to participate with him in some such activity, and although he didn't always mandate it, there were very few people who would refuse the "invitation" and thus risk losing their standing in his eyes.

About eighty-five percent of the students came to the session on Sunday. Exactly how many actually made spiritual progress, and how many went to sleep during the prostration, was hard to judge, for it was a silent time; but I distinctly remember hearing somebody snoring not far from me, and soon afterward came a discreet whisper: "Brother, Brother—wake up!"

I lay face down on the cold tiled floor and concentrated on relaxing. Slowly, I emptied my mind of its pressing and frenzied thoughts. I wanted so desperately to rid myself of all my doubts and to touch God. I begged forgiveness for anything I might have done wrong and quietly turned my heart and confidence toward my Creator. I lay still, allowing my deepest desires to reach upward. I was surprised at how rapidly the time passed, and when five o'clock came around, I did feel somewhat quieted within, although not resolved.

The next week we did it again, and then it became regular practice, until the principal encouraged us to spend at least one hour in quiet prostration each morning from five-thirty to six-thirty. It was during these times of meditation and contemplation that I began to pray specifically "To the God of Abraham, Isaac, and Jacob." Day after day,

I lay on the floor, pleading with the One True God to draw me closer to Him, to lead me along the path of truth and righteousness. I had imagined so naively that God was here in the palm of my hand, but my instincts told me I had a far way to go before I could even begin to understand Him, let alone walk with Him. This one desire began to eclipse every other whim in my life. I could think of nothing else.

Early one Sunday morning, I was sitting in my room, reading my Bible that contained all the Scriptures. I turned to the Book of Psalms, and it fell open to Psalm 119, the longest one of all. This Psalm had never been much emphasized in college because it spoke of the commandments, which did not apply to us since we were under grace. In years gone by, I had always flicked right past it, but I was feeling more and more of an attachment to it lately. I decided to learn the entire Psalm 119 by heart, and as I repeated the words aloud, tears welled up in my eyes and streaked down my cheeks.

> *Depart from me the way of lying*
> *I will run the way of Your commandments...*
> *Grant me Your law graciously....*

Those were the very words my own soul was crying out to God. But even as I clutched my Bible to my heart, and recited the words in prayer, I did not understand them completely. Had I not left the "way of lying," the false life of the outside world? Surely the way of vanity and deceit was a consuming fire for anyone who dared to venture outside of Jesus, and I had abandoned that life when I made the decision to come to the college and dedicate myself to God. What was the Psalmist really talking about?

And what was the significance of the commandments? Somehow I knew this must be referring to more than the Ten Commandments. If only I could understand those words—understand their true meaning—I felt my searching would be complete. But how was one to learn their meaning when only the words themselves were on the page?

I was not going to play games anymore, I decided. I was going to find *the truth* even if it killed me.

≤∞

My schedule kept me moving constantly. There were children to be picked up for Bible school, sermons to be prepared, literature to be designed, daily chores to attend to. I never allowed anyone to see my unrest. Instead I slipped into a mechanical mode; I did everything I was supposed to do, said everything I was supposed to say, but my emotions were on hold. I clicked off, and I think now that this was an involuntary defense that may have saved me then from losing my mind.

As time went by, I became more and more irritated with the routine, for it was beginning to lose its meaning. A certain sense of abandon crept into my behavior, and I was less careful with my words than I had always been. No longer was I the little lamb who had arrived at the college with the artlessness of youth stamped all over her. I was a minister now; I had fired up many souls with my sermons, and I was not quite as afraid of my superiors as I had once been.

I was very often accused during that time of being "sharp" with the other students, and was forever getting called into the office because this sister or that had complained that I was behaving too harshly with them, or making them feel uncomfortable in some way or other. Sister Bertha was the most irritating in this band of grumblers. She was a frightfully insecure and overweight woman, about ten years older than I, who had wormed her way into "pet" status with Daddy Raymond. She whined frequently to him that I was giving her an inferiority complex. It was almost as though I had to apologize for anything I did that turned out nicely!

Whenever I was faced with these reports, I would say I had simply been truthful, but Sister Victoria's words for my behavior were "cutting and caustic." I think my superiors were all disappointed that they had lost their lamb.

One day at the office, Victoria drew me onto her knee and cuddled me. I always bristled when this happened, which probably prompted her to do it even more.

"How are you, Joy?" she asked solicitously, rubbing my arm.

"If you want the truth, I don't know," I answered plainly.

"You know, Joy, I've been reading a book on schizophrenia, and I think this is your problem. It was caused in you by rejection in your childhood." She was trying to speak as sweetly and as gently as she could.

I remained silent.

Daddy Raymond entered the room. They had apparently been discussing my problem beforehand, for it was obvious that the whole approach had been planned.

"Joy, I want Victoria to be the shepherd of your soul right now," the principal announced. "Whatever she tells you to do, do it. I really feel that if you work with her, she will be able to help you."

I nodded in silent response. He turned and left the room.

"How do you feel about it?" whispered Sister Victoria, drawing me close to her and giving me a kiss.

"Okay, whatever you think," I replied mechanically. I wasn't even sure that I fully understood what a schizophrenic really was, but a part of me was ready to grasp at a solution—any solution.

"Come to my room tonight instead of going back to the office," Sister Victoria instructed me. "First I want to pray for deliverance for you."

"But I've already had the spirits of rebellion, unbelief, scorn, ridicule, and a million other things cast out of me about three times now!" I answered doubtfully. "Why haven't they left me already?"

"Do you believe that they will leave you?" she asked.

"Of course I do," I answered quickly.

"Then tonight they will leave you," she concluded.

My heart was full of hope as I knocked on Sister Victoria's door that evening.

"Come in," she beckoned in her singsong voice. She told me to make myself comfortable on her bed and offered me a cup of tea. Then we knelt down.

"Joy, you are brutal and mean. You are selfish and proud. You are stubborn and bad," she said gently, and I believed her because Sister Victoria *knew.* "We are going to cast out some spirits tonight. We'll go a few at a time—I don't want to exhaust you."

Daddy Raymond was called in, and one by one the spirits were cast out. I was very excited and very hopeful—as hopeful as I had been when the hundred demons had been exorcised from me so many years earlier, as hopeful as I had been during the months when I had tried to convince myself that I was a gentile. Perhaps those things were only minor aspects of the problem, and I actually was a schizophrenic. Oh, if only that were true! If only this were the answer to the pain in my life! A swelling anticipation rose within my heart.

"Oh, God, thank you!" I cried when the ordeal was over.

The rest of the evening was spent discussing how we were going to find the real "Joy." There were no concrete guidelines, just an instruction that I had to be close to Sister Victoria, and if she felt anything about me through "the spirit," she would let me know.

I slept well that night. I was a very happy young woman. It didn't occur to me that since I had been called out as a prophet when I was ordained, I was just as capable as Victoria, if not more, of receiving messages through "the spirit," and I trusted myself in her hands.

The next day, when I called in to the principal's apartment on my way to the office, he asked me how I was feeling.

"I feel fine," I responded positively.

"I have a new surname for you," he said with a twinkle in his eye. Mother looked on curiously, for he had obviously not confided the news to her. I waited expectantly. He liked the drama of the moment and chose to hold his silence for a time.

"Tell me already," I requested eagerly.

He swallowed hard before saying quietly, "Israel."

Mother shot bolt upright in her chair. "*Raymond*—and after all you've said!" she declared in exasperation.

He smiled and closed his Bible. "Do you like it?" he inquired.

"I don't know," I replied. "'Miss Israel' sounds a bit weird." But on the way to work, I consoled myself, thinking of two girls I had known in junior school whose names were Pamela England and Anne French. Maybe it wasn't too odd to have such a surname after all. And in another way, it was a good sign, for it meant that Daddy Raymond finally considered me purified enough to enter "New Covenant Israel" and receive a Jewish name.

But at the same time, it was strange. Very strange. I was so confused.

I decided to buy myself a notebook and record my feelings as I set out on a search to find this person called "Joy Israel."

August 2, 1980

Today I realized something. Before today, I knew I hated. Not anyone or anything in particular, just everyone and everything in general, but today I realized it's not anyone or anything, everyone or everything—it's just me. Wherever I am, I hate, whatever I do, I hate, because I hate me.

But anyway, somewhere inside is a person called Joy. I don't know her, but I'm sure I won't hate her because she is going to be all I've ever wanted to be. I'll love Joy. I know I will, because just thinking about her brings tears to my eyes. I so much want to be her. I know it will be a hard struggle and that I will have much to learn, but in the end it's going to be worth it all because I'll be "normal." I'll be a normal functioning citizen. I wonder how long it will take? Tomorrow I must ask Jesus to help me recognize her.

August 4

So far, I haven't seen Joy at all today. I've been unkind, mean, almost brutal. It's a shame really. I am tired. I could blame my behavior on my tiredness, but I won't. I will blame it on nothing but myself.

I look at the plaque on my wall. It says, "He is love." I like the plaque because it is my only hope in life. My only hope is the fact that He is love, and He loves me.

Father, thank You for helping me to overcome.

I love You, Father. I think I love You. Well, as much as I am able to love in my condition, that's how much I love You. One day, I'll love You more. One day, I'll see You, and when I do, I'll be Joy.

August 16

It is Sabbath. I get up and get ready, and I go to the meeting. I go through all the motions. I wonder, if I had a choice, would I go to church today? I don't think I would. But I don't think about it for long. It's too dangerous. I go because I am expected to go, it is required of me. So I must meet the requirements.

Is heaven really real? Will I really walk on golden streets one day? I'm not excited about it. Somehow it's lost its awe and wonder.

Maybe I'm not Joy at the moment.

September 5

It's Sabbath evening. We have been in the lounge.

I don't feel any peace tonight. I only feel like screaming at the top of my voice, screaming until I'm hoarse; I feel like lying on the floor and kicking and bashing my arms and legs. I think I started to get like this yesterday, but today at the office, it got worse. I stuck the Tabernacles song sheet up wrong, and when I realized it was backward, I tore it in half and threw it on the floor. I paced the office, a raging furnace deep within, clenched fists, gritted teeth, tears ready to spill down...but I restrained myself...I didn't do it.

Maybe that's why I feel like I do now. Maybe if I'd screamed loud and long, the raging furnace inside would be gone, the tensions would have died away, and I would be at peace.

Peace, you are far from me and yet you are within me. I can't feel you. But theoretically you are there, so you must be. Bible theory doesn't lie.

Tonight I hate. I'm going to sleep.

September 10

It is the eve of the Feast of Tabernacles. I don't look forward to the feast. I'm not looking forward to anything. Right now, I'm just not looking forward.

I wish people would leave me alone and stop demanding of me. I wish I could be alone for a long time. It would be glorious. There's only one snag—I wouldn't be able to forget.

October 2

The Feast of Tabernacles has come...and gone.

I have heard comments like, "This has been the richest feast yet," and "Hasn't it been a lovely feast?" and I realize something quite sad: I have been through the feast, but I wasn't there. I don't know where I was, but I don't think I have benefited at all. There are no words from the ministry resounding in my heart, no songs, no testimonies ringing within. The concert and banquet might have been just fairy-tales.

October 3

People have been talking lately of marriage and parents, mothers and fathers. I haven't the faintest idea whether I want to be married or not, so I leave that to God, but if I did marry, I would want him to be a Jew and really zealous for the things of God. I would like him to be a good preacher and well-versed in the Scriptures. I would also like him to be a hard worker and intelligent.

I would like one child and it must be a boy.

However, I am not sure that I really want all this in my heart. All I really know is that I want God's will.

I have given up searching for earthly parents now. I have sought after so many and have only been disappointed. I wonder now—did I expect too much from my natural parents? Maybe I did, for I have never been satisfied with any others.

I cling to You, God. You are to me both mother and father. You will never disappoint me. You take such good care of me. I belong to You, and I will not seek for any other now.

Only one thing I ask, and that is that You change me thoroughly and utterly that I may bring only joy and pleasure and credit to Your name.

October 8

It's just a laugh when I think of Joy.

Why? She's just a million miles away! But maybe she's just around the bend.

Maybe I've given up. I'm just a horrible person. Horrible, despicable to the core. When I look at myself in the mirror, I hate what I see.

I must keep striving. I was warned it would be a hard battle, but I must keep walking through the blackness. The valley of death is all around me. I almost shiver when I think of its eeriness.

The fact that You are with me gives me courage to go on. Strengthen me, God, help me, that I may one day be normal and truly a joy—especially to You.

I love You, Father. I think I love You.

November 2

I feel alone in a big world.

I still woke early every Sabbath morning. Depressed, I would lie in bed or sit and stare silently out the window.

"Come on, Joy," my roommates would encourage me. "Cheer up." But my thoughts and heart were far away, and I barely heard their words.

Week after week, I watched the clock and thought of the synagogue. Now they would be taking the Torah out of the ark. Now the rabbi would walk up to the *bimah* and place the scrolls on the table, and then he would stand straight and recite *"Shema Yisrael"* in his resonant voice.

"Joy, whatever are you thinking about?" one of the girls said, breaking into my reverie.

"Oh, nothing," I replied nonchalantly and busied myself around the room. Inside I was screaming.

Resentfully I dressed for church. I always made sure I was not too early, for I didn't want people approaching me. I was sick of the plastic smile that I was forced to wear, the plastic words, the marionette actions. My heart was yearning for something of worth, of good quality, something lasting that would not let me down.

I had trained myself to sit upright in my seat in church and to appear as though I were drinking in every word of the service. As I was always on the platform, I had a great responsibility to set an example for the younger students and to seem involved. However, the truth was that many times I just clicked off, and when the service ended, I had not a clue about what was said or even who had said it.

After the service, it was the custom to go around and greet people with a "holy kiss." I had loathed this from the time I was a child and tried to avoid as many congregants as possible. Sometimes a few would come up to me and demand a greeting, and I would have no choice but to respond, but inside I was rigid as a board, with a heart of stone.

Hurriedly, I would scurry up to my room, flop down in the chair, and breathe a sigh of relief. My room was on the third floor, overlooking the front lawn of the college, so I could look down from my window at all the people arriving and departing from church. They laughed and chatted happily with one another; the young with the old, the black with the white. They were a unique people, but for some reason being a part of them sickened me. I tortured myself for being such an arrogant snob that I could not allow myself to fit in with such a holy community. What the principal and his daughter had told me must be true; I must be very selfish and proud. I would have to crush out this ego of mine in order to belong—but on the other hand, I wasn't sure I really *wanted* to belong.

My mind drifted again. I thought of a "Jews for Jesus" recording that we had heard recently during a fellowship. Many of the group's songs were versions of old Jewish ballads, and there was one about a schoolhouse called "Around the Oven" that had left a haunting impression on me. I thought of the sparse, dimly lit room described in the song, the hard wooden chairs that the children sat on as they huddled around the little fire in the oven and chanted the letters of the alphabet. I was lost in the imaginary world of the Torah.

My roommates were coming up from church.

"Come on, Joy," I told myself. "Be normal. Pull yourself together."

It was getting hard—very hard. I didn't want to be here anymore.

NINETEEN

THE snow billowed down from the sky and settled in thick blankets beneath our feet. The wind howled and bit mercilessly into our flesh. It was a hard and very cold winter, which seemed to reflect the wasteland in my heart.

The first Sabbath of every month we had a fellowship meal. Everyone in the congregation who lived in the neighborhood would bring in food to share, and we would all sit down after the service and eat the meal together. Afterward, we would sometimes see a religious film or two.

That week, there was a film called "Samson and Delilah," the Hollywood version of the Biblical story. The college dining room buzzed afterward with talk of the film.

Sister Victoria asked me what I thought about it. I told her that the part that was most outstanding to me was at the end when Samson's eyes had been gouged out and he was down in the cellars grinding corn. A Jewish girl, who was supposed to have married Samson, according to the film, turned to a Philistine girl and said, "You can do whatever you want, say whatever you like, but there is a higher call on his life, and he will always answer it!"

"Never even noticed it," Victoria answered tartly, and moved on to another table.

I finished my drink alone, lost in my own thoughts of a "higher call" and what exactly that meant. Samson had suffered, but at least he had found some purpose. I was still looking for mine.

I soon returned to my room. It was so cold outside that icy drafts had seeped through the cracks in my window and left me as chilled outside as I was inside.

ঞ

The filing system at the Administration Center, which housed correspondence from every corner of the globe, had become totally disorganized. At one of the weekly office meetings it was decided that I would be the lucky one to put it all in order. I was presented with a huge roomful of chaotic material and was given unlimited time for the task. For once, I did not feel pressured and thoroughly enjoyed the change.

One evening, I was in for a very pleasant surprise, for at the base of one of the filing drawers, I found a large folded card. It turned out to be a wall chart of the *Thirteen Principles of Faith*, a set of fundamental Jewish beliefs which had been codified by the famous rabbinic sage, Maimonides. The chart was written in both Hebrew and English. Where it had come from, I had no idea. I skimmed through the English part and quickly reburied my treasure. Oh, what a find! The principles didn't seem to make much sense, but that didn't worry me. Now at least I knew what the Jews believed!

The next day, at five o'clock, the van arrived to take us back to the college for the evening meal and our two-hour break, but I said I had too much work to do and that I would skip dinner. No sooner had the van pulled away than I ran down to Sister Victoria's office and took out my hidden prize. Meticulously, I copied down each Hebrew letter and vowel onto a paper. It was a laborious process which took much longer than I expected; I had to miss a considerable number of dinners before my masterpiece was completed. Finally I replaced the chart in the drawer for the last time and hid my copy in my room. It felt good to have the chart, even though I had no conception of its meaning.

I was soon to have another opportunity to find out more about the Jews.

My brother was very excited. His evangelical efforts in the Polytechnic had paid off, and he had finally recruited one of the Jewish staff members, a computer programmer named Jacob Fine. Jacob was a soft-spoken, dark-featured young man, and he began to come for tea and to attend services occasionally.

I had very few chances to meet Jews and was immediately interested in him. He was quite a nice boy, and at times, I toyed with the notion that I wouldn't mind marrying him, but it was a distant thought which I did not entertain in a practical way.

Whenever it was my turn to stay up the whole of Thursday night and bake bread for the college, I would always make a small portion of *challah* and set it aside for Jacob. I had no idea what real *challah* looked like, nor did I even know how to pronounce the word properly, but I knew it was a Jewish recipe. I had found it in one of my old club cookbooks from school; "Jewish Egg Bread," it was called. I would often add grated cheese to make it tastier and went to great lengths to obtain the necessary poppy seeds to sprinkle on top. I would sneak the *challah* up to my room while the college slept and hide it at the back of my wardrobe. Then, when everyone was in the lounge for Friday fellowship, I would slip out, redeem my little labor of love, and drop it into the pocket of Jacob's coat, which always hung in the front conservatory. He knew it was from me and would find a way to thank me without letting anyone else in on the secret.

I saw Jacob frequently at college over the course of the next six months and never missed an opportunity to bombard him with questions about Judaism. His mother was an Eastern European immigrant, and even though she was not at all religious, Jacob had some basic notion of traditional Jewish practices from her. His concept of Judaism was mostly of the chicken soup variety, but it was worth gold and diamonds to me. I wanted to know about the synagogue; about the *megillah*; about *Yom Kippur*.

"Did you fast on *Yom Kippur*?" I asked.

"As a matter of fact, I did," he replied.

I felt cheated and had great difficulty concealing my aggravation. *Yom Kippur* had become a recognized day in the Church some years ago, after one of Daddy Raymond's revelations, but we didn't fast because we were taught that Jesus had already forgiven our sins, and consequently it was a day of rejoicing. I had wanted very much to truly observe the day in the Old Testament style.

"Why didn't you *tell* me?" I complained to Jacob in mock consternation. "I would've fasted with you!"

"Sorry," he grinned apologetically. "Next time."

Jacob's mother lived in London, and he would frequently drive down to visit her. Late one Sunday night, when I had finally completed my day's work, I found him sitting in the kitchen, chatting with my brother.

"Joy, I have something for you," he said with a smile.

"I thought you were going to London today," I queried.

"I did," he said, "and I brought you something you'll like." He handed me a brown paper bag that was saturated with grease. I peeped inside. A small ring of weatherbeaten bread sat wearily at the bottom of the package.

"Oh, wow, thanks, Jacob," I said teasingly. "Well, what is it?"

"It's real Jewish bread. They call it a bagel."

"Oh! I'm going to eat it right now."

I found a scrap of margarine and tucked it into my prize. Jacob watched me with amused interest as I fought to twist and prize the bread away from my teeth with each bite.

"I'm sorry it's not so fresh, Joy," he added with a grin. "I've had it in the car the whole day. Well, at least you've had a bit of a taste of what real Jewish things are like."

"So Jews are made of tough stuff, eh, Jacob?" I asked wryly, holding my jaw.

"Never mind," he laughed. "*Purim* is coming. I'll get you some *hamantashen*."

"Some what?"

"Some of Haman's ears," he explained.

"Oh, it's quite all right, Jacob. Don't trouble yourself. I don't think I want any!" I responded, thinking to myself that the Jews certainly had very strange taste in delicacies. Jacob laughed affably.

It was well past midnight when I cleared up the last of the dishes and disappeared to my room. Everyone was sleeping already. Within minutes, I drifted into a genial slumber, dreaming of Jews eating people's ears.

I suppose that in some mild way, my interaction with Jacob constituted flirting—certainly the closest I had ever come to it—but in equal measure, it was a flirtation with Judaism. I wanted information, *real* information, and the Church's diluted version of Jewish customs was rapidly losing its glamor for me.

The snow crusts began to crack and dissolve into slush, and a weak March sun cast out a few feeble rays to warm our bones. Gradually, the wind lost its bitter force. The spring always seemed to hold out a promise of renewal, and I went about my tasks with a flicker of hope inside.

One day, as I was crossing the parking lot behind the college, I noticed the first spring flower. A tiny snowdrop which had pushed its way through the cement and was swaying peacefully in the breeze. I was astonished; the flower had ignored all natural rules and had insisted on blooming in the midst of a thick layer of hardened tar. I wished desperately that I could do the same, that I could somehow lift the iron ceiling from above my head, and allow my own soul to blossom.

In fact, as Passover approached, I did begin to feel a change taking place, a change I did not understand. I only knew that this year I had no desire to renew my vow never to sin again, and that I did not want to partake of the Paschal lamb. I was too afraid of revealing my inner doubts, however, and so I compensated by throwing myself into my holiday tasks with a frenetic energy; but I felt something bristling inside, something exciting and a bit dangerous. I felt I was being driven along by an intense striving, a yearning from the deepest crevices of my life, and that something "big" was about to happen.

Sister Victoria was planning an elaborate musical entitled "*Hamoshea.*" It would contain scriptural verses and songs telling the complete story of the Messiah from Genesis through Revelations. The theme was taken from the song I had written years before, "He Is a Hiding Place." I was given several verses from Jeremiah to set to music. They were somewhat inspiring, and I tried as best I could to immerse myself in the musical composition.

At the office, I also had my usual job of designing all the programs, song sheets and leaflets we would need for the Passover evening festivities. I put every ounce of creativity I possessed into those pieces; I wanted no one to point a critical finger at me and say that my mind was far away and that I was not doing my job properly. By the time the sheets were off the press and compiled, even Daddy Raymond was impressed with my efforts. It was the nicest design work I had ever done.

I was happy too that my assignment during the holiday week was waitressing. That would keep me so busy that I would have little time to talk, and would therefore not have to engage my plastic smile and forced words any more than necessary.

And so, without too much dread in my heart, I entered Passover. I was greatly relieved to get through the detested foot-washing ceremony; and when the time came to renew my vow, I mouthed the words without sound and pretended to eat the bread of the "body that was broken for me" and to sip the wine which was the "blood shed for my sin."

It was more difficult to avoid eating of the lamb without causing a stir, and I did not want to attract attention to myself in any way, so I ate a morsel and hoped no one would notice my feeble enthusiasm. I did not *want* to separate myself openly from the congregation, to put an obvious stamp of withdrawal on my behavior. I didn't want to feel so estranged, so repelled by practices that had always been sacred to me, but I couldn't shake my aversion. I told myself that I just needed some time.

The feast swung into high gear the next day, and there was a festive atmosphere as congregants from far and wide mingled with friends they seldom saw. The Norwegian brethren were full of their usual zeal and unique flavor. They were a very rugged and hardy band, and their liveliness provided an amusing contrast to their more staid British counterparts. Sister Inga, a petite, energetic woman who had once been the skipper of a ship, was the bounciest of the Norwegians and could be seen strumming her guitar with fingers of lightning at every opportunity. Ever since I had hosted the Norwegians years ago, during Passover, she had liked me, and she often gave me little treats of chocolate and cakes.

During one of the services, Sister Inga was asked to speak. Although she knew English, she preferred to give a formal talk in her own tongue, and Brother Johann, the leader of the contingent, stood by to translate. She told of how she and her friends had contacted a group of religious Jews in Oslo with the intention of missionizing. They had befriended them by claiming that they too were Jewish, and since the Norwegians had beards and knew enough to come with their heads covered, they were able to fool the Jews. Everyone laughed.

Sister Inga continued her humorous tale. The Norwegians had said they were on their way to England to observe Passover so the Jews had given them an address in London where they could receive information about the holiday. When the Norwegians arrived in London, they were early for their connecting train to Portfield, so they decided to actually look up the address they had been given. They found themselves at the Lubavitch House headquarters in Stamford Hill.

"*Shalom aleichem,*" Sister Inga had greeted them.

"*Aleichem shalom,*" replied the Lubavitchers.

"We are Jews from Norway," explained Brother Johann.

It was obvious to the *Chassidim* that the Norwegians were not very religious, for they seemed to know nothing of the upcoming holiday; so they generously handed out leaflets explaining the laws of Passover, or "*Pesach*," as they called it. Happily, the Norwegians made their way to Portfield.

The entire audience was now laughing hysterically over the fact that Brother Johann and his little band of followers had succeeded in fooling a houseful of religious Jews. Sister Inga handed out the Lubavitch leaflets to anyone who was interested. I was up on the platform at the time and was not able to take a leaflet as I had been banned from anything Jewish. I desperately wanted one.

For the entire week, I was following Sister Inga around the campus trying to speak to her alone. On the last day of the convention, I found my chance. I ran to Sister Inga.

"I don't have any more," she informed me. "Well, actually, I do have one left, but it's mine." She took it out of her bag and looked at it longingly, as if she were remembering all the trouble she had gone through to get it.

Finally, seeing the pleading look on my face, she said, "All right, you can have it," and handed it to me.

I thanked her profusely. I knew it was hard for her to part with the pamphlet, and normally I would never have pressed my advantage, but I wanted it so badly. I ran back to my room and hid it under my mattress. That night, when my roommates slept soundly, I took out my prize. It was written in English but was difficult to understand. What was an *afikomen*? How strange! And what was this about the rabbi in town buying everyone's leaven? He must have a huge storehouse in order to keep it all! A peculiar and rather droll scenario formed in my mind of an entire procession of fancy Jews, in their latest designer clothing, staggering out of Rolls Royces with packages of bread to give to the rabbi.

I decided right there and then to write to the address at the bottom of the leaflet and ask if any similar material were available on any of the other Jewish holidays. I wrote that I would pay for them if necessary, and as an afterthought I added that my mother was a Jew.

I mailed the letter with an inner feeling of contentment on another score, for I knew that someone, somewhere would be encouraged. Hadn't I always felt pleased myself when, after the thousands of pieces of literature that we constantly pumped into the world, one person took the time to write and say that he had enjoyed reading it? And if that someone was in a place where we had no congregation, such a letter was doubly heartening.

I anxiously awaited a response, but days turned into weeks and I heard nothing.

Once again I had new roommates: Charity, a West Indian from London who was quite musical, and Mahajra, a Pakistani. They were both quiet, committed and very sweet, and we got along well.

Mahajra was dusting my bookcase one day when she noticed my book on the Holocaust. "Joy, will you read it to us, a little each night?" she inquired.

I wasn't so sure this was a good idea. No one had yet bothered me about the book, and I didn't want to get into trouble.

"It's really horrible," I said, "sick, gory and cruel."

"I still want to know about it," she persisted. "Please, Joy."

"Oh, all right," I said, "but don't go around telling everyone. I'm only reading it to you two, and I don't want anyone else to know. You know I have been banned from anything Jewish!"

They promised to keep the secret, and that night we settled down to read the first few chapters together. It must have been a strange sight—a Pakistani, a West Indian and me, sitting in a Christian Bible college with our noses in a book about one of the worst sagas in history, a holocaust which had been aided and abetted by Christendom's forefathers. We had no idea that we ourselves shared responsibility for that calamity.

Charity and Mahajra found the book fascinating and made me

continue our nightly reading until we had completely finished it, but they did not take it to heart. However, it affected me in a much stronger way than it had on my first reading. Each night, when I had closed the book and my roommates were asleep, I wept silently, without tears. This hurt was too deep for tears. Slowly, slowly, it began to dawn on me that it was in the name of Christianity that so many Jews had gone to the gas chambers, and what was I doing? I was in a Christian college, killing myself to be a part of these people! I felt that just by association with them, I was whipping and torturing the Jews afresh.

But *why*? That's what bothered me. Why should I feel like this? Why should I have such a sense of sympathy for the Jews? Just because my mother was a Jew? So what? My father wasn't, and he was the one who counted.

I felt alone, helpless.

Deep inside, I had a feeling that to go with the Jewish people would mean hardships, alienation and persecution, but nevertheless I had a sense of security in that thought. There was an urgency, an intense pushing from within me to get to the Jews. I must hurry.

Then I would come to my senses and try to snap out of it. Whatever was I thinking? The whole idea was preposterous! I was becoming obsessed with these thoughts, allowing my mind to race away with me, and it was destroying my soul.

"Dear God, I am sorry," I would pray quickly whenever these stray notions would flit through my head. "Please forgive me."

What was happening to me?

May 31, 1981

It's a very long time since l have written in this book. My thoughts have been so vast, and I have been so tired inside, weary of trying to analyze them. I feel numb and sad.

Dear God, You have stolen my life. You have robbed me. I have never had the chance to choose for myself. You say I have, but I haven't really—for You made sure I was brainwashed from birth.

I fear You. And You want me to love You. How can you love FEAR?

I don't understand Your pathways. I don't feel anything for them anymore. I'll keep Your commandments, but not from love—from fear. Tonight, my eyes are blinded and I cannot see good in Your ways.

I won't say I hate You, but I can't say I love You.

June 8

There is an answer to my problem. It's a simple answer—in fact, it's only one word. It begins with D. I won't even mention it, but if I don't do it, I'll go MAD. I feel like I'm going mad. I mean it. I can feel it coming. I can't go on much more. I hate living.

I know it's the same old record; but why was I born? Why couldn't someone else have been given my job to do?

Life is hell. Life is one big trap, and I hate it with all my heart.

June 12

My life is being driven by an unknown force. I must allow myself to be driven, because if I don't, I fear the outcome. My whole life has never been what I wanted, but always tainted with what He wants. Sometimes, it has only been slightly colored, other times fully dyed, but there has always been at least a tiny show of color somewhere.

Dear Father in heaven, You know all about me. You read me like an open book. I see myself as a dirty, crumpled book, tattered and torn. The contents of the book are superb, for Jesus is inside of me, I know; but the only thing is, the pages are so dirty you can hardly read the writing. But You can read it, Father. You know every word. Only You in this whole wide world can help me. I think I'm in a bigger mess than I imagine. I know it's my fault. I don't blame You for one moment. I don't blame anyone. Only myself.

୬

We heard that a group of Jews for Jesus was coming to sing at a Bible College about seven miles away, and Daddy Raymond thought the performance might give us a healthy boost. Sister Victoria made the travel arrangements, and everyone on campus was planning to attend. About an hour before we were scheduled to leave, the principal's wife crossed my path.

"Are you going tonight?" she inquired.

"I thought we were all invited," I said.

"We are, but I don't know why you want to go," she replied with an indignant sneer. I didn't answer. She was one person who always had to have the last word, and it would have been a total waste of breath for me to say more. I continued on my way, but inside I was steaming.

All along I had accepted the discipline as a matter of course—the constant injunctions and reprimands that were meant to keep me in line, the accusations of doubt and unbelief. I felt it was my lot, that I had a great many spiritual "demons" to overcome, and would simply have to work harder to truly refine myself. But lately, I was beginning to feel singled out. Why was it always *me*? This matter of the Jews especially made my blood boil. The symbol of the *menorah* hung on the wall of our chapel; everyone in the college was learning Jewish dances and Jewish phrases; they were allowed to be the "new Jews," but I wasn't! In fact, there wasn't one other person on campus who had gotten so much as a disapproving look from Mother for wanting to see the Jews for Jesus concert.

Well, I didn't care. I would go to the concert anyway.

I must have been quite annoyed, because right before the van departed, I decided on impulse to call the rabbi of the synagogue that I had visited so frequently before the principal's ban.

The call was very disappointing. The rabbi had the title "reverend," just as my father had, and in my ignorance, I expected this gentleman to behave in the way I had known all other reverends to act. Whenever an "outsider" phoned my father to ask for an appointment to discuss religion, his answer was always welcoming: "Come over to my home, have tea, and we'll sit and talk together!" But it seemed the Jews were different.

After rehearsing my opening line so many times that it sounded like utter nonsense, I dialed the number.

"Excuse me for disturbing you, my name is Joy Israel," I spouted all in one breath, "and I was wondering if you could spare me a few moments to ask you some questions about Judaism."

"Oh, well, I'm very busy," came the reply in a distinctly pompous tone, "but I suppose I was utterly shocked and could think of nothing to say, so he continued. "Tell me, are you thinking of converting to Judaism?"

The question threw me. I giggled nervously and said, "Oh, no, it's just that I read a leaflet on the Feast of Passover, and I would like to ask a few questions about it."

There was no response.

"Where exactly shall I come, and when?" I asked awkwardly, breaking the silence.

"Well, you can come tonight if you like. We can talk in the lobby."

"Thank you," I replied, "but this evening I am going out to hear a Jewish group sing."

"That's very interesting, because we have a Christian group coming here to sing to us tonight," he said with a little chuckle. Not wishing to be impolite, I laughed also. We made another arrangement for a meeting, which I knew instinctively I would never keep, and I put the phone down.

In just a few moments, my mind had been totally blown. Christians going to sing in an Orthodox synagogue? Somehow that didn't seem right. I knew it was an Orthodox synagogue because the sign outside had said so, even though some of the congregants drove to the services on Saturday. Why on earth would the rabbi invite a Christian group to sing there?

And furthermore, his abruptness had seemed totally inappropriate. At home, we had never turned anyone away from the fold, and I couldn't understand why the rabbi had shown almost no inclination to talk to me. None of it made sense. I scolded myself for even having the idea to phone him and tried to convince myself that this was proof from heaven that the principal had been right all along.

I pushed the incident out of my mind and went downstairs to the bus.

❧

The concert was held in a huge, oblong auditorium. Hanging from all the walls were brightly-colored posters with slogans such as "Jesus the messiah" and "he is alive." We sat in a semi-circle, absorbing the words around us and flipping through brochures advertising the group, who were known as "The Liberated Wailing Wall." Finally the lights went out and the group appeared. There were two men and four women.

The first thing that struck me was the women's immodest attire: floor-length royal blue dresses that were low-cut and tight-fitting. As they sang, they flicked their long flowing hair, fluttered their wispy eyelashes, and swung their hips in a seductive manner. I was terribly embarrassed.

I listened to their songs. A few were traditional Israeli songs, such as "Jerusalem of Gold," but most were Jewish melodies that subtly conveyed Christian teachings. One song entitled "Tradition" belittled all the ancient customs and practices of observant Judaism. The singers wiggled around and spat forth their empty words in an offensive display of scorn and ridicule. My expectations for a pleasant evening were rapidly being drowned. Perhaps the ancient traditions of the Jews were "dead religion," as my father had always claimed, but the sight of Jews disparaging their own heritage in such a vulgar way was appalling to me.

After the songs, a woman in the group gave her testimony. She had apparently been brought up in a secular Jewish home which paid lip service to the traditions, but even though she had been a straight A' student and had led an outwardly successful life, she had felt unfulfilled—until Jesus had "set her free from bondage." From her words, it was obvious that the group kept Christmas, Easter and other holidays that Daddy Raymond had taught us were pagan, and that they ate non-kosher food.

All I could think was, "What a terrible shame!" Here in front of me was a full-blooded Jewish woman who had been brought up with Judaism in some form, yet had chosen to give up her heritage for the "freedom" of Christianity. And here I was, brought up in such "freedom," and yet hungering and thirsting to sit at the feet of a rabbi and learn of the "bondage" that she was so eager to cast aside!

At the end of the evening, the group encouraged us to fill out the forms in the brochures they had distributed so that they could keep in touch with us through correspondence. My brother was right behind me and saw that I was sitting idly with the form in my hand.

"Aren't you going to give it in, Joy?" he inquired. "They'll send you their magazines and letters."

"I don't want their correspondence," I replied without turning around.

The audience broke up, and people clustered together to chat in small groups, while others went around collecting autographs.

"Joy, did you enjoy it?" my friends asked. "It was okay," I replied. "I liked the songs on Israel best." Actually, I hadn't enjoyed it at all, but I was afraid to speak the truth. I sensed with an incomprehensible clarity that there was simply no such thing as mixing Jews with Jesus. They didn't belong together. The Jews had something, some kind of unknown treasure, and it shouldn't be contaminated by other influences. Why couldn't people mind their own religion and leave the Jews alone?

And to top it off, I could not understand why no one—not even the principal—had expressed one word of disapproval about the group's provocative attire and sensual style, after all the lectures we were constantly receiving about modesty and all the stringent college requirements about dress! Where *was* everyone?

I was totally dazed and felt like a droplet in a foreign ocean.

The next morning, Sister Victoria came up to me and repeated the question for what seemed like the millionth time: "It was really a wonderful performance last night, wasn't it? Did you enjoy it?"

"It was okay," I replied like a broken record, "but I liked the songs on Israel best."

Her attitude immediately changed. "It was *all* good," she said angrily, as if trying to send out some kind of verbal venom that would squash every Jewish emotion out of every cell in my body. I knew it was pointless to argue, and walked away stewing to myself about aggravating people who asked questions only to express their own point of view. What was the big problem, anyway? Even if I liked Jewish things, why couldn't I be a good Christian at the same time? What difference did it make?

❧

On Sabbath mornings, I was in the habit of getting up early to collect the mail for our building and post it under people's doors. I was surprised to see a letter for me in a plain brown envelope from Almington. I hurried back to my room and opened it, careful not to awaken my roommates.

My mouth dropped open. It was from a rabbi, in response to the inquiry I had made over four months ago. I had long since given up hope of receiving a reply.

The note was brief:

Your letter has been passed on to me from the head office in London. I will be in Portfield for a short time on July 3. My schedule is extremely hectic, so you must forgive me if I do not have much more than twenty minutes to spare, but I will be happy to answer some questions on Judaism. Please contact me for an appointment.
Sincerely,
Rabbi Shmuel Arkush

He had been clever enough to use an envelope that had no Jewish insignia on the outside, for if the letter had come on any day when I did not collect the mail, I would never have received it.

Good Lord, I thought, I had only wanted a leaflet. I didn't want to see a rabbi. My call to the reverend of the Portfield synagogue had been made on an impulsive whim, and in a way I had been relieved when the meeting hadn't worked out. My heart started to beat faster. I was afraid.

I folded the letter up, replaced it in the envelope, and hid it under my mattress. However, it took me only one cup of tea to regain myself, and the idea of actually making an appointment began to tantalize me. I smiled to myself as I sipped and thought of how I could wangle my way to get out and see him. The flimsy possibility turned quickly into an imperative; I just *had* to go. After all, if the rabbi could tell me about Judaism in twenty minutes, then he was worth listening to!

But that weekend, Daddy Raymond informed me that he wanted to open another Bible shop in Almington. This was an important new enterprise, for in addition to selling all the Sharon Rose goods and Bibles, the branch would house a coffee shop. He wanted to take Sister Victoria and me that Wednesday to view the premises. What a blow! That was the day the rabbi would be coming to Portfield. I would miss him altogether.

Secretly, I went into my office at the Administration Center and dialed the number that he had jotted at the bottom of his note.

"Look, I have to tell you the truth," I explained breathlessly. "If anyone finds out that I've contacted you, I've had it. I've already been banned from having all contact with Jews, but I'll tell you what. I have one friend from outside whom I have been allowed to keep in touch with. She's an old school friend named Anita, and if ever I'm talking to you and someone comes into the room, I will immediately pretend that I am talking to her...."

I felt rather stupid explaining all this to a rabbi I had never met, even though he sounded quite pleasant and very friendly. "He must think I'm crazy," I thought.

We could not make another arrangement to meet, but I agreed to be in touch with him by phone whenever I could. The initiative would have to be mine completely, of course, for he could never contact me.

THERE was much work to do in Almington. The premises were large, and most of the interior design was left to my discretion. As a final touch, when the construction was completed, I made the sign for the store myself and nailed it up for all to see. The shop was an immediate success, especially since it was located on Ferris Road, a main street in a very dilapidated area of the city. Many people stopped by to comment on the sheer pleasure of having such a beautiful shop in the district.

The minister, Brother Paul Markham, was very grateful for this boost to the church work in his lonely corner of England, and I became very friendly with him and his wife. In fact, I was so comfortable that I inadvertently confided to them one day when I was in their home that I had thought of contacting a rabbi, just to get some information on the Jewish version of the holidays. The Markhams did not register any surprise, and it did not occur to me that I had made a "slip."

I worked very hard that first week of the shop opening, and Victoria allowed me half a day off to do whatever I wanted.

Now was my chance, I decided. The letter from the rabbi had come from Almington. That meant he was right here in the city, and I had to find him. But there was a problem: I only had about one pound to my name. I took a bus to town, which wasn't too far, and that ate up a quarter of my money. I asked a few people on the street which bus

I needed to get to Charinghouse Road, but I couldn't get a straight answer out of anyone. This person told me one number, that person another number, until finally I thought I had found someone who seemed to know exactly what he was talking about.

I waited over an hour for the bus to arrive and was just about to give up when it finally turned the corner. About fifteen teenagers disembarked, all dark-haired, swarthy and fashionably dressed, and speaking a very sophisticated English. Instantly I backed off, my pulse racing. "They must be Jews," I thought. "They're rich and well dressed. This must be the right bus. I have to go to the place they're coming from." But I couldn't move. I looked down at my dowdy, old-fashioned clothes and touched my hair, scraped back and tied up in two braids around my head. And my ugly face! I couldn't, I just couldn't.

I let the bus pull away.

Oh, this was so ridiculous! Why did I think I could fit in with the Jews? I had to forget it—I *had* to. The whole business was making me neurotic.

I decided to take a walk around the city to cheer myself up and turned into a Laura Ashley store, dolefully drinking in the elegant surroundings. "If only I could get some money," I thought, "I could buy some decent clothes, and then I could go to see the Jews."

Of course, when I got back, Sister Victoria wanted to know exactly where I had been. I had cleverly sprayed perfume on my arm in Laura Ashley's.

"Oh, I looked all over the town. I had a good time. Smell." I held out my arm for her to take a whiff of the heavy scent.

I was relieved that Brother Paul Markham did not ask me to participate in the weekend services. I was still preaching at home in Portfield about twice a month, along with regular duties that included singing or giving a "thought," but my heart was cold and distant. It was becoming increasingly difficult to play the double role, and I was so thankful that I did not have to put my synthetic image into action in Almington as well.

As we headed back to the college, Sister Victoria thanked me in a very solicitous tone of voice for everything I had done for the Bible shop. I was shocked. It was the first time anyone had thanked me for anything in nine years.

It was understood in the college that all the work you did was for the sake of God, and it was your call to do it, and there was no need for any human being to thank you for it. I felt somehow that I was being patronized, and the only possible reason for this would be a suspicion on the part of the administration that I might be slipping "out of the fold." It turned out my hunch was right. The Markhams had apparently repeated to Daddy Raymond the comment I had made about wanting to contact a rabbi, and there were no secrets between him and his daughter when it came to student affairs. Victoria's manner was unusually gentle during the entire drive home.

Back in the college, I found everyone else being polite to me as well. The "word" had obviously gotten out, and many of the students fasted and prayed for my spiritual well being. I was still too naive to understand the full implications of this situation. The simple fact was that Daddy Raymond couldn't afford to lose me for many reasons. The size of my contribution to the church at that time was inestimable: the artwork, the Sharon Rose goods, the Bible school—not to mention my growing influence as a minister in my own right. In addition, the principal was no doubt nervous because my father had entrusted me to him at a very young age, making him responsible for my welfare. What would he say to my parents if I went off with the Jews? Worst of all, what would he say to God? If he lost a soul, he'd have to answer for it on the Day of Reckoning. Daddy Raymond was certainly in a bind.

I did not openly respond to the wooing in the college and continued to work harder than ever. Everything I did was impeccable; I did not want there to be a single blemish on any of my handiwork, not one speck of dust that could be a cause for reproach. I achieved even greater heights than ever before in all areas of my work, but inside my heart remained closed.

I was totally confused and decided to contact the rabbi again.

"Hello, this is Joy Israel. Is the rabbi in?"

"Yes, how are you?" came his warm response.

"Okay, I suppose," I said without conviction.

We exchanged pleasantries, and then he got down to business.

"Listen," he said, "I have an uncle who lives in Portfield in Haverly Court. How about if we arrange a time next week when we can get together at his house and discuss Judaism? I'll be in Ryster, and it won't be too difficult to get there."

"All right," I said eagerly. "Wednesday is best, and I think the only time I could be there is after five-thirty—and I would have to be back before seven."

"It couldn't be Tuesday?" Rabbi Arkush queried.

"Okay, I'll try," I promised.

He gave me directions to Haverly Court, and I replaced the receiver. I knew I had a difficult task ahead of me. First, I had to think of an excuse to use one of the cars. Secondly, I wanted to look halfway "normal" without anyone in the college wondering what was going on, and thirdly, I had to keep my wits about me and remain cool and collected.

For the next few days, I laid the foundation of my plan. "I have to go to the library in town next week," I reminded the principal on a few occasions. "I'll need a car because the design books I need are bulky and hard to carry. I think I'll go Tuesday after work," I concluded innocently.

Over the weekend it was announced that band practice on Tuesday evening would be moved up one hour, to eight o'clock. "Even better," I thought. "I will have more time with the rabbi."

The Monday before "The Tuesday" arrived. It so happened that several designs I had worked on were completed that day, and I had to take them to the principal to have them checked. From the moment I walked into his office, he began digging. He showed little interest in the designs and asked question after question about my spiritual welfare. How was I? What did I think about this? What did I think about that?

For about two and a half hours, I tried to satisfy him with small talk, but he was stubbornly persistent. Finally, out of sheer frustration, I said calmly, "All right, so I'll tell you! I've contacted a rabbi!"

The room went dead.

He leaned forward, thumped his fist down hard on his huge oaken desk, and in a ferocious voice bellowed, "*You what?* Did you pray about this, child?"

"Pray about it?" I replied indignantly. "What was there to pray about? I simply have some questions to ask about Judaism. I *want* to see him!"

"Well, why in the world didn't you come and ask *me* about them?" he sputtered. "Haven't you seen all my books on Jews?"

Angrily, I retorted, "Ask you? I hardly dare mention the word 'Jew' to you! And anyway, if you are so sure that the Church is the right way for me, why don't you let me go and see him? What are you so afraid of?" I was on a roll and headed on blindly. "I saw a poster the other day that had a picture of a young horse running free out in the fields, and the words on it were, 'If you love something, let it go free; if it comes back to you, it is yours for eternity—but if it doesn't, it was never meant to be.' If you love me as much as you say you do, why don't you let me go free? All my life you've told me, 'This is the right way, believe it, live it, give yourself to it, and you will find your place and fit in.' And what have I been doing for twenty-five years? Believing it, living it, preaching it! How much more can I give myself to it? I'm burned out from the effort I've poured out, and still, *still* I don't feel I fit in. Repeatedly, I come back to this same place where I feel I cannot go on anymore, and to tell you the truth, the older I get, the more embarrassing it is to cope with it. You have never given me a chance to find out for myself. I feel like a rebellious puppy dog being dragged along on a tight lead."

By this time, I was crying hard. He gave me his handkerchief, grasping awkwardly for any gesture that would draw me closer.

I stood there. He sat there. Just a desk between us, and yet already a vast ocean.

His face was bright red with anger and his voice intense. "I'm telling you, child, you're playing with fire. Leave it alone! Do you hear me? *Leave it alone!*" he screamed, then looked at me long and hard before continuing. "Do you know, there is something the matter with your soul, child, and it makes you walk on the edge of a cliff all the time, and I just can't put my finger on what it is!"

"Even if you tell me I can't go, I'm still going, because I don't see anything wrong with it," I firmly insisted.

"The choice is yours, child, but you're playing with fire!" He glared at me for a moment and then stormed out of the room.

All afternoon, he kept coming up to my office and telling me repeatedly that I was "playing with fire" and I should "leave it alone." I remained silent. I so much wanted to talk to the rabbi, but I was afraid. This was Daddy Raymond talking to me, a person I had looked up to my whole life. How could I want to disobey him? I had never fought him at such length on any issue before.

That evening, I telephoned the rabbi and said that I wanted to put off the meeting for now.

"Wednesday, we'll make it Wednesday," he offered.

"No, please," I replied. "I'll tell you the truth. I hate to be deceitful, and I finally told the principal that I had contacted you. He said he wasn't telling me not to see you and that the choice was mine, but that I was playing with fire. I just feel that I want to let it go for the time being."

"Well, I still think we should get together and talk," he insisted gently. "Think about it, and when you feel ready to contact me again, please feel free to do so."

His kindness impressed me greatly. I had totally messed him about, letting him go to all the trouble of organizing a meeting, and then I had let him down; and yet he still wanted to make some time for me. He was very different from the rabbi of the Portfield synagogue, who had made me feel that I was burning up his money for every minute it took to get my question out. Deep down, I had a fear that at some point this rabbi would also say to me, "I'm sorry, but I don't have time," and I would be left out in the cold.

I was so lonely. Night after night, I saturated my pillow with tears, I had no one to talk to. Sister Victoria was in Brazil with her father visiting long-time correspondents, and anyway, I knew she would never understand my feelings. I'd almost given up trying to explain them.

I was surprised to find that leaving the college was no longer just a vague, untouchable fantasy, but actually a possibility. I had lost confidence in the fruits of my spiritual labors in the Church and had come to the point where I just couldn't preach the message anymore. My heart was filled with disappointment at the realization that Sister Victoria's schizophrenia theory not only hadn't worked, but was *making* me crazy instead! I did not even have the strength left to convince myself that the fault was only with me. How could it be? What had gone wrong?

I wanted so terribly to serve Jesus. Hadn't I tried with all of my being to love him and to be faithful to him? My father had taught me from the time I was a little girl that once you accepted Jesus into your heart, he would never leave you, no matter how wayward you became, for he had promised that even though we might deny him, he would always remain faithful. It was so difficult to understand, and so worrisome to me that everyone else seemed to be able to believe it. Why couldn't I believe it? With my whole heart I wanted to.

I was afraid to leave the college. I had been told time and time again that hell did not begin when you died, it began when you left the Church, and that concept was very real to me. I was petrified of God and of the end of times described in the Book of Revelations of the Apostle John. The verses portrayed the New Jerusalem, the City of Gold, that would be built after Jesus had come to save the earth. He would sit on a throne in the center of this most sublime and perfect city, a holy paradise filled with green trees and healing waters, children playing merrily in the streets, and a light so bright there would be no need for the sun and moon. Angels with flaming swords would guard the gates of the city, and the only ones who could enter were those who had their names inscribed in the Book of Life.

And woe to those who could not enter! For they would spend eternity in the company of the warmongers and sorcerers who hovered outside the gates, doomed to torture and torment, flung to everlasting darkness. Those inside the city would not be able to see past the gates, but those outside would see in; and therein was their ultimate punishment.

When I was about ten or eleven, I had asked my father, "What's so bad about hell? If it burns you up, then you die, and that's the end!"

"No," he had replied, "the fires of hell are different and special. They can burn a person without killing him and will keep burning him forever."

I remember that after he told me this, I took a box of matches from a shelf in the kitchen and struck one, determined to see how long I could hold my finger in it. Of course, the heat frightened me and I never got close enough to hurt myself, but the image branded itself instead on my soul, and I had carried that brand till this day.

I wanted to be on the *inside* of those pearly gates, not lost among the unbelievers and warmongers on the outside. But most of all, I was heartbroken because the dearest relationship in my life was crumbling, and the one whom I loved most, the savior for whom I was willing to die, was slowly becoming estranged.

In the very depths of my life was a quiet whisper of a feeling that I should be with the Jews, and that in so doing, I would find the security and completion I was so desperately seeking. But this tiny feeling sent my inner being into turmoil, contradicting every teaching and doctrine of my youth. My emotions were in chaos.

People started to say I was melancholy, but that hurt me. I knew it wasn't true. I hadn't been melancholy when I'd come to the college nine years ago; I'd been a bright, boisterous, fun-loving girl. The injustice of all these smug pronouncements on my spiritual condition was gnawing away at me. I wasn't sure how much longer I could take it. Many times I wondered if I even remembered how to laugh.

I let several weeks pass in numbness before I contacted the rabbi again. I was relieved that he sounded delighted to hear from me. We decided on another date for a meeting, and as I had to get off the phone in a hurry, I promised I would mail him directions to our neighborhood.

His last words to me were, "And don't tell anyone this time!"

"I won't," I promised, and replaced the receiver.

It was only Monday. It would be another nine days before I would get to see him. A mixture of anticipation and fear churned in my stomach.

During the week a lucky coincidence boosted my excitement. The college owned a large garage and workshop in the heart of an enormous industrial estate on the other side of town. The two college coaches had recently been resprayed, and Brother Bartholomew asked me if I wouldn't mind going down to the garages with him and decoratively painting the name and address of the college on the back of each vehicle. I agreed, and to my delight, the route Brother Bartholomew chose to cross town was exactly the route that Rabbi Arkush would need to take when he pulled off the motorway. I put my memory into operation, noting the directions in my head as we drove along, and as soon as we arrived home that evening, I wrote down the information as accurately as I could remember it and mailed it off to Rabbi Arkush.

Since it was impossible to take two or three hours off work without anyone noticing, I once again formed a plan. This time, I told all my colleagues at the Administration Center that I had to go to town to buy materials for Sharon Rose, and the idea went over smoothly.

A quarter to one the next afternoon found me rushing along toward an arboretum that was not too far from the college. I had directed Rabbi Arkush to the entrance of the park because it was an easy landmark, but it was also inconveniently located on a main street. I ran along frantically with my head down, hoping that no one I knew would see me.

"Oh, God, let him be there," I prayed.

My eyes searched anxiously for the orange car he had described on the phone. "There's a yellowish one, I'll try that," I told myself. I peered inside and saw a kindly-looking man reading a book. He had a beard and could not have been past his early thirties.

He opened the door for me. "Are you Joy Israel?" he inquired.

"Yes. Are you Rabbi Arkush?"

"I sure am," he answered with a broad smile.

"Oh, thank God," I spluttered, diving into the car and reaching out to shake his hand.

Startled, he shrank back against the windowpane. I wondered what I had done wrong and awkwardly took my hand back.

"Is it all right to stay here?" he asked.

"No, we have to get away from here as fast as we can. It's too close to the college." I was really afraid. There were now about eighty students in the college and a congregation of at least three hundred. I needed only one of those pairs of eyes to spot me, and I was doomed.

He turned the car around slowly, pulled onto a side street that was not quite so busy, and switched off the engine. My heart was thumping violently, and I was amazed at his calmness. All during our talk, I kept ducking my head every time a car passed by. It was still a busy road.

"Tell me about yourself," he said with that same pleasant smile.

As clearly as I could, I explained that my mother was a Jew who had been brought up in an Orthodox home in Alexandria. When she was twenty-one years old, she and my grandmother had been influenced by some people from the Salvation Army mission, and they had both converted to Christianity. My grandfather had been furious and had said the prayers for the dead for them. That was really all I knew about my mother's Jewish life.

I went on to tell of how my mother had met my father during the war when he was stationed with the British Army in Alexandria, and how they had married in England after the war was over. My father had always been a believer, and after he came through the war unharmed, he decided to devote his life to God and became a Pentecostal preacher. By the time I was born, the congregation in Greenborough was well established, and I'd grown up within the church.

"At sixteen I came to the theological college in Portfield, and now nine years later, I'm still here," I concluded.

"So why did you contact me?" Rabbi Arkush asked.

"Well, for years...well, sometimes it seems as though from very far back—ever since I was a little girl—something in me has been struggling to click. All I want to do is to serve God wholeheartedly, and I constantly find myself fighting to be able to give myself completely to the doctrines of my youth. I was never really interested in Jews at all, but over the last few years I found myself involuntarily thinking about them and about my mother. I just keep having these feelings out of the blue, and I wanted to know who the Jews are, that's all."

"You know what I think you should do?" he offered. "You should go and stay with a religious family for two weeks in Manchester or in London, and then you'd get a taste of what Judaism has to offer."

"But I could never do that. We don't have any vacation, or any time off at all."

"Well, can't you just have a mad moment?" he asked.

"I can't, you don't understand," I said quietly. "In nine years, I've never left the college for a personal reason, not even for a minute. Nobody would buy the 'mad moment' idea."

I sat for a few minutes, thinking seriously of the offer, and Rabbi Arkush waited patiently. No, it was impossible. It was far too much to ask. I would have to throw away twenty-five years, and for what?

"No, I can't," I broke out. "It's too complicated. If I leave, I can never go back. Maybe, and only maybe, I would be accepted again in the church, but I would never be accepted back into the college, and certainly not as a minister."

"Look, I promise you, I won't leave you on the street. I'll find you another Christian group that you'll like. You won't be left alone."

I knew he would never understand that I believed my group to be the ultimate in Christianity, the closest possible way of serving God. I could never be satisfied with the Anglican Church or any other mainstream branch whose methods of worship were tepid compared to ours. For me, there would be total commitment or nothing.

"No," I sighed. "I just can't."

We chatted a while longer. Rabbi Arkush told me gently several times that I was really Jewish, quoting several verses from the Bible that showed how the Jewish sages had arrived at the principle of matrilineal heritage. He told me to think about his offer and to let him know. He understood that it was a very difficult decision for me, but maybe somehow I could think of a way to work it out.

An hour had already passed in what seemed like just a matter of minutes.

"I have to go," I said. "I'm sorry."

"Wait, let me at least take you a little closer to town," he offered kindly.

"Okay, thanks." It was a long way for me to walk to town, and the ride would save me valuable time. I stood on the curb and watched him drive away. The first thought that passed through my mind was that I had actually laughed a good hearty laugh. I still remembered how to do it!

As the little yellow car disappeared into the distance, I felt rooted to the pavement. Every fiber of my soul was screaming out to him,

"Wait! How can you leave me here? *Take me with you! Please, let me come with you, now!"*

I tried to pull myself together. My emotions were running away with me again. How could I so readily throw away my life? I must calm down and think rationally.

I had to hurry. I ran to a shop in the center of town and quickly picked out the material I had told my co-workers I needed for Sharon Rose, only to be reprimanded for my choices when I got home.

As I sat on the platform facing the congregation in the prayer meeting that night, I found it extremely difficult to concentrate. After the service, one of the students approached me and said, "Do you mind if I ask you a question?"

"No," I responded nonchalantly.

"What were you thinking about tonight?"

I was startled. "Why do you ask?"

"Because I was watching you, and every now and again you would break out into this beaming smile."

"Ah, that's my secret," I answered teasingly with a raised finger to my nose, and quickly scooted away before she could engage me in further discussion.

❧ TWENTY-ONE ❦

I HAD a secret, and I did my best to keep it under lock and key. It was important that not one soul should guess.

Over the next two months or so, I was in touch with Rabbi Arkush whenever I could steal five minutes of private time at a phone. I never had trouble reaching him, and I learned much later that he had bought a beeper and instructed his wife to page him whenever I called. Our conversations were never very long, or in-depth; mostly he would just ask me how I was doing. But it was my lifeline to the outside, to the possibility of a new world.

I continued to work hard, instinctively feeling that I might not be around much longer. In a very inconspicuous manner, I gradually taught all my workmates at the Administration Center how to produce all the Sharon Rose goods that were under my supervision, including the screen printing and candle-making, and worked every spare minute to build up a stock of those goods that were in the greatest demand. I had made up my mind that if I did leave, there would not be a single stain on my record. Not one person would be able to point a finger at me and say I had been slacking or had been in any way sour or malicious. I would carry through my responsibilities in an exemplary fashion to the very last second.

One girl was keen-eyed.

"You're up to something, Joy," she told me. "I've been watching you, and you've never worked like this. You've been churning out products by the dozen."

"Maybe," I said flatly, "but then again, maybe not."

Daddy Raymond and Sister Victoria returned from Brazil. She had bought me a present, which surprised me, as I had not written to her during the entire six weeks that she was away.

"Hug me," she demanded as we passed on the stairs.

"What for?" I asked.

"Because you've missed me, that's why," she said, leaning on me and putting her arm around my waist.

"Thanks for telling me," I responded, wriggling away and running down the stairs while she shouted after me that I was "cutting and caustic."

Shortly after her return, we were sitting together in Daddy Raymond's office discussing the upkeep of the Bible shops. Sister Victoria announced casually, "As manager of Sharon Rose, I think I should have a special devotional headscarf. Would you make me one, Joy?"

It was only a lifetime of internal discipline that saved me from doing her damage. I had built those shops by myself, and every single product that was sold in them was the work of my soul. Where had she found the arrogance to appoint herself the "manager"?

Even Daddy Raymond could not duck the vicious irony of her remark. In an unsympathetic tone, he said to me, "How come you are so quiet?"

"I'm refraining from saying my words," I answered, looking straight at Sister Victoria, "lest they be *cutting and caustic.*" The remark silenced her for the time being, but it did not silence my growing bitterness.

❧

The Sabbath services began that week with a song, and I sat dutifully on the platform with the other members of the band. Everything was proceeding normally, until suddenly the principal stood up and announced that he could feel a special presence of Jesus in the service and that everyone should kneel down and worship him in deep communication. I was relieved that I was in the band, and therefore could not join in, but the situation intensified.

Daddy Raymond spoke again. "I want everyone to do this," he encouraged, "every child, every minister. Even those in the band should stop playing their instruments now and kneel down." He beckoned to Sister Martha, his secretary, and she slipped out of the chapel. I knew that she had gone to bring the bread and wine for communion, for Daddy Raymond usually asked us to take communion at times that were particularly "holy." By the time she returned, the entire congregation was prostrate on the ground, worshipping Jesus. Only I remained in my seat, with my clarinet in my lap.

"Everyone can do this," the principal coaxed. "It doesn't matter how you feel, you can still do it. Reach out to heaven!"

But I couldn't. "I can't go to see a rabbi one day and kneel down and worship Jesus the next," I told myself. "I have to get to the bottom of this once and for all."

The principal set up the communion table and carried it across the platform, setting it down immediately in front of me. Silently, I stood up and walked off the platform, down the main aisle of the chapel, and through the back doors.

Within moments, about six of the old ladies in the congregation were chasing after me and begging me to go back in. "It's right, it's right," they pleaded.

"I know," I said sweetly and with equanimity. "It's right for you. You go back and worship Jesus. Don't worry about me, I'll be okay."

I sat quietly in my room for a while and tried to collect my thoughts, but they refused to assemble in any kind of orderly fashion. On a sudden impulse, I got down on the floor and began ruffling through my drawers, looking for important papers: my driver's license, birth certificate, address book.

While I was doing this, Mary entered the room suddenly without knocking.

"What are you doing, Joy?" she asked.

"Nothing," I replied calmly. "I'm just looking for one or two things." I ignored her and continued my search.

"Come down to my room for tea," she invited. I knew the service was still in full swing.

"No thanks, Mary, I'm just not in the mood."

I lay on my bed after she had left and wondered where my life would take me; where I could go; what I could do.

But I had not seen the last of the visitors. Sister Samantha had come in from Bloomington for the service, and it was not long before she showed up at the door. This woman who had beaten me so many times in past years now knelt down by my bed and took hold of my hand.

"Tell me why you didn't kneel down today," she pleaded softly.

I shook my head and stared at her blankly.

"Joy, I'm not going to get off my knees until you tell me," she urged strongly.

"I'm sorry," I said, "but you're going to be there an awfully long time."

"You are breaking the principal's heart!" she cried. "Can't you see what you are doing to him? You're worrying him so much, you're making him ill. Doesn't it bother you?"

I remained silent. I had no desire to communicate. Eventually she got up off the floor and left.

The next day at Bible school I mouthed all the words to the songs, but not a sound came out. I just couldn't do it anymore. My preaching days were over.

❧

During that week, the minister in charge of the church in Denmark returned from a business trip to Israel. It just so happened that Sister Victoria was very close with his family, and he had brought her a present. Like a spoiled child, she bounded straight up to me and said, "You don't know what I've got!" in a taunting six-year-old voice.

Instinct informed me. I looked her straight in the eye and said forcefully, "If that's a *mezuzah* and you put it up, I'm warning you there's going to be fireworks in this place like you've never seen before. I've had one from my uncle for more than two years and was not allowed to have it up."

She went bright red, shocked that I had guessed what her gift was and doubly shocked at my anger. Could this be Sister Joy—the former "lamb"? Flummoxed, she hurried off to her room without another word.

But the interchange left me feeling very frustrated. This place was making me more and more sick as each day went by. Sister Victoria was thirty-eight years old, an international spiritual leader and mentor, privy to every secret in the college—and here she was, behaving like a catty adolescent! She had always had a nasty streak; I still remembered vividly the time she had come waltzing smugly into the bank in her glamorous fur coat after she had forced me to wear that horrid red relic. It dawned on me how pathetic she was.

And besides, this whole issue of the Jews was becoming intolerable. Sister Victoria wore a Jewish star around her neck, and she was spiritually advanced enough to have a *mezuzah* on her door because she could "handle" it. Why did they want to be Jews? And why wouldn't they let *me* be a Jew? Wasn't there anyone in the world who could tell me why?

On Friday afternoon of the following week, I was in my office at the Administration Center with Sister Josephine and another young girl from the neighborhood who sometimes came to help out. Sister Josephine was slowly hooking her into the fold, and the girl confided to Josephine that she had a headache and didn't feel well.

"Tell Auntie Joy and she will pray for you," announced Josephine authoritatively. I was sitting right there in the room, busy with screen-printing.

"I'm sorry, but Auntie Joy won't," I said firmly.

Josephine glared at me, so furious that she did not know what to do. "And why not?" she bellowed.

"Because when I'm finished, she'll still have the headache, that's why," I said calmly. So Josephine prayed for her.

This was another game that I was tired of playing. The Pentecostals really believed in prayer as a quick treatment for even minor ills, basing their practice on the verse in the New Testament that says, "Those who believe shall lay hands on the sick, and they shall recover." The problem was that if the sick person didn't recover, either party would be blamed for not believing hard enough. No matter what you did, you could never get away from this pressure of "belief," from the endless guilt that was always being thrown back in your lap.

I did not yet have it in my heart to challenge the Church teachings directly; my belief in the Scriptures still fueled the most mechanical of my actions. It was just that I had questions, and lately I had become brave enough to ask them, but nobody seemed to have answers.

I had no doubts about the many spiritual experiences I had had over the past nine years, about the reality of spirituality in the Church. I did not know what the source of it was, but I knew it was there. I had seen things that could not be denied. Josephine had once had warts covering her entire left hand, and Daddy Raymond had prayed for her. The next day she came into the services without a single wart on her hand, not even a trace. She said she had searched her bed when she woke up in the morning but had found nothing. And her story was not an isolated one.

There was a cane hanging up in the chapel of the college which had once belonged to a man who was paralyzed from the waist down. Daddy Raymond had prayed for him too, and there were people in the congregation who had actually seen him get up and walk away from the chair without so much as a limp, and who could report that he'd been fine ever afterward.

But then there were other stories—of prayers that hadn't worked, of people who'd died of cancer in spite of the most fervent supplication. And that was the part I didn't understand. Jesus had promised in the New Testament that his powers would *always* heal. And if that was a blanket guarantee, why didn't it work every time? The answer couldn't be simply that the sick people hadn't "believed"; this seemed too easy an excuse, and it wasn't fair.

I continued working, and that was the last I saw of Josephine for the weekend. On Monday evening, about half an hour before we were due to go home in the minibus, she came marching into my office without warning and started shouting at me.

"If you really feel like you do, why don't you leave?" she screeched. "You're no example to the young people, and you're a disgrace to the ministry!"

I was so furious I couldn't even speak. My fists were clenched, and my body shook with anger. I wanted only to flatten her, but would not allow myself the privilege for two reasons: first, I knew she bruised easily, and second, I did not want anyone saying that I had been forced to leave the church because I had gotten into a brawl. I wanted my record to be absolutely immaculate.

How *dare* she tell me to leave? What had she contributed to this place? She hadn't even come into the church until she was fourteen years old, after her parents had died in the car accident. And on top of that, what had her parents given to the church? Nothing, absolutely nothing! If my father hadn't given away his last dime, there wouldn't have been half the facilities or services that existed today; and how much had we children suffered so that my father could give so freely? Oh, I was so angry! I'd done *nothing* but give; Josephine had done precious little but take. She was always the last person to go an extra mile for anyone, and she of all people—this little spitfire who had once been expelled from the band and the ministry for a year because she'd been caught in the basement with another minister—this low-life upstart who had had a full-blown affair with her boss and had been caught with him in a mobile home—*she* had the audacity to tell me to leave!

Such thoughts raced through my mind at a rapid pace, but all I could do was scream, "*Leave*? Where shall I go—to the gutter?"

She turned and flounced out of the room.

I stood alone in the middle of the floor, tears of fury and frustration pouring down my face. I couldn't go home on the minibus with everyone else tonight. I didn't want to see people. I decided I would walk back to the college and that I would not go back to the Administration Center until everything was sorted out.

I couldn't face the dining room either, and so I missed dinner and went straight to my room. At ten minutes to seven that evening, my roommate Charity reminded me that it was time for me to go back to the office, and that I should hurry or I would miss the bus.

"I'm not going," I said simply.

With a start, she asked, "Are you on kitchen duty?"

"No."

"Are you on laundry duty?"

"No."

"Well, where *are* you?"

It was unheard of not to work. There wasn't a soul in the place who passed an idle moment during the nearly eighteen-hour day.

"I'm just going to stay right here," I said.

Charity was kindhearted. She knew that I'd been going through a rough time, and she respected my privacy. "Okay, I won't tell anyone," she promised, and was gone.

I busied myself around the room, ironing, dusting and reading. At about ten-fifteen that evening, there came a knock at the door. It was Sister Victoria, who had just come from evening prayers.

"Where were you tonight?" she inquired.

"Right here," I replied.

"Rather against tradition, isn't it?"

"You could say that, I suppose."

She was greatly put out by my pleasant, tranquil manner. "Well, I'm downstairs. Come down and talk," she demanded sternly.

About ten minutes later, I sauntered into her room.

She was naked. "Do you want me to tell you the truth about your-self?" she began, and then plunged in without waiting for a reply. "You're selfish, you're proud, you're arrogant"—the list included several other items which I fail to remember now—"and *that's* why you feel the way you do," she concluded.

I didn't comment or argue; we were past the point where we could discuss things. Her angry accusations continued well into the night. At about one-thirty in the morning, I stood to leave.

"Anyway," I said in parting, "I'm not going back to work in the office until I have discussed things with your father."

"Well, it will have to wait!" she snapped with a contented smirk. "He's going away tomorrow."

"It's okay. I'll just wait in my room until he has time to speak to me."

"Oh," she stammered, seeing that I really meant what I had said, and that her threatening stance was having no effect at all. "Well, maybe he'll see you before he goes. I'll try and make you an appointment with him."

"As you like," I said coolly, and left the room.

The sun shone brightly the next morning, and after a quick cup of tea, I dressed and went straight to the principal's private quarters. I had already given up on morning devotions.

"May I speak to you?" I inquired.

"At the office," he responded without looking up. His wife was sitting by his side, and it was obvious their daughter had already made a full report to them.

"No, I'm sorry, but I'm not going back to the office until I have spoken to you," I said firmly.

"Very well. Is now a good time?"

"Yes."

"Alone?" he questioned. Mother rose to leave.

"No, no, it's quite all right for both of you to hear what I have to say." I told them matter-of-factly that I simply could not go on anymore. I tried to explain that I felt as though a heavy, oppressive blanket were suffocating me, and unless there was a real change in the very depths of my life, I just couldn't continue to fool myself anymore. I also told them that I had seen a rabbi who had offered me two weeks with a Jewish family, and that I was seriously considering taking up his offer.

Daddy Raymond cried all the time I was speaking. "What the Jews have is down here," he whispered hoarsely, placing the palm of his hand toward the ground, "and what we have is up here," and his hand went above his head. "You know what's wrong, Joy? You never repented in the first place. You have to go back and meet Jesus at the crossroads. He's waiting there for you!"

"I've done nothing but repent my whole life," I reminded him. "I *meant* it. I was so sincere, I believed—don't you understand? It's like being full to bursting point with food, and then someone puts a four-course meal in front of you and demands that you eat it. It doesn't matter if the flavor is good. I can't even look at it anymore."

He was heartbroken. I knew that part of him would miss me personally if I left, but his sense of failure was eating away at him too.

"I'm going to give you the rest of the day off from the office, Joy. I want you to go upstairs to your room, kneel down by your bed, and contact Jesus."

I knew it was no use arguing. I went upstairs and lay on my bed like a broken, empty shell, my eyes swollen and froglike from so much crying. After about two hours, I took my headscarf, knelt down beside my bed, and tried to pray, but it was no use. I knew that was not the answer anymore.

I remained in my room all day. The next morning, I dressed to go to the office, in spite of my warning that I would not go back to work until the situation was resolved. I purposely missed the van again and walked instead, wanting to air out a little, and on the way I pleaded desperately with God.

"Dear God, can't You give me a word, a verse, a promise, *something* to let me know if this is all real? I don't want a miracle. All I want is to have the quiet confidence that this is the right way of life. I'm twenty-five years old, and I've devoted my entire life to the Church. I don't *want* to leave. I don't *want* to turn my life upside down. I have so many accomplishments here. Just please let me know that it's *right!*"

When I was about halfway to the Administration Center, words from a scriptural verse suddenly came to my mind: "Seek peace and pursue it." I knew the words were from Psalms, but I couldn't quite place them. I had a sudden feeling of inner satisfaction.

Eagerly, I rushed the rest of the way to the office and went straight to look up the verse in Young's Concordance. "Depart from evil and do good," it began, "seek peace and pursue it." If only I knew for sure what the "evil" referred to! Rabbi Arkush had told me in his own quiet way that Christianity was evil; Daddy Raymond had said that Judaism was evil. How could I be sure which of these paths was really "playing with fire"? But even though I did not understand the verse completely, I felt lightened inside; I sensed that somehow God still heard my prayers and that He was close by.

During the course of the day, the principal came into my office several times to ask me if I had made up my mind. He seemed relieved that I had come to the office in spite of the ultimatum I had given, and he kept pressing me for an answer. My reply to him was always the same: all I wanted was to feel peace inside so that I wouldn't have to continually beat my brains out trying to convince myself that what I was doing was right. That was all.

"The reason you feel like this is because you have one foot on either side of the fence, Joy. You have to turn around completely, and then it will be fine," he promised.

All right, I decided. One last time, I would completely turn around, just as he had said. I would forget all about the Jews, forget even that my mother was a Jew, and I would *serve* Jesus.

❧

Sister Victoria wept openly when she heard my decision. "I was so worried you would leave," she admitted with a tear-stained face. But her tears did not move me, for I knew they were tears for herself, and not for me. Being in charge of the Administration Center was a huge burden on her, and I think she felt there was no way she could keep it afloat without me. Victoria was intelligent and conscientious—but who would do all the work if I left? There was no way she could continue to produce all the Sharon Rose goods and all the artwork without me, and there was no one else around who was creative enough to supply her with ideas.

The principal behaved in a surprisingly weak fashion. In an effort to secure my "reinstatement," he suddenly began to relieve his conscience to me in a way that was totally unexpected. He tried to explain his actions concerning my parents over the years and apologized for the cruel way he had treated them. He probably thought that I might secretly have been in contact with my parents despite my ban, and that perhaps they had voiced their own complaints about what the church had done to them. It wasn't so much the apology itself that was shocking, however; it was his choice of words.

"I only did what I thought would be good for them," he explained desperately. "I had no idea what it would do to them."

I didn't comment; I was speechless.

Maybe I hadn't heard him correctly.

He had done what he *thought* would be good for them? What he *thought*? What had happened to God? What about all the divine revelations he had supposedly received concerning the matter, the voice of the spirit that was supposed to be guiding him? Hadn't it been *God's* directive that my parents give up every last possession and leave the town they'd lived in for over twenty years; God's voice that had pushed them out of the congregation altogether?

I was livid. There had been no revelation, only Daddy Raymond's "thoughts." He'd ruined my parents, and now he was trying to justify himself to me.

I thought of an incident a week earlier in his office when he'd been in discussion with Sister Bertha, one of his pets, about the new moon and the holidays. She had been giving him all sorts of advice about the calendar, and how to determine the dates of the festivals, and he was listening attentively and nodding at her suggestions.

"Wait a minute," I'd piped up in a sudden flash of brazenness. "Who is determining all of these things? Isn't God supposed to decide? I thought you had revelations about the holidays!" The two of them sat there stone-faced and said not a word.

And now it suddenly made perfect sense. These people were not doing God's bidding—He was doing theirs! All of this ripped through me with lightning pain as I sat in front of the principal, thinking about my parents, contemplating their wasted suffering. I knew that Daddy Raymond was terribly embarrassed, for it was plain to see that he was cringing inwardly. I think he really did believe in his own powers of spirituality, but somewhere along the way, he had lost the fine line between God's will and his own.

I sat still and did not press the issue. I think my silence was sharper than anything I could have said, and I knew that he was intimidated. Fortunately for him, the phone rang, and he was saved any further humiliation for the time being.

Even Brother Bartholomew had a confession to make. One day when he was driving me to the church garage, he mentioned that he had ignorantly abused my father's generosity in years gone by, not realizing that our family was not wealthy. He'd taken money, time, and sometimes even the food right out of our mouths!—and now all he had to say was, "I'm sorry."

"I know that you children suffered because of it," he admitted, "but I was oblivious and just took your father's kindness for granted."

Again I said nothing. There was nothing to say. Those times were gone now.

๛

That weekend, my parents called the principal and asked special permission for me and my brother to meet them at Margaret's house. My aunt and her daughter were visiting from Israel and wanted to see us. Margaret had been ostracized from the church upon her marriage and my parents were still officially under the ban, but Daddy Raymond was pressed to the wall on this issue and he had to agree. He did not want to appear "the harsh Christian" in front of our Jewish relatives. The meeting was arranged in McKenley Park, a huge park in the center of Portfield.

My brother did not want to go, but he allowed me to take along his three-year-old son Raffy; and so the two of us set off on our adventure.

I had not seen my parents or been in contact with them for several years. I knew that they were still living in a mobile home in Cornwall, unable to afford a regular apartment after the church had dismissed them. My father was still preaching and doing odd jobs—gardening, painting, wallpapering—and my mother was still sewing and doing alterations. I had no idea how they were managing now that they had given up their pension, but I did not want to pry.

The visit was casual and quite pleasant. I was glad to see my parents and we got along nicely, although there was no real closeness between us. Our conversation remained very general. I knew that they had been deeply hurt by my decision to break with them and stay in Portfield, but they did not mention one word about it. Neither did I mention that I had made contact with a rabbi.

I also enjoyed meeting my Aunt Jacqueline and her daughter, both of whom spoke good English. Jacqueline's husband, my mother's brother Solomon, had passed away two years earlier and her friends had advised her to get away and travel a bit, so she'd come to England. She knew Raymond Webster; in fact, both my uncles had known him in Alexandria during the war, and he always visited their homes on his trips to Israel. Aunt Jacqueline had no idea, though, exactly what kind of institution he ran, and I suppose my ways and dress must have seemed a bit odd to her.

We ended up going home to Margaret's for a meal, and it was a very pleasant interlude. I told my teenage cousin that I had been learning Hebrew from a Linguaphone kit, and she helped me out with some tips which I greatly appreciated.

Toward the end of the afternoon, I plucked up enough courage to ask my mother for a copy of her birth and marriage certificates. "I would just like to have all the papers together," I explained. "I never know when I might need them." A practical hunch had prompted this request. I knew that if I ever did leave the college, there might be a number of circumstances in which I would need to prove my own Jewishness, and I didn't know when, if ever, I might see my parents again. My mother did not show any suspicion at all at the request. She was eager to please, and wanted to show her love for me in spite of my previous rejection, so she promised to send the papers out immediately.

The next day was Sunday. I had begun going to morning devotions again and spent time in prostration in a final hope that I would once again be able to contact Jesus, but the gates had thus far remained closed. However, I had never once allowed any of my doubts or "backsliding" to interfere in my work with the children at Bible school. I kept an enthusiastic demeanor toward them at all times, and they would literally cling to my fingers and skirt.

That morning I was playing a game with them in class when Sister

Bertha, the whiner who had so often complained of my "harsh" treatment of her, came prancing up to me. "I've just seen the roster. You're on open-airs this afternoon and you have to preach—*ner, ner, ner, ner, ner!*" she sang childishly. As an "insider," she was obviously aware that I was going through a rough time, and her words were an open taunt.

In fact, I was no longer actively preaching. I had only had to speak twice in the past three months, and on one occasion, I had done nothing more than rattle off a bunch of memorized verses. I knew the principal was trying to force a decisive reaction in me by putting me on the roster, but I preferred to cope with my situation in a quieter way, by giving myself time and working through the conflicts internally.

I looked Sister Bertha straight in the eye and said, "Well, I'm not preaching."

Taken aback by my sharp retort, she strutted off, singing over her shoulder, "Well, you have to—*ner, ner, ner, ner, ner!*" Sister Bertha was a public school teacher of about thirty-two years of age, but neither of those facts seemed to have any bearing on her behavior. She was a hopelessly insecure person who never managed to become a permanent staff member at the college because she never excelled at anything; and so she compensated with her loud voice and her stool-pigeoning for Daddy Raymond, whom she always referred to in a jealously sweet lilt as "*my* Daddy."

Would these people ever grow up?

As it turned out, my name was listed on the roster for open-airs, but I was relieved to find that Sister Bertha had made a mistake. The principal had not put me on preaching but on outreach, the simple task of speaking on an individual basis to any people who came to their doors and expressed an interest in our group. This was much less difficult, and I spent the outing quietly distributing copies of our children's Christian comics to all the young people who gathered around to listen.

I went to morning devotions every day that week and quietly pleaded with God to fill me with the peace I needed. But no answers came, only the same hollow echo in the inner chamber of my heart; and I knew that no great change would take place within me. I had made one enormous, last-ditch effort, but my intuition had been correct. This method of serving God was not working for me anymore. Why? I did not know. I felt that I did not understand anything at all anymore, and I had no idea what I would do.

✌ TWENTY-TWO ✌

O N Thursday, an envelope arrived from my mother with copies of all the official papers I had requested. She had also sent me a surprising gift of five pounds, something my parents had rarely ever done.

Friday evening arrived. Little did I know that this was the last time I would sit at dinner with these people. I remember exactly where I sat and with whom. We didn't talk much, just polite chatter. Had they realized that I would not be in the college much longer, our conversation would certainly have taken a different course, for three of the ministers sitting nearby were pastors whose job it was to insure that no sheep strayed from the "flock." For the time being, I sat quietly within the fold; somewhat distant, perhaps, deeply sad and very isolated, but my feelings were carefully disguised.

Sister Martha, the principal's secretary, called me into his office after the meal and showed me the order of service for the next day. I scanned down the list, looking for my name, and there it was again, next to last: "Joy, half an hour."

My heart sank. "Oh, God, help me!" I thought. How could I preach? And for half an hour! That was an excruciatingly long time when you had nothing to say! I felt a sense of desperation at being backed into a corner like this, and I was incensed at Daddy Raymond. I was still a minister of standing as far as the college was concerned, and he knew that I could not very well refuse to preach; it would be a scandalous flouting of authority.

Sister Bertha had also seen the list and was overly delighted that this time she had not made a mistake. I had really been put on the spot! She ran excitedly into the entrance hall where many of the young people were chatting, and announced with glee, "Joy's on preaching, Joy's on preaching!"

It didn't pay to make a scene. Silently I went into the lounge for the evening fellowship, but I was worried. What was I going to say? Maybe I could get around it. After all, the roster hadn't clearly stated "preaching," it had only given a time slot, and the rest was understood. Perhaps I could sing.... No! That was ridiculous. How could I sing for half an hour? And anyway, someone else was slated to do a solo right before me. Maybe I could read the Scriptures or learn part of them by heart. But that was absurd. I would never be able to memorize enough verses to last half an hour by the next afternoon. What else was there to do? A testimony, perhaps. In a way, I felt that was exactly what the principal really wanted, but what could I testify about? I was still in the valley.

The evening dawdled on until finally the principal motioned that it was time for evening prayers. We all stood up in the lounge and prayed together. I walked alone to my room, burdened and heavy of heart. In times past it had never been a problem to preach; in fact, I thoroughly enjoyed the incentive for extra study and was forever brimming over with ideas and real-life incidents to illustrate my thoughts. But tonight, everything was dead inside, all shutters down, all communications closed. I scanned my bookshelf in an effort to rekindle a waning light and took down several Bibles and study books: *New American Standard, King James, Amplified, Jerusalem, Young's Concordance, Bible History*. There had to be something I could say, but as the night progressed, I knew I was rapidly getting nowhere.

"Maybe I'm just tired," I encouraged myself. "I'll get up early in the morning and try again."

I don't recall having much of a conversation with my two roommates, but I do remember being very irritable and tense.

In the twilight hours of the morning, I was still lying awake in bed thinking, but every idea which sprang to mind seemed to contradict the previous one. "How can I take people from A to B when I'm on a merry-go-round myself?" I concluded in despair. I groped around within the blackness in my heart, but there was not one spark of enthusiasm, nothing. It was a total vacuum.

I marvel now that I was somehow able to cope with such a gruesome realization and to face the reality of failure so calmly. For months, I had been weighing the possibilities of leaving the college, but where could I go? And to do what? From infancy, my life had been directed toward the ministry, and I had spent nine concentrated years achieving that goal. How could I throw it all away—and so easily, too? The idea was totally absurd.

Nevertheless, in the early gray hours of the Sabbath morning, those distant thoughts were taking shape. I told myself that I mustn't rush into anything and rationally went over a list of options in my mind.

I could go to the service and not stand up when it was my turn, but that would be an open disgrace, a stain on the whole ministry. Thanks to Sister Bertha, the majority of the young people knew that I was scheduled to preach today, and if I didn't get up, the principal would be forced to punish me openly; otherwise, if he asked any of the young people in the future to do something, they could say, "Auntie Joy didn't do it, and she's a minister, so why should I?"

Another possibility was that Daddy Raymond would see that I was not moving, and he could very well stand up and announce, "*Now* we are going to hear from Sister Joy." Then I would have two alternatives. The more mature response would be to walk calmly to the pulpit and say, "I'm very sorry, but I waited on the heavenly Father and did not receive anything to share with you," and then go back to my place. The immature response would be simply to walk down the aisle of the church and out the main doors, as I had done once before. Somehow, neither of these two ideas was appealing.

Another option was to stay in my room and not attend the service at all. But that was no solution either, for surely at least half a dozen of the elderly women in the congregation would feel it their duty to seek me out, fall on their knees, and plead with me to repent and attend the service. No, I definitely couldn't face that.

And so, what next? I could leave the college temporarily and return in the evening. That wasn't such a bad idea, but it would have annoying results: lengthy discussions, repentance prayers, the casting out of evil spirits, all of which I'd been through so many times before. Only one option remained—to leave the college for good.

"If I'm going to leave, it has to be now," I reasoned. I was amazed at my calm and peaceful demeanor.

I immediately shifted into a practical gear and took a mental inventory of all the clothing I possessed. I would need to wear something warm, something that wouldn't crease easily and that looked as "normal" as possible; also, flat, sensible shoes in case I had to run. It wasn't too difficult to make a choice, for I didn't have a very large selection of presentable outfits.

Silently, I tiptoed across the room and dressed. I gathered together my toothbrush and toothpaste, my papers, and all the money I had— the five pounds my parents had just sent me. I had one cheese sandwich and a few green olives which I packed in a tupperware container. I put on my duffel coat, took one last look at my roommates, who were sleeping peacefully, and smiled to myself. I thought about leaving a note but decided against it. Never could they have imagined what was happening while they slumbered. The sun was just rising as I took a final glance out of the window. "If I have to sleep in the gutter or do any kind of menial task, I will do it," I resolved, "if that's what it will take to find the One True God."

I closed the door gently behind me and sped lightly down the stairs and out of the building. The college was totally dark; there was no movement anywhere, no lights shining. Hurriedly, I passed the gates and swept through the murky shadows of the slum streets. I was almost excited, and totally at peace.

I decided to go to the Administration Center, which was about a mile and a half away. Fortunately, I had the keys to the front door and several of the offices, and I knew that no one would be working in either of the buildings until Sunday morning. Just maybe no one would consider the possibility of searching for me there, and it was a chance worth taking. I had nowhere else to go, and I needed time to think. I knew I couldn't phone the rabbi on Saturday, and anyway I had only met him once for a couple of hours. Maybe he wouldn't want to be bothered with the problems of a runaway. I held not the slightest expectation from him to come to my aid.

I went upstairs to the attic of the main building and sat down on the floor, still toying with the idea of returning to the college in time for the service. I was on safe territory and had a few hours to make up my mind. Perhaps I could still think of something to preach, something that wouldn't contradict my experience, and then I could simply show up without anyone knowing of my previous intentions. Even if I missed the service altogether, I could still go back to the college in the evening and redeem myself. I would probably be "out of favor" for a while, but the damage would not be irreparable.

But morning turned into afternoon, and still I could not think of anything to say. Even after the service started, I was thinking that I could go in late and still be up on the platform in time for my slot. But the real dilemma, I realized, had nothing to do with preaching; what I was asking myself was, "Can you handle that whole scene?" And I knew I couldn't.

Evening descended upon the town, and the service ended. The sky turned black, the wind howled, and the rain crashed down from the sky amidst flashes of lightning and blasts of thunder. I remained crouched by the attic window, shivering from cold. I could not turn on the light, for it would arouse suspicion in the neighborhood.

Mice scratched around behind the cupboards, and I clutched my coat tightly around me. I was very hungry; I had been fasting along with everyone else in the college for the duration of Thursday and Friday, and the cheese sandwich and olives were the only food I'd had since then.

"Maybe I should phone the principal," I thought. "He'll be so happy to come and get me. All will be forgiven...." I had the feeling that I was ready to do that only because I was so tired and cold. I decided that if I still felt the same way in the morning, I would call him—but if not, I'd phone the rabbi.

Content with my decision, I lay down on the floor, and in the midst of praying to God that He would not let the mice run over me, I drifted into an exhausted slumber.

The storm passed with the dawn of the new day. Freshened somewhat from the few hours sleep, I realized that I had no desire at all to call the principal. Quickly, I leaped down the many flights of stairs to the ground floor to telephone the rabbi, only to find that he was out at morning services. His wife said that she could not page him on the beeper during prayer and that she did not know when he would be back, and besides they were leaving at noon to go to London for a few days. My heart sank. This was terrible! I had to get away, and fast—otherwise I was doomed.

I left my number and begged her to make sure he called me the minute he stepped into the house up until nine o'clock. While I waited, I retraced my steps in the building to make sure that I had left no mark whatsoever of my presence. The minutes ticked by. It was already five minutes to nine; by nine-thirty, Sister Victoria would arrive to work on her correspondence.

"Come on, Rabbi. Please, wherever you are, *come on*! Oh, God, let him call me," I silently begged.

The phone rang.

"What's wrong, Joy?" Rabbi Arkush asked softly. His voice was a ray of sunlight.

"I've run away."

"Good for you!" he shouted excitedly. "I'll come and pick you up. Where are you?"

"No, no," I explained, "you can't come here. I'm hiding out at the church's Administration Center, but I must leave right away. It's much too dangerous to stay around. I have just enough money for a ticket, but...I don't have anything," I added awkwardly.

"What do you mean, you don't have anything?"

I had no idea how to break the news that I had not brought anything with me except for the clothes I was standing in. Finally I said, "All I have is what I'm wearing."

"Oh, oh," he responded understandingly. "Don't worry about that. My wife will put some things together for you. Just come, and we'll sort everything out. I'll meet you at the Almington bus station. Give me two minutes and I will call you right back."

Those two minutes felt like eternity.

"Joy, do you know what an au pair is?" It was Rabbi Arkush again. "No."

"It's someone who takes care of children. There is a wonderful family in London who are waiting for an au pair to arrive from Europe. They have agreed to take you in for a while to look after their seven children. How about it?"

"Seven children? Well, I have taught children in the Sunday schools, I suppose I can handle it," I said warily. Little did I know that the eldest was only eight.

"Good! Just come!" Rabbi Arkush exclaimed excitedly.

With fumbling fingers, I ploughed through the phone book to find the number of the bus station. There was a bus leaving for Almington in twenty minutes. Two seconds later, I was tearing through the streets.

The air was still, the alleyway deserted and ghostly, except for a random vagrant or two sitting on a stoop; but the sun shone brightly, too brightly for comfort. I had only twenty minutes to cover more than two miles. As I lifted my flowing skirts and flew along, each foot screamed, "Faster, faster, faster!" My heart panicked and I cried silently, "Dear God, *please* don't let anyone see me now!"

I thought of the ultimate nightmare: being caught by the college students on their way to pick up children for Bible school. I should have been out with them this morning, making my own rounds! For this reason, I was careful to run on the right side of the road, facing the oncoming traffic, so that no one would be able to stop right next to me and forcibly drag me into his vehicle. The fear of being caught gripped my heart, but the pushing from within strengthened me, and I quickened my pace. Over a wall, across two fields, and—thank God—I was nearly at the bus station.

As I ran under the shelter, everyone stopped to have a look at me, for I was an intriguing sight. Perspiration trickled down my beet-red face, and my long brown hair had escaped its tight bun, and was straggling wildly in all directions. I was panting and gasping for breath like a hunted animal looking for refuge in the crevice of a rock or furrow, and that's exactly how I felt.

My conscience was screaming at me, "You can go back now. It's not too late. There's still time! You can repent."

The bathroom attendant was absently singing the words of a well-known hymn that sent a dart into my heart: "Amazing grace, how sweet the sound that saved a wretch like me." I stood there dazed, and still as a stone, but deep inside, a silent voice was calling me forward. There could be no turning back now.

It was the greatest good fortune that I had the five pounds my parents had sent me, or I would never have been able to get away. I purchased a ticket to Almington, which was sixty miles away, about a two-and-a-half-hour ride; and before I knew it, I was aboard the bus and we were slowly pulling away.

I sat back and tried to relax. Gradually my heartbeat slowed down and I was able to catch my breath, and within a few minutes I was thoroughly enjoying the journey. Once out of the city, the bus wended its way through luscious green meadows, past golden corn-fields awaiting harvest, over tiny village bridges. The sun rippled playfully through the streams that bubbled beneath us. It was an intoxicatingly beautiful day.

It was hard to imagine that to the elderly ladies we passed gossiping on the country roads, and to the young couple sauntering along beneath the trees, it was just a normal day. The gentleman sitting behind me who was blowing his cigarette smoke into my hair, the West Indian lady in the seat across from me who rustled among her multitude of packages—they knew nothing of my daring escapade. I had finally jumped off the cliff into uncharted territory, and not a soul in the world knew. I was alone. I thought about it often as we bumped along, but strangely enough, I was not afraid. I was at peace within.

As we pulled into the Almington bus station, I looked anxiously for Rabbi Arkush. Thank God, he was there! Just as I was heading for the shelter, my heart stopped beating; the first person boarding the bus back to Portfield was a woman from the congregation. I put my head down and ran in front of the bus and onto the road. Rabbi Arkush was walking slowly up and down, keeping his eye out for me and peacefully smoking his pipe. I bounded up to him.

"Rabbi Arkush, quickly," I called, "*run!*"

Once we were in the safety of his car, he said with a smile, "Excited? You must be!"

I searched inside myself. No, I definitely was not excited; more numb than anything else. I sat quietly, and he tried again to make conversation.

"My wife is looking forward to meeting you," he offered as we pulled onto the road.

I looked down at my crumpled clothing. "Rabbi Arkush," I whispered, "I feel like a cross between a tramp and Mrs. Noah!"

He laughed heartily. Within five minutes, we were outside his house, and the door was opened wide by a smiling lady. She sat me down without ceremony in the living room and brought me tea and cakes.

"Thank you, but I'm not at all hungry," I lied. Actually I was starving. I'd had only one decent meal in three days, but I was much too shy to eat anything. I took a few sips of the tea, but my hands were shaking so much I spilled most of it in the saucer, and ten minutes later we were on our way again.

Rabbi Arkush had already arranged for me to stay for two weeks with the Weinbaum family in London, so that I could experience Orthodox Judaism. The timing was very convenient as he was on his way to London to visit his in-laws; and so I piled into the car along with his wife and two children, and we set off for the seventy-mile drive. As we sped along, I marveled at the bit of providence that had pushed me to phone him from the college in the nick of time. If I had waited any longer, he would already have left for London with his family. God only knows what I would have done then.

Surely He was still guarding me.

I felt as though I were in a whirlwind, a spinning carousel of unreality. Houses, trees, colors whipped past the windows in a blur, and they all seemed to belong to another world. Was this me in the car, going to London to stay with a strange Jewish family, or was I imagining it? Oddly, I felt no sense of personal loss at all about leaving the college, only a pang of remorse at having abandoned the children. I thought of them clinging to my skirts and realized that they would be waiting eagerly for "Auntie Joy" to come to Bible school that day, and would suffer terrible disappointment. I tried hard to push that picture out of my head. I could not go back now.

We drew to a halt outside a large and beautiful home in Hampstead Garden Suburbs, one of the most affluent neighborhoods in London. No sooner had the rabbi announced, "We're here," than an exuberant, dark-haired young woman came running out to the car.

"Come in, come in, you must be very tired," Sandy Weinbaum said cheerfully. She looked very young, in fact, not much older than me. I smiled and followed silently, still in a daze.

"This is my husband, Binnum," she said as a friendly-looking gentleman came into the front hall. I put out my hand like a polite English girl, but he only smiled kindly and said, "We don't shake hands."

I hastily apologized and followed Mrs. Weinbaum up to the room that had been prepared for me. Relief swept over me, for I had the room to myself. I closed the door quietly and stood motionless. What a day it had been! "God help me," was all I could think.

About ten minutes later, Rabbi Arkush knocked on the door. "Joy, are you all right? We're going now, but don't worry—you'll be fine. I'll phone tomorrow to see how you are."

I raced to the door. "*Going*? You can't go. Please don't leave me!" I pleaded. Didn't he realize he was the only person I had in the world now?

He laughed warmly. "Don't worry. You're in very good hands, and you can call me whenever you like."

"Rabbi Arkush, why didn't Mr. Weinbaum shake my hand? Is it because he's not sure I'm Jewish, or is it because I come from a Christian background?"

He laughed again and assured me it was simply because Orthodox men and women had no physical contact outside of marriage. "See, you've been here only a few minutes, and you've learned something already," he said with a smile; and the next minute he was gone.

I withdrew into the shelter of my room and stood looking out the window at the rolling green garden that lay peacefully below me. It was hard to believe the distance I'd traveled in such a short time. Little did I know it, but I'd crossed an ocean.

I sat down on the edge of the bed and tried to relax. The room was equipped with everything I needed—sink, wardrobe, dressing table, pretty light shade and fitted carpet, as well as the large picture window with the charming view.

I was petrified.

After a few more minutes, there was a gentle knock on the door.

"Hello, my name is Chana Feiga," came a sweet young voice. "My mother said if you need anything you should let us know."

"Thank you," I replied softly.

Half an hour later there was another light tap at the door.

"Hello," said another young voice, this time a boy's. "My name is Shmaryahu. My mother says to ask you if there's anything you need."

"Thank you very much, I'm fine," I replied, amused but still too uncomfortable to accept the offer.

After yet another little messenger had been sent to determine whether or not I had evaporated from the room, I decided it was time to venture downstairs. I washed and changed into Rabbi Arkush's wife's clothes which happened to be far too big. There was no help for it; this was the best I could do for now.

I heard voices coming from the kitchen and headed downstairs. The children crowded around me like a miniature battalion, eyeing me suspiciously. I smiled at them as they told me their names: Chani, Shmaryahu, Ettel, Sorah, Rivkah Henia, Nechoma Dina and Yehuda Leib. I was *sure* I would never remember them. I couldn't even say them. Where did they get these names from?

They warmed up a bit and asked me *my* name, and a barrage of questions followed. Where had I come from? How old was I? I tried as best I could to parry some of the questions and befriend the children at the same time. In the midst of this hurricane welcome, a huge tin of chocolate cake somehow materialized on the table in front of me, but even though my stomach growled mercilessly, I couldn't eat. I was too shy to have anything more than a glass of water. Sandy Weinbaum handed me an envelope from Rabbi Arkush containing a short note and ten pounds. I was silently grateful, though a little embarrassed.

The family tried to put me at ease, asking me a ton of questions to get me to talk. I appreciated the attempt, but I was totally disoriented. I had no idea what to say or even think.

Later in the afternoon, I realized that Rabbi Arkush had indeed been busy behind the scenes, and that he was looking after me in more ways than one. He'd arranged for a skilled anti-missionary worker to come visit me. Rabbi Yitzchok Sufrin was a very kindhearted and intelligent man, and as he sat at the dining room table and chatted with me, I was relieved to find that I could express myself to him about my background without fear of consequences. This was only the first of many occasions when he would sit and listen patiently to my confused and frightened talk of fire and brimstone, the Second Coming, and a thousand other points of Christian doctrine. By the time he left it was well into the evening, and I was glad to have a suitable excuse to retire.

The next day, I busied myself trying to help Sandy out around the house. I felt awkward and did not know what else I should be doing. It turned out that my judgment about Sandy had been right; she was only two years older than me, but she seemed worlds away—confident, bright and talkative, settled in her family, in her religion, in her community. I felt like an ignorant street urchin.

She tried to make pleasant small talk during the morning and mentioned her involvement in a newly formed local Jewish organization. I inquired politely about the nature of this new club. "It's a service organization geared toward children," Sandy explained. "We want them to be involved in creative religious activities and to feel that they are in *Hashem*'s army, so to speak."

"Oh, can I join?" I asked enthusiastically.

She laughed and said, "You're in it already. All Jews are part of it."

I smiled, wondering to myself if I really was a Jew.

Sandy's children were playing a record on the stereo that sent a shock down my spine, for the words that I heard strangely echoed my situation. The singers were a Jewish folk duo called "*Megama*," and their song never ceased to haunt me:

> *Dear God, here I am, asking for another day,*
> *I want to change my life right now,*
> *Learn to live Your ways.*
> *Dear God, here I am, calling myself a Jew.*
> *I can fool my friends and my neighbors*
> *But there ain't no foolin' You.*

I knew there was no fooling God, and it worried me enormously. We had been cautioned all our lives in the Church not to go "after the lusts of our hearts," to do only what God wanted us to do. Perhaps this yearning for the Jews was only a "lust" of my heart that I had followed heedlessly, turning a blind eye to my responsibilities as a minister, and to the gutter children starving for attention whom I had left behind.

Besides the guilt, I lived in a pool of torment about whether God accepted me as a Jew or not. If He didn't, my reckless escapade had been totally wasted.

❧ TWENTY-THREE ❧

BY Friday morning, I learned that Raymond Webster was looking for me. He had cleverly put a few facts together, one of which was the slip I had made months earlier in Almington, when I had told Minister Markham and his wife that I wanted to contact a rabbi. Webster happened to have a Jewish podiatrist who had pictures of sagely rabbis hanging on the walls of his office, so he called this doctor and asked him if he happened to know of any rabbis in the Almington vicinity. The podiatrist replied proudly that his very own nephew was a rabbi in Almington—none other than Rabbi Arkush himself!

Webster immediately phoned Almington and found that he had stumbled on the right track. He told Rabbi Arkush that he was "like an uncle" to me and was very worried about me. "What shall I tell her parents?" he wanted to know. Rabbi Arkush told him only that I was safe, and then he called to ask me how much information I wanted to divulge.

I was tremendously afraid of the mental and emotional pressure the principal would subject me to, and told Rabbi Arkush that I preferred to be left alone to work out my feelings. I certainly did not want my address given out. At the same time, I felt isolated and bewildered, for in the act of putting Webster off my trail, it seemed I had burned a bridge behind me that could never be repaired.

"Dear God, what have I done?" I cried inside. "Whatever made me do such a stupid thing? I've ruined my whole life!"

The children had been in the midst of giving me a detailed and cheerful explanation of the procedure for lighting *Shabbos* candles, but I excused myself from the kitchen hubbub and disappeared upstairs to the safety of my room. "I'm not going to light a candle this evening," I decided. "I'm not going to do anything. I'm just going to have Sandy tell the children that I don't feel well, and I'll stay in my room the whole *Shabbos*. I've made a mistake. I must get back to the college somehow."

After a while, I managed to collect myself. I reasoned that since I was already here, I might as well go along with the idea. "I'll stick it out for another week," I told myself, "and then I'll know for sure that there is nothing in it. This Jewish business will be out of my system, and then I can go back to the college with a free heart, and be a good Christian minister."

Satisfied with my decision, I trekked back downstairs, figuring that I would light the candle after all.

"Would you like to take a shower now and wash your hair?" Sandy inquired.

"It's all right," I said, taking a look around the kitchen, which was still in an untidy state. "I don't mind helping you a bit more." I planned to take a long hot bath after *Shabbos* came in and things had settled down a bit.

The minutes ticked by, and Sandy asked me again, "Are you *sure* you don't want to take a shower? The bathroom is empty now—it's really no problem."

She must have thought I was a dirty little pup! "No, thank you, it's quite all right," I answered politely.

We were still pottering around the kitchen, taking care of a dozen odd jobs, when Sandy finally declared, "Okay, children, time to light candles."

Excitement filled the air as little people came running from all directions to congregate in the dining room.

"Well, I don't think much of this," I said to myself. "How can I light a candle? I'm still in my dirty clothes, and we've worked right up until the last minute! And this is a religious home?" In the college, we'd always stopped work completely an hour before sunset on Fridays to have time to unwind. We'd change into our good clothes and sing soft songs, slowly entering the *Shabbos* spirit. There was a conscious effort to separate ourselves from the physical environment and to enter a state of spirituality. The abrupt change in this household did not suit me at all. How did they expect to truly prepare for the *Shabbos* in a split second?

I followed Sandy into the dining room and was amazed to see the transformation that had taken place under my nose. I had not been into the room all day. The table was extended, draped with a beautiful white linen tablecloth, and set with gleaming china and silver. Dotting the settings were several embroidered velvet covers which hid loaves of freshly baked bread.

So *that's* what that oblong cover was for! I remembered with a twinge of surprise the one my mother had brought me from Israel so many years ago. I had left it behind in the college decorating the back of my chair.

The sideboard was covered with silver candelabras and candlesticks. The children scrambled on and off the chairs, taking turns saying the blessing over their candles and lighting them. Sandy pointed to the candle that was to be mine, and the children argued over who would help me say the blessing. Sandy instructed me to wave my hands three times over the light and then cover my eyes until I'd finished the blessing. In embarrassment, I repeated the meaningless and strange-sounding words as best I could.

"Good *Shabbos*," she said then, and kissed me on the cheek. I smiled gently. So little ceremony, so little intensity—the Jews did nothing more than light a candle, and they had *Shabbos*! Very odd.

"Well, finally, *Shabbos* has arrived! Is it all right if I take a shower and wash my hair now?" I asked.

Sandy looked at me open-mouthed. "I'm sorry, but I thought you understood. We don't do that on *Shabbos*. That's why I asked you beforehand if you wanted to wash your hair."

I was devastated. Why hadn't someone *told* me? I couldn't believe this. I was filthy! Sandy had encouraged me during the week to let my hair down, as it wasn't customary for single girls in the community to wear buns on top of their heads, and I had done so. But my hair was extremely long, for strict Christian women never had their hair cut, and now it dangled around me in limp strands. There was no way I was going to spend the next twenty-five hours walking around like that!

I stomped up the stairs, grumbling to myself that I was going to take a shower anyway. It wasn't *my* fault—they should have explained it, and if they thought I was going to set foot out of the house with my hair reeking down the block, they had better think again, and....

I was so angry! Images of the Jewish women in the Portfield congregation flashed through my mind, and it dawned on me that I would have to face another crowd of fancy Jews in the synagogue the next morning. I thought of them, all dressed up in the latest fashions, inching away from me in disgust as I sat there with dirty hair in my frumpy borrowed clothes that were two sizes too large. My father's words rang in my ears: "First impressions are very important!"

"I can't, I can't," I screamed inside. "I just can't! This is awful. Oh, God...." My eyes filled with tears.

As I opened the door I stood back, somewhat startled. I couldn't go in. Something was in that room....

Peace. The room was filled with a peace so thick you could touch it. I stood still for a moment, and then I noticed that the whole house was filled with this peace. I remained motionless on the landing for a while, allowing the storm to calm within.

God was in this home. In twenty-five years, I had never sensed His presence so strongly.

"I only lit a candle!" I whispered to myself. I knew beyond a shadow of a doubt that God was really with these people, these religious Jews tied to "ancient, dead traditions"—these people who were supposed to be living in bondage!

They didn't need quiet meditation, they didn't need to unwind and enter into the "Sabbath spirit." It was as though they were saying, "We don't have to leave the world or change spheres. We can have God right here." They could be hectically busy right up until the last minute—and then all they had to do was light a candle, and suddenly the whole house was transformed into a blissful haven of rest. I sensed instinctively that there was more spirituality in their simple action than in trying desperately to "contact" God through fasting and prostration—because He'd been here all along.

I was absolutely astounded.

I didn't want to wash my hair anymore. I didn't want to take a shower. I would go to the synagogue just as I was; it didn't matter anymore. I felt God was embracing me in that room, and I didn't want to let go of His clutches or do anything at all that would disturb this peace.

I also felt then that I would do anything I had to do, suffer any torment, to find this God of the Jews.

The formalities of *Shabbos* were a little bewildering, but everyone in the family was helpful and patient, and they did their best to explain. I clumsily stumbled through all the alien rituals at the meals like a bull lumbering through a china shop; the *kiddush*, handwashing, dipping the *challah* in salt. The children explained to me that the *challos* had sesame seeds sprinkled on them because they resembled the *mon* that God had given the Jews to eat in the desert, and that they were covered before *kiddush* so as not to embarrass them in front of the wine, whose blessing came first.

The table stretched the entire length of the dining room, accommodating not only the Weinbaums, but also Sandy's parents, the Raders, who lived around the corner and were almost constantly in the house, as well as a number of other guests. The meal was lively and merrily chaotic, with much singing and an abundance of excellent food.

Little Shmaryahu Weinbaum, who was seven years old, got up and recited the *Chumash* he had learned that week in three languages. I began to feel smaller and smaller, sensing the enormity of the gulf that lay between me and my past life, between me and any future life. I knew the Bible inside and out, and yet here was a seven year old who could recite verses in three languages, and who seemed to understand them better than I ever had.

One of the children sat next to me during the Grace after Meals, or *benching*, as they called it, and pointed out the place to me in a little booklet. The English translation was printed on the left-hand side, but I didn't say anything, only followed along politely.

There were few occasions in my life that had been more humbling. In a matter of hours, I had gone from my status as a respected and powerful minister, who had held hundreds of people spellbound in my sermons, to being *nothing*. I found myself back at square one. My clothing was strange, my speech was strange, my ideas were foreign, and there was no mistaking the odd looks I received from more than one person over the next few months, questioning my normalcy, and even my Jewishness. I would have to start all over again and learn everything from scratch, like a child, and I prayed that God would give me the strength to see it through.

I braced myself for another ordeal in the synagogue the next morning, but was pleasantly surprised. It was nothing at all like the synagogue in Portfield, either in appearance or in atmosphere. In fact, the building itself was nothing more than a converted school room, and I did not see any pressure or formality at all.

A few women were there with their daughters, and they sat quietly the entire morning and prayed. There was no chattering, no distractions. Sandy had stayed home with the baby, so the older Weinbaum girls had brought me, and they patiently pointed out the place to me in the *Siddur* and *Chumash*. I liked the singing and I liked hearing the Torah being read, even though I did not understand anymore than I had in Portfield.

I felt quite scruffy, and was very embarrassed by my dirty hair and shapeless clothing, but, surprisingly, no one stared at me. In fact, the women were quite friendly, and some of them even came up after the service to say hello and ask me my name. I was somewhat taken aback by this and also very relieved; and the rest of the day passed fairly smoothly.

On *Motzei Shabbos*, Rabbi Sufrin came to visit me again from his home in the Stamford Hill neighborhood of London, this time bringing his wife. He impressed me again as a warm, fatherly person with a straightforward manner and a great deal of energy. I learned that anti-missionary activity was only a small part of his work. He did a great deal of traveling for his organization called "Friends of the Small Communities," visiting towns in the south of England which had no more than a handful of Jews, and giving classes there. Apparently, Rabbi Arkush had put me on his itinerary, for he continued to visit me regularly all the time I was in the Weinbaums' home.

That evening, we discussed many topics at length, most of which were initiated by the rabbi, for I found myself so simple in the knowledge of Jewish matters that even though I was eager to learn, I had no idea even of what to ask.

The *Shabbos* experience had given me a lot of confidence, and I no longer had the frantic desire to return to the college that had sent me into turmoil on Friday morning.

For the rest of the second week, I mostly helped Sandy around the house and assisted with some of the paperwork that was involved in getting the new youth organization off the ground. Even though I did not understand much of what I was doing, I was glad to be kept busy, and Sandy did her utmost to make me feel comfortable. Once she even asked me if there was any type of food that I missed. I answered simply, "Bread and cheese," not realizing at the time that kosher cheese in England was prohibitively expensive, which explained its absence from the Weinbaum refrigerator. Sandy made no mention of this, but immediately ran out to buy a package of cheese and made me a delicious cheese sandwich on the spot.

Such gestures impressed me deeply, especially since no one had ever done things like that at the college, and in spite of my awkwardness in the household, I felt drawn toward the Weinbaums' lifestyle. I wondered what would happen when my adventure was over, and I did not have long to find out.

I felt like a weed in a flower bed, but I had become quite friendly with the children when Sandy approached me.

"Don't worry," she said, "I know you have nowhere to go and I want you to feel settled. I will not put you out onto the street. If you would like to take the position of au pair, you are welcome to stay with us."

I certainly could not turn down such an opportunity. Besides, I really had nowhere else to go; returning to the college was no longer a practical option.

When the arrangements had been settled, Sandy suggested casually that I could start out by helping to make the children's breakfast in the morning.

Immediately I froze. "Oh, God, no," I thought. "Anything but breakfast!" It had been nine long years since the breakfast catastrophe in the college when I had burnt half the food, but the shame and bitterness of the entire incident welled up inside me with a fresh intensity. I could see Sister Martha's nasty leer and feel Mother's fingernails digging into my arm.

"No, please," I blurted out in panic, "not breakfast. Please don't ask me to do that, if you don't mind."

Sandy looked rather startled at my bluntness, and, of course, she hadn't the slightest idea what had prompted such a nervous reaction. After a moment, she ventured, "But it's only cold cereal. You just pour it into a bowl."

I felt quite silly. "Oh, in that case, it's no problem," I said with relief. As far as I can remember, that was the only momentary hitch in the plan, and I was soon settled into a regular routine. With seven children—the oldest eight and a half years old—the household was understandably hectic and the work never-ending. The children learned to trust me very quickly, and I soon became indispensable to them. I was up at six-thirty in the morning and had them on the bus by eight, after which there was laundry and cleaning up to do; then in the evening, I would help with dinner and get the children bathed and into pajamas, and afterward, their father would come in to read them a story and say *Shema* with them.

The children had strong personalities and were quite verbal, right down to little two-year-old Dini, who would hop into my bed in the morning and chant, "Tova Weinbaum, get me dressed!" (She assumed I was an inherited family member.) There was never a dull moment with this clan, and they had their own individual methods of getting attention. These ranged from little Etty's strategy of lying on the floor across doorways, waiting for someone to pick her up, which she ingeniously devised from the knowledge that no one in the house ever stepped over a person because of the "evil eye," to the nightly collective demand for "just one more story." The children loved their picture books filled with tales of righteous sages, and it seemed that I was forever being clambered upon, and tugged at, by endless little pairs of hands and feet.

But the truth is that although I was taking care of them, they were taking care of me in a different way. In their own totally ingenuous manner, they helped me to adjust to life in a religious community, from Chani, the eldest, who at only eight years of age was an excellent guide in *shul*, to Shmaryahu, who would patiently and sweetly explain to me everything he'd learned in school that day. Even the baby adored me and made me feel comfortable.

With the adults, this feeling of acceptance did not come as easily. I knew they were aware of my odd story, and perhaps they were not even quite sure I was Jewish. Rabbi Arkush had told the Weinbaums that my mother was Jewish, but everything about me belied that fact; I did not look Jewish, and I did not even speak the same language they did. Whenever the subject of religion came up, I found myself speaking in terms of the "heavenly Father," the "holy spirit" and the "Scriptures"; and there was no mistaking the skeptical glances I received on more than one occasion.

My housewarming with Jewish observance was equally slow, a process through which I tiptoed with a great deal of caution. I had come to find out about Judaism, but I did not walk into the Weinbaums' home and start doing *mitzvos* without further ado. I had made up my mind that no one was going to tell me what to do until I was really sure that it was the right thing for me, and until I was ready to take it on. I wasn't about to simply shed my old skin and "believe" something new. The very word "believe" gave me an oppressive feeling in my stomach.

For the first few weeks, I mainly observed the doings in the household and occasionally participated. Sandy and Binnum politely explained all their practices to me, but they did not pressure me or react with hysteria if I made a mistake.

Binnum was a dentist by profession but a teacher by nature, and quite a passionate one. His subject was Judaism, and his students were any Jews who had the slightest interest in their heritage. He was involved in several educational and outreach programs, and this activity took up most of his spare time. In the London area, there were several rabbinic authorities whom the Weinbaums consulted, but a rabbi in America, whose picture hung in the living room, was their mentor. He was referred to as the "Lubavitcher Rebbe," or simply as "the Rebbe." One of Binnum's pet projects was the Hebrew language, and he began to teach me the *aleph-bais* almost as soon as I arrived. My experience with Linguaphone had provided an excellent background, and within a month, I could read and say *Shema*.

After the first week, he introduced me to the *mitzvah* of washing my hands with a cup in the morning, and other practices followed slowly. I had no idea how much I was absorbing until I was standing in the bathroom one morning with my toothbrush in my hand. I was just about to put it into my mouth when I thought, "Oh, no, I forgot to wash *negel vasser!*" Then I thought, "But I'm too tired. Never mind, I can't be bothered with that."

But I couldn't brush my teeth. I just stood there for a few moments, and then I realized I wasn't going to get anyplace unless I washed my hands. I was shocked that it really meant something to me. It had sunk in almost by osmosis, very slowly and innocently, without the painful pressure of "believing" that had always been launched at us in the college, without any wrenching of the insides; just a series of simple actions. Amazing.

Cultural adjustment was much more stressful. The issue of clothing was still horribly embarrassing for me, as I possessed nothing but the few outsized garments that Mrs. Arkush had given me, but Sandy was able to round up a few other outfits. She tried quietly to convince me that my skirts did not need to reach the floor and that it was all right to wear more conventional clothing. I was encouraged to lift up my head a little, and to leave my hair down, for I was always tempted to scrape it back into the tight bun I was so accustomed to, and after a while I began to look a bit less like a "weed." But my shyness was more difficult to overcome, and it took me about six weeks before I could look Binnum in the eye when I spoke to him and call him by his first name. At the college, we had been strongly discouraged from looking a man in the eye.

I did not even like to go outside the house, for the neighborhood was extremely wealthy and exclusive, and I was very self-conscious about my borrowed clothing and flat, clumpy, lace-up shoes. It only served to intensify my sense of not belonging, and my fear in general of tackling the outside world, and Sandy had to literally push me out the door once a week to order the fruits and vegetables for *Shabbos.*

The lady at the fruit shop once phoned Sandy to ask her if I had come to London after a broken love affair, as I always looked so sad.

"Well, I suppose you could say that," Sandy answered with a chuckle, and she was not so far wrong. It *had* been a love affair, broken after a lifetime of commitment. It would take me a much longer time than I expected to get over it.

❧

Rosh Hashanah was upon us in the blink of an eye. What astonished me most about it was the sound of the *shofar*—not at all the sophisticated silver trumpet tones that I had imagined, but instead a raw blast that hit you squarely in the heart. There was something so solid and direct about it, as though Judaism were saying, "This is the way it is— no trappings, no frills, nothing extra. This is everything you need." The Jews did not need to contrive their "holiness" or to adorn themselves with "spirituality," for their observance itself, in its simplicity, was innately holy.

I was not, however, prepared for the extent of the bizarre activity that I witnessed over the next few weeks. The *Shabbos* meals and the synagogue were more or less what I had expected, but I had no idea that Jews engaged in such weird practices. The idea of emptying our pockets of sins, and throwing them to the fish in the river, seemed absurd, but that was mild in comparison to what happened next.

A few days before *Yom Kippur*, several live chickens were brought in and housed in the garage. Binnum tried to explain to me that we would use them to perform a ceremony in which our sins would be transferred to the chickens' heads, but this preposterous discourse far outreached my understanding. After several malodorous trips to the garage to collect food from the freezer, I was relieved when *Erev Yom Kippur* arrived and the chickens finally made their debut.

To my shock, Sandy somehow mustered up the nerve to stand on a chair in the back yard and wave one of them in the air over her head! I had absolutely no intention of parking myself beneath a live, swinging bird, and so I slipped away to my room and watched the proceedings from the window.

I was not too concerned about fasting; I had done it often enough in the college, although never without water, and of course I had always brushed my teeth and taken a shower. But I was sure I would manage. The most impressive sight came at the advent of the holy day, when I watched an entire community of grown men float through the dusk dressed in eighteenth-century white cotton nightshirts, carrying candles in their hands, as though on their way to a séance! I was a bit embarrassed at having to walk through the streets of London in bedroom slippers, but no one else seemed to share my discomfort, and once I got over the shock of the whole scene, the day passed without problem.

I spent most of the time in the synagogue trying to pick out my Hebrew name in the *machzor* and thinking about the Jewish method of repentance. How different it was from the way I had always been taught! In the Church, there was only one way to atone: believe in Jesus. But the Jews had so many ways to get rid of sins—every week a new one. First they threw their sins to the fish in the river, then they swung live, squawking birds over their heads, and then they marched to the synagogue in ghostly outfits and spent the entire day fasting and praying. The Jews were so inventive!

I did not understand much of what happened in the service that day, and at times was bored, but I had a feeling of deep satisfaction at having finally observed *Yom Kippur* in the correct way.

Immediately after Binnum finished his meal on *Motzei Yom Kippur*, he dashed out to the garage and began rummaging through boxes of old toys, bicycles, and other junk. Finally he emerged with boards for the "*succah*" and stacked them at the back of the house.

Over the next few days, I watched the *succah* take shape with great interest, and was equally amazed to see the *lulav* and *esrog*. My imagination could never have conjured up anything quite like them, and it was difficult in particular to see this wart-ridden lemon as beautiful.

The wind howled and spat forth icy droplets when *Erev Succos* arrived. Binnum's *succah* was finally completed and was busy holding its own against the bitter blasts when the telephone rang. The caller was a less fortunate neighbor whose *succah* had been flattened to the ground by the wind. Binnum, Sandy and the children immediately went across the street to offer their services to the distressed family while I remained in the warm shelter of the house with the babies.

As I sat down, sipping a steaming mug of coffee, I stared through the kitchen window at Binnum's sturdy and spacious *succah*. It had become increasingly hard to believe that I was still living in England and had not been magically whisked away to an unknown planet. I was still totally bewildered. I had no idea what would happen next, but after the chickens, anything seemed possible.

They were strange people, these Jews. So refined, so cultured, so *English*—and yet they did outrageous things, like taking dirty birds into their homes and swinging them in the air, building little sheds and keeping house in them for a week in the nastiest weather, and paying a fortune for a pair of ordinary tree branches and a lemon with warts, which they cared for as lovingly and tenderly as if they were made of gold! There were no open manifestations of peace or spirituality in any of these doings, but that didn't seem to bother them in the least. They went about their tasks with a natural tranquility, totally secure. It seemed almost like a great musical presentation with magnificent harmonies and arrangements that everyone was "tuned" into—everyone except me, for I was tone deaf.

Eyes streaming from the cold, faces red and radiant, the family soon came home triumphant. The *succah* had been rebuilt, and the children were cheering about the "big *mitzvah*" they had performed, for without their help the neighbor would never have managed to accomplish the feat in time for the holiday. The children danced and jumped, alive with the excitement that was in the air. They had good news to tell their friends that night at *shul*.

Within a few hours, we were wrapping ourselves in thick layers of clothing and warm woolen cardigans as we made our way in to the *succah* to hear *kiddush*. The candles fought to retain their strength against the wind, and the pleasant fragrance of the green branches above our heads mingled with the sweet aroma of the wine. I shivered from cold, but I was calm. There was actually nothing very odd or difficult to digest about the *succah*, and if it rained, I knew we could go inside.

Sandy's parents were with us as always. Her mother's sweet borscht was too foreign for my Anglicized taste buds, and the smell of the kasha I found nauseating, but my nine years of training at the college had served me well; I cleared my plate and graciously thanked my hosts for the delicious meal. By the end of the week, I was adept at shaking the *lulav* and reciting the blessing, and I was even beginning to enjoy the festival when *Simchas Torah* arrived.

Binnum and Sandy always held a party for the entire synagogue in their home and this year was to be no exception. The proceedings began in the synagogue, and it was well into the night before the guests began making their way to the Weinbaum residence. Once again, I was astonished at the Jewish approach to the service of God. Having come from a strict puritanical background, it was hard enough to accept the idea that people could smoke and still be religious, but never in a million years could I have imagined what I witnessed on *Simchas Torah*.

As I peeked through the door into the men's section, my mouth dropped open in amazement, for many of the men were totally drunk. Some were lying across the tables, spilling cups of brandy and other strong drinks, while others careened around the room, singing and laughing and having a jolly old time. From time to time, someone stood up to make a *"l'chaim"* or to give over a *dvar Torah*. This was considered the height of the holiday, but it dumbfounded me. Sandy tried to explain that throughout the entire year the men were very restrained in their handling of alcohol, but twice a year they had a chance to "relax," and to use their drinking as a way of expressing their joy of Torah.

I thought back to the times when my father had gone "pubbing" in Greenborough when I was small. He had never allowed us to come inside on these trips, so I had never seen anyone really roaring drunk before, but I had a friend whose parents owned a pub, and her stories echoed in my head. The men used to drink "meth," or methylated spirits, a liquor so strong it was almost like kerosene, and then they would go home after a night of carousing and beat up their wives. I remembered one older woman in particular who used to come to the church black and blue every week.

But the Jews weren't like that at all. There was no trace of violence about them, no vulgarity. They were relaxed and joyous, their singing was heartfelt, they spun giddily in rapturous circles with their arms around each other's shoulders. There was love of all kinds in that unruly meleé—love of Torah, love of God, love of community—and yet it was all so foreign to me.

By the early hours of the morning, I was numb mentally and physically. My body moved mechanically to help Sandy clean up the mess, but I was asleep on my feet.

"Well, what do you think of this whole experience of *Tishrei*, Tova?" asked the *Zeidie* of the family in a kindly tone.

"It was fine, thank you," I replied politely. I was still too closed to take in a completely new understanding of worship, too held in to open up and explain what was going on inside me—if I even knew at this point.

"You know," *Zeidie* continued, "you're a very lucky girl!"

I smiled softly. I wanted to believe him, but in reality I didn't think of myself as lucky.

I was beginning to feel angry with God. Why had He brought me here, of all places? What about the Jews in the synagogue in Portfield? They were supposedly Orthodox, but they did not behave like this. They seemed so much more normal. I knew for a fact that the majority of them drove their cars or took public transportation to the *Shabbos* day services, and in the afternoon, they either watched television or went to the football stadium. They were still Jews, I argued to myself, and I was sure their overall way of life could not be as extreme as *this*! Why couldn't God have taken me to that kind of community?

I felt so angry, so lost, and so totally trapped; and on top of everything, I felt guilty for not bubbling over with happiness. Hadn't I begged God to let me be with the Jews? Now I was here. They were friendly, warm, generous beyond measure, and they had opened their arms and accepted me. Sandy was at a loss to understand why I always seemed so tense and sullen. I had wanted Judaism, and now I had it, so why wasn't I content with it? She never voiced the question openly, but the look in her eyes spoke worlds, and the truth was that I couldn't answer that question myself.

I thought of the college and of my life there. Perhaps going back was really not such a farfetched idea after all. Even if Daddy Raymond did not want to accept me as part of the college itself, I knew he would never throw me out of the Church entirely. I could rent a flat in town, go back to my wonderful job at the bank where I had been so appreciated, attend church in the evenings, and still give all my free time to the organization. Or I could go to my parents or my sister Margaret. I didn't have to feel so alone, I told myself. There were places to go, options to pick from.

But the truth was that I simply did not want them. Somehow, as difficult as it was, in the depths of my life there was a deep desire to persevere, a sense of "pushing" that kept me from giving up. Instinct told me I had not seen it all, nor did I understand what I *had* seen, and I desperately wanted to.

I never quite had a rest from this struggle, and sometimes all I wanted was to be rid of this religion business altogether. I was so sick and tired of *believing* things! I just wanted to be left alone. Often, when this mood overcame me, I would get the urge to prove to myself that there was life outside of religion, and occasionally I would act on it.

I remember that one night when the children were asleep, and

Binnum and Sandy were out, I decided to make myself a cup of coffee. I looked in the refrigerator for a little something to go along with it. The leftover frankfurters from supper sat on a plate smiling at me—beefy, fat and appetizing.

"There's nothing *really* wrong with eating meat and milk together," I reasoned. "And anyway, I've done it all my life."

I laid a place mat down on the kitchen table and piled the frankfurters onto a *fleishig* plate. Then I took a *milchig* cup, made coffee with cream, and placed it on the other side of the table, setting up a book as a division. After making the appropriate blessings, I heartily ate the frankfurters, then moved to the other side of the table and drank the coffee; I washed the dishes on the respective sides of the kitchen, being fastidiously careful not to mix anything up. Then I retired for the night—or so I intended.

My poor stomach refused to accept the transgression. In the early hours of the morning, I ran to the bathroom to throw up, and when dawn finally arrived I felt so weak I could not get out of bed.

"What happened?" Sandy cried. "You were fine yesterday!"

"I don't know," I lied. "I really don't know." But I never mixed meat and milk again!

Surely there was some conspiracy from above to keep me going. The "pushing" from within was perpetual. And sometimes there were signs of providence that were so graphic they could not be ignored.

One day after *Succos*, I was talking with Sandy in the kitchen about the volunteer projects that she was involved in. Sandy's English was quite polished and her skills were often in demand. In addition to the youth work, much of her spare time—what precious little of it there was—went into writing and preparing mailing kits for the various festivals. This interested me, as I had produced dozens of similar kits myself at the college.

Sandy showed me some of her handiwork, and as I leafed through the material, I suddenly let out a gasp. There in the pile was a copy of the Passover brochure—the very one that Sister Inga had shown us in the church when she had told her tale of how the Norwegians had fooled the Jews! I could barely stammer out my story, and Sandy beamed with amusement and delight. She had worked nights on end to design that brochure right here in the living room; and it was the phone number on the back that had brought me to her house!

Within a few minutes, I learned that this astonishing coincidence was not an isolated one, and that a confluence of well-timed events had conspired to change my life. It seemed that the Weinbaums' relationship with Rabbi Arkush was not a long-standing one at all. In fact, he had only met them a few weeks before I left the college, and in a most unlikely manner.

The Weinbaums had taken the children on vacation to a beach area at the beginning of the summer. At the last minute, they had changed their plans and chosen a new and unfamiliar place in the hope of finding better weather. The children had scampered ahead on the beach one day and had come back to report to their parents that there was a man with a black beard and hat a little further along. The man turned out to be none other than Rabbi Arkush, who had also brought his family out for the day; and while the two couples chatted, he mentioned to the Weinbaums that he had been in contact with a Jewish girl in a Christian theological college. Only a few weeks later, they were the first family he called when I escaped.

But that was not the only interesting piece of information that had been exchanged. Binnum told Rabbi Arkush that the Lubavitcher Rebbe had given him a blessing ten years earlier to teach the *aleph-bais*, and that although he'd been teaching diligently, he'd had no opportunity yet to publish. Rabbi Arkush mentioned an advertisement he'd seen in the *Jewish Chronicle*, placed by the London Board of Jewish Education, which was looking for anyone with a new method of teaching the Hebrew alphabet.

"Now's your chance, Binnum," Sandy had urged her husband. "Call them up and show them your material!"

And so Binnum had contacted the Director of Education and had invited several staff members to his home. I remembered the meeting well, for I had been a bit awed by the sight of so many religious dignitaries and had escaped to the safety of my room. But I could hear them from upstairs and listened as they expressed their frustration with their current inadequate method of teaching reading in primary schools around the country. They were very impressed with Binnum's kit, and by the time the meeting ended, they had agreed to publish the entire package, including a text and workbook, cassette tapes, videos and wall charts. Binnum was elated; his dream would finally become a reality.

But the providential interlude was not quite over. By the time Sandy finished putting together the pieces of this very compelling chronological puzzle, she was looking at me with a mischievous twinkle in her eye. She produced scrap of paper and drew an *aleph* on it.

"Here," she said, handing me the pencil, "copy this shape, and draw a little girl to go with it. I want to see what you can do."

I drew a quick, simple picture that I thought would be appropriate for younger children, and she grinned delightedly. "You will be the illustrator of *Lamdeini*, the *aleph-bais* book. Binnum," she called, "we have our artist!"

I was reluctant to commit myself, and protested that there were many other people who could do a superior job, but Sandy had already made up her mind. She reminded me of all the experience I had in designing and illustrating children's literature, and here was a chance to put it to excellent use!

It was difficult to refuse, especially in light of the astonishing chain of events that had brought me to this point. A leaflet designed by Sandy herself had led me to her home—and at exactly the time when they were looking for someone with my capabilities. It seemed that I was meant to do the job.

The prospect of earning a little money was also exciting, but even more than that, I was thankful for the opportunity to give something back to the Weinbaums after all they had done for me. Binnum and Sandy explained to me exactly what pictures were needed, when the next meeting was scheduled, and how much work I would need to produce by that time. With exuberant hearts, we all retired for the night.

And so for the next two months, my schedule became even more demanding, for as soon as the children were in bed, I would begin work on *Lamdeini*, often not finishing until one o'clock in the morning. I had no time at all to think or plan, and it did not occur to me that my situation could change again so quickly; but change it did.

Just when I thought I had settled into a routine, Sandy approached me one day and mentioned a winter learning program in America that she felt might suit me. "Would you be interested?" she asked.

"Yes," I responded immediately. I had little idea what a "program" was like, but I did want to learn more about Judaism and thought it would be nice to do so in a structured setting. However, it was already December, and as I had only my few bits of borrowed clothing and no money, I felt sure she must be talking about next winter. It was no problem to make a decision about next year; but it dawned on me slowly that Sandy was speaking about *this* year, and what's more, the program was to begin in two weeks.

"What?!" I screamed. "I can't!"

"Calm down, Tova," Sandy said. "I'll organize it for you."

And organize she did. She took out loans for me, bought a plane ticket, and arranged places for me to stay, first in New York, and then in Minnesota, where the program would take place.

I worked furiously on *Lamdeini* during those next few nights, hoping that with the money I earned, I would be able to make at least a partial repayment on the loans and to buy myself some clothing for the trip. The pace of the arrangements was frenetic, and one day I found myself alone on the London subway for the first time, venturing out across the city in order to put in a passport application. The officials looked at me indulgently and assured me with smug smiles that I would never get a passport in less than two weeks; but fortunately, they were proven wrong.

In no time at all, I was sitting in my room amongst my little pile of possessions, trying to decide how much I could fit into the one small battered suitcase I was taking to America.

A month or so earlier, Raymond Webster had finally put together a package of all the items I had left at the college and sent it to Rabbi Arkush. He had never been told where I was, and probably assumed I was in Almington, but after his initial phone call to Rabbi Arkush, he'd made no other attempt to contact me.

I was glad to have my clarinet, guitar and sewing machine back, as well as several smaller items I had missed, but there were also a number of things in the package which didn't belong to me at all. I learned later that Webster had sent them because he didn't want anyone at the college to be contaminated by the evil spirits that apparently possessed me, and I disposed of them in due order.

I sat on my bed now, cramming my few treasures into the suitcase. At last, there was only one tiny space left, and I looked down hopelessly at the clutter with my last two valuables in my hands.

"Well," Sandy said, looking on with a wry smile, "you can't fit them both in. Which will it be—the clarinet or the bear?"

I debated. The teddy bear had been given to me by my Jewish grandfather when I was one year old, and it was the only thing I had left of him. "The bear," I said, and handed her the clarinet.

It was with mixed emotions that I arrived at the airport—bewildered by the fast changes that were taking place, relieved to have a break from the hard work of the past three months, excited at the prospect of doing some formal learning. I also felt disconcerted, for I'd left *Lamdeini* half done and had no idea if I'd ever return to finish it—or indeed what my future held at all.

"Now, if you want to change your plans and stay in America, it's quite all right," Sandy was saying to me. "It's up to you. Don't worry about the book—you are under no obligation whatsoever." She assured me that I was, of course, very welcome to return.

Before I knew it, we had said our good-byes and I was behind the barriers.

❧ TWENTY-FOUR ◈

THE entire trip was like a dream. Most of the time I sat rigidly in my seat. I was totally exhausted, but we were passing through storms over the Atlantic, and the bumping and swaying of the plane kept me from sleeping.

At the last minute, Sandy had found someone in the airport from the Stamford Hill community who was traveling to New York on the same plane. About halfway through the flight, she located me and helped me to unwind a bit. She was very kind and never left me for a minute, and when we arrived at the airport, she insisted on taking me in her taxi and delivering me to the door of the home in Crown Heights where I would be staying for the weekend.

As soon as I walked into Rabbi and Rebbetzin Baumgarten's house, I felt comfortable. They were relatives of Sandy's, very warm Chassidic people who welcomed me with open arms. Guests were a part of their lifestyle, and having newcomers from all parts of the world was apparently quite routine to them. It amazed me that I had traveled so far and yet could still find myself in a Jewish home so much like Sandy's—so congenial and pleasant, so *settled*. I sensed among these people that same feeling of comfort with Jewish observance, a security in simple practices that they knew beyond a shadow of a doubt were the will of God.

I felt I was coming from the moon.

But at least I was not alone. There was another guest staying in the house, a girl of about my age named Rebecca who was also attending the weekend seminar. She had been sent by a rabbi from her neighborhood in Long Island, and in a way she was coming from the moon too, so she made me feel less isolated.

Rebecca came bouncing cheerfully into the living room to meet me on Thursday afternoon, wearing pants, sneakers and *tzitzis* which hung out over her pockets. I watched her curiously the next morning as she donned a *tallis* and *tefillin* and put a small knitted *yarmulka* on her head to say the morning prayers. She seemed completely unabashed by the fact that her practices were slightly different from those of the people around her, and she was quite outgoing. She appointed herself my guide for the weekend and dutifully shuffled me to all the right sessions at the proper times, making sure I had everything I needed. I was still dazed and suffering from jet-lag, and I'm not quite sure what I would have done without her.

About forty girls had come to the seminar from all over the world. The weekend was designed to rekindle a Jewish spark in our hearts and to recruit anyone who was interested in coming to the longer program in Minnesota. On Friday morning, we were all taken to a local girls' high school to bake *challah*. The dough had been prepared already, and we did not have to do much more than shape it, but I found myself hopelessly butterfingered. We had never had to do anything quite as elaborate as these twists when we had baked bread for the college in Portfield!

That evening at the *Shabbos* table, much to my chagrin, Rebbetzin Baumgarten held up our *challos* in innocent good will and proclaimed, "Look what Tova and Rebecca made!" Besides the embarrassment of seeing a "Show and Tell" exhibition at my expense, it was quite apparent, even to an amateur, that in comparison to Rebecca's *challah*, mine looked like a deformed pretzel. I felt like crawling on the floor, but I must say that the company was very polite and no one laughed.

The meal was as inviting and down-to-earth as the Baumgartens themselves. There were several guests and a never-ending supply of food and song. A few of the sons in the family were cantors, and their *zemiros* were breathtakingly beautiful. The atmosphere was altogether warm and accepting.

The Baumgartens had their own *shul* in the adjacent house, but on *Shabbos* morning, we went instead to the service at the main Lubavitch synagogue, affectionately nicknamed "770" after its address. We sat up in the balcony in the women's section, behind colored glass partitions that allowed a view from our side only. The interior of the *shul* was very simple; it was made entirely of wood and showed evidence of many years of hard but loving use. I sat mesmerized in the huge hall, soaking up the atmosphere. I was amazed that I felt so much at peace with my surroundings, like a battered ship returning to the safety of the harbor after a long and exceedingly perilous journey.

Several lectures were given over the course of the weekend, and the speakers included a number of women who told stories of their return to Judaism. One was a professor who, I learned with interest, had come all the way from England to give her talk, and another held a prestigious job in the broadcasting industry. Their stories were intriguing, and I was beginning to see that there were quite a number of people who were in the same boat as I—all struggling, all fumbling in the dark for a deeper truth.

On Sunday afternoon, right before the plane left for Minnesota, I attended the *Chanukah* rally at 770. The *shul* was even more crowded than it had been on *Shabbos*, and there was absolutely no place to sit. Many of the men were singing and the Rebbe was speaking at intervals in Yiddish, but despite the discomfort, and the fact that I did not understand a word, I had that same satisfying feeling of being in the right place. I was hoping simply to have a glimpse of the lighting of the enormous *menorah* before I had to leave for the airport.

I looked anxiously for a foothold and managed to find a perch on the edge of one of the benches, right next to the narrow aisle. I stood there precariously for a few moments enjoying the view, until I was suddenly pushed from behind; and having nothing to grasp, I sent about ten people in front of me careening forward in a heap. I could-n't help laughing as we all staggered to our feet, and I did apologize to them, but unfortunately no one was willing to share my humor.

Before the festivity was over, I rushed out with two other girls to catch the plane West. My traveling companions had already been to Minneapolis, and thanks to them we were met at the airport by Rabbi Manis Friedman, a thin man in his mid-thirties with a long, silver-streaked beard and a relaxed but confident bearing. I soon learned that he was the pillar of the entire program.

His welcome was a bit strange, for it was not much of a welcome at all. It was bitterly cold outside and we had just been through a har-rowing journey, and yet he merely got out of his car and stared straight into my face without smiling. His look was not cold or harsh, but very intense, and I returned the glare a bit defensively, indignant that he chose to speak not one word of greeting.

We traveled to the school with the voices of *Megama* booming from the cassette deck in the car. It seemed that this duo was determined to follow me to the ends of the earth, peppering me with messages.

"Jewish child, you're out there on the streets running wild," they sang; and I surely felt "out on the streets," but I was far too exhaust-ed to be wild.

The program, officially called "Bais Chana," was located in the Lubavitch community house, a huge converted stone mansion which was used for year-round activities. It was completely equipped with a large dining room, kitchen, library, *mikvah* and several classrooms. Twice a year, the upper floor was turned into a girls' dormitory for the duration of the month long learning program, once in the winter and once in the summer.

The first shock was the free and independent way in which the dor-mitory was run. There were no rules at all as there had been at the college. You found a bed in any room you wanted—with whomever you wanted. You found your own sheets, blankets, pillows and pillow cases—if you were lucky enough to get to the linen closet before everyone else—and made your own bed. The accommodation was sparse, with six people to a room, but by this time, I was used to anything. I was very happy just to have a bed and blanket, and was relieved at the total absence of pampering. No wooing, no one urging me to accept a religion of "love," no one slobbering "holy kisses" all over me. The message seemed to be: if you want it, take it; if you don't want it, leave it. I felt totally drained and was content for the time being to be left alone and remain simply an observer.

The course itself was run in a similarly free-hand manner. Rabbi Friedman gave two classes a day, one in the morning and one in the evening, both of which focused mainly on Jewish outlook and philosophy. During the afternoon, there was a wide range of classes available on everything from the Hebrew language to *halacha*, but attendance was not mandatory and you could more or less create your own schedule.

On the morning after I arrived, the course began. One of the girls in my room wanted to tape the lecture and persuaded me to sit with her in the front row. About ten other people had also brought tape recorders along.

Rabbi Friedman walked in without ceremony and began to speak. I had a sudden twinge of doubt about the crazy impulse that had sent me tumbling halfway across the world on money that didn't exist to hear some strange man lecture, a man who didn't seem to know how to smile! Who *was* this bloke, anyway?

Rabbi Friedman's eyes were intense and his presence commanding. He seemed to stare right through me, and within a matter of minutes, I found that his words as well were piercing through my heart like fiery arrows. He opened up a book and began to talk about the essence of a Jew and his relationship to God, of the difference between the Jews and the gentiles. He was informal and blunt, but the vibrant energy of total conviction emanated from every fiber of his being.

After two days, I asked my roommate to please excuse me and found a new seat about two-thirds of the way back. I breathed a sigh of relief. I could get lost in the crowd here, and if Rabbi Friedman stared at me, I felt at a safe enough distance to return his glare.

His evening class was open to discussion and covered any suggested topic, from marriage to meditation. Some of the girls in the class were dating or married to non-Jews, and he had no qualms about telling them plainly that they should quit seeing their boyfriends or get divorced. He had a steady supply of relevant case histories about people he had met, some of whom had been through the program, and he was never at a loss for words. For every question, he had an answer; for every statement, a rebuttal.

I began to cringe inside. In the Weinbaums' home, I had simply followed their lifestyle, trying to absorb Jewish tradition in an emotional sense, without really understanding the philosophy behind it. Rabbi Friedman made one unequivocal statement after another about the foundation principles of Judaism, and not one word that came out of his mouth supported the very least precept I had grown up with. My experiences were all I had in the world. How could it be possible that *every single one of them* was based on untruth? It was so unfair!

I began to hate this rabbi who could lean back so casually in his chair and, without lifting a finger, smash my whole life to smithereens. In the bottom of my soul, I knew that every word he uttered was true. I don't know how I knew it, but I did; and I *wanted* it to be true, but at the same time, the injustice of it killed me. I had worked so hard, given my emotions, my time, my energy, my *entire being*, for a path of falsehood and vanity. Sometimes I would walk out of class, run to my room, and silently sob my heart out. I was so confused and terribly frustrated. I couldn't eat or sleep, my life was in utter turmoil. I felt that I couldn't respect this rabbi. After all, wasn't I superior to him? I was a prophetess, I had led an entire congregation only four months earlier. I was sanctified and filled with the holy spirit—I was *spiritual*! And what did *he* have? Only some ancient traditions and practices which were devoid of fervor.

I drove myself crazy. I knew that I desired what he had with all of my heart, but the idea of accepting point-blank a completely foreign set of values and ideas was absurd. Things hadn't seemed quite so drastic at the Weinbaums', and I wondered when I was going to wake up from this nightmare.

One evening, Rabbi Friedman came in to class and began talking about Mickey Mouse, Superman, and other childish fantasy heroes. I listened innocently to his humorous illustrations, having no idea what was in store. He explained that a child can really believe in Mickey Mouse, or dress up in a Superman outfit, and convince himself that he can accomplish fantastic feats: the human mind is capable of believing anything. It sounded correct, but when he went on to say that Jesus was none other than such a fantasy figure, it was too much for me to take.

From the back of the room, I destroyed my image as a quiet little girl, thumping my hand down on the desk and screaming out loud, "How can *you* say that? You have never had an experience of Jesus, and you say yourself that you've never even read the New Testament! So what right do you have to pull it apart?"

He smiled calmly, which made me even more furious. For hours we argued back and forth. Other students joined in occasionally, but slowly most of them left, and by the early hours of the morning, only six students remained from a class of nearly seventy. I was exhausted and had nothing more to say, no other arguments to offer.

It seems to me now in retrospect, that the terrible anguish I felt inside was not at all because I disagreed with him. I saw clearly that what he was saying was true. What stung me was that I had devoted my entire life to Jesus and felt that I had personally experienced spiritual revelations from him; and Rabbi Friedman, who had never toiled to understand Jesus, and who, on the contrary, was *proud* that he had never even read his words, was flying way above my head in his understanding of the issue. I had labored all my life to achieve an understanding, and of what avail was all my hard work to me? I thought bitterly of the parable about the man who had discovered after twenty years of turning a grindstone wheel that it was not attached to anything and had died from the utter despondency of a lifetime of futile activity. I understood exactly how that man had felt, and it seemed monstrously unjust. I couldn't bear it.

But it was etiquette that dictated my next move. The following morning, I ran downstairs to Rabbi Friedman's office.

"I'm sorry," I told him. "I really did not mean to monopolize the whole class. It was very rude of me to just call out like that."

"No, no," he responded with his maddeningly casual grin, "it's quite all right. It was an excellent class."

As I lay in bed that night, my pride stepped in, and I called myself a fool for having played right into his hands. I realized that he'd known all along exactly what kind of reaction he'd wanted during the discussion, and had put out the appropriate bait to provoke it; and I, like an imbecile, had bitten. But I had to admit that I was beginning to feel a grudging respect for him. He held the key to many doors, and I realized that I was not giving him the credit he deserved.

The screaming match had actually done me a lot of good, and I soon found myself more willing to participate in class, and a bit more open to receiving. This was partly due to the unexpected freedom I was given to voice any of my questions, and the even more astonishing realization that people accepted me in spite of them—and maybe *because* of them. To me, that was one of the most outstanding facets of the learning process in Minnesota, and it spun my mind like a heady wine.

In Portfield, questions had been a sign of doubt, but here they were a sign of involvement. In fact, it was never considered enough that we were learning Torah and accepting it, or even that we were able to regurgitate information accurately. These people were not at all interested in hearing their words parroted back to them, for they were not propagating a path of blind faith. They encouraged us not only to understand *what*, but to understand *why*. They expected us to take their words and expand them with our minds, to dig through the implications of the principles we were taught, and to live our lives accordingly.

Rabbi Friedman slowly became less of a threat to me, and more of a human being, with a warm side that I had not guessed at. One day, I found myself in his office, telling him a little about my life.

"Rabbi Friedman," I said, "you don't understand. I'm filled with the holy spirit."

He seemed to make a tremendous effort to restrain himself from laughing and responded, "What makes you think *I'm* not?"

"You're not!" I giggled.

"No, really," he said seriously, "I am. How do you know I'm not?"

"Because I *know*!" I said, and laughed again.

"All Jews are the children of God. We're all 'spirit-filled,'" he returned in his typical no-nonsense manner. I thought the whole idea was bizarre, but once again, I simply could not refute him. He never went to great lengths to appease our indignation, but his manner was so invincible, and his conviction so airtight, that you had no choice but to swallow his words and hope you wouldn't choke.

It took me many agonizing hours to come to terms with several issues dealing with Jesus and to reconcile my former training with the Jewish teachings about the Messiah. Slowly, slowly, I broke through the crumbling bonds of my old beliefs and came to accept that Jesus had been simply a false prophet who had abused his own heritage, and that in writing his story, the Christians had had to be quite imaginative to cover the tracks of their own inconsistencies. They claimed that Jesus was the Messiah and that he had already come; but they also believed firmly in the divine origin of the Old Testament, which declared that the Messiah's arrival would herald an era free of warfare and disease in which all the peoples of the world would serve God.

Of course, Jesus had not accomplished any of these things in his lifetime, so the Christians invented the idea of a "second coming" which would complete his mission, and presented the New Testament as a fulfillment of the Old. But since there is no indication anywhere in the Old Testament of a "second coming," the entire concept had no basis at all.

A person of average intelligence would have been hard-pressed to defend Christianity after facing a firing squad whose ammunition only consisted of a pure and powerful logic. The more I learned, the more I understood that many of the Bible verses which the Christians used as proofs of their doctrine were taken entirely out of context, and that if one read the surrounding text, he would find that the subject matter had nothing at all to do with the proposed meaning of the particular verse. In fact, the coveted Thomson Chain Reference Bible, considered such an invaluable asset for preachers, was based on nothing more than an arbitrarily composed network of orphaned verses whose true meanings bore no reference to each other whatsoever.

I also discovered that many fundamental Christian beliefs were the result of errors in translation. The most classic case is the verse in Isaiah (7:14) upon which the entire Christian establishment is based. The verse reads, "And the young lady will conceive and give birth to a son." The Hebrew word *alma*, meaning "young girl," is mistakenly translated as "virgin," for which the correct Hebrew equivalent would have been *besulah*. And from this error stemmed the Christian proof of Jesus' divinity and their claim that his mother had conceived of God and not of a man.

I thought back to all the times in the college when I had come across teachings that didn't seem to have complete explanations. Whenever I would ask someone to clarify, I would be told, "Oh, that's not so important, you just have to believe," and if I was not so lucky, I'd be told, "Believe it or burn in hell forever." No one said things like that in Minnesota, and on top of it, I was getting answers that actually made sense.

The one question that lingered in my head, though, was the source of the spirituality in the Church that I knew I could not have imagined. Rabbi Friedman explained to me that I had not been hallucinating, but that God had unleashed two sources of spiritual influence in the world, and the one in the Church came from the *tamei,* or impure source. It was this unholy spirituality that had empowered Pharaoh's advisors in Egypt, giving them the capacity to perform a limited degree of magic; the same source that had empowered any of the gentile prophets and sorcerers over the ages. This dual structure had been created by God in order to maintain one of the cornerstone principles of the world—the possibility of man's free choice.

Unfortunately, I discovered that knowledge is not synonymous with comfort. I was developing on two levels simultaneously, the emotional and the intellectual, and they did not keep pace with each other. Although I knew that what I was learning was true, the absorption of those ideas into the spinning gears of daily life was a colossal task, and I was constantly pained by the fact that I had wasted twenty-five years of my life. I was in a whirlpool of change that left me dizzy and winded. At times, I felt totally distant and locked, at others, extremely close and content.

There were spaces of delight in this box of philosophic confusion, and one of them was the total lack of restraint in the lifestyle of the school. This was the first time in my life that I did not have someone looking over my shoulder and telling me what to do or holding me accountable for every minute of my time. I spent many afternoons browsing through the library and enjoying the books, or sometimes simply walking around the neighborhood or going shopping with the girls. After nine years of suffocation in a barracks, the freedom was a breath of fresh air.

And the girls themselves were a joyous experience. I was too exhausted emotionally to form very close relationships with anyone individually, but for the first time I felt at ease in a group as a whole. In high school, I had always been the "odd man out," the one whose skirts were too long and whose practices too weird; and in the Church, in spite of all the "hugs and kisses," I had always found myself chafing against the grain. This new sense of belonging was an incredible relief, a beam of light in a tunnel.

All of these girls were searching as I was, we were at loose ends together; and above everything—they were *normal* people. I wasn't even sure what a normal friendship was supposed to be like, and this was the first chance I'd had to choose my own friends and simply have fun with them without feeling a sense of constrained formality or overbearing duty. I felt as though my personality had been taken out of a dark and mildewed storage crate and had all the dust shaken out of it.

The girls in the program were mostly in their mid-twenties, but there the resemblance ended. They came from every walk of life and were at various stages of development in Judaism. I had never seen such a motley crew of characters in one room before, so different and yet all so sweet and giving.

Laura was a very lively girl from a tremendously wealthy home in Uruguay. She was still not very committed, but she talked often about marrying "this rabbi" she had met. Then there was Amy, a girl from Miami who'd been divorced from a non-Jew and was engaged now to a Jewish doctor. She'd come to Minnesota to learn more about Judaism before her marriage. Tina was a feminist with a frizzy mop of hair, a heart full of confidence, and a head full of plans for all the projects she wanted to accomplish in life.

On the other end of the spectrum was a girl named Ricki, who was already strictly observant and would get mad at us if we didn't wash our hands before eating bread. She'd been asked to teach in the *cheder* and was very tense about it, so she decided to be in bed by ten o'clock in the evening. If there was any noise in the room, she'd get very upset but wouldn't be able to do anything about it because she'd already said *Hamapil*! We called her "Miss Frummie" behind her back, and I'm afraid we gave her a very hard time, but none of us was quite at that stage yet, and we resented the imposition

One girl with whom I got along famously was Karen, who came from a Reform background in Beverly Hills, California. She amazed me, as did all the others who came from affluent families, for in spite of her wealth, she was as down-to-earth and simple as if she'd been "the girl next door." I wasn't accustomed to this kind of behavior, for in England the sense of class was very rigid, a strong cultural implantation that persisted even amongst the Jews. I appreciated Karen's openness and informality, and we teased each other constantly.

She was a somewhat typical laid-back Californian and used to walk around in culottes and sneakers, chewing gum and playing her guitar. I think she was intrigued by my more sophisticated British demeanor and liked to wheedle me into reading aloud all the time so that she could enjoy my accent. To her I was a "Miss Prissy," the neatness fanatic whose bed could be spotted a mile away because it was the only one in the room that was always made. Cultural habits were another mutual source of deprecatory amusement; I thought her chewing gum was disgusting, and she thought my use of a lace handkerchief equally repulsive.

It was so nice to be a human being.

One night, we had a *farbrenghen*, the first one I had ever attended. It was just a simple get-together where we sat cozily, chatting and singing songs, but it was light years away from the "fellowship" gatherings at the college. I had always felt so empty after having a spiritual high during my years as a minister, with nothing to fill in the gap; but here in Minnesota, there were no gaps to fill in. There was a natural closeness amongst us, a feeling of being in the right place, a contentment that needed no artificial "highs" to sell itself. The evening was so beautiful that I wanted it to go on forever. That night, while everyone in the dormitory slept, I put my thoughts to paper.

January 1981

Tonight has been the most beautiful night of my life. It seems hard to believe that my life has changed so much in so short a time. Tonight was filled with tenderness and love. We sat around a table, a group of girls from totally different backgrounds, different walks of life, different cultures—and yet one people. Contentedly we watched the flickering lights of the candles, each one reminding us of the flickering light within us that had brought us all together in harmony.

Lovingly, we sat together, sharing thoughts, songs, even our very lives. The coldness of the night outside only enhanced the warmth and beauty within. Is it possible that only four months ago my life was so cold, dark and lonely—almost eerie at times? I was "outside." But thank God, He led me home.

The most beautiful thing about tonight was that it was not a "spiritual high"—here today, then gone tomorrow. It was so natural, so down-to-earth, so much a part of me. To be at peace is like finding priceless treasure.

Each moment of the evening sank into my being, telling me over and over again, "You belong, you belong, you're a part, you're a part—this is your home."

Rabbi Friedman encouraged me to write to my mother and explain what had happened to me. He felt it was important to maintain family ties to whatever extent possible. "It will hurt her," he warned me, "but deep down she will be very happy."

And so I sat down quietly one afternoon and composed a letter.

Dear Mummy,

I am writing to you in the hope that you will understand. Try and listen to what I am saying.

For many years, it has bothered me—"Am I Jewish, or am I not?" Why the question was so important to me I really don't know, but it was, and therefore I felt that I needed to seek for an answer. When I look back over my life, I realize I began searching at a very early age. I remember sitting in our living room on Parkville Drive, just seven years old, staring at photographs of Uncle Sammy's children, and wishing I was like them, longing for black hair and dark skin. I prayed many nights as a child, "God, please will You make my hair go black and my skin go dark?" In the morning, I looked for results, and the fact that it didn't happen never deterred me from asking. I knew He could do it if He wanted to. Why was it important for me to make such a request? Then I didn't understand, but now I do. Uncle Sammy's children were the only Jewish people I had seen, and in my heart of hearts I was crying out to be Jewish, and to me that meant black hair and dark skin.

Another thing is that I can't count the number of times I asked Jesus to come into my heart, to forgive my sins, to cleanse my life—dozens of times—and yet, at over twenty years of age, I was still wondering deep down, "Has he really come in? Am I really saved?" Something wasn't blending inside and I couldn't place my finger on it. Don't say I didn't try, Mummy. What else could I have done? How much harder could I have tried to accept the teachings that you brought me up with? I tried to lay down my life, to be a living sacrifice, to surrender my all, and yet in so doing I became a rigid, disciplined robot. I wound myself up every morning to do everything that was expected of me, but I never allowed myself to dwell on the fact that the love, joy and peace I preached to others was not a reality in my own life. Eventually there comes a time when one must sit down and reconsider what has gone wrong and why.

Mummy, if I dare say so, something went wrong many years ago in Alexandria when a Jewish lady married a non-Jewish young man. True, he was a very kind, loving, handsome young man, but no matter how hard we try to ignore it, we must face the fact that Jew and gentile don't mix. I know there are many Scriptures in the New Testament that say there is no Jew and gentile in Jesus—that we are all one. I would like to believe it, but my soul tells me that there is a difference.

Mummy, when you bore me, you transmitted something precious to me, and that is my Jewish soul. The very essence of my life came from you, and that part of me was crying out to be in its natural environment. I tried to suppress the feeling, telling myself, as I had always been taught, that I was a gentile because Daddy is gentile, and yet the more I told myself, "I am a gentile," the more Jewish I felt.

Believe me, I couldn't understand it. I'm only just beginning to understand it a tiny bit, but I dared to follow it and explore it, and in doing so, I would like you to know that I have never been so happy in all my life. I feel accepted. I feel I belong. I feel I've come home, and to me that is everything. My soul has finally found its place of safety.

Another thing that has become clearer to me is the fact that I have always felt an orphan. I know this sounds stupid, since you could never have provided any more for me than you did, and for that I am eternally grateful. But the truth of the matter is that I could never "click" with Daddy. I've been screaming out all of my life for a Jewish Daddy. It's not Daddy's fault. There is nothing more he can do for me, I just cannot relate to him. Many people have tried to fill the father figure role in my life, but it hasn't worked.

This one factor has made a tremendous gash on my personality, and I have to contend with it daily. It cannot be helped now, and believe me, I don't tell you all this to purposely inflict pain on you, but I want you to please understand that I want to be Jewish! I want to get back to my roots and to find my place in the house of Israel.

I always said that I would never marry, but what I was really saying was that I would never marry a gentile—and because there were no Jews around, that meant I would not marry at all! Why? Because I would never want my children to go through the hell that I have been through in my life until now.

For this reason, I am studying Judaism at present in Minnesota, in the United States. And if, please God, I am granted the blessing of children, I want them to be whole and to be brought up within the stability of a Jewish home. Believe me, this doesn't mean dead religion. The Judaism that is rapidly becoming a part of my life is joy, love, life itself. It is not anything "spiritually high." It is a practical way to live life, with a strong faith in God.

And I have finally found love. For twenty-five years, people told me over and over again, "We love you, we love you, we love you," yet I could not believe them. Here no one says "I love you," but they don't have to. You can feel the love all around, and I believe them. Mummy, they care, they really care. I fit in here, and that's all I need, simply to be a square peg in a square hole.

Mummy, I love you. I miss you. Listen to me with a Jewish heart and try to understand.

Your daughter,

Tova

About two days before I left Minnesota, I mailed the letter to my mother, though I had little hope that she would understand. But I did want her to know how I felt, and I was happy that Rabbi Friedman had prompted me to do it.

As the program drew to a close, I made up my mind firmly that I wanted to continue learning. A woman had come to speak to us about a women's *yeshiva* called Machon Alte in Safed, a beautiful little country town way up in the hills of the Galilee, and it sounded like paradise. The opportunity to learn Torah in Israel was a dream that I could not pass up. I decided that I would return to the Weinbaums' long enough to pay back the money I had borrowed, and then I'd be on my way.

It was with mixed emotions that I found myself preparing to leave Bais Chana. It had been a very difficult time on the one hand, and I felt as though I'd been shaken around inside a glass paperweight, buffeted from all sides; and yet at the same time it had been a cozy haven of acceptance.

Almost as if he could read my thoughts, Rabbi Friedman called me aside on the evening prior to my departure, and tied the whole experience together for me. "Don't think we treated you this way because we didn't care," he told me, "but rather because we *did* care. We disliked the foundation of your life to such an extent that we wanted to tear it down so that it could be rebuilt afresh."

Even so, as I sat on the plane, I marveled at the gumption he and the other teachers had displayed, wondering how they could dare to rip someone apart like that and then wave good-bye! I thought back to my initial clandestine meeting with Rabbi Arkush, when I'd stood on the curb watching the little yellow car pull away, every inch of me crying out inside not to be left alone. I felt just the same way now, as though I were being forcibly removed of the refuge I'd sought so desperately. "Don't kick me out into the big wide world again!" I thought anxiously. "This is where I'm supposed to be!"

It was only once I arrived in England, and was back into the routine of daily life at the Weinbaums' house, that I realized what an extraordinary thing had happened to me in America—and how much further the road stretched out ahead of me.

ॐ TWENTY-FIVE ॐ

I HAD been so careful with my money in America that I arrived back in England with presents for everyone in the entire family, including Sandy's parents, and forty pounds to spare. I was terribly anxious to begin paying off my loans immediately, but when I tried to give Sandy the forty pounds, she admonished me firmly.

"What did you buy for yourself?" she pressed.

I had to admit sheepishly that I had not bought myself a thing. Twenty-five years of discipline and denial had taught me to keep my own needs on the back burner, and coupled with the urgency of my debt, it had not even occurred to me to spend an extra penny on myself. Sandy insisted that I begin to repay the loan only after I had treated myself to something, so I took her advice and bought a beautiful piece of fabric to make myself an outfit for *Shabbos*. But that was the last time I indulged myself for quite a while.

The next six months turned out to be even more hectic than my initial stay. I took on three jobs in order to pay back my loans and save enough money for the trip to Israel. I was up at six-thirty every morning to get the children on the bus. Then I'd do some work around the house, and at noon I'd catch a bus to Lubavitch House on the other side of town, where I did secretarial work for Rabbi Sufrin, the kind anti-missionary worker who had spent so much time with me when I'd first arrived in London. In the evening, after the children were in bed, I would sit down to work on *Lamdeini* and soon found that my bedtime had crept up to two or three o'clock in the morning.

It was an exhausting time in all ways, but that same driving force from within, the "pushing" that I had felt so frequently over the past year or so, kept me in top form.

Shortly after I arrived home, I received a letter from my mother in reply to the one I had written, but it had very obviously been composed by my father; his voice and convictions came through clearly in every line.

He told me that I was estranged from the heavenly Father and that I desperately needed a life-changing experience with Jesus. I could not agree, for when I had sung in years gone by with the "anointing of the spirit," or preached like a powerhouse, would anyone have told me then that I needed a life-changing experience? No, simply because I was living and breathing the experience. And how many of these "experiences" could I continue to have before the right one came along and "changed" me for good? There was something wrong with the spirit, the power, the house, or all three, and I had to find out the truth.

The letter also reprimanded me for daring to mention that my parents' marriage was not made in heaven; that the very thought itself was outrageous and obnoxious in God's sight; and that by rejecting my earthly father, I was deliberately violating the commandment to honor parents, a fault which must be put right if I were ever to know God's blessing in my life.

My father also criticized me for being primarily concerned with my own personal happiness and peace of mind, but this in itself seemed to contradict the statement he had just made about finding "God's blessing in your life." He was telling me, on one hand, that it was only important to do God's will, regardless of your own satisfaction, but on the other hand, that the clearest sign of God's acceptance would be that very satisfaction! And that was exactly the complaint I had: in twenty-five years of serving God in Christianity, I had never felt an inkling of this promised "peace and blessing."

It was my father's next line that seemed to put the whole issue under a sparkling magnifier. He wrote that Abraham had not been saved by any of his own deeds, but merely by faith in God. To the Christians, faith was the entire foundation of life, the only key to salvation.

What struck me so clearly was not the obvious difference between this system of "faith" and the diametrically opposed structure of Jewish observance, which was based on practical adherence to the commandments. What struck me was the altogether nebulous basis of the Christians' faith. What exactly *was* it they were supposed to believe? They had no concrete set of guidelines to follow, so the only other possible explanation was that they believed whatever they wanted to!

I remembered so many times as a youth in the church having heard gospel-filled congregants declare fervently, "I *believe*! God is leading me!" If you had strung out a mile-long line of hard, cold proofs against the validity of any point of Christian doctrine, they would not have been moved, and would only have repeated with ardor, "God is leading me!"

And now I thought, yes! God is leading them; He's leading them wherever they want to go! Even their abstinence and suffering were of their own choosing, devices that somehow satisfied their deepest psychological and emotional needs. If God had said to them, "Serve Me by taking nothing except the clothes on your back and sitting out on a raft on the ocean for the rest of your life," perhaps their "belief" would have taken a different tack.

I thought also of the varied strains of belief that characterized the Christians. One would have been hard pressed to find two neighbors who "believed" exactly the same thing and who did not disagree on any point of doctrine. And yet here were the Jews, whose laws had not changed in three thousand years, every letter of whose Scripture was identical, no matter where in the world it turned up, and whose belief in the absolute binding power of the law was undiminished despite differences in culture and custom. Was there a Jew anywhere on the face of the globe who put on triangular phylacteries? His diet might be different, the tunes he sang might be different, but in the essential laws of the Torah, he was one with his people.

I knew in the depths of my heart that God must be more absolute than a vague, undefined "belief," that His message to us, in an unbroken chain of solid dictates, could yield *only* the "peace and blessing" I wanted so hungrily in my life.

The letter ended by saying that I did have a "Jewish Daddy" and His name was God, and that the only way to contact him was through Jesus.

It was not an easy letter to receive. Religion aside, they were still my parents. In my letter, I had expressed rejection of them; in their letter, they now expressed rejection of me. Neither party was happy; each was desperately longing for the other to conform, to open the eyes and "see." The accusation that I had broken the commandment to honor my parents stung me in particular, for I had tried my best to be as respectful as possible. In all honesty, I did respect my parents very much as people but still felt that I had to speak the truth for myself, and it pained me that they could not separate the two issues.

I thought about the letter for quite a long time before I replied. Rabbi Arkush encouraged me to answer it so that they would at least know that I was receiving their correspondence. He advised me to show my reply to an esteemed rabbi who was the principal of the girls' grammar school in London at that time, and this kind gentleman assured me that my second letter was most respectful.

Dear Daddy and Mummy,

Thank you for your letter and all previous correspondence.

I write to you both because your last letter was so obviously a joint effort. I must say it was not a surprise to me. I could not expect you to react in any other way than you did. It is not my purpose to go through the letter and argue out each point because it would only mean letters of this caliber going back and forth indefinitely, and personally I do not feel that this is a step in the right direction.

However, I would like to point out that I have always believed that a person must do what he himself inwardly feels, for at the end of my life I have to give an account of myself—what I, Tonica Marlow, have done with the divine inspiration that has ignited my soul. Similarly, you and Mummy must give an account of yourselves. It will be no good for me to say, "My father did this, therefore it is right for me," because maybe God is requiring you to act in a certain way, but that is no guarantee that He wants me to act in that way also. I cannot say what is right for you, for I cannot look inside you, at the deeper motives of your heart. Only God can do that. And may I say also that you too cannot truthfully say what is right for me. You may have a theory—but not an absolute conclusion—because you cannot see into the depths of my heart.

Although you may say that my words and actions prove otherwise—nevertheless I will close by saying that I love you and honor you to the best of my ability according to the Torah.

Wishing you well, take care,

Tonica

Trials, it appeared, operated conspiratorially, for one had barely subsided when a new one emerged.

It seemed that while I was in Minnesota, a Jewish journalist had gotten wind of my story and had published it in England's national Jewish newspaper—without revealing my identity, of course—and it had sparked a controversy among the Orthodox rabbis in Almington. Rabbi Arkush was closely affiliated with the main synagogue there, which was quite a large and influential one, and several of his colleagues were taking him to task for spending time and money on a non-Jewish girl. The British Orthodox community certainly did not want to be publicized as a proselytizing religion.

After the article appeared, the Chief Rabbi of Almington contacted the *Bais Din* in London and asked for the verdict on my case. Was

I a Jew or a gentile? The only problem was that the *Bais Din* had not even heard of me.

Rabbi Arkush had told me long ago that I would need to clarify my Jewish status with a *Bais Din*, but he did not say when and he did not pressure me. I presumed that I would have to do so before I intended to get married, and as I had no desire to get married at that time, I had put the whole matter aside.

Now I was in a predicament. Sandy advised me to contact the *Bais Din* immediately and get a certificate from them once and for all, so that I would never have a problem in the future. She told me they were waiting to make an appointment with me, so I called up and arranged a date. *Zeidie*, who had always been so sweet and protective of me, kindly offered to drive me to the appointment and do anything he could to help me.

I was not afraid. I knew without a shadow of a doubt that my mother was Jewish, but as the day approached, Sandy began to warn me that the rabbinical authorities would not treat me very gently until they had proved my identity. The London *Bais Din* was a long-standing, respected establishment that was recognized by all of British Orthodox Jewry, and even by the government, and its halachic policies were stringent.

"Judaism does not want converts," she explained. "We are not like other religious groups. We don't proselytize. Since you do not have many documents that show your mother is Jewish, they may want you to go through conversion. How do you feel about that?"

Her words were well-intentioned, but they pierced my heart like daggers. Convert? On one hand, I felt I would have no choice. On the other hand, if I didn't convert, I knew I could never go back to Christianity. I was almost twenty-six years old, and all my life I had known something was wrong. I thought I had finally found out what it was, and even then, there was just the tiniest thread, almost invisible to the naked eye, holding me to these people—my mother's Jewishness. What if they would tell me now that there was no thread after all, that all these feelings of wanting to be with the Jews had been in my head? If that was the case, then nothing was real. I would just have to forget about serving God altogether. The disappointment I felt, only He knew.

In the car on the way to the *Bais Din*, *Zeidie* warned me afresh that I was probably in for a hard time, and he too asked me how I felt about conversion. I started to cry. I felt so desperately alone; now that I was finally with my own people, they were going to reject me!

I tried to pull myself together. We walked slowly through the streets of the West End and up the stairs of a big stone building. There was a bench in the sparse, dingy entry hall, and we sat down to wait. The building seemed empty except for a clerk who scurried past us, his heels leaving a clacking echo in the cavernous corridor.

About ten minutes later, two heavy black rubber doors swung open, and some men beckoned to *Zeidie*. He went inside to tell them we had arrived, and then we waited about fifteen minutes more. Finally, a gentleman opened those two enormous doors again and called me in. *Zeidie* rushed forward to accompany me but was asked to remain outside. I was in this alone.

The gentleman and I silently walked along a narrow hallway. I looked at the closed doors: Court One, Court Two, Court Three. He opened the fourth door and we walked inside. The room was very long and poorly lit. Its walls were lined from ceiling to floor with bookshelves holding volumes of all shapes and sizes, and in the center of the room stood a heavy oaken table and several imposing bear-like chairs.

"Sit down," the gentleman ordered. "The rabbis will be with you in a few minutes."

I felt lost beside the magnitude of the table, and the silence seemed to deafen me. Finally, five aged rabbis walked through the doors and took their places at the head of the table. I did not know that I should have stood up; rather, I put my head down, for I was afraid to look at them. Everyone's words were ringing through my mind: "They are not going to be nice to you; they don't want converts."

But as it turned out, I had no need to fear anything at all.

"Why don't you come and sit a little closer to us?" one of the rabbis said with paternal kindness. I smiled shyly, slipped off my chair, and came forward.

They had all my documents in front of them and asked me many questions to ascertain their authenticity. Every now and then, they would converse with each other in a language I had never heard before. I knew it was not Hebrew, and I could not decide which country had such a language.

I was completely taken aback when one of the rabbis asked me suddenly, "And how is your sister Esther doing?"

My *sister*? How did they know my sister?

The rabbi went on to mention that Esther too had some documents that had come through the *Bais Din*. How was she? Where was she living? Was she religious? I told them all I knew: that Esther had gone to Israel and had married a Jew, but I had not seen her in many years.

Their voices were kind and they smiled at me, each one trying to relax me with gentle words. I felt that if I had been twenty years younger, they would have taken me on their knees with their own grandchildren and told me stories of the beauty of our heritage. They welcomed me and wished me success; but there was an element of uneasiness in the fact that they knew so much about me.

My mother's birth certificate had been signed by the Chief Rabbi of Alexandria, which I'm sure lent a great deal of credence to my story, and after about fifteen minutes, they were obviously in agreement that the documents were authentic.

"Now, tell us," one of the rabbis said. "Do you have a boyfriend?"

I laughed and replied, "No."

"Now, come on, tell us! You do have a boyfriend, don't you?"

I was really amused. "No, really, I honestly don't."

"We only want to make sure that you have someone to take care of you. Come now, you *do* have a boyfriend, don't you?" the rabbi persisted.

"I promise you," I told him seriously. "I do not have a boyfriend. I'm not interested in getting married right now. I want to learn more about Judaism and how to run a Jewish home."

They were finally satisfied and chatted on to each other in the strange-sounding language. Finally, one of them said, "We accept your Jewishness from birth, but we will require you to immerse yourself in a *mikvah*, and you will not be allowed to marry a *kohain*."

I thanked them and rose to leave, although I was a little disappointed. Why couldn't I marry a *kohain*? It wasn't that I wanted to, but I didn't understand why they had to impose this restriction. Was my status somehow not as good as everyone else's? I was accepted, and they had been so pleasant to me. What more could I have asked for? But somehow I did want more. I felt like a second-class citizen.

I called in at the office to make arrangements for the *mikvah* and received instructions as to where I should go. "There will be a lady there who will tell you what to do," the secretary informed me. "Don't worry."

In a moment, I was bounding back through the huge black rubber doors. "*Zeidie, Zeidie*, I'm kosher!" I exclaimed with delight.

He was astounded. "So soon? They told you already that you are Jewish?"

"Yes, yes," I continued eagerly, "they told me that I'm Jewish from birth, and all I have to do is go to the *mikvah* and I can't marry a *kohain*, and that's all. I'm kosher, *Zeidie*—even for *Pesach*!" I could hardly contain my elation.

Everyone at home was as shocked as I was. They had not expected the process to be so easy or quick, and yet here I was—an accepted Jewess.

When I thought later about this unusual occurrence, together with the fact that my mother had miraculously managed to send me the documents I had requested only a couple of days before I left the ministerial college, it seemed clearer and clearer to me that there was a God who was indeed involved in my daily affairs and who was carefully guiding my footsteps.

By the time I left the *Bais Din* after my verdict, I was already late for work. *Zeidie* dropped me off at an underground station so that I could hurry to the Lubavitch House across town. When I got there, I openly expressed my disappointment to Rabbi Sufrin at being told that I could not marry a *kohain*. "So you won't marry a *kohain*," he said cheerily, trying to perk me up. "There are too many problems marrying a *kohain*, anyway. What do you need that for? Besides, there are plenty of other Jews for you to marry!" He told me not to worry about it, and so I disciplined myself not to dwell on it anymore.

I found out later in Israel that the reason for this stipulation was based partially on my falling into the category of someone who has been "captured" and brought up by Christians, a circumstance which makes a woman forbidden to a *kohain*. But I think Rabbi Sufrin probably felt that trying to explain these *halachos* to an already bewildered and overwhelmed young woman would only exacerbate tensions, and he wisely kept them to himself.

As the day approached for me to go to the *mikvah*, I suddenly got cold feet. It was usually hard for me to explain my doubts and worries to the Weinbaums. Even though they were pure gold and had helped me beyond measure, in certain ways, I still felt a million miles away from them.

I went to my room and wrote in my diary.

February 28, 1982

> On Tuesday, I hope to go to the *mikvah*. If it was just that I would get wet, it wouldn't bother me. I'm not afraid of water. But in a subtle way, it's much more than that, and that's what bothers me. It's a denunciation of all that has passed in my life. It's an act that will say, "All my old life was unclean—and now I wash it away."

But do I really believe it was *tumah*? In my heart of hearts, do I believe it? I'm honestly not sure. I wish I was; but to be truthful, I'm not, and it's scary.

And yet, even while I sit here contemplating, I know I could never go back to where I was before. I get a sick feeling just thinking about it. Why can I not forget it altogether? The truth is, it's clinging to me, sucking my strength, draining my vitality. It really is *tumah*! Please, God, when Tuesday comes, let all of it be washed away, that I might be thoroughly cleansed—new!

The next day found me standing outside a small *mikvah* in London awaiting the rabbis. I still felt alone—alone in sorrow and alone in joy. It was very hard to go through so many changes and mixed emotions in solitude. Of course, people were kind to me, but when it came to the nitty-gritty of dealing with internal challenges, I was on my own, and I knew that all the basic decisions were mine.

I could do whatever I wanted, go wherever I wanted, wear whatever I wanted...I was free. It was somewhat frightening after being held so tightly for so long. I was slightly amused at myself; with the wide world at my doorstep, I had chosen instead to stand in a parking lot outside a *mikvah*, awaiting a group of rabbis whom I did not know and a strange ritual I did not really understand. But I was calm. My decision was a complete one.

Soon, about ten *rabbonim* arrived and accompanied me to a small room. They sat on chairs against three of the walls and looked at me.

"Tova," one of them said, "I want you to know that when you go into the waters of the *mikvah* today, you are not going to convert. You are Jewish and we accept you as a Jew. You are going into the *mikvah* so that you can be cleansed of your past life. You will be newborn, like a child. Just as a child inside its mother's womb is encased in water, so

the waters of the *mikvah* will cover you. Today you will be born again."
I smiled a little at this, for the rabbi had used the term "born again"
quite innocently and had no idea what he was saying. They gave me a
siddur and asked me to recite the three paragraphs of the *Shema* aloud
in front of them. I was accustomed to saying only the first paragraph,
so I braved that one in Hebrew but asked permission to say the
remaining two in English. I was relieved when they agreed. I was then
sent into an adjoining room to see the *mikvah* lady, who told me to
shower quickly and to wash my hair. I did not have to make any of the
official preparations normally required of a convert; I would simply
immerse myself in the water. The voice of the rabbi who had spoken
to me before came floating gently through the door.

"Tova, remember everything we have talked about. You will be like
a child in the mother's womb. Dip now under the water." The *mikvah*
lady instructed me to submerge myself twice under the swirling
waters.

The rabbi spoke again. "Tova, do you hear me? Now you are all
new! Always remember to give *tzedokah*, for this is the mark of a
Jewish soul," he concluded in a delighted tone of voice.

I stepped out of the water to the amazement of the *mikvah* lady,
who blurted in confusion, "What? No *brochah*? You are Jewish? What
happened?" She threw her arms around me and wept.

That deep and beautiful peace had returned, the same peace I'd felt
six months earlier when I'd opened the door to my bedroom in the
Weinbaums' house on Friday evening and found God in the room. I'd
been baptized three times, and never once had I felt like this. I had not
come to the *mikvah* expecting anything, but only to keep an appointment, and I'd met God again. There was such a sweet and special
atmosphere in the room that it was indescribable. The *mikvah* lady
hugged me again, unable to contain her tears, and I too wept from
happiness. I had come home.

I didn't go straight back to the house afterward. I sauntered around
the shops in the neighborhood, wanting to buy something that would

remind me of this day. I felt that I should celebrate somehow, but it was hard to celebrate alone, and I wandered around aimlessly. Finally, empty-handed, I decided I had better return home, only to find Sandy frantic about my absence.

Zeidie's only comment was, "Tova, you must be Jewish. Here we are worrying whether you've gotten lost or run away, and you've only been out shopping. Now, *that's* Jewish!"

THE *aleph-bais* book was nearing completion. Once it went to press, I would get paid, and then I could pay off my debts and purchase a ticket to Israel. The discussion of plans for my future made me feel that I was really heading somewhere, making progress. Many people had expressed the opinion that I should marry first and then learn, but I really wanted to learn and was determined to get to Israel. I eagerly awaited a reply to the letter I had sent to Machon Alte.

The weeks swam by in a dizzying routine of work. Although I was constantly busy, there was a nagging loneliness inside me, a feeling that although I'd come so far, the road ahead still stretched halfway around the world. I couldn't shake the realization that everyone around me was high up on a mountain someplace while I was still down below, groveling in the dirt.

The need for familiarity was so strong that it occurred to me one day to make contact with one of my old friends from the college. The idea was very comforting; and so I called Jacob, the Jewish boy whom I had liked. I knew he had a position at the Polytechnic in Portfield, and it was not hard to track down the number.

When he realized who it was on the phone, he couldn't contain his astonishment. "Where *are* you?" he asked incredulously. "We all thought you had disappeared off the face of the earth!"

I made him promise he wouldn't tell a soul of my whereabouts, and

I knew I could trust him. We made arrangements to meet the next time he came to London to visit his mother. In the meantime I baked a batch of *hamantashen* and sent them off to him by post. I knew he would be amused at this subtle reminder of our old joke about "Haman's ears," and the thought of his reaction kept me entertained as I anxiously awaited his visit. It simply felt good to *know* someone, to meet anyone who was familiar to me, no matter who it was.

On the Sunday Jacob arrived, he telephoned first to inform me that he would be coming over to the house in the evening. Sandy said she didn't mind, but she preferred that he wear a *kippah* in the house in order not to confuse the children. Jacob refused, so we went out for a drive instead.

He had brought some interesting items along with him: an expensive bottle of perfume for me, which quite surprised me, and a package of the literature that had been published at the church since my departure. He brought me up to date on the current college news and wanted me to keep the literature, but that much I declined.

"You can't imagine what it was like after you left," he informed me. "It was just like someone had died. Raymond Webster left all of your things perfectly intact, as though you were coming back any day, and then finally he announced that none of it could be touched. Everyone's spirits were dampened, and it was really quiet everywhere. The mood lasted for a few weeks.…"

I didn't have anything to say. I knew they felt let down and hurt, that I had greatly disappointed them, but there was nothing I could do. I hadn't asked to be born a Jew. I simply couldn't help it.

After a time, we parked the car and walked around, and eventually we held hands. Although we had never touched before, it seemed inevitable that it should happen now. Back in the college, there had been limits, but those standards were gone now and no one was watching us. I was so naive. All I remembered hearing in the college was that men and women had to be kept separate or else they would wind up doing "that"—but I wasn't even quite sure what "that" really was. Jacob was very sweet, and our hand holding seemed innocent enough. After all, wasn't it normal to touch?

We walked for a while through a quiet suburb in London, hand in hand; but later when we were sitting once again in the car, his affection suddenly became heated. I was caught between a sense of alarm and a yearning to be wanted, and I allowed him to kiss and cuddle me. Fortunately, we did not go further, but it was enough to make me feel absolutely vulgar. I pulled back abruptly, confused and angry—at Jacob, and, even more, at myself.

"Let's go back now," I told him, "it's getting late."

Jacob was dazed with emotion and told me in strong terms that he wanted to marry me. He had a house, a car, a good job. He declared that he loved me and would live anywhere for me and that he was sorry he had not asked me before I left the church. I didn't know what to think. I did like him, and it was very tempting to accept an offer from someone in my lonely world who wanted to care especially for me; but at the same time, I felt so disgusted.

When I got back to the house, I told Binnum everything. I was mortified that I had allowed such a thing to happen, and even though I was by nature extremely reserved about my personal feelings, my first instinct now was to talk about it. All my life, I had been brought up in a strict moral environment, sheltered from any exposure to the topic of sexuality. I had the impression only that it was a "dirty" thing, and it disturbed me deeply that after twenty-six years of such training, I could have slipped so drastically. What had gone wrong?

With time, I began to see that my training had been preventive rather than independently virtuous. At college, the women had been adjured constantly to exercise extreme modesty; hence, the long skirts, headscarves and multiple layers of clothing. But the reason we were given for such caution was that life was very difficult for the men, and that if we gave them the least provocation, they wouldn't be able to control themselves. The Christians—whether they were Protestant Evangelists or Catholic nuns and priests from "over the wall"—treated modesty not as a virtue or value in itself, but as a protection against the appetite they would succumb to the minute no one was looking. They were not pious because they were so pure; they were pious because they were so vulgar!

In a way, their minds were on the subject all the time, right down to the books on the college library shelf, which had been carefully "censored" but still managed to include some reading material which subtly sanctioned alternate outlets for an unnaturally restrained urge.

I began to see so many other Church practices in a new perspective, everything from "holy kisses" to the many times when our ministers had been reprimanded for behavior that was considered a "weakness." I thought of what Raymond Webster had almost done to me, and I realized that he was no better than any of the others—merely an animal temporarily off the leash.

And what about *me*? I was shocked to discover the same base impulses in myself and was repulsed by my own vulgarity. "Sister Joy," the former prophetess, was just as degraded and unrestrained as anyone else in the church! It hurt deeply and sent me crashing down.

Jacob continued to write me love letters at the rate of one per day. But even though I was so tantalized emotionally by his attention, I knew I had not left my former lifestyle just for Jacob. There had to be more; I could never be satisfied by taking the easy way out. After a week, I wrote to him and told him that we were not meant for each other and asked that he please stop writing to me. Of course he was hurt. I received only one more letter, telling me that I badly needed deliverance from the evil spirits that bound my life, and only then would I really experience Jesus.

Binnum offered to take me along in the car one Friday afternoon when he went out to run errands for *Shabbos*. "I see that you still feel very badly about this whole incident," he said gently. "I thought you might want to talk more about it." I deeply appreciated his fatherly concern and sweetness, and was grateful for the opportunity to sort my feelings out. By the time we returned home, I was glad to find that much of the self-hate I had felt had drained out of my system.

But the residue of the episode lingered behind, and for weeks afterward I tossed about this idea of modesty and what it really meant. Sandy had also been very firm with me when it came to modesty, but in the early days, I did not understand the difference between her approach and the Church's. She had screamed at me once when I came downstairs in a tee shirt with sleeves cut above the elbows and had ordered me to change immediately. On another occasion, I had brought home a dress with short sleeves, thinking that I might alter it, and I remember her words clearly: "Never try to fix up a dress that doesn't cover you properly; it will never look right. Just leave it on the hanger—*it's not for you.*"

Those words, "It's not for you," left a subtle but deep impression. There had never been any talk of "sinfulness," or of "how hard it is for the men"; the modesty was for *me*, a manifestation of my inner refinement, a mark of self-respect. That meant that some clothing was automatically "for me," while other clothing simply did not fit into my set of values.

What fascinated me was the idea that being modest in no way contradicted being attractive. In fact, I had been encouraged from the time I'd set foot in the Weinbaum home to brighten up my image and to dress more conventionally, and recently I had even had my long hair cut and permed—a radical change from my church days! I learned that attractiveness for a Jewish woman was considered a virtue, especially when it reflected inner beauty, but that this did not fall into the same category as being provocative.

I thought about the shapeless, handmade skirts I had worn at college, the dark brown sweaters, the shabby headscarves. No wonder I had felt so ugly! Ironically, that clothing and that waist length hair, which had been considered so modest by the Christians, were immodest in the Jewish community because they set me apart and aroused too much attention!

Slowly it sank in that Jewish modesty was something innately beautiful and precious, something that guarded the ability to have a deeply meaningful and holy relationship, and that perceiving it as a device to prevent crime demeaned its worth completely.

The Jews had treasures whose depth and richness I was only just beginning to perceive.

Pesach was approaching, and again I was totally overwhelmed by the proceedings. I had absolutely no conception of what was going on, although after six months of orientation, I had expected that something would penetrate. The house was turned upside-down, the schedule changed from day to day, and there was a whole new set of bizarre rituals. I had always been used to so much order in my life, and the stress was too much for me to handle. To Sandy, my silence must have seemed like ingratitude, and I could find no way to alleviate her frustration.

One of the most amazing—and amusing—episodes of this hectic pre-festival period was the afternoon I found Binnum, clad in thick rubber gloves, rummaging through the garbage bins in the front yard. I watched him silently for a few moments, wondering whether the sun had gotten to this usually immaculate DDS. Every now and then, he would hand me a piece of corrugated cardboard and say, "This is all right," and then he would bury the top half of his body again in the depths of the bin. I thought perhaps he was just tidying up the yard in honor of the festival, but that didn't seem to necessitate the systematic categorization of the garbage, a task which he seemed to be treating with the utmost urgency.

Finally, I could take it no longer.

"Binnum, what are you doing, exactly?" I queried innocently. With perspiration dripping from his brow, and hands laden with refuse of various aromas, he smiled at me and said patiently, "Tova, the dustbin men are on strike. I'm sorting out the *chometz* from the non-*chometz*, and everything that is *chometz*, I'm going to take to the district dump. The car isn't large enough to load all these bins, and I can only afford to make one trip," and down went his head again to search for more of the criminal material.

"Oh...." I replied vaguely, trying desperately to take it all in. Once again, I was confronted with the odd paradox of Jewish behavior. Here we were, in one of the most affluent areas of the country, and the gentleman of the house—a gentleman in every sense of the word—thought nothing of burying himself waist-deep in rubbish bins, all for the sake of a *mitzvah*, which took precedence over any temporary dirt or discomfort. While on the outside, such behavior seemed rather eccentric, I had been living with this family in their home, and I knew that they were not in any way strange or unbalanced. In fact, they were very normal and down-to-earth people, intellectual and refined, and their practices had to be more than a haphazard pile of superstitions.

It was incidents like the rubbish bins that kept me going, and I needed all the motivation I could get, for the next few weeks were a swamp of tension. The *Pesach* preparations and restrictions, especially those in the kitchen, sometimes seemed extreme. According to their family custom, Sandy made practically all the food from scratch. She made her own mayonnaise and squeezed lemons to make lemonade for the children. The tea was sifted, the sugar was boiled, and all the fruits and vegetables were purchased before the night of *bedikas chometz*, so that any speck of *chometz* which could possibly have been brought in with them could be nullified. This alone was a source of worry, because the food that was bought had to last the entire eight days; nothing would be purchased during *Chol Hamoed*.

It seemed like everything I touched I messed up, and everything I did turned out wrong. Sandy used separate knives for peeling and chopping the vegetables in case there were any *chometz* particles on the skin of the vegetables which could transfer to a knife. It was the Lubavitch custom also not to use any item which had touched the floor. I seemed to be constantly mixing up knives and dropping utensils; and that was in addition to my almond cookies, which turned into a mush and did not look half so nice as little Chani Weinbaum's. I spent a lot of time in my room just trying to escape the possibility of further mistakes.

It was a relief when the first night of *Pesach* finally arrived. The pressure evaporated, and I enjoyed the *Seder* much more than I had expected. It struck me again that the Jewish way of doing things seemed so much more "tame" than that of the Church, and yet its impact was so much more profound. At the heart of these age-old rituals was a deep security and strength that I could sense clearly, even though I did not understand all of them completely.

One thing that was immediately obvious was the marked difference in emphasis. The Passover night at college had centered around "the lamb." The students received almost no meat the entire year, and in comparison to the Weinbaums' table, their celebration seemed in retrospect more like an orgy than a spiritual event. They would renew their vows to God—and then rush straight to the dining room and stuff themselves!

In this house, the emphasis was on the story, on remembering the miracles that God had made for us, with the meal itself occupying only a small portion of the evening. The atmosphere was so much more sedate on the outside, so dynamic and meaningful within.

I also remembered a few occasions in which Raymond Webster had announced at the end of the *Seder*, "Everyone's very tired, so we'll go to sleep now and recite the *Hallel* in the morning." What an odd service to God that seemed now, almost tantamount to saying, "We're sorry, God, but we're exhausted. We've had a hard night of eating lamb. You'll have to wait till tomorrow." The Weinbaums' reading of the *Haggadah* was complete; it would never have entered their minds to put some of it off until the next day just because they were too tired. Judaism didn't cater to people's fatigue, or any other feeling of the moment, for that matter. It was absolute.

It was during the latter part of the festival that I made a great mistake. We were walking home from Yom Tov dinner at *Bubbie* and *Zeidie*'s house, and we had to cross a main road where a multitude of cars and trucks were whizzing by. Rivkie, the three year old, was holding my hand. As we approached the traffic signals, I totally forgot it was Yom Tov and said, "Look, Rivkie, the signal button. Press the button and the green man will appear."

I held up her hand, and instantly everyone screamed, "No, no, don't touch the button!"

But it was too late. The movement could not be retrieved, and the button was pressed.

Binnum and Sandy tried to hide their dismay at my total lack of thought, but the children were not quite as tactful and began to taunt their little sister.

Poor Rivkie began to cry. It hurt me badly to see her so upset, and I shouted at the children not to annoy her. "It's not Rivkie's fault," I told them, "it's mine!"

The children quieted down, and thankfully we reached home. I went straight upstairs to my room and cried for hours. It was hopeless, totally and absolutely hopeless. I would never in a million years get over the wall and understand this way of life.

Way into the night, when the house was asleep, tears of frustration continued to flood down my face. In my mind, I debated the idea of going back to the college. What about *Shabbos?* I wondered, and told myself that somehow I would work it out. As far as *kashrus* was concerned, I could become vegetarian and then I wouldn't have to eat *treif.* But what about *Pesach* and *Rosh Hashanah*, and all of the other rituals? Oh, it seemed impossible; but somehow I felt I had to get back to Portfield.

Suddenly, in the midst of this heated "discussion," a fresh thought appeared like a bolt of lightning: "But you're a Jew." I realized that no matter where I would go, I would carry my heritage with me. I could never ignore it. I started to cry all over again, and I knew then that I would get over that wall somehow.

And so *Pesach* of 1982 left us. It had already been a year since Sister Inga had given me her Passover leaflet. How much had changed since then!

Just one week after the holiday, I spent *Shabbos* in the home of the Lews, a Lubavitch family who lived in Stamford Hill. On *Shabbos* afternoon, while the mile-long table was expertly and efficiently cleared by many eager helping hands, I sat chatting with eight-year-old Sholom Ber. I was wearing a pale green woolen suit that I had sewn myself. It was decorated at the shoulder with a black and white feathered brooch, which Sholom Ber fingered with interest.

"Be careful you don't spoil it," I said gently. "I won't be able to buy another feather."

"Where did you get it from?" he asked.

"My brooch? From Portfield," I replied.

"*Portfield?*" he screeched with delight. Breathlessly he spluttered out question after question. "Do you know about this girl? She ran away from a place called Portfield and she was living in the Weinbaums' house. Her father's a priest and she ran away with nothing, and no one in the world knows where she is, and...." He caught his breath and looked at me seriously. "Do *you* know who she is?"

"I think I might," I said in a dramatically soft tone, not wishing to spoil his story so abruptly. I wondered where he had heard it; little did I know that Shmaryahu Weinbaum was his classmate.

He jumped up ecstatically. "YOU KNOW HER!" he screamed. "Where is she now?"

More than a little amused, I whispered, "She's sitting right here in this room."

"Where?" he stammered, looking around the empty room.

"Right here, sitting next to you!" I whispered again.

It took a moment for the message to sink in before he burst out, "*Naah*! It's not you!" He was a bit put out with himself for having been carried along by the joke.

"It is, Sholom Ber, that girl is right here in front of you!"

"It's *not* you," he responded adamantly, determined not to be teased.

"Why do you think it's not me, Sholom Ber?"

"Cuz you're *Jewish*, you are," he said in exasperation.

To me those words were like a little emissary of love from God. There was absolutely no doubt in his pure young mind that I was Jewish, so the story couldn't possibly apply to me. Well, maybe my Jewishness was becoming obvious. I was so thankful!

I felt more and more heartened about my rapidly approaching trip to Israel, and there was only one small hitch in my plans: the school had not replied to my letters.

"They may have gotten lost in the Israeli mail," Sandy told me. "But schools like this are usually run very informally, and they will probably take you on the spot when you arrive—even without formal registration." The choice was mine: wait indefinitely for a reply, or take the plunge and hope for the best. If it didn't work out, Sandy assured me that I could stay with her relatives for a while, and at least have a holiday in Israel before I came home.

A happy coincidence helped me make up my mind. Shortly before I was scheduled to depart, two people from the Lubavitch community in Safed just happened to be passing through London, and they came to the house, one to collect money for the *yeshiva* and the other to see Binnum about his teeth. They had a very encouraging report to give about Machon Alte, and I was so glad to receive any information, especially since no one in London seemed to be familiar with the school.

"Oh, you'll be all right," one of them assured me. "They are a nice group of girls, and if you get stuck, here's my address at home. In fact, you can go straight to my wife and she'll take you over to the school. I'll phone her and tell her you're coming!"

This bit of good fortune was a great relief, and happily I went about my packing.

ॐ

Exactly a week before my departure, Rabbi Arkush called me from Almington to say that my sister Esther was visiting from Israel and had called to tell him in quite forceful terms that she was not going back home until she had seen me. Apparently Raymond Webster had given Rabbi Arkush's phone number to my parents, and Esther had called him from their home. She had practically screamed on the phone that she was prepared to search the world over until she found me.

"You had better phone your parents," he advised me quietly. "It's best not to upset them, and I think it would be a good idea for you to see your sister. She really sounded quite concerned."

This was the first time I had spoken to my parents since I had left the college, and I was really nervous. The call was brief, and I talked mostly with Esther, who sounded somewhat formal, but very sincere. We made an arrangement to meet in Rabbi Arkush's home in Almington, as I still did not want anyone to know that I was living with the Weinbaums in London. I thought apprehensively of how my father would react to my permed hair and make-up.

Before I left, *Zeidie*, who had always been right beside me during my transformation, and who was my dearest friend in time of need, wrote me a poem:

WHY BOTHER, TOVA?
When it's so hard to be a Jew,
So many things you have to do,
Why bother, Tova!
When it's so easy to be free

Of every statute, each decree,
Why bother, Tova!

When Hashem in heaven appears remote
And mitzvos we just do by rote,
Why bother, Tova!
Do you think that God can care
About the type of clothes we wear?
Why bother, Tova!

And can we make the heavens bright
If one small candle we do light?
Why bother, Tova!

And can we Hashem above entreat
By what we say and what we eat?
Why bother, Tova!

But what of those who went before,
Who gave their all to keep this law?
The millions who their lives did lose,
So we could practice, we could choose?
They showed a disregard of self
So we'd inherit this Jewish wealth.
From every grave in which they lie
To us this truth they always cry:
You must bother, Tova!

Benzion Rader
Rosh Chodesh Sivan 5742

৵

Thank God, the meeting was not so terrible. Margaret and her husband had come to Almington along with my parents and Esther. (Philip had stayed behind, as he was still observing the church ban on communication with my parents.) Our talk was cordial but distant, and consisted mostly of light banter, which I think was a blessing in disguise. It was too dangerous to touch on any serious subject or anything of a religious nature, and no one wanted to reveal truthful feelings.

We walked in a local park for a while and took some photographs, and then went to Rabbi Arkush's house, where we sat chatting in the living room. Esther was the most voluble of all; her personality had not changed a trace in sixteen years. She was vivacious, energetic and full of laughter. She told me confidentially that she thought my new hairstyle was very attractive, and in general, she was still somewhat motherly toward me, in spite of the passage of time and the great changes in both our lives. She tried to open up a deeper channel between us by telling me that she was Jewish too, and that she always scoured her house for Passover. I knew that in her heart she still believed in Jesus, but I set the issue aside and enjoyed her company very much.

"Listen, Tonica," she asked unexpectedly at one point, "do you have any plans to come to Israel? Why don't you come and visit me? I'd love for you to meet my husband and my little boy."

I was very hesitant, still afraid that if my parents found out I was going to Israel they would do everything possible to track me down and put more pressure on me to abandon my new lifestyle. Even the thought of having to deal with my father's letters was difficult for me.

"I'm thinking about it," I lied to Esther, "but I might go to America first for a while." I knew I would need time to settle down in Israel before I could muster up the strength to defend myself, and I thought my vague statement might put Esther off the trail. I was so apprehensive that I had no idea then what a good friend my sister really was, and if I'd been less suspicious, I might have had more of a chance to develop a relationship with her. But at the time, my vision was very narrow.

My father sat quietly in a chair the whole time, and thank goodness, he never said a word about my appearance, but I was sure he would want to pray at the end. He never left any place without first praying there. I knew it was coming, and so for the last time in England I was "committed into the Father's hands"...or so at least my father thought.

୭

There were many last-minute preparations to make for my trip. I was happy that over the past few months I had earned enough money to pay back all my loans and to buy my ticket to Israel, but I did not have much left for pocket money when I arrived there. Sandy suggested various Jewish organizations that might help me out with a scholarship, but to no avail—I was too old! Such funding was available to high school graduates who were planning to spend a year in seminary, but to these sponsors, twenty-six years old was simply ancient. I decided to go on to Israel anyway, with the hope of finding a part-time job when I arrived.

I completed the last touches on the *Lamdeini* alphabet book at about two A.M., and my plane left at eleven that same morning.

Binnum, Sandy and the children drove me to the airport. It was not easy to say good-bye, and the hardest one of all to leave behind was Rivkie. How that little girl had helped me, she will never know. So many times when the going had been rough, seemingly out of the blue she had come up to me, raised her chubby little arms, and said, "Tova, I want to hug you,"—or "Tova, I love you," and my heart would soften and the tension would fall away.

All of the children, so precious, so sincere, so pure and innocent, had been like little angels coming to my rescue, over and over again, helping me to make a difficult and, at times, almost impossible adjustment; and now I had to leave them, a family who had become my family, and go on alone. I tried to be brave, but it was hard to stop the tears from cascading down my face.

❧ TWENTY-SEVEN ❧

I FELT as if my stomach as well as my heart had been left behind, and it was a difficult flight. My face must have been ghostly white because the attendants repeatedly asked after my well being. By the time we landed, I was in such a smoky daze that even the frenetic scene in the airport seemed dreamlike. Somehow I managed to locate my luggage and a taxi.

Sandy had arranged for me to stay the first night at her brother-in-law's family, who lived in a small village called Kfar Chabad. The half-hour drive was uneventful, but a quick glance in any direction was enough to let me know that I had arrived on a different planet. Miles and miles of barren land zoomed past us, parched terrain that stretched for miles under a vast canopy of empty sky, relieved only by the occasional appearance of a solitary palm tree. The hot June wind whistled heavily through the open windows of the taxi. I seemed to be swimming through a sky-blue and brown dream.

The picture changed abruptly when we turned into the outskirts of Kfar Chabad at about six in the evening. Lush greenery sprang up suddenly to greet us on all sides, and the village was so picturesque that one could easily fall in love with it. We wound through narrow, meandering roads flanked by quaint, cream-colored stone houses, each bordered by a large porch and carpets of green grass. The streets were dotted with flickering patches of fading sunlight, and except for the buzz of mosquitoes and the incessant chirping of the crickets, the atmosphere was quiet and peaceful. If Safed was anything like this, my stay at school would be a pleasant one indeed.

Sandy's relatives made me feel very welcome. Although they spoke only Hebrew, they had two grown daughters who knew English, so communication was not too difficult. They owned a successful chicken farm and were apparently well-to-do, for their home was spacious and equipped with modern conveniences. I desperately needed a good night's rest and fell asleep in minutes in the soft, roomy bed; and it was a good thing, because the next day it took me five hours and four buses to reach Safed. I was so worn out by the time I boarded the last bus that I could not load my suitcase by myself and had to ask for assistance from a man standing nearby who had only one arm! I had the sensation that I'd been traveling almost continuously for an entire year, and I could hardly believe it when the bus driver finally announced, "Kiryat Chabad."

I looked around. I knew that Kiryat Chabad was the neighborhood in Safed where I was supposed to get off, but the only thing in front of me was an off-white, multi-storey concrete building rising out of the jagged side of a steep mountain. A pine grove languished on the other side of the road, and in the distance, I could barely make out a cluster of crowded buildings with laundry flapping from the rooftops in the hot breeze.

"Where?" I queried hazily.

"Right there," he said impatiently, pointing to the enormous white building. "*Nu!*"

I staggered off the bus and heaved my luggage up to the first set of stone steps, searching the maze of doors for the number I had marked down on a scrap of wilted paper. Finally, I found the right door all the way on the other side of the huge complex, but I could tell by the face of the woman who greeted me that her husband had forgotten to inform her of my arrival.

"Is this the Antians' home?" I asked weakly. I got a nod in response, but no flicker of recognition. "I'm Tova, from England," I explained. "I think your husband forgot to tell you I was coming."

"Come in, come in," she encouraged warmly, "it's quite all right."

Thank goodness she spoke English! She poured me a cool drink while I told her that I had come to attend a school called Machon Alte. I did not know any details about the school, or who was in charge, but her husband had informed me in England that she would be able to help me. Immediately she got on the phone and arranged a meeting for that evening with Rabbi Rosenfeld, the principal. Fortunately he lived right here in the complex, as did several of the other teachers in the school, so I would not have far to go for my interview.

Without warning, I burst into tears. I was so drained and confused, and now it seemed that after my struggle to get to Israel, I might not even be accepted! I knew I had taken a risk when I left England, but in Sandy's house it had seemed like a risk I could handle. Now I was in a foreign land where I had not one friend and did not even know the language, and suddenly I felt that I would fall apart if they were to reject me. What then? I had no strength left!

In the comfort of this humble home, I fell into an exhausted slumber, and it was well into the evening when I awoke. I was late for my interview with Rabbi Rosenfeld but relieved to find out that I would indeed be accepted. In fact, he told me that he had replied immediately to my original letter of some weeks ago, so Sandy's hunch about the lost mail had been correct after all. Thank God! The tension vanished.

Rabbi Rosenfeld informed me that I had arrived during the last week of the term, after which there would be a ten-day break before the summer session began. He told me I was welcome to attend classes that week, even though I would be entering in the middle of the program, and might not be able to follow the discussions completely.

Right after the interview he drove me to the school, which was several minutes' drive away, in the old city of Safed. We turned into a dim, narrow alleyway and then through two towering iron doors into an ancient cobble stoned courtyard. Three small buildings formed a "U" around the courtyard; one housed the library and Rabbi Rosenfeld's office, the second contained the kitchen and classrooms, and the third was used as a dormitory.

The evening class was in session when we arrived. Before I knew what was happening, a few girls spotted me through the windows and came pouring out into the courtyard to greet me. I couldn't believe my eyes! Here were four of my friends from Minnesota, whom I had never expected to see again: Rebecca, my "guardian angel" during my first weekend in America, Taibke, Miriam, and a girl from South Africa named Sharone. Familiar faces in the wilderness! My heart breathed a massive sigh of relief. The sun was going to shine once more on my life.

Miriam and I had been in the same room in Minneapolis and would now share one again. We were overjoyed to see each other. There was no time to be tired now; we had so much news to catch up on, and we stayed up chatting throughout the night.

The first class I attended at Machon Alte was on *halacha*. They just happened to be in the middle of a series of discussions on relationships with non-Jews. My first reaction was that these laws were absolutely outrageous and that the entire approach was openly abusive toward gentiles. All I could think of was my father. Perhaps he was a gentile, but he was still my father, and it hurt me to think of him being treated in so condescending a manner.

"Pardon me for saying so," I interrupted the teacher in mid-sentence, "but do you really believe what you are talking about?"

The rabbi only stared at me for a moment, obviously trying to figure out who I was; I'd flounced into class without even identifying myself! When I repeated my question, he explained gently that these laws were much more complex than they appeared at first glance, and that the Torah was in no way inhumane, and he advised me not to worry about it. I tried to follow his advice, but the next *halacha* class was almost as preposterous as the first.

"You should not invite a non-Jew to eat with you. Why? Because he will end up marrying your daughter."

"That's stupid," I called out, but I had no idea of the irony in my words, for I was still ignorant of some key elements of my family background, and could not understand just how meaningful the rabbi's statement was. What amazed me at the time was the realization that I was not nearly as well-adjusted in my new lifestyle as I had presumed, and that the Church still had quite a fierce hold on my thinking. It was no small feat to shake a lifetime of training out of one's pockets. The full-time, intensive program at Machon Alte would aggravate my sensibilities in ways I had never dreamed of.

I found myself challenging the teachers fearlessly. I'd certainly come out of my shell in the past year, and was determined that no one would spoon-feed me anymore. It was not easy to hear such contrary ideas, and my supply of questions was never-ending.

History was sometimes just as difficult as *halacha* because it focused a great deal on the gentiles' persecution of the Jews throughout the ages. I had had some introduction to this idea from the Holocaust book I'd read in Portfield, but the idea of Jews being oppressed during the French Revolution seemed extreme. How come nobody had ever mentioned such things in history lessons before?

Classes in *hashkofah* were much easier to digest, for these dealt mainly with philosophical subjects that did not touch our daily lives in as practical a manner. I loved learning about such broad Jewish concepts as God's relationship to us, the meaning of trials and troubles, and life after death. The view of the latter in particular was so vastly different from the Christian outlook and nowhere near as horrifying. Philosophy helped me to feel at least intellectually integrated into the

Jewish people, but when it came to *mitzvos*, my first instinct was always to cry out, "That is stupid and pointless!" I had spent a lifetime "under grace," and it would be several years before I would be able to really cherish the *mitzvos* rather than simply going through the motions.

However, I was still very glad that I had come to the school. In spite of everything, I knew, as I had known in Minnesota, that the Torah was absolutely true and that I was in the right place.

Once again, my friends cushioned the blows. Some of the girls in the dormitory were lifesavers, and they helped to absorb some of the shock of a new adjustment. At that time, there were about thirty girls in the school, from America, England and a few other countries as well, and—just as in Minnesota—it was a great relief to me that we were all in the same rough waters, thrashing out a new life together.

༄

The dorm was sparse and conditions somewhat austere. People in England had warned me, "Tova, don't forget, you're going to Israel— things are different there," but I didn't know what they were talking about until the first time I had visitors. Shortly after my arrival, an entire tribe of ants chose to take advantage of my hospitality and made themselves cozily at home in my bed. Fortunately, one of my friends had gone back to America for the month of *Tishrei*, and I slept in her bed until the troop decided to search for friendlier quarters elsewhere.

However, there must have been some strange attraction about our room, for as soon as the ants left, the mosquitoes came. During the hot months, they kept me company constantly at night, and for the first time in my life I discovered I was allergic to them. Miriam spent quite a lot of time rubbing lotion into my swollen ankles, and whenever I tried to thank her, she would say warmly, "Oh, Tova, my mother would do it for me!" She was a very sweet, bubbly girl, and her company was a delight. I think now that I was in constant wonderment over the pleasure of having good friends who sincerely cared about my welfare.

There were a number of other unexpected things to contend with, including the cold—it snowed three times that first winter, a record for Safed—and the food, which was completely different from anything I was accustomed to. I thought fondly of the time Sandy had made me a cheese sandwich when I'd first arrived at her house; I was just beginning to realize what a great comfort it was to have something familiar to eat! The Israeli custom of having a large meal in the middle of the day—and a very small one at night—was particularly difficult. Supper was not an official meal at the school, and we used to scrounge up whatever scraps we could find. When I had been at school a few months, the cook became ill and I took over the kitchen. I would get up at four in the morning to make lunch for all the girls on a tiny two-burner stove, rushing to finish cooking in time for classes. I was constantly fatigued from the schedule but satisfied at the same time, partly because the girls loved my cooking, and partly because the school had accepted me without tuition, and I was thankful to have a way to repay this kindness.

I also found a job as a cleaner for one of the families in the community on my one free afternoon from school. I did everything from laundry to washing the floors, and the few *shekalim* I earned provided me with just enough pocket money to get by during the week.

I had had a lot of practice living on practically nothing, and I'm proud now, when I look back, that not a soul knew of it. Once the school took us on a trip to the Banyas in Tel Dan, and some of the girls went wading in the pools at the foot of the waterfalls. Someone noticed me pulling off my knee-high stockings and asked, "Why are you doing that?"

"I don't want to get holes in them," I replied.

"So?" she said with a shrug of her shoulders. "You'll get more."

I would never have admitted to anyone that this was the only pair of knee-highs I owned, but inside, I couldn't relate to her response. To me, anything extra was a luxury, even ice cream; but I would walk down the streets of Safed with my head up and never let on that I had not a thing in the world. The only precious possession left to me was my self-respect, and I wasn't about to part with that.

I knew there were plenty of other people who'd had a hard life and had come through. I made up my mind that I was not going to be bitter, that I would never say to myself, "Well, life treated me rottenly, so I'm justified in giving up." I was determined to make my life over.

Occasionally I used to wonder why I simply hadn't gone back into banking when I'd had the opportunity. With my credentials from the job in Portfield, I could certainly have gotten a decent position, rented my own apartment in London, and lived very nicely. But I knew that if I had taken the easy way out materially, I would not have developed as much spiritually, and that my present experience was providing me with a secure internal sense of Judaism. I was not over the rapids yet by any means, but I never for a moment regretted my decision.

Two months after I arrived in Israel, my appendix flared up, and I was rushed to the hospital for an emergency operation. I had had intermittent pain for over a year, and in fact one of the girls in Minnesota, who was a nurse, had tried to convince me that it might be my appendix, but I had dismissed it as indigestion. By the time I returned to London, the discomfort was so severe that I finally got myself to a doctor. All he'd said was that I was too tense and needed to relax, so as always I blamed it on myself. But my attempts to "relax" were fruitless, and it was simply a miracle that I had the operation before any damage was done.

The hospital stay was frightening and uncomfortable, but fortunately, I had friends around me constantly. The dorm counselor slept in a chair next to my bed at night, and the girls were like family and came from school to see me every day. Rabbi Rosenfeld took complete charge of all the arrangements and stayed on top of the medical staff at every moment, making sure that I was properly cared for. Somehow he even managed to have the hospital fee waived, which was a miracle in itself, for I had no medical insurance and no idea how I could have managed such a financial crisis.

There were three other Israeli women sharing the room with me. One of them had just undergone a Caesarean section, and had tubes running into every part of her body, and another had been in a car accident in which two out of five passengers were killed; so I tried hard to count my blessings.

Thankfully, the surgeon had done a good job, and after I was discharged from the hospital, the Rosenfelds took me into their home until I was well enough to return to school. It was there that I saw the true meaning of giving displayed at every turn, from Rabbi Rosenfeld himself, who made sure that a private doctor monitored my recovery, to his nine-year-old daughter Hindy, who insisted immediately that I stay in *her* room, in *her* bed. Blanketed by the family's warmth, I quickly recuperated and regained my strength.

Sometimes, as I lay on the couch, I marveled that the pain had gone. After more than a year, I had almost become accustomed to the nagging hurt in my body, but now it had evaporated. It felt wonderful, and I prayed to God to make that deep inner hurt in my life disappear too. "Oh, please, God," I thought fervently, "can't You somehow, sometime, take it away?"

All too soon, the summer program was drawing to a close, and we began to discuss the High Holidays and the concept of repentance. Apprehension rose in my heart as I learned about the judgment of God and the awesome sanctity of the day of *Yom Kippur*. It all sounded very frightening, and tension engulfed me. Why did everything still seem so foreign? I wanted very much to feel a part of what was going on, to fit into the framework, but I was so closed inside that it was almost impossible.

Finally *Rosh Hashanah* arrived, and I was relieved that it was not so terrible. God judged and life went on, but in my case I wasn't exactly sure what "life" meant and where I was "going." People everywhere in the synagogue were furiously reciting *Tehillim*, but I just couldn't do that. I still had little faith that anything was going to help settle this festering confusion inside me, this sense of being adrift on a raft under heavy skies. I didn't have enough confidence to approach God at this point to pray for a change of plan in my life, to ask for anything better. In effect, I said to Him, "You do whatever You decide." Either I'd chosen the right path or I hadn't, and only He knew the answer, but I was so emotionally exhausted I could hardly worry about it anymore. I knew that if God so wanted, He could effortlessly squash every bit of life out of me, or He could continue to sustain me, and I simply left myself in His hands.

On *Erev Yom Kippur*, I ate the *seudah* in Rabbi Rosenfeld's home.

"Eat more, Tova," he encouraged me, half in jest, as various rich dishes were passed around the table.

"I can't," I replied. I had already eaten more than I was accustomed to, and my stomach was full.

"You must!" he teased. "Every mouthful you eat today is a *mitzvah*. Eat more!"

I took his teasing quite literally, and by the end of the meal, I was disgusted with myself. I had never eaten so much at one time in my life, and my skirt wouldn't even fasten anymore. I was very angry with myself. How could I have indulged like that? What had happened to the refined and disciplined Sister Joy?

There was no room in my frustration for the concept Rabbi Rosenfeld had been trying to get across—that the Jewish idea of abstinence was totally different from the Christians'—focusing on the spiritual use of the physical world rather than on withdrawal from it.

Even when God asked us to fast, He did not do so in a punishing way, but gave us to eat beforehand so that we would have strength.

I didn't care about that now. All I knew was that I felt repulsive, and I went to the synagogue in an angry mood. The scene there only depressed me further, for the women's section was crowded and so full of noisy children that it was impossible to hear *Kol Nidrei.*

I looked around the room in amazement. "This is the holiest day of the year?" I thought to myself. "First they feed me up like a pig, and bring me to a marketplace, and then they tell me *this is holy*?"

A distinguished lady from the other side of the *shul* noticed the distress that must have been written on my face and came over to help out. I learned that she was Rebbetzin Hendel, a much sought-after teacher in the girls' high school here in Safed, and that her husband administrated all of the Chabad elementary schools for boys. She was very kind, and patiently showed me the prayers, trying to explain what was happening; but although I could read the words, they had no more meaning for me than a stream of gibberish. I didn't understand how all of these devout Jews could hope to atone for their sins by reading words from a book. We had always said our own prayers in Portfield. Why weren't my own heartfelt words good enough? I found it nearly impossible to get into the proper mood of remorse, and in the middle of the silent standing prayer, I could tolerate it no longer and walked out.

This just couldn't be God.

Alone I trudged back to the school. The whole city of Safed had come to a reverential halt. Not a single car could be seen along the roads in this ancient city. The birds twittered their goodnight song in the uppermost branches of the motionless trees, and the air was still.

I was so tense, I couldn't think. All of a sudden, bells chimed and the spell was broken. I stood still and looked around.

Bells? In Safed? I hadn't known there was a church here. I decided I wasn't going back to the synagogue tomorrow until I found that church and sorted this out with God once and for all.

The next day, I awoke early and lay in bed for a few minutes, trying to decide whether I should go to the synagogue first or to the church. Suddenly I reminded myself of a promise I had made to someone the day before, and I put on my robe and went to the kitchen, only to find more trouble waiting for me.

One of the women from the Kirya had asked a favor of me the previous afternoon. Her husband and son would be staying in the city over *Yom Kippur* night so that they would not have to walk twice all the way to and from the Kirya. She wanted to know if I would take some sandwiches along for her little son in case he became hungry during the long day in *shul*. Of course, this was a simple thing to do, and I had readily agreed, knowing that it would be permissible to carry the sandwiches since there was an acceptable *eiruv* around the main area of Safed.

But when I opened up the paper bag, I discovered to my horror that the sandwiches were full of ants. There was no bread or anything else to eat in the kitchen, and I was scared out of my mind. This woman had entrusted me with her son's food, and now he would starve the entire day! I didn't know what to do, so I ended up picking out every single ant from the sandwiches with my fingers, all the while thinking, "I must be committing a big sin, because I don't even know if I'm allowed to take these things out on *Yom Kippur*." I felt worse and worse with each passing minute.

I sent the sandwiches to *shul* with another girl, and I can only hope the child didn't eat them, for a night outside the refrigerator had left them in a sorry state to begin with. I felt awful, and it boded ill for the day to come.

I crept back into bed and tried to decide what I should do next. I wanted to find the church whose bells were still ringing in my head; but how could I go afterward to the synagogue and tell God I was sorry? No, I couldn't do that. So I wouldn't go to the synagogue at all. But that wasn't good either, because it was *Yom Kippur* and God might cut me off from His people. I was afraid.

I slipped into another uneasy slumber and dreamt I had discovered a Pentecostal church, but when I went inside I found that it had been converted into a gymnasium, and children were playing there. As I walked out, dogs of all shapes and sizes jumped on me, and I tried desperately to push them away. Finally I found a Catholic church, but the door was chained shut and the interior was dark. I tried to take a bus, but there were none to be found on *Yom Kippur*; and someone in the street kept trying to sell me cloth, but I knew it was forbidden to buy on *Yom Kippur*.

I woke up tossing in my bed. The midday sun was already beating down through the window of my room, causing heavy beads of perspiration to trickle down my brow. The school was silent. Everyone was in the synagogue, no one had missed me. Perhaps they thought I had gone to the synagogue in Kiryat Chabad, while those in the Kirya thought I was in the old city. Somehow I didn't want to go to church anymore, but I just couldn't get myself together to go to the synagogue either, and the day passed by as silently as it had arrived.

Yom Kippur was over. The cars raced once more along the high street, the shops opened, people went about their business in the markets.

Rabbi Dovid Turkoff, the very kind school counselor, met me in the courtyard the next day. He saw that I was so tense I could barely speak, and insisted that we sit down in his office and have a talk. Almost involuntarily, I spilled out everything: my frustration, anger, fear of God, and my doubts about leaving Christianity. I told him that I had a tremendous pull to find God in the Church because I so desperately needed the comfort of a familiar mode of worship. I even told him that I could still speak in tongues if I wanted to.

"So do it," he said unexpectedly. "Do it now."

"No," I replied.

"Why not?"

"Because it's *ridiculous!*" I burst out.

After about three hours, I had talked myself out and was a little calmer. Rabbi Turkoff told me that I couldn't go on like this, dragging Christianity at my ankles, and feeling guilty all the time about whether God was angry with me or not. He encouraged me to take a break before the new term commenced and go away with the girls to Jerusalem for *Succos*.

My friend Taibke had plans for the holiday and urged me to go with her. She was eager for new experiences and wanted to see the way Israeli families lived, but I was not excited. I didn't want to go to other people's houses, I just wanted to be alone, but after a great deal of persuasion, I wearily agreed.

For the first days of *Succos*, we were set up with a family in Givat Shaul in Jerusalem. They were of French origin and were very sweet, but the first question put to me by the lady of the house was, "Are you religious?"

I was flabbergasted. No one in my entire life had ever had to ask me such a question before. It had always been so blatantly obvious that I was religious. I took stock of my appearance—my permed hair and make-up, sleeves rolled up to the elbow, skirt just a bit below my knees—and I wondered what had come over me during the course of the past year that I had allowed myself to "fall so low." What in the world had happened?

I still had not totally absorbed the idea that modesty was an internal, as well as an external, virtue, and I hadn't completely divorced myself from my identity as "Sister Joy," the rigid disciplinarian and dependable role model who could be counted on to maintain the highest standards. It seemed clear to me that my hostess's question could only have been prompted by my "unchaste" appearance, and it caused me considerable alarm.

I can't say that I did much more than go through the motions those first few days of *Succos*. Taibke and I moved on to Meah Shearim for the remainder of the week, and there I was utterly astounded. The visit was a mixture of abject culture shock and absolute delight at the warmth and sincerity of religious Jews.

Never before in my life had I seen such Jews, not even in photographs. It was like walking into a museum, only this was a real setting and these were living people. The houses were simple and sparsely furnished, with rickety stairways and sagging walls that looked as though they had been resisting the temptation to collapse for the last hundred years. All the men wore knickers and what I thought of as "pajama coats"; the women wore headscarves rather than wigs, and all the girls had long braids.

The family we stayed with spoke Yiddish, but their kindness and hospitality needed no words, and the warmth they generated was immeasurable. There were thirteen children in that house, and they were all beautiful. All of them had pure, beaming faces, and they were very excited to have guests, fighting each other to give us the best seats at the table and the choicest portions at the meals. I thought back to all the times I had felt deprived when my father insisted that I give up my lunch for one of the vagabonds he was always bringing home. But the behavior of these children bore no resemblance at all to my experience. There was no sense of deprivation among them; on the contrary, the children were delighted to have company, and their joy in doing a *mitzvah* was untainted.

Their mother was constantly inviting us to eat, but in spite of her generosity, decorum prevented us from taking up her offer freely. The people in this neighborhood made all their own food from scratch, right down to soup nuts, and there wasn't a packaged item to be found anywhere. One day, I came into the kitchen and found the mother stuffing a pair of cow's lungs which lay in a huge metal tub. She was sitting there quite calmly, stitching up the lungs with a needle and thread, as though it were no more unusual than putting the kettle on to boil; and although I was quite sure that similar procedures took place in the back rooms of fancy restaurants where no one could look on, I could not convince my stomach of this fact.

On another occasion, Taibke and I were in the kitchen with a bunch of the children, and she said to me with a mischievous wink, "Look in the pot on the countertop!"

Apprehensively, I lifted the lid of an enormous pot and found to my horror that it was full of chicken feet sitting peacefully in water. I giggled for Taibke's sake, but I didn't dare tell her that my mother loved chicken feet, and any moment she knew that my father would be out of the house, she would cook some, but I had never tasted one myself. Needless to say, Taibke and I did not eat much in that house, but fortunately we were out most of the day, and our schedule left us a polite escape hatch.

The poor mother of this well-meaning family did her best to communicate with us without the benefit of English, and tried to show us her photo albums, but although we were made extremely welcome, I couldn't relax. I kept hoping that Taibke would just leave me alone for half a day so that I could seek out the Christian quarter of the city and find a church to pray in. Ever since *Yom Kippur*, this urgent need had filled my mind constantly. What a long time it had been since I'd seen the inside of a church!

But as though she knew my thoughts—or perhaps on Rabbi Turkoff's instructions—Taibke never left my side. We went together to the Wailing Wall, but my heart was far from it; and each night she dragged me to the *Succos* water-drawing ceremonies in the many synagogues in the neighborhood. Here and there, I managed to peep through the cracks in the *mechitza* into the men's section, and was struck again by the sparks of purity I saw there: young boys arm in arm with aged men, slowly moving around and around, like droplets in a vast ocean of Torah, of time, even of life itself. But it was so hard for me to connect this awesome and timeless beauty with the shock of the totally foreign lifestyle of these people. I didn't know if I would ever be able to combine together the two facets.

Before we left Meah Shearim, I had a very elaborate and strange dream. Rabbi Rosenfeld came to me and said that he had found a nice boy for me to marry, a person of sterling character, but there was only one problem—the boy was very ugly. Would I agree to go out with him? I said yes, and while I was sitting at the Rosenfelds' table on Friday night, there was a knock at the door.

The warning I had been given did not properly prepare me for the boy's appearance, for he was so obese that he could not even enunciate his words properly. I said to Rabbi Rosenfeld, "Just one moment—please ask the gentleman to sit down, and I'll be right back." I ran to the bathroom and cried. How could he do that to me? I wondered in anguish, but I decided that the very least I could do was to spend some time with the boy in order not to hurt his feelings.

I pulled myself together, went back to the living room, and offered the young man a glass of tea. We chatted for about half an hour, but even though I was getting restless, he made no move to go. Finally I stood up and was just about to excuse myself when I saw him fumbling around under his hat.

"Tova," he said, "before you go, I just want you to know something," and he began to pull off his outer covering, peeling it away like the skin of a banana. I did not see exactly what he looked like as I awoke at that instant, but I knew he was stunningly handsome and that the entire spectacle had been enacted as a test to see if I was willing to look beyond the surface and see true beauty within.

The dream left a startling impression on me. Marriage was the furthest thing from my mind at this point. The only issues that concerned me were the culture shock I was going through, and the atavistic Christian impulses that had come back to haunt me, both of which were more than I could handle. I had no idea what the dream could possibly mean and stored it in a vacant chamber of my mind.

For *Simchas Torah*, we moved on to Kfar Chabad, where Taibke had made arrangements to stay with another Chassidic family. By this time, the strain of unfamiliar surroundings had become unbearable for me, and I did something totally un-English. I politely excused myself and walked all the way across the Kfar to the home of Sandy's relatives, with whom I had stayed on my first night in Israel. It was the first time I had ever showed up uninvited on someone's doorstep, but I was desperate to see anyone or anything familiar. I was very relieved that they were so happy to see me, and of course to accommodate me, and so I spent the last night of my holiday vacation between crisp American-style sheets and had a breakfast which consisted of recognizable foods. I was sorry that I could not keep in closer contact with the family and at least have a home base of familiar faces, but they had no phone and lived over four hours away from the school.

When I arrived back at Machon Alte, I was in no better a condition than when I had left. Although I had been moved by the generosity and purity of the *Chassidim*, I felt extremely lonely, and still wanted to go to a church to pray. Rabbi Turkoff finally decided to send me to see a rabbi in Jerusalem named Shlomo Bergman, who had also spent most of his life in Christianity.

I was reluctant. "Look," I argued, "I'm only going if he's been through the same things as I have. If he was not Pentecostal and spirit-filled, then I don't want to see him."

Rabbi Turkoff suggested that I speak to him first on the telephone. I was more than a little abrupt during the phone conversation, but he seemed quite understanding, and so I went to Jerusalem.

Shlomo Bergman had been born into an observant Chassidic home in Eastern Europe shortly before the war. At the age of five, he had watched his parents being buried alive, and the family maid somehow managed to nail him into a crate and ship him off as cargo on a boat sailing for England. There he was met by a group of Christian missionaries, who took him under their wings and raised him.

When he was fifteen, they told him the truth of his family background and gave him the option of returning to his roots. He decided, however, to stay in Christianity, and went off to India, where he worked as a missionary for close to twenty-five years; but gradually the "message" died out on him, and he began slowly to search into his Jewish heritage. During this period, he became very ill and journeyed to Jerusalem, promising God that if he recovered he would dedicate his life to rescuing other Jews from Christianity, and he was now in the midst of keeping that promise. He had a wide network of friends and was involved with several Jerusalem rabbis.

We talked for hours. I was so relieved just to be able to sit down and speak in my own "language" about a heavenly Father, the gifts of the spirit, the Messiah, and goodness knows what else. He understood me completely; and when he said, "I just came to a place where I couldn't preach it anymore," my heart relaxed for the first time in more than two years. Those were exactly the words I had said to myself in Portfield when I knew I had nothing more to give as a minister. It was also comforting to speak with someone who was older and more experienced than I. All of the rabbis I had dealt with until now were so *young*—they were my brother's age, or even my age, and I found it very uncomfortable. Here was an old pastor who was the same age as my father, and who even looked a bit like him, but who wore a *kippah* and spoke of Jewish things in a way that only a Jew can. He blew my mind away.

"Don't feel alone," he encouraged me. "There are a lot of us who were entrenched in Christianity and are now coming back to Torah."

It was good to hear, and I finally dared to believe that the voice of God had really and truly resonated in the depths of my life, and felt that I had been led by Him, rather than by some misguided whim of my own.

Rabbi Bergman was about to host a session for several of his "returned" friends and asked me to stay and meet them, hoping that I would become involved in his anti-missionary activities. I did stay that one time but found the gathering very disconcerting, for I discovered that our approaches were quite different. The subject matter of the discussion was acceptable, but the style of the meeting bothered me; it was conducted in a typical Christian manner and even began with an introductory prayer.

My feeling was that I wanted pure Judaism or nothing. I didn't want it mixed with anything Christian, whether they were innocuous stylistic elements or not. Rabbi Bergman wanted to bring a little of that "Pentecostal fire" into Judaism, while I wanted to search for it on its own terms, to find that deeper flame that I knew had held the Jewish people together for centuries through the worst disasters.

I admired him, though, for the tremendous work he was doing, and was very glad that I had seen him. All along, I'd been learning about Judaism, but subconsciously I was always holding on to Christianity in the faint hope of being able to fall back on it if Judaism wasn't the right thing. After seeing Rabbi Bergman, any doubts that I had harbored about my choice disappeared. My entire past slid off my lap; I let go of the Christians. I felt as though a tightly locked valve somewhere in my soul had sprung open and a tremendous pressure had been released; the only task now was to fill up the vacuum that had been left behind. I had torn down my old, decaying house but had not yet put up the new one, and so in the meantime I was standing out in the open air, shivering.

Everything about me had been Christian except for one delicate, fragile thread of Jewishness, and now this thread was all that was left to me. I had nothing else. As the new term at school commenced, I resolved to strengthen that tiny thread to the best of my ability, to try to refill the empty chamber in my life.

We went on a trip to the Diaspora Museum in Tel Aviv, and it was there that I saw before my eyes what the Christians had done to the Jews repeatedly over hundreds and thousands of years; so many *shuls* burnt to the ground, so many communities ravaged, so many people tortured and killed. I stood near the exhibits for hours, reading, thinking, copying down bits and pieces of information. It was almost too much to absorb.

I began to understand the world I had come from and to appreciate the amazing tolerance the Weinbaums had exhibited by accepting me in such a raw state from a culture which had done their people so much damage over the ages. Their courage was compounded by the fact that they had not even been quite certain in the beginning that I was Jewish or that my story was authentic. Once again, all I could think of was that I wished I could beg forgiveness from all the Jews for having been associated for twenty-five years with their oppressors. I simply hadn't known.

I was humbled when I returned to school from the trip and looked afresh at the rabbis and all the people in the community who had opened their arms wide in order to help me. At times, it still seemed a dream that I was among Jews. Often, I would look around the classroom at all of the girls and tell myself, "These are all Jews, every one of them, and I'm here among them, and this is a rabbi who is teaching us"; or I would sit in the Rosenfelds' home on *Shabbos*, trying to take in the beauty of the table, the candles and *kiddush*, and the royal presence of the *Shabbos* queen herself. My heart would melt with the sheer pleasure of having come home.

I was growing and learning fast. Even *halacha* was no longer a problem. Thirstily I drank from the well of truth and absorbed the words of Torah with relish and delight. The education at Machon Alte was excellent and all the teachers first-rate. Rabbi Rosenfeld never lost an opportunity to teach me words of Torah personally or to share stories of his own life. I remember as well with much gratitude the totally different sort of education his wife gave me during innumerable cozy Friday afternoons when we talked about many different aspects of life while I helped her prepare for *Shabbos*. All of these people were living examples of the life they were teaching, and I felt greatly indebted to them.

It was about this time that Rabbi Friedman came from Minneapolis to speak in Jerusalem. We all went down to hear him, and I was thoroughly surprised that he recognized me even though I had cut and permed my hair. During his stay, he visited Safed for a *Shabbos*, and I was lucky enough to be able to speak with him.

He explained to me that my struggles over the past year resulted from my attempt to serve God with a Christian approach, and I realized that he was right. I thought of the disappointment I had felt in the synagogue on *Yom Kippur*, where the entire atmosphere of worship seemed so inappropriate. I had expected to see people silently weeping tears of remorse, to sense around me the agony of regretfulness that I had experienced in Portfield, and instead had found myself amidst a hum of fervent, energetic, hopeful prayer. I thought of the old instincts that had haunted me for so long: the urge to go to the hills of Safed and meditate, to speak in tongues, to seek out the familiarity of a church and form my own prayers rather than read words by rote from a book. I had come into my new life with a set of old expectations which had tripped me up again and again. I understood this much better now.

Rabbi Friedman also told me that it would take a miracle for me to get married.

"Marriage is a miracle anyway," he explained, "but for you it will take a slightly larger miracle. But don't worry," he added with a reassuring smile. "If a miracle is going to happen, you are in the right place."

I was afraid to ask him exactly what he meant. We both knew I would never have married had I stayed in the college, and I think that if I had known my new life would necessarily lead to it, I might never have left. Although I deeply desired it in my heart, the idea of marriage terrified me. I had grown up solidly grounded in the notion that the institution was nothing more than a tolerable compromise designed for people who could not control their impulses, and Rabbi Friedman must have understood that it would be very difficult for me to overcome this mindset.

His words sank deep into my heart. I thought of the dream I had had in Meah Shearim. Perhaps there was some significance in it. I was content to wait and see how my "miracle" would actually come about. In the following months, many people suggested I should think about going to America to find a suitable partner in life: but I never replied. It was my secret. I would stay in Israel and wait. Rabbi Friedman also encouraged me to write my story down. "Tova, I have learned Torah my entire life, lived it and teach it, but when I see it alive in front of my eyes, I can not tell you what it does to me. You must write it down."

It was good to speak to Rabbi Friedman and to hear his encouraging words. Things were finally coming together.

❧ TWENTY-EIGHT ❧

SOME time ago, I had received a call from a woman who told me that my sister Esther was dangerously ill. I knew that Esther lived in Bat Yam, but I had not contacted her since my arrival in Israel. I was fairly sure that if my parents discovered my whereabouts through her, it would only be a short time before letters would begin to arrive telling me that I was wasting my time, and I simply wasn't prepared to deal with that yet. I no longer had any doubts about what I'd done, but I knew that my father was displeased with me, and his letters were always a difficult challenge.

For the same reason, I had not contacted any of my mother's relatives in Israel, not even my Uncle Sammy. None of them were religious, and I was going through so many inner conflicts that I did not want to add outer ones to the fire.

In my paranoia, I assumed that my parents had asked Esther to locate me, and that the phone call was a ruse to find out if I had really arrived in Israel or not. I was very brusque with the woman and told her to leave me alone and stop telling me lies. I put down the receiver, but five minutes later, she called again and repeated that my sister was gravely ill.

I decided to let the matter lie. Hadn't I seen my sister in England only a few months ago? There was definitely nothing wrong with her then. She was bonny and as full of life as she'd always been. I decided that if she were really sick, the caller would tell her that I was at

391

Machon Alte, and Uncle Sammy, who lived only thirty minutes away by car in Kiryat Shemonah, would contact me and confirm it. But I heard nothing for a few months.

Shortly before *Chanukah*, while I was sitting in class, I happened to glance up at the doorway of the classroom. Standing there, to my utter amazement, were Uncle Sammy and his wife, a lovely Moroccan woman whom I had never seen before except in photographs. They had given me no warning or hint at all. At first, I was nervous, for I thought they would be angry with me for not having contacted them sooner; but then my uncle winked at me, and I knew that there were no hard feelings.

I got up quietly and left the classroom. My uncle wept with the sheer joy of seeing me in Israel, away from "those crazy people in Portfield," as he called them. He mentioned that my sister Esther had not been very well but that it was nothing to worry about. It turned out that she had given him my address and had asked him to visit me, but my parents were not involved at all.

He and Aunt Maria invited me to their home, and I promised that the next time we had an "out *Shabbos*" in the school, in which case there were no classes on Sunday, I would use the Sunday to come visit them in Kiryat Shemonah.

Sure enough, one *Motzei Shabbos*, the telephone rang in the dorm. "Hello, Toni," my uncle said cheerfully. "I hope you haven't changed your mind about tomorrow."

Of course I hadn't, and I spent the remainder of the evening preparing myself for the next day. My aunt would be disgusted if I did not eat anything, but since their home was not kosher, all my food and eating utensils had to be packed. I was looking forward to meeting all my cousins, whom I had heard so much about and had seen grow up in photographs, but I was a little afraid of what they would think of my strange ways. I hoped they would accept me.

৯

The sun glistened on a snow-peaked Mount Hermon as the bus twisted its way north the next day, and the other mountains of the Golan shimmered in the distance. Valleys and hills, alive with fresh vegetation, flashed by us, surrounding open, airy fields and an occasional army base. My thoughts ran away with me, and the time flew by. True to his word, my uncle was at the bus station to meet me, and during the drive home, he talked proudly of the history of his town and the role he had taken in its growth.

Uncle Sammy was still a stocky, energetic man with a mind and will as active and powerful as his physique. He was exactly as I remembered him. Still the old-fashioned Zionist, fiercely proud of being Jewish, and intensely proud of the state of Israel. He was beyond himself with excitement that I was actually in Kiryat Shemonah. He reminded me of how they had started out in tin huts, one hut per family; how he had worked so hard to help dig two huge canals to drain the swamps; how he had ploughed the fields and worked the soil and built roads. Now the town boasted many beautiful orchards, fresh vegetable gardens, fine houses, a university and a *yeshiva*. He had also lobbied with protective zeal to make sure political measures insured the welfare of Kiryat Shemonah's citizens. He was very proud of his accomplishments, and I could not blame him.

"Look at the little ones," he said, pointing to some children playing nearby. "We've fought and worked hard so that these children can play happily and peacefully in the streets."

Sammy had worked equally hard to build a successful career as a chartered accountant and had clients all over the Galilee. He was extremely charitable, and his home was always full of guests. He had never really believed in God, but his heart and feelings were Jewish to the core.

My Aunt Maria had an equally feisty history. She was from a wealthy Sephardic family who had come to Israel from Morocco, and her family had been among the "tent people" who lived out in the open until there were enough developments to house them. They had been strongly religious before they emigrated, and spoke Ladino at home, but even though my aunt was no longer observant, her Jewish identity was just as strong as her husband's. I was soon to find out that anyone who questioned her faith was asking for trouble. One didn't get onto the subject of God with Aunt Maria!

Uncle Sammy excitedly told me that he and Aunt Maria had recently been chosen for a special honor. There had been a particularly difficult week when dozens of Ketusha rockets had fallen on Kiryat Shemonah. As a consequence, the President of Israel, Yitzchak Navon had announced that he wanted to go to Kiryat Shemonah and meet an ordinary family there and speak with them. Uncle Sammy was beside himself with joy when he and Aunt Maria were chosen. City Hall said they would pay for food and refreshments and any expenses my uncle and aunt incurred to prepare for the President's arrival, but my uncle would not hear of it. He paid for everything himself and was ecstatic for weeks. It so happened that a Ketusha fell right before the President arrived and my uncle had to greet him with a flashlight as the electricity was still out. In true Morrocan custom, my aunt met him at the door with warm milk, fresh mint and sugar. Many of their personal friends and neighbors were also invited, and as both Aunt Maria and the President were of Spanish/Ladino descent, they all conversed in Ladino.

"Toni, it was in *my* home that the President of Israel came! Do you know what an honor that was? I will never forget it my entire life."

Soon we were ascending the steps to their humble, yet tastefully decorated, home on Herzl Street. The atmosphere was distinctly Middle Eastern and glowed with the comfort of material security. Big round leather pouffes sprawled restfully on Persian rugs, brass knickknacks adorned the shelves, and a variety of plants filled the small conservatory next to the living room. Through a stone archway, one could catch a glimpse of the grapevine which canopied the garden, and beyond that, the avocado trees and cacti standing motionless against the pure blue perfume of the afternoon.

Uncle Sammy took great pleasure in giving me a tour and pointing out the family treasures. One of his daughters was an art teacher, and her paintings and macrame baskets dotted the living room walls. He showed me a pencil drawing of my grandfather that he had done when he was a boy, and a *menorah* which my grandfather had lit in Alexandria. Grandpa had died while I was still in Portfield, and this *menorah* suddenly took on a special importance. I stared at it for a long time; so old, so beautiful, but a slave to the wall.

"Uncle, why don't you use it?" I inquired. "It's much better to use oil on *Chanukah*."

"Yes, Toni, I know," he said quietly, "but candles are quicker, you know...."

My Aunt Maria, true to her Moroccan upbringing, wanted to feed me immediately. Proudly, she brought her wares out of the cupboard: a soup bowl, side plate and dinner plate carefully packed in plastic wrap, labels still intact, with a big "Made in Israel" stamp on the underside of each piece. "See—new," she said with delight. "We bought them especially for you."

My uncle chuckled. "Come, Toni," he said, "we are going to the grocery store and you can choose whatever food you like. We want you to feel at home."

I insisted it wasn't necessary, thinking of the food I had brought along in my handbag, but I did not wish to offend them in any way.

We drove to the store, and I chose just a few simple items which I knew had the correct seals of rabbinic supervision. My uncle also urged me to take a few chocolate bars, and any other treats I wanted, so that I would have something to take back to school.

We happened to run into one of his old battle comrades in the aisle, and Uncle Sammy introduced me. The gentleman politely held out his hand to me, but I quickly dunked both of mine into my pockets. "I'm sorry," I said with a sweet smile. "I don't shake hands but I'm very happy to meet you."

"You don't *shake hands?*" my uncle responded in a shocked tone.

How fanatical had his little niece become? He stood there for a moment in numb silence, but his comrade was not the least bit perturbed, and we chatted for a while before parting amiably.

Lunch was very pleasant—and fortunately, not as awkward as I had anticipated. I sat with my own little goodies while the rest of the family dove into my aunt's delicious cooking. I remembered Raymond Webster telling me years ago that he had traveled the world over but had never tasted food like my Aunt Maria's. I had always longed to meet her and eat her delicacies; and now I was here, smelling the beautiful aromas but not the slightest bit upset that I was not tasting them as well.

My uncle was watching my every movement.

"Toni," he asked, "do you know all the prayers by heart?"

"Oh, no," I laughed. "Only the short blessings before and after eating, but there are much longer ones which I read from the prayer book."

"Do you know them in Hebrew?"

"Yes, Uncle, in Hebrew," I answered.

He seemed overwhelmed and his eyes filled with tears. We sat quietly for a few moments, and finally he said, "Toni, I never would have thought, I never would have dreamt, that you of all people—you would come into my home and teach me Judaism."

After lunch, we sat and talked for a while. Still somewhat awed, Sammy said wistfully, "I wish that Grandpa could see you now. He wanted so much for someone in the family to be religious. He wanted it from me...but I just couldn't do it. And to think that it should come from his own daughter who went astray, that she should have a child like you! If there had been some sort of tiny flame and it was rekindled, I could understand it, but there was nothing. Absolutely nothing."

"You know, Toni," he added softly after a moment's thought, "you are experiencing it, and we are observing it—and for us it is the greater thing." His eyes were full of tears again. It was a moment made precious by all the years of rebellion, struggles and great distance that had preceded it. For me, it was another wondrous episode in my living dream.

෨

Having fought in all the wars since the 1948 War of Independence, my uncle was keen to show me all the local places of military interest, and after lunch, we went out for a drive. He had a full stock of stories and historical information to keep me entertained. I particularly liked his account of the battles he had fought with Aunt Maria by his side, she loading up the ammunition and he firing.

He took me to Tel Hai, Metulla and the Lebanese border, and our chat led us to the subject of the Arab-Israeli wars.

Uncle Sammy had a daughter who was also named Toni, and her husband worked in a rehabilitation center, counseling boys who were addicted to drugs and alcohol. One boy had been a particularly bad alcoholic, and after Toni's husband had finally put him back on his feet, he'd gone off to fight in Lebanon and was killed.

"My son-in-law still feels terrible about this," Uncle Sammy told me. "He thinks that if he had left the boy alone, he might still be alive today."

"And do you know what the worst part is?" I rejoined. "So many boys just like him have gone to battle—and you would give back the very land they fought for! Their deaths might have been totally in vain."

"We give back the land because it is not ours," my uncle said.

"What do you mean, it's not ours?" I retorted. "In the *Chumash*, it's ours! *Hashem* gave it to us from the very foundation of the world!"

Sammy laughed. "Oh, Toni," he said, "you are so religious! I am proud to have such a religious niece. I say, God bless your soul."

"And I say, God bless yours!"

My uncle was fun. I felt lucky that he was so proud of me, and from that time on, I went often to see him. He always insisted on giving me pocket money and buying me lots of treats, and he even told me that when he had returned home from his trip to England, he'd saved up money for a ticket to bring me to Israel—"just in case" I asked him.

❧

It was after one of these Sunday visits, while we waited in the station for my bus back to Safed, that I asked my uncle about our family history. I was totally astonished by the things I heard.

Patiently, he told me of my mother's Spanish origins and of how the family had fled to Greece when the Jews were expelled. They had settled among Jewish refugees from Italy on a small island called Zante, and had stayed there until a blood libel in the latter part of the nineteenth century forced them to flee again, this time to Egypt.

That explained why my mother's first language was Italian. "But, Uncle," I asked, "if Grandpa was religious, how did he allow my mother to marry a non-Jew?"

"Well, Toni," he continued, "for humane reasons during the war, Grandma and Grandpa opened their home to the young boys in the army who didn't smoke, drink or use bad language. There was nowhere for them to go in Alexandria except to drinking places and gambling halls, so your grandparents allowed them to come in to have a meal and sing songs.

"Of course these were all Christian boys, but they were good boys," he added emphatically. "Your father just happened to be one of them. In fact, all of the boys wanted your mother—she was a pretty girl, quiet and pleasant too. She liked to stay at home and help her mother, and she was excellent at embroidery and things like that. Everyone liked her."

By now, he was on an inner journey, dreamily picturing the past in his mind. "Actually your father was not the first one. Your mother liked another boy before him, and when she mentioned it to Grandpa, he took a stick and chased her all around the room. I'm sure he didn't intend to beat her, but he was so horrified that he didn't know what to do. While he was running after her, he tripped and broke his leg. It took a long time to mend, and I think maybe he took it as a sign from God that it was not so terrible for his daughter to marry one of the soldiers. After all, they were good, moral, clean-living boys. And so when your father came along, Grandpa had already learned his lesson—and while he did not agree to the marriage, and would not give his blessing, he did not forbid it.

"In fact, Toni, your Grandpa would never have seen your mother again, except that I managed to persuade him after many years to go to England and visit her. I paid for his ticket and made all the arrangements, and I had to literally force him to get on the plane," he concluded.

A shock of remembrance shot through me suddenly and set a voice ringing in my head: *"Do not invite a non-Jew to eat with you, for he will end up marrying your daughter."* And then, with a pang of irony, I heard my own voice screaming out, *"That's stupid!"* I had been so angry with that rabbi, only to find living proof of his words in my own family!

The bus for Safed arrived, but I couldn't go on board. I wanted to know more. We watched it pull out and remained by the railings, our minds far away in a small house on a street called Thompson in the heart of Alexandria.

"But Uncle, how did Grandma come to believe in Christianity?" I asked.

"Well, Toni," he said, "I am embarrassed to tell you that we were very poor. *Very* poor! It was much worse than you could ever imagine. Grandpa was not an aggressive person, even though he was talented. He knew nine languages fluently and could write them beautifully too, but even though he was a printer by trade—and a very good one—he preferred to stay at the same job he had held for years instead of finding better-paying work. We were so poor that we didn't even have enough soup bowls to go around, and the ones we did have were all cracked and broken. Often, I would come home from school and say, 'Mother, I'm hungry. What is there to eat?' and she'd reply, 'I'm sorry, but there's nothing.' Sometimes there would be a little weak soup, and she would tell me to fill up on bread. It was hard for Grandma to keep kosher because of this. The kosher butcher was a long way from the house, and the prices were twice as high as those of the non-kosher butcher, so she stopped going out there—and then she stopped keeping *Shabbat*, simply because it was too difficult and expensive. By the time the local missionaries befriended her, she was barely observant.

"Your grandmother was not a wicked woman, Toni," he stressed quietly. "It was just incredibly difficult for her. She was also very clever and knew English perfectly, so she was hired at a private Christian school in Alexandria to teach English. In place of a salary, the headmaster agreed to take me and my brother into the school for no money. You know, Toni, if I hadn't had that education, I wouldn't be where I am today," he added.

I knew everything now; but I was amazed that the Torah I was learning in school had once been so real within my own family. Hadn't we learned that *Shabbos* and *kashrus* were the foundations of the Jewish faith? With those gone, it was no wonder my grandmother had become easy prey for the missionaries.

It was then that my uncle asked me why I did not want to contact my sister Esther.

"Because I don't trust her," I said without hesitation. "I'm not worried about Esther—I'm just afraid that she might tell my father where I am. I don't want my father preaching at me. I've had enough of it."

"I just want to tell you one thing," Uncle Sammy said seriously. "You don't know your big sister."

The bus arrived and I boarded it, waving happy good-byes to the uncle who was becoming more and more of a father to me.

≈ TWENY-NINE ≈

JUST a few days later, Rabbi Rosenfeld called me out of class. This was not his custom, and I wondered what could be so urgent. He sat me down in the kitchen and told me that my sister was not well and that my uncle wanted to take me to Bat Yam to see her. His tone was very grave, and I waited for Uncle Sammy to arrive with no little apprehension.

When I had last seen Esther in England, she was glowing, her cheeks were rosy, and her eyes were glittering with laughter and fun. What had happened in these six months?

"You understand, Toni," Uncle Sammy said as we headed south in the car, "Esther has been very sick. She is not the Esther you are used to. But she doesn't know exactly how sick she is, and you have to act normally—as though everything is fine."

I thought back to the days when Esther and I were children and tried to picture her as a young girl. If ever there had been a maverick in our family, it was she. With only eleven months difference between her and my sister Margaret, they were constantly being compared, but the balance always tipped in Margaret's favor. She was the shining star, always impeccably neat and much more hardworking at school. Esther, on the other hand, could never sit in one place for long, and was so full of life and mischief that she would do the most outrageous things simply because she could not resist an adventure. Despite her lack of academic achievement, Esther had a tremendous personality, but unfortunately that quality did not rank as high in the Church as discipline and obedience.

I was only ten years old when she left home to go the ministerial college in Portfield, and that was the last I had really seen of her for almost seventeen years. Aside from two brief meetings, all I knew about her were the random stories I had picked up over the years. I had heard that her name had always been on the black list at college because she would not submit to those in authority over her. Her departure from the Church had always been a mysterious blank in our family history, and until now it hadn't occurred to me to ask for the details.

What I found was no "black sheep," no heretical outcast; what I found was a sweet, tender rose whose beauty I discovered too late. In later years, my experience with Esther reminded me of a parable I had once heard about a king who had a beautiful garden filled with a tremendous variety of plants and flowers. Every day, he would walk in this little paradise and enjoy its wonderful perfumes; but there was one flower that he particularly liked. He would stand and behold its beauty for a few extra moments, watching it grow more and more exquisite as time went by.

But then, one day, when the king was taking his usual stroll, he noticed that the beautiful flower was spoiled. The petals had all fallen off, and the stem hung down limply. The king in the story, of course, is God, His garden this world, and His flowers the creations within it; but unlike the king in the story, He knows exactly the right time to pick each flower before it loses its luster.

To me, this was Esther, a radiant flower who had sprung up amongst a thicket of briars and thorns. She had the strength of character to bloom where she was planted, even under great difficulty, and when she achieved her goals, there was seemingly no one around to admire and appreciate her sweet perfume and tenderness—that is, until the King of Kings, God Himself, stooped down in His garden and mercifully picked her before she was finally trampled into the ground and thoroughly spoiled.

Esther was rare and beautiful. I found out too late, but I will never forget the tiny glimpse I had of her.

&

When I entered the house, I was met with a very cold reception from Esther's husband, Rammy, and her father-in-law, who were obviously displeased with me for not having visited her sooner.

"Tonica, is that you?" came a pallid voice from somewhere in the distance. I waited nervously, and about five minutes later Esther appeared at the door of her bedroom. Not even my uncle's warning could have prepared me for the sight I beheld.

She was a standing corpse, skin and bone, so white she was almost transparent. She breathed with difficulty and could barely walk. She said nothing, but her obvious joy in seeing me shone through her weak smile. I ran over to her and hugged her, tears streaming down my face.

After a moment, she managed to gasp out a few questions. What would I eat? Would I please drink something? She had a new dress that she had saved for me and a pair of boots to go with it. Even in her condition, she wanted only to be a big sister to me and to care for me as she had done when I was a little girl.

I suggested she get back into bed and sat down next to her. An enormous oxygen cylinder was her constant companion. Every time she tried to talk, she would break into fits of coughing that turned her face purple. We sat there together holding hands, something we hadn't done since we were children. I tried desperately to maintain my composure, and she tried desperately to make me feel at ease, assuring me that everything was all right and that she was going to get better.

Later, my uncle clarified my doubts as to the nature of her illness. Two years earlier, she had been diagnosed with breast cancer and had undergone a radical mastectomy. The surgery was seemingly successful, but the disease had struck again four months ago. The doctors said it was just a matter of time now, that there wasn't a cell in her body that wasn't infested.

If ever I had seen ugliness in this world, I saw it in my beautiful sister. Each time I visited her, she was eaten away a little more, but she struggled and fought continually.

She once insisted on taking me to a shop in Tel Aviv that sold dress patterns so that I could make myself something nice for *Pesach*. She even wanted to buy the pattern for me. The bus ride was half an hour each way, and I didn't know what the trip had cost her until we returned home and were sitting in her kitchen.

"You see, Ton," she said, "I did it! I never thought I would be able to make it, but I did it!" Something in her voice gave me the feeling that she had doubted whether she would even survive the journey, but that hadn't deterred her. She was the same Esther I'd known seventeen years ago—putting others first, herself second.

I began to go down to Bat Yam regularly, as often as I could make the trip, about once each week. When I spoke to Rabbi Rosenfeld about it, he asked me some questions about Esther's husband. I told him that Rammy was a diving instructor in Eilat and only came home on weekends. This fact, together with the non-religious nature of the home, troubled the principal, and he advised me not to stay in the house overnight.

There was only one time that I did not heed his wishes, and that was on the occasion of Avishai's birthday. Esther's little son was turning six, and she asked me to come to the party she was planning for him at his kindergarten. I brought along a cake I had baked and a huge, handmade birthday card, and helped Esther out with the preparations. That night I slept in Avishai's room, and I could tell by my sister's face how happy and grateful she was that I had come.

The next morning as we were jolting along in the bus on the way to the school, Esther whispered, "Tonica, you don't know how hard it is for me to get one breath. I'm so sick of this stupid cough. For *one* breath, it's a fight that nearly kills me."

I slipped my arm through hers. I didn't know what to say. I wanted to fight it for her, but I couldn't; I just had to stand by like a helpless rag doll and watch her struggling to survive a losing battle. It was the most horrible thing I'd ever experienced—watching someone I loved, my own flesh and blood, whither away, and feeling that a part of myself was disintegrating too.

When we arrived at the school, Esther tried to dance with her son. She almost fainted once and fell down, but she got up and continued. Avishai only laughed, for he did not understand, and like a good mother, she tried to laugh too. Some might have said that she was reckless and had probably shortened her life by taxing her strength so much, but I admired her courage. All the other mothers in the kindergarten danced with their children at birthday parties, and Esther was not about to disappoint her son. Right up until she died, she made sure Avishai never missed anything. He and her loved ones and friends were always first on her list.

During the course of my visits over the next few months, she told me many stories about herself, and I was finally able to string together all the pieces of her past. It seemed incredible to me that at age twenty-seven I was still finding out so many astonishing secrets about my family.

Esther had gone to training college at sixteen, and she confirmed the reports I had heard of her rebelliousness. In her own words, she had been "treated like dirt" there. Victoria Webster had dealt harshly with most of the novices, but Esther felt she had been singled out because she was always laughing things off and could not be put down easily.

Four years later, when she was twenty, she was sent to help out in a congregation in Shenley, a town in the south of England. She was assigned no permanent quarters and was shipped around from family to family, until one day she arrived home from work and found all her belongings in the street. The old couple with whom she had been staying decided that they didn't want to attend the services anymore, and so consequently they didn't want Esther either.

Heartbroken and in tears, she telephoned my father, who at that time was ministering in Southford. He drove to Shenley immediately and took her back home with him. This caused a big stir in the church, for apparently Raymond Webster did not approve of my father's action. I don't know whether he expected Esther to stay in the street or not, but he had sent her on the mission and could not afford to have other people interfering with his orders.

Esther never did return to Shenley, but instead made plans to go to Israel. Before she left, Brother Bartholomew, the most respected "prophet" in the college, tried hard to persuade her to give up her plans by pronouncing his prophecy of doom: "The moment you step on the plane, there is no way back." I realized now that the Church had to engage in such spiritual browbeating in order to pump fear into the hearts of any other "wayward sheep" who might be edging out of the fold.

But Esther was equipped with a stalwart personality and sheer guts. She went anyway. I can't say she wasn't afraid, but she went. She crossed an ocean and entered what was for her a new world, a new culture, and a new people.

In Israel, she stayed at Uncle Sammy's home for the first six months and afterwards met and married Rammy, a secular and affluent Jew whose father was a bank manager in Tel Aviv. Esther was not openly practicing Christianity then, and since Rammy's father was religious, she agreed to have her documents authorized by the *Bais Din* in London in order to satisfy the family. She even went to the trouble of asking my parents to write a detailed letter to the *Bais Din* explaining the circumstances of their own marriage and testifying to my mother's Jewishness. Now at last, I had an answer to the strange mystery of almost a year ago, when the rabbis who interviewed me had told me that they knew my sister!

Unfortunately, Esther's gesture did not do much to heal an ailing situation, for her husband was quite disturbed when he subsequently found out how strong her Christian convictions really were; and once he even took a Bible that my father had sent her, and ripped it apart in front of her.

This issue was unfortunately not the only stress in the marriage, for Rammy was unfaithful as well. In spite of all her difficulties, Esther persevered and stayed at home to raise her little son, and she never complained. She had been deeply hurt by so many people, but she never expressed an ounce of bitterness and never took her anger out on anyone, concentrating instead on making new friends and helping people. She had always been very close to my parents, and I learned now that it was she who had supported them for several years when they were living in a mobile home on someone's lot in Stornwell, after having been ousted from the church. She had faithfully sent them hard-earned money from her job at the Israel Discount Bank in Tel Aviv, where she had worked for many years in their international department.

Even now, lying weightlessly in bed with almost no strength in her wasted body, she was still shining.

My last visit to Esther was the only time in my life that I ever saw her depressed. Her sickness had spread throughout her entire body, blinding one eye and blurring the other. "Ton, I'm so glad to see you," she told me. "I've been so depressed. I don't know what's the matter with me, I just can't stop crying. Night and day I cry. Usually I get over things and get back on top, but you just don't know how much it has upset me to lose the sight in this eye."

As usual, I was completely at a loss for words. I don't know what I did that day to lighten her load, but a few minutes before I left, she sat up in bed and said, "You've cheered me up so much, Ton. I'm so happy you came."

I was torn between staying with my sister and getting all the way up to the north of the country before the last buses stopped. I thought of Rabbi Rosenfeld's warning not to stay in the house overnight, and I was worried. This was a totally non-religious community, and I did-n't even know where I could buy food. It was Thursday; if I stayed, I would have to stay over *Shabbos*, and I didn't know how I could keep *Shabbos* in this home. I felt so tired and so low that I wasn't even sure I would make the effort.

Finally, I moved to leave. I will never forget Esther's eyes—so far away, so pleading, yet so undemanding.

"Are you going now?" she asked.

"Etty, I'm sorry, I have to. I'll come again soon." I think perhaps she knew that this was the last time we would see each other, and perhaps I did too. All the way to Tel Aviv I kept thinking that I should take the next bus straight back to Bat Yam, but I was too drained to make a decision. I refused to listen to the inner call and continued on my way.

Three days before she died, she telephoned me. Where was I? Did I have enough warm clothing? Did I have enough to eat? When was I going to visit her? She was so worried about me. I told her I was coming to the south on Friday and would head straight to her house the minute *Shabbos* was over.

And I did. But it was too late.

On *Motzei Shabbos*, the rain was coming down in torrents, and it was very windy and cold. I set out to her home from Kfar Chabad and arrived totally drenched. When I opened the front door, I found the room filled with silent people. Rammy was sitting in the middle of the group, and I saw my parents.

"Where's Etty?" I cried. "Where's Etty? *What happened to Etty?*"

No one answered. My parents motioned me into the kitchen, and my father said in an irritable tone, "Do you want me to tell you what happened to your sister?"

I obediently replied, "Yes," as he so obviously wanted to tell me.

"She went to meet Jesus in the sky," he said.

My only instinct was to spit in his eye, but I managed to control myself somehow. I ignored his statement and replied harshly, "God takes the best first, and we're the rubbish. That's why we're still here."

They went back into the front room and left me in the kitchen, alone. Esther was gone, and I had only managed to catch a faint glimmer of her. My uncle had been right; I never knew her. I was totally numb, and I never cried.

At such a time, you are not left with reason or teachings, and all the philosophy in the world will not come to your aid. A person can spout anything from Buddhism to Communism when things are going well, but in the heat of the test, he is left with nothing but the very foundation of his life, his most fundamental belief. It's then that he finds out who he really is.

There had been so many times in my life when I'd looked for an opportunity to "curse God and die," as had been suggested to Job, but I'd never been successful. Now I had a perfect excuse, a reason to leave religion once and for all. How could there be a God who would allow such a beautiful person to be so ravaged? How could He have allowed Etty to die? I was sick of religion, sick of everything.

But I couldn't give it up.

Could I really, really believe there was no God? No, I couldn't believe that. Could I believe that God was bad? No, I couldn't believe that either. So I was left with my most basic and deepest belief: that God existed and that He was good, and it was only I who didn't understand. That was the bottom line.

Esther fortunately had a Jewish burial on the insistence of Rammy's father. After the funeral, I was standing alone by the water fountain in the cemetery grounds when my father came up to me. He put his arm around my shoulder and said, "It was nice, wasn't it?"

I couldn't answer. He was my father; it was the funeral of his eldest daughter. I couldn't think of one nice thing about the way she had died or the way she was buried.

My mother's only reaction was to say to my father, "Jeem, for them it is a tragedy, but for us it is victory."

I was sickened in the pit of my stomach. My parents were not even allowing themselves to feel any grief, because the Christian teaching dictated that the reunification of a soul with Jesus was a joyous occasion. To them, Etty's death—or anyone's death, for that matter—was the best thing that could have happened. To me, their entire conception was warped.

I longed to be back again with my own friends, with Jews who were real people. They felt pain. They cried. They had *simchas*, real *simchas*, and real sorrows too, for Torah was big enough to allow you to be a human being. Christianity was not for human beings, it was only for the saints and the "righteous."

℞

Rammy pressured me to stay and sit *shiva* in his home, hinting that I should move into the house to take care of Avishai. I was still quite naive, but he made it clear that this suggestion included a proposal of marriage, although perhaps not in the immediate future. I knew that there had to be something perverted about a man who would propose to his dead wife's sister so soon after the funeral, and, in fact, Rammy did not look very upset. He even cracked jokes during that first day of *shiva*.

I think the only reason I could have toyed with his offer was because of the state I was in. I had barely any resources left with which to cope. All I could think of was how isolated and lonely I felt, and of how primitive the living quarters were in Machon Alte. Rammy had everything: plenty of money, a beautiful home filled with exquisite paintings and every modern convenience, two large balconies that overlooked the sea. He had everything but Torah.

I desperately wanted my struggles to end, but thank God, I had enough clearheadedness to tell him, "Rammy, it would never work. One of us would have to change."

"I know," he said, "and it wouldn't be me."

"I know," I replied, "and it wouldn't be me either."

Rabbi Rosenfeld had long since foreseen the situation, and had wisely sent down a couple of my closest friends to be with me for the funeral and to encourage me to go back to Safed and sit *shiva* there. Uncle Sammy waited anxiously for me to say something, but I was too numb to think, much less make a decision. Finally my friend Taibke, who had always been a sort of guardian angel for me in times of distress, made my decision for me. "She's coming home to Safed with us," she told Rammy firmly. My uncle drove me straight back to the Rosenfelds' house, where I sat *shiva*.

I was very angry and tense when I arrived, not in love with Torah, God, or anyone at all; but as the week progressed, I was deeply touched by the warmth and concern of the community. Even friends from England called and wrote to me, and my stone heart melted once more. I was back in the safe nest of my own people.

When the week was over, my parents came up to Machon Alte to visit me. My father told me quite bluntly that I was going in the opposite direction of what God wanted for my life. He begged me to go back with them to England, where they had a beautiful room for me, newly decorated; I could forget everything that had passed and start life anew. They would help me find a nice Christian boy to marry.

When I did not respond, my mother wept. "Leave her, Jeem," she cried, "leave the girl alone. Maybe the Almighty will open her eyes another way."

But my father was not about to give up, and he never left me for one second. With tears streaming down his face, holding me tightly in both his arms, he begged, "Promise me, *promise me, right now*, that you will never marry a Jew."

"Daddy, please don't upset yourself so. Everything will work itself out," I responded as gently as I could.

Even on the bus, he was calling out to me from the window that the main idea of the approaching festival of Passover was "the blood."

"When I see the blood, I will pass over you," he quoted. "Make sure you have Jesus' blood on your life—on your heart!"

I was not going to argue with him. There was no point. I knew that until his death, he would be fasting for my "sin" and praying for my return to the "fold." I knew I could never change his attitude. It was hopeless even to try.

In my loneliness I decided it was really true, life was "the pits."

"I could have ended up with the stalks and the leaves," I reprimanded myself for feeling a twinge of self-pity. "I must plant the pits and build my own tree."

Pesach was almost upon us once more. I begged God to let me go out of my own Egypt this year, out of my "place of bondage." I had seen enough bitterness and tears.

I said only one prayer for a husband, and God heard. Alone in my room, I sat on the edge of the bed and sighed from the depths of my heart, "I've been on my own long enough," and one week after *Pesach*, I met my husband.

❧ THIRTY ↬

CHANANIAH Mordechai had been born Jonathan Walter Clark in Sacramento, California, to an Episcopalian couple who raised him in the church. He was the elder of two sons.

His father, born in Chicago, was a rocket scientist who had worked with Erik von Braun and the other German rocket engineers to develop America's first ballistic missile, the Redstone. His mother was born on a farm in western Pennsylvania and was a nurse by profession. The Clarks had a proud lineage dating back to Abraham Clark who signed the Declaration of Independence for the State of New Jersey.

Young Jonathan had carried the cross as an altar boy after being confirmed at the age of fourteen. At that point, he decided to become more serious about Christianity and for the first time read the complete King James Bible from cover to cover. His studies turned up many things that did not make sense. He realized that the New Testament could not be understood by itself, but only within the context of Judaism. He had always heard that the Jews were the chosen people of God and they did not eat pork, and that the Christians were a continuation of that selection, but they do eat pork. How was it, then, that the chosen could suddenly change and now permit that which was forbidden? He went to his priest on numerous occasions to discuss this and other "bothersome" matters such as the Sabbath having been displaced by Sunday, while all the time feeling that he was not receiving satisfactory answers. He spent hours at a time in the public library delving into these matters and trying to understand the meaning of the conflict between Jesus and the Pharisees.

At school, Jonathan had always been known as the "guru," but after he began asking these questions they started to call him "the Jew," which became extremely embarrassing.

More than anything on earth, Jonathan wanted to understand the people of the Bible. He wanted to know all about Moses, the Prophet Samuel, King David, Isaiah and Jeremiah. He felt a burning desire to know what clothes they wore, what food they ate, how they thought, and what words they used. He knew they did not say, "Thou" and "Thee" and he intended to find out what they really did say. He started by memorizing the Hebrew alphabet, alone, at age fourteen. He then progressed onto Hebrew grammar, and by the age of sixteen, he enrolled in an adult class at the local synagogue to learn conversational Hebrew at which he excelled.

About this time, he came to the conclusion that the Pharisees were right and he considered Jesus to be a thief who had stolen the *mitzvos*, and thus, he abandoned all contact with Christianity.

By age seventeen, he was attending synagogue services regularly and joining in their entire after-school educational program. There were some parents who expressed concern about having a non-Jewish boy attending the youth activities but since he knew Hebrew and his Bible studies better than anyone else, the concerns soon faded.

Jonathan's mother told him, "You are throwing away your own heritage the way Esau threw away his birthright for a bowl of beans." She respected the Jews but felt that her son was getting into something that was way too big for him. "All of the dumb Jews got killed hundreds of years ago and all the Jews of today are very smart; you will never be able to keep up with them," she warned him.

Jonathan, on the other hand, felt that to uphold his own heritage was to settle for an unviable compromise, and so, after completing high school at age eighteen, he went to Israel on a one-way ticket. His six-year stay there took him through a kibbutz, conversion, and *yeshivos*, until he'd finally landed at Ohr Someach in Zichron Yaakov, learning under the auspices of Rabbi Asher Reich who happened to be a Tzanzer *Chassid.*

Chananiah had come to Safed a few months earlier to see what the Chabad *yeshiva* was like, with the hope of delving a little into the deeper esoteric principles of Torah, but had been dissatisfied. He was ready to pack up and go back to Ohr Sameach one *Motzei Shabbos* when he heard that Rabbi Manis Friedman from Minneapolis was in town. He delayed his trip in order to hear him speak and was so impressed that he ended up staying in Safed for another six months.

The lecture took place only two days after Rabbi Friedman had told me that it would take a miracle for me to get married.

The dorm mother at Machon Alte had had Chananiah in her house as a *Shabbos* guest, and suggested the match to Rabbi Rosenfeld; I was very much against it. I wasn't ready to get married, and certainly not to a convert. The old longing for a Jewish father was still embedded in me, and I was nourishing the vague hope that if I married a Jewish boy, his father would be mine too. But Rabbi Rosenfeld encouraged me to try it, and so we met in the home of the dorm mother after the Friday night meal that week.

It so happened that Chananiah's glasses broke shortly before. He debated within himself whether to call the meeting off, but finally decided in favor.

From my part, I decided that I would simply speak with him for an hour or so, say "No thank you" to Rabbi Rosenfeld, and continue with my studies unhindered.

All evening I had the strange feeling that I had somehow met Chananiah already.

We sat in our hosts' private library for about an hour and engaged in obligatory chit-chat. I was impatient of the formalities, and I remember thinking, "Oh, for heaven's sake, let's just finish this."

He must have sensed my restlessness, for he asked, "What would you like to do now?"

I didn't want to offend him, so I replied, "Oh, whatever you want to do."

He wasn't sure what that meant and took it as a sign that I probably wanted to talk more; and we ended up sitting in the library until about two-thirty in the morning!

Once we got past the preliminaries, the tone of the conversation changed. I felt more relaxed and found myself talking about my sister Esther and her illness. We never once spoke about religion, and he never once said to me—that night—or in any of our talks afterwards—"Tova, I understand you." My teachers had always told me that they "understood" me, whatever that meant; but with Chananiah, I sensed it in such a deep way that he never had to say it. I felt that I'd finally found a friend.

The following Sunday morning, I happened to see him passing in the street, and was utterly amazed. He did not look anything like the well-groomed, suited fellow who had shown up at the door on Friday night. His sweater was dirty and sported a large, gaping hole at the elbow, and his pants were hopelessly creased; they seemed to have shrunk in the wash as well, for his socks were eminently visible. Obviously the clock had struck midnight and he had turned back into a pumpkin!

We saw each other several times during the next two weeks, taking long walks through the old city of Safed or sometimes just sitting in the city park. It was on one of those occasions that Chananiah let out the secret that he normally wore glasses but they had broken, and since the services of an optician are not so easy to come by in a place like Safed, he actually had no idea what I looked like for about ten days! I kept teasing him, "You realize that when you get your glasses it's all going to be over, don't you?"

But he told me later that he knew he wanted to marry me even before the glasses were repaired.

People tried to discourage me while we were going out. They saw me as the proper English girl with the lace handkerchief tucked neatly up her sleeve, and assumed that I needed someone in a crisp, three-piece suit, carrying an attache case. I decided we just needed to go shopping. They said that Chananiah was unsettled, that he'd flipped around from place to place too many times, that he was cold. One woman told me she thought he was the type who would never bring his wife flowers for *Shabbos*. Chananiah eventually brought me so many flowers that I had to ask him to stop. Fortunately, I took my own time making a decision and used my own judgment, but it made me realize with alarm how easy it is for people to kill a perfect match with senseless blabbering.

We were engaged on the fifteenth of *Tammuz* and I realized I now had a huge dilemma. Should I tell my parents I was getting married to an Orthodox Jew?

I knew my father would come to the wedding and cry.

My sister had just died. They would surely feel like they had lost two children in a very short period of time.

No. I could not bring myself to do it. I would simply get married and afterwards I would break the news to them as gently as I could.

I did take Chananiah to meet Uncle Sammy and Aunt Maria in Kiryat Shemonah, and, needless to say, they fell in love with him immediately. Uncle Sammy proudly showed Chananiah a family heirloom—three beautiful leather bound prayer books preserved in a handmade tin box, passed down through the family for over one hundred and thirty years—a *Haggadah*, and the two prayer books for *Rosh Hashanah* and *Yom Kippur*. They were amazing masterpieces. On one side was Hebrew, and on the other was Ladino, but more interesting were the carefully handwritten notes in Italian. These were my ancestors. They read the *Haggadah* and had their own *machzorim*. It was a great feeling.

Shortly before the wedding, Chananiah told me about a dream of his own that had affected him deeply. Although he was very young at the time, he still remembered it vividly. In it, he was sitting with his mother, brother and some other family members in a large tree. There was another tree nearby, and he had the urgent feeling that he was in the wrong place and should get to the other tree as quickly as possible. He knew it would not be easy to climb down from the tree alone and try to scramble up the other, but deep within himself, he sensed that his life's mission demanded it, and so he did.

୭

As it was the height of the tourist season in Safed, none of the hotels would rent us a hall for the wedding as we wanted to bring in our own kosher caterer.

"Never mind," I told Rabbi Rosenfeld seriously, "We can just get married in the courtyard of Kiryat Chabad. It will be a garden party." I actually thought the idea was rather cute but Rabbi Rosenfeld would not hear of it. He personally went around the city to seek out a place, and finally he found an elderly gentleman who had the key to a former discotheque in the historic Metsuda Park, high up in a forest near the old city of Safed. I had one hundred dollars to my name. With that, I made my own wedding gown and several outfits for *sheva brachos*. Had it not been for the self-sacrifice of my sister, Esther, when she took me on a shopping trip to Tel Aviv, I would never have known where to begin to look for fabric and patterns. Etti was still helping me!

Chananiah had a nest egg that his grandfather had saved for him, and he paid for everything else, even my wedding shoes, *sheitel* and the apartment we rented.

On our wedding invitation was printed the *posuk* from Isaiah (57:19), which reads in part: "*Shalom, shalom larachok v'lakarov...u'refusiv*"—"Peace, peace, to him that is far and to him that is near...and I will heal him." The commentaries explain that the person who is "far" is the convert, and the person who is "near" refers to one who was born Jewish but not raised Jewish.

On the afternoon of the wedding, I got dressed in Rabbi Rosenfeld's home. The one florist store in Safed was not able to make me a bridal bouquet, and so for photographs, I used Mrs. Rosenfeld's silk flowers from her kitchen!

When we were just about to leave for the hall, there was an unexpected knock on the door—and standing there, laden with boxes and bags of all shapes and sizes, was Rabbi Sufrin! He had come all the way from England as a special surprise, bringing me the good wishes of the London community, my sewing machine, and a host of gifts. Among these treasures were poems, letters and photographs from the Weinbaum children, who considered me part of their family and were so happy for me. I'd kept in touch with the Weinbaums all during my stay in Israel, mainly through a warm correspondence with *Zeidie*, and these additional love notes from little hands were like sparkling icing on my wedding cake.

And so I went to my *chasunah* alive, excited and determined to enjoy myself, and completely unprepared for the additional surprises awaiting me.

Firstly, in the midst of the *kabbolas ponim*, Rabbi Rosenfeld sent over to me the most beautiful bouquet of roses and carnations in various shades of red, pink and white. To this day, he only smiles when I ask him where he got it from. Secondly, Chananiah and I had predicted we would be lucky to have a *minyan* at the wedding, as we had few contacts and didn't belong to a community; but the affair unfolded in a spectacular way. The hall was in an open, public area, and Jews of all types and opinions began to pour in from nowhere. Some of them had never seen a religious wedding before, including my own relatives who were extremely moved, both by the ceremony itself and by the warmth of the atmosphere. An entire tour of Bnei Akiva boys from England decided to "crash," and by the time the dancing was well under way, they could be seen bouncing on the shoulders of *Chassidim* they had never met before. A whole group of Chananiah's friends from Zichron Yaakov rented an Egged bus and showed up without warning, and several girls from various seminaries came up to me and said, "I know we don't have an invitation, but my friend was coming, so I came along too." The girls from Machon Alte performed several beautiful dances for me, and they were even equipped with a lavishly decorated maypole.

My wedding was very special and very joyous, even though I did not know the names of most of the people who were there.

૭

When I was five months pregnant with our first child, I decided it was time to tell my parents I had got married. I wrote a postcard home:

Dear Daddy and Mummy,
How are you? I am having a great time in Israel. The weather is good and I'm meeting a lot of wonderful people. Trust you are both well,
Love Tova.
p.s. I got married.

About ten days later, I received a telephone call from my sister, Margaret.

"Daddy and Mummy are planning an emergency trip to Israel," she forewarned me. "Daddy is furious! He cannot believe you had the audacity to do such a thing. He is horrified. And this '*so-called husband*' of yours did not even ask for your hand in marriage! Daddy is disgusted! He is coming to Israel to see who this person is that you have married. Don't say I did not warn you."

After thanking my sister for the call, I replaced the receiver. Shortly afterwards, the telephone rang a second time. It was my father telling me to prepare for his visit and that my mother would be joining him. They would be spending most of their time between the homes of my mother's two brothers in Acco and Kiryat Shemonah, but they would spend one night with me.

૭

Chananiah was the best sport, especially when the only gift my father gave him was a cheap plastic pen. Whilst the preacher and my rabbi conversed, I went into the kitchen to prepare supper. My mother soon joined me.

"Tova," she whispered. "Do you know what prayer I said when I was on the operating table?"

Nine years had passed since my mother's operation. For twenty-seven years I had only known her as the "completed Jewess," the "Christian of Jewish origin." My mother had sat for hours upon hours each week in her husband's church and never spoke one word of her life as a Jew before she converted to Christianity.

"No, Mummy. I do not know what prayer you said," I answered.

"I said *Shema*," she confided.

It was my turn to be flabbergasted. I had absolutely no idea that she even knew the *Shema*. And now she had admitted that despite all the so-called proclamations of faith in a foreign deity that had passed her lips over the past forty years, when it came to a life-and-death situation she had not chosen to waste the moment on a useless god. She knew exactly where her strength lay—in the only true God, the God of Israel. And she both knew and remembered how to reach Him as a Jew.

Just one month before our first child was born, Uncle Sammy died of cancer. In his last moments he called to his side his youngest daughter, Shirley, who was serving in the army at the time. He asked her to speak for him and tell everyone that he was sorry he had not had the opportunity to die in battle. Death from illness he considered a total waste. He requested that he be covered with the Israeli flag and his grave should be covered only with the stone of the Golan Heights. Inscribed upon it were the words he spoke so often, and totally lived by:

To serve the country is an obligation,
To love the country is a privilege.

He was fifty-two years old.

Our son was born on the fifteenth of *Tammuz* which coincided with the *yahrtzeit* of the famous kabbalistic rabbi from Morrocco, the "Ohr haChaim." We decided to call our son Chaim, followed by Raphael Shmuel, after my grandfather. It was after we had already named Chaim that my aunt Maria told us the most interesting story.

Shortly before Uncle Sammy's passing, his family had brought to their home the famous kabbalist from Ashkelon, Rabbi Pinto. As he examined Uncle Sammy's soul, as part of his spiritual investigation, he discovered a difficulty in Sammy's name.

"Does he have another name?" he inquired.

"No, Sammy–Shmuel," my aunt immediately replied. "This is the only name I know of."

Shortly afterwards, Rabbi Pinto inquired if "Chaim" was his name and instructed my aunt to go to his bedside and inquire.

"Yes," my uncle confirmed. "My name is Chaim Shmuel."

All of a sudden, my mother's story about how the rabbi in Alexandria had chosen his name—in the promise he would live—made so much more sense, for Chaim means "life."

I continued to cook for Machon Alte, as well as doing secretarial work, and in the beginning, I also sat in on classes as often as I could, taking my baby with me. Chananiah stayed in *kollel* for a year and a half until he received his rabbinical ordination, and then he began teaching part-time in Machon Alte. He had a broad span of knowledge and was very articulate, and because of his background, he was able to get through to the more intellectual girls who had been brought up with a rational, scientific outlook on life.

Our relationship was miraculous in more ways than one. In spite of our non-Jewish histories, we had both grown up in morally strict environments. Chananiah had been less sheltered than I, but in spite of his exposure to American culture, he never drank, smoked or had a girl-friend, and when he was once asked why he didn't take drugs, he'd replied that it was too expensive! In our own way, we were both still so pure and innocent, and I thank God to this day that we did not have to deal with some of the adjustments that even a "mainstream" couple often has to make when the partners come from dissimilar backgrounds.

But Chananiah was my miracle in more ways than abstinence from drugs and alcohol. What I really needed was a "nun" rehabilitation center before I was fit to try to begin a marital relationship. I became moody and untouchable in an effort to protect myself from further "sin" and "disgrace." As it was so personal an issue, it did not occur to me that I could get professional help, and sadly to say, it took me well over ten years of marriage to learn to allow myself pleasure.

M Y entire life I arrogantly thought I knew how to serve God. I had no idea it would take me another fifteen years to learn exactly what God wanted from a Jew.

I had no idea that having a baby was what God wanted from me. That educating a child and caring for his needs was serving God. That maintaining a kosher home and preserving the sanctity of *Shabbos* was highly esteemed in God's eyes. I was ignorant and very heavily brainwashed. This was not Raymond Webster's vision. Children were a hindrance to God's call on a person's life. They took up time, energy and resources and did not give in return. And so, about two weeks after giving birth to our first child, I was back at work. It was not because we needed the money—nor was it because the school could not manage without me—it was simply because I needed to work in order to be acceptable before God.

Our lease had run out in the furnished apartment and we did not want to renew it again for another year. To find an apartment within Kiryat Chabad available for a minimal rent from the housing authorities, and not to have to sub-let from a tenant who had moved away, was unheard of in those days. Upon serious investigation, however, we found out that there was one. It had been unoccupied for over a year. It was so unbelievably filthy no one wanted to deal with it. And so when Chaim was just four weeks old, we moved in.

It was on the fifth floor of a thirteenth storey building, and was fifty-five square meters, including the laundry room and bathrooms. When Chananiah stretched his arms out wide, he touched both walls! Broken filthy furniture scattered the floor of every room. Strange, cave-like drawings in black paint covered most of the walls, and the windows were covered with dark, colored stick-on plastic, rather like cheap imitation stained glass windows. The kitchen sinks and bathtub were dark brown. But most of all the entire apartment was occupied with gigantic two and three inch black bugs which would not die even when sprayed with a whole can of bug spray. A long, hot, wash cycle in the washing machine did not finish them off either. By accident, one was in the machine one day for a full hour of heavy revolutions and boiling hot water, and after the cycle, it simply crawled out and trundled away.

We set about cleaning the place up. It would have made perfect sense for us to hire some *bochurim* to help us move the furniture, but at the time we did not think of it, and so struggling, the two of us carried down the stairs, and through the huge courtyard of Kiryat Chabad, every piece of junk in order to throw it down into the wadi. This was after a long hard day's work of cooking and doing secretarial work at school, nursing the baby, and changing him with cloth diapers which we washed ourselves each day.

The housing authorities painted the walls with cheap white paint. The floor was so filthy Chananiah washed it three times with the strongest detergents and bleach, but alas, each time it looked no better than the first. To remedy the problem, I took a knife and laboriously scraped the dirt off each and every tile in the entire apartment. I sewed lace curtains for the windows and we bought couches. We had no beds, tables or chairs but we had what I considered necessities for a home. A couch and an iron and ironing board! Eventually, Chananiah made wooden bookshelves and a table, four chairs and four stools, and lastly we purchased beds!

❧

That *Rosh Hashanah*, I was sitting on the couch in the living room when I felt a sudden nameless shifting inside me, a release. I felt that someone was letting go of me, and I realized it was God. For three years, I'd had a frequent, urgent "pushing" from within, a feeling that God was holding me by the hand and dragging me along a path. I had deeply desired the truth on my own, and I had searched; but there were so many times when despair had virtually throttled me, and I knew that without that "pushing" I would never have climbed out of the ditch. There on the couch that day, I suddenly felt that God had let go of my hand. I floundered for a moment, and my insides were crying out, "No, wait—don't leave me—I'm not ready yet!"

It was as if God were saying, "You asked Me to show you, and I've shown you, I've brought you here. Now you're strong enough to go out on your own and choose for yourself. It's up to you."

I never felt that pushing again. I was lonely for a while afterward, but I realized that this was the way it should be. I'd had my initiation and was now in the same boat with the rest of the Jewish people. My *Yiddishkeit* would be exactly what I made of it.

There are moments when I look at my present life in comparison to the past, and the contrast strikes me as utterly bizarre. The Christians gave me a fairy tale. They led me through a noxious fantasy, making me all kinds of wonderful promises which never materialized. They set themselves up as models of humility, the "meek" serving God, but when I was in *yeshiva*, I began to realize that the very words "I am spiritual" were a contradiction in terms, and a display of outright arrogance; for if a person is really close to God, there is no "I," there's no self.

For years in Portfield, I struggled constantly with the availability of God. I knew that we were "buddies" walking "arm in arm," but in spite of His closeness, I couldn't explain the emptiness I felt. If He was so "available," how come I couldn't feel Him? Afterward, I understood that the Christians fill up their space with so much of themselves that there's no room for God!

Daily I faced the truth, and I knew that I had much work to do before I was even fit to stand in the outer courtyards of God. Judaism is hard work. Torah is hard work, but it's real work. I can't imagine what would have happened to me if, God forbid, I had woken up after eighty years in the Church and discovered, like the man in the fable, that the wheel I was turning was not attached to anything, that all my toil had been in vain. I think I too would have lost my mind.

I took nothing for granted, and I wanted always to cherish *Yiddishkeit*, and never suffer the innocent arrogant complacence I saw in the Church that could allow a person to presume an intimacy with God that did nothing more than feed his own ego.

But I still had a long way to go.

Firstly, I did not know anything at all about babies. I certainly knew nothing about being a nursing mother. I thought it was all so natural and obvious. You bring the baby to your breast, he sucks and is fed, and that's all there is to it. I never liked making a big deal about things and could not understand what the fuss and commotion was about. I do not know where I picked up in life the notion that everything is just straightforward and simple, but unfortunately it was not so easy.

Chaim cried. I breast-fed him. He sucked hard and long with perspiration covering his tiny face, and after about half an hour, he was screaming again. We thought he was colicky, so we swaddled him tightly with cotton fabric and took turns pacing the floors for hours to try to settle him.

When I took him to the baby clinic, they screamed at me and insisted I give him formula and cornflour, which was fine by me. I sensed my baby was hungry, but when I arrived back in Kiryat Chabad, all the mothers adamantly insisted that if I did anything other than breast-feed, I was affecting the *emunah* of my child. Rabbi Rosenfeld's wife, Rochel Leah, the one person I really trusted, was in America for the High Holidays. I decided I would wait until she returned to Safed, and whatever she told me to do would be the way to go. However, that took longer than expected. Chaim was born on the fifteenth of

Tammuz and the Rosenfeld's came back only after *Shabbos Bereishis*. By that time, Chaim was his same birth weight. Chaim's weak high-pitched cry had a desperate edge to it.

Mrs. Rosenfeld took one look at him and sprang into action, as did her eldest sister, Gittel. Gittel fed Chaim—anything and everything. She made cereals and patiently spooned them into him and we gave him bottle after bottle of formula. We had him checked privately by the head doctor of the pediatric ward in Rivkah Siev Hospital, Dr. Cohen. Dr. Cohen reminded me of my own pediatrician when I was a child. He was old enough to be my father and experienced enough to exude confidence and security. An added bonus was his South African origins, fluent English, and cultural compatibility, all of which is priceless when living in the Middle East.

After listening intently to the entire saga, checking Chaim and finding him, thank God, healthy and responsive, despite his low weight, he asked to watch me nurse the child.

Instantly he saw the problem.

"Madam, your breast is obstructing the chin of the child, preventing him from sucking. He is working much too hard simply to obtain a few drops of milk. This is the reason he is sweating excessively and falling asleep prematurely," he announced delightedly. He felt my breast.

"There's plenty of milk in there," he declared triumphantly as if he was looking over a prize-milking cow. "Now, pick it up! Pick all of it up. That's right!"

I thought I would die of embarrassment, maybe I had read too many James Herriot books. It was a tall order for a former Miss Priss, but then, on the other hand, it was a real relief to know that Chaim was fine.

I was exhausted. Each day I dragged myself out of bed, prepared Chaim to come with me for the entire day to work and ran to catch an eight o'clock bus into the city. I made lunch and supper for over fifty students with no help at all. I was responsible for cooking and cleaning up all the huge saucepans and kitchen floors, leaving the place in good shape for the next day. Chaim stayed in a cubbyhole in the kitchen in an effort to shield him from the multitude of draughts. I propped his bottles and changed his cloth diapers as often as needed, and awaited the times when students would run into the kitchen between classes to take him out for fresh air and fun.

Besides the kitchen work, I took care of the office and taught sewing classes to the students. Wearily, I got us back home between eight and eight-thirty at night when Chananiah would help me to do laundry and clean the apartment.

Until about eleven at night, the door did not stop with desperate people needing help with one thing or another. Problems ranging from help with graphics and art, to sewing or cooking, to speaking or singing, all of which I initially answered in the negative, but all of which I ended up doing. I was a prize catch for the Middle East and a total "*fryer.*" They pleaded and begged at the door. They insisted, demanded, imposed. It was a *mitzvah. Tizki leMitzvos!* On the other hand, I was still running on Raymond Webster's gas. I could have said no, but it would be years before I would have the inner confidence and strength to do so. From eleven-thirty at night until six o'clock in the morning, I awoke as any mother with a newborn infant, several times for bottles, nursing and changing diapers.

My body was already back to its natural cycles and Chaim was less than three months old. Birth control is frowned upon in Orthodox circles for many reasons. Firstly, according to Torah, the commandment to be fruitful and multiply refers to Jew and non-Jew alike. Secondly, the belief that the key to fertility lies in God's hand alone is deeply rooted, and comes together, with the faith that each child brings with it into this world its own supply of blessing and sustenance.

I was deeply exhausted: body, soul and mind. My reservoir of energy had been drained many years previously by Raymond Webster. The enormous weight of the stress of leaving the Church, reestablishing myself amongst Orthodox Jews, moving to Israel, marrying and having a child was taking its toll, not just physically, but emotionally as well.

The thought of bringing another child into the world was daunting.

I plucked up courage and went to my rabbi who happened to be a halachic authority. He in turn called his *Rav* and they discussed the situation between themselves. The verdict was that I could abstain from having children for two weeks!!

Instantly my blood boiled as anger rose up in my being. I turned and fled to our apartment, feeling trapped and overwhelmed.

I should have spoken up. I should have discussed the situation with my husband. I could have done many things but I was too well trained by Raymond Webster. Mine was just to do or die.

DIE, DIE! I would burn in hell. I would go to eternal damnation if I did not procreate. Like a lamb to the slaughter, I prepared myself in the necessary way to be together with my husband. We still did not have any beds. We slept in the living room. My bed was the couch; Chananiah's bed was a thin mattress belonging to Chaim's playpen. There, on that hard floor, in that corner, with overwhelming anger in my soul, our second son was conceived.

Each day, I continued to work at the same frenetic pace, and would *shlep* Chaim, with his carriage and baby equipment for the day, on the bus to Machon Alte.

Nausea overtook me. I vomited at least fifteen to twenty times each day. Many times I would be literally up the entire night emptying my guts into the toilet bowl, but I always went to work the next day, and the next. I continued to be swayed to subserviance and self-sacrifice until one day, my body finally screamed at me, enough!

It was a few days before Passover. We had planned to go to England to spend Passover with the Weinbaums, and Chananiah's mother was going to meet us there so that she could see Chaim. I was five months pregnant. The morning of the departure I knew that there was no way I would be able to make the journey. I started having contractions at a steady pace. My doctor wanted to hospitalize me instantly, I had such serious dehydration, but I begged him to let me stay home as I did not want to spend Passover in the hospital. He finally agreed and prescribed heavy duty medication to stop the contractions, giving me clear instructions that I must remain in bed for two weeks. I promised but knew there was no way I could lie around on the eve of Passover.

Immediately upon our arrival home, I went downstairs to the vegetable store to prepare for a few Passover necessities, saddened that we could not go to England, but thrilled not to be in the hospital. Suddenly I began to tremble, a little at first, then more visibly. The storekeeper called Chananiah to come down and help me and he got me safely in bed. We chuckled at the intelligence of the doctor. He knew exactly who he was dealing with and had prescribed a dose of medication strong enough to keep me grounded.

It was obvious I would not be able to continue with the kitchen work, and so after Passover, I went back to work in the office only. I still took Chaim with me each day and another couple of months passed by. In my ninth month of pregnancy, Chaim became very ill with a stomach problem and was so seriously dehydrated he was hospitalized for a week. The day after we brought him home, he came down with dysentery and as soon as he was over that, he came down with measles and had such a raging fever he was almost having convulsions. All night long, we bathed him and watched over his trembling form until finally the fever broke. For a few days, all was calm.

Less than one week later, at almost midnight on the fifteenth day of the month of *Av*, when the moon is full and round, I gave birth to our second son. He was circumcised eight days later and was named Nechemiah. He was such a quiet, undemanding baby—I thought he was an angel. When he awoke, even as an infant, he waited patiently until I went to him.

There was only one problem. My body refused to heal, and without warning, just five weeks after birth, I awoke one morning and could scarcely move. My joints were so stiff and awkward, I could not lift my baby. I could not bend my fingers or my knees and my body was ravaged with fever.

Shortly afterwards, I was diagnosed with rheumatoid arthritis. We took on full time home-help to care for the boys and manage the home, including such tasks as shopping and cooking.

I was so frustrated that no sooner had the inner pain in my life been annihilated than physical pain took over.

Chananiah was always extremely patient and sensitive with me, and he allowed me to be myself, to express all facets of my personality; he kept me company in everything I wanted to do, whether it was having a philosophical discussion or giggling and laughing like a pair of young children. I was in a position where I would have remolded myself to fit the standards of the family I married into, done anything in order to be accepted as an Orthodox Jew, and in the process I know that I would have crushed out parts of my personality. My husband was much further advanced in *Yiddishkeit* than I was when we met, but he never pressured me in any way.

A year or two after we were married I would still occasionally have the urge to sing a hymn—a *"parev"* hymn about God but nevertheless, a hymn. I'd turn to Chananiah and say, "Listen, I just have to sing," and he never panicked. I had horrific visions of the average husband dashing off to the local rabbi, screaming, "I need a divorce!" But Chananiah was wise; he knew that I would sing one or two hymns and then it would be gone from me, and he was right. Gradually these impulses died out completely.

In spite of the fact that I knew I'd found truth, it took me a long, long time to convince myself that the Church had not only been the wrong place, but actually an evil place, and that Raymond Webster had been nothing more than an arrogant glutton obsessed with his own power. It was very difficult for me to view the whole experience objectively, and two years later I was still telling my husband that perhaps Webster had simply been misguided. I thought I might have been fantasizing about my life in the Church, creating a black myth in my head which hadn't actually been all that severe. And then, my brother came to Israel with his non-Jewish wife and son, and when I looked at him, I was speechless. The Church had a stranglehold on his entire personality; there was a white cobweb of sterile holiness blanketing his features, his mannerisms, even his speech. A stinging chill went through me, for I could see so clearly that the Church had actually been much worse than I'd suspected, and I had forgotten.

I had premeditated that I was going to ask my brother if he wanted to be circumcised and had refreshed my mind with the verses I would need to support the importance and validity of my offer.

I was in total shock at my brother.

"Do you really think I could?" he answered with immediate interest.

"Of course," I replied immediately, "there are plenty of Russians who come to Israel and are older in age and have never been circumcised. I can arrange it in Jerusalem."

Holding back tears, he answered simply, "I would love to."

"You know," he continued, "I have never told anyone what I am going to tell you now."

Philip told me that he had been sent to Gateshead many years earlier to missionize. He was one of the select few whom Webster had assigned to recruit Jewish converts, and he had gone to visit the local synagogue on Saturday morning.

"An old man came up to me in the synagogue and asked me if I was a newcomer. I said, 'yes.' Then he asked me if I was Jewish, to which I replied, 'my mother's Jewish,' and then finally he inquired if I was circumcised, explaining that he would like to have me called up to the Torah, and somehow I couldn't bring myself to lie to him. Tonica, I will never forget the look of pain in that old man's eyes. It has haunted me day and night for years, and that's why I wanted Rafi circumcised. I knew the Jews did not accept him as a Jew, but if anyone would ever ask him in his life if he was circumcised he would be able to answer in the positive."

Philip's *Bris Mila* was the highlight of his entire trip. We arranged for him to be given a Jewish name and to be called up to the Torah, so in a way he had a *bar-mitzvah* at the same time!

With tears streaming down my face, I begged him not to go back to Raymond Webster.

"I'll be fine," he promised. "I'll find my way. Don't worry."

Raymond Webster was not impressed with Philip's physical attachment to the Jewish faith, and soon after his return to England, Philip, together with his wife and son, moved to Seattle as an assistant pastor in a "Messianic Temple."

Back in Safed, a group of high school girls had heard about my odyssey and begged me to speak to their class. I finally consented and invited them over to our home for the evening. It was the first time Chananiah was to hear the entire saga.

About four hours later, when the girls had finally left, Chananiah innocently asked, "Tova, why did you stay there? I wouldn't have lasted a week in that place. How did you remain for nine years?"

"Chananiah, I was so naive—an innocent baby away from home. I thought I would become a holy person, and as a result make the world a better place."

"Tova, I have never told you this, but when I was in *yeshiva* I had the most disturbing dream. In it I saw a girl in church with a huge cross around her neck and the *Rosh Yeshiva* kept on telling me that this was the girl I was to marry. I was so disturbed by this dream. I searched within myself to see the reason why, even though I had been living in Israel for several years already and was fully committed to Torah and *mitzvos*, I would have such a dream. The worst part was that this dream kept on recurring over the course of a year until finally, the girl took the cross, broke it off of its chain and threw it onto the ground. I never had the dream again."

I begged my husband to think back and work out exactly when that year was, and to our utter amazement, it took place during the last year that I was in the church—as I was prostrating on the floor for hours at a time, begging the One True God to allow me to find Him.

&

That year after *Simchas Torah*, I looked around at the drunken "corpses" in the *shul* and realized that every single one of those men would get up the next morning and *daven shacharis*, that each one was doing his utmost to serve God. How different from a life of abstinence! When I saw them, I thought of my dream about the man who peeled off his outer covering to reveal an inner beauty. The outer guise of Judaism, much of which had initially seemed so inappropriate to my uninitiated eye, really sheltered a greater holiness than I could ever imagine. I had finally learned what these men had always known: that remaining in tune with life, elevating the physical world by using it to do God's commandments, was much harder work and required a much deeper level of devotion than retreating behind high walls and trying to be "spiritual."

Sometimes, people say to me, "Don't you think you've just changed one set of clothes for another? One religion for another?" And my response to them is that I'm not religious at all anymore. I was before, but I'm not now. Religion to me is self-righteousness. It's an outer garment that people don and shed at will, and it can take any form—anything from Hinduism to macrobiotics. People are very religious about their diets, their clothing, their careers. It's a crutch that they latch onto, not something that is intrinsic to their existence.

A Jew does what God wants, and that is his entire essence. It's not an outside, extra thing, it's the meaning of his being. When he does a *mitzvah*, he has done what he was meant to do; it is a natural act, totally apart from his ego.

Each day now, when I say *Shema* or make a meal for my family, I come a little further into the courtyard. Each week, when I light my

Shabbos candles or do any of the other *mitzvos,* I come nearer to God than I ever was from a lifetime of fasting, praying, lying on the floor, meditating, holy spirits, or any other device that takes a person further and further away from the reality of the world. God is more real and close to me now than He ever was in the first twenty-five years of my life.

❧ NOT THE END, BUT JUST THE BEGINNING... ❧

TO Play with Fire does not have a fairy-tale ending; to walk hand in hand with God requires a mammoth amount of stamina. And so, dear reader, having emerged from my experiences new, enriched and totally whole, I share with you now some of the conflicts and dilemmas that I continue to wrestle with along life's way, and valuable lessons and insights that I have gleaned from the many challenges that I have faced.

Since my return to Judaism, my relationship with my family, in particular my parents, has been fraught with difficulty. I love my parents deeply—they are amongst the most amazing and beautiful people I know—and it pains me to see their pain. I know that in her heart of hearts, my mother is very happy that I have embraced my Jewish roots, but at the same time, she cannot believe that I have chosen this path without any qualms.

My father continues to fast for me twice a week, in the hope that I will return to the Christian fold. He often cries over the prospect that all the family will be in heaven with the exception of me. He simply cannot come to terms with the fact that for all eternity he will never see me again. I was always a "daddy's girl," and having to live with the knowledge that I have so deeply hurt my parents, my father in particular, in order to find personal fulfillment, is tough to live with. I persisted in the college for two extra years in an earnest attempt to make it work, because I couldn't bring myself to crush my father. In the end, though, I simply had to escape so as to preserve my own sanity.

My first reunion with
my parents since my
break from the Church,
spring 1982, Midlands.

Our wedding day,
August 8, 1983, *Rosh
Chodesh Elul,* Safed.

My meeting with the Lubavitcher Rebbe, November 4, 1991.

My sister Margaret (left) and me
during a visit to England in the 1990s.

Uncle Sammy (center) with the President of Israel, Yitzchak Navon (far right).

My father (far right) at a family celebration.

Nechemiah's *bar-mitzvah*, 15 *Av* 5758, July 20, 1997. From left: Nechemiah, Chananiah, me and Chana Batya (10 days old).

Yosaif's *bar-mitzvah*, 29 *Nissan* 5761, April 11, 2000.
From left: Chaim, Chananiah, Chana Batya, me and Yosaif.

As for the rest of the family, one brother and one sister have sadly passed away. I continue to have a wonderful relationship with my remaining brother and sister, even though my sister is married to a non-practicing Catholic. We have all endured so much trauma that we give each other the space and freedom we each need to find our individual paths. I actually call my sister from time to time, and we roll about with laughter as we reminisce over our years with the Websters. Each one of us carries huge amounts of pain, my parents included, but we are looking forward, thank God, not back.

People often ask me if I ever experience any doubts. The answer is no. Certainly, I have felt overwhelmed at times, but I feel secure in my existence as a Jew in the eyes of God. To live within the confines of the Torah is, for me, the greatest freedom of all. With my return to Judaism, I have abandoned the idea of perfection. The Torah was not given to angels, but humans: humans who are fallible and who, yes, do occasionally err. True strength is the courage to admit one's weaknesses, and to grow and change as a result.

❧ ACKNOWLEDGMENTS ❦

IT has not been an easy journey to get the odyssey of my life back into print. It was while standing in one of Rabbi Menachem Mendel Schneersohn's infamous "dollar lines," amidst tens of thousands of other individuals, that the Rebbe turned to me personally, thanked me for publicizing my story and gave me a *brochah* to spread it. This task of bringing the story of my life back to you was made all the more easier by the generosity and care of four outstanding individuals, Harvey Finkel, Joseph Jacobowitz, Max Munk, and Mitch Zahler, to whom I will be forever indebted.

My profound gratitude goes to Binnum and Sandy Weinbaum and their beautiful children for nurturing the Jewish embryo within me for nine months and allowing me to grow into my new identity as a Jewess. Equally, my deep appreciation goes to Rabbi Joseph Rosenfeld and his dear wife Rochel Leah, for not only taking me into Machon Alte (Safed, Israel), where I truly learned what it means to be a Jew, but for opening up their lives and home to such an extent that their families became mine, and in due time, my husband and children's also.

My sincere thanks to Rabbi Shmuel Arkush for his diligence in seeking me out, to Rabbi Yitzchok Sufrin for sorting me out, and to Rabbi Shmuel Lew for helping me out.

My heartfelt gratitude to Rabbi Manis Friedman for only ever seeing me as a Jew, and whose confidence in my capabilities launched me into this project. It goes without saying that without his fatherly advice and guidance, I would not be what I am today, nor would this book ever have been written.

Last but not least, my deepest appreciation to Mr. and Mrs. Abraham Rubashkin for giving so freely and so selflessly of themselves; for teaching me through example the principles of *tzedokah* and *chesed*, and for extending such tremendous warmth and encouragement during this very difficult transition.

And to the myriads of you, so many it is impossible to name each one—you mean so much. You taught me abundantly and shared so freely. Thank you—I will be eternally indebted to you all.

Tova Mordechai
Safed, Israel
Kislev 5762 / December 2001

Afikomen. *Matzoh* eaten as dessert at the end of the *Seder* meal

A"h. Abbreviation of *Alav Hashalom*, meaning "may his soul rest in peace"

Aleph. First letter in the Hebrew alphabet

aleph-bais. The Hebrew alphabet

aliyah. The act of settling permanently in Israel; literally, "going up"

Bais Din. Rabbinical court

bedikas chometz. The search for leaven particles which takes place on the evening before Passover

benching. Grace After Meals

bimah. The podium in the synagogue on which the Torah scrolls are placed for reading

bris. Circumcision

brochah. Blessing

Bubbie. Yiddish for grandmother

challah. Bread eaten on the Sabbath and holidays

chasunah. A Jewish wedding

Chassidus. Hassidism

Cheder. A primary grade school in which Jewish subjects are taught

Chesed. Act/s of kindness

Chol Hamoed. The intermediary festival days

chometz. Leaven or any substance containing leaven

Chumash. The Pentateuch

daven. To pray

eiruv. A legal physical boundary around a private or public area which allows for the transporting of objects on *Shabbat* or *Yom Kippur*

Erev. The day preceding *Shabbat* or a festival

esrog. Citron, used on *Succos* along with the *lulav*

farbrenghen. A gathering or get-together

fleishig. Containing meat or used for meat products (e.g. utensils)

frum. Religious

Haftorah. Oone of the biblical selections from the Books of the Prophets read after the weekly Torah portion in the synagogue on *Shabbat*

Haggadah. The text used at the Passover *Seder*

Halacha. Jewish Law

Hallel. A prayer comprising Psalms 113–118 which is chanted on many Jewish festivals

Hamantashen. A three-cornered pastry eaten on the festival of *Purim*

Hamapil. The final evening prayer, said immediately before going to sleep

Hashem. God

hashkofah. Philosophy or outlook

havdalah. The "separation" prayer recited at the end of *Shabbos* or holidays

kaddish. A prayer said at certain points in the service and by mourners

kashrus. The kosher status of one's home or of a product

kibbutz. An Israeli collective farm or settlement

kiddush. The blessing recited over wine before the meals on *Shabbos* and festivals

kippah. Head covering for males

kohain. Priest, descendants of Aaron, who performed the holiest Temple rituals. Today the priests' primary function is to bless the congregation

Kollel. Talmudical seminary for married men

Kol Nidrei. An Aramaic prayer nullifying vows which is chanted in the synagogue on the eve of *Yom Kippur*

Lamdeini. Literally, "teach me"

Leshanah Tova. Literally, "To a good year"

lulav. Palm branch, used ritually on *Succos*

machzor. Festival prayer book

Maimonides. The Rambam, Rabbi Moses ben Maimon, Spanish-born philosopher and Torah scholar (1135–1204)

mechitzah. A partition separating the men's and women's sections in the synagogue

megillah. Scroll containing the story of Esther, read on *Purim*

menorah. Lamp lit on the eight nights of *Chanukah*

mezuzah. Parchment scroll inscribed with Deuteronomy 6:4–9 and 11:13–21 and placed in a case affixed to the door post

middos. Character traits

mikvah. Ritual immersion pool

milchig. Containing milk or used for milk products (e.g. utensils)

minyan. A quorum of ten men required for group prayer

mitzvah. A commandment or Jewish law; also, a meritorious act

mon. The food miraculously supplied to the Jews during their forty-year sojourn in the desert

Motzei Shabbos. Saturday night; literally, "the outgoing of *Shabbat*"

negel vasser. Ritual washing of the hands upon arising in the morning

posuk. Scriptural verse

rav/rabbonim. Rabbi/s

rebbetzin. Yiddish for a rabbi's wife

Rosh Chodesh. Literally, "the head of the month"; the one-or two-day minor festival celebrated at the beginning of each Jewish month

Seder. Jewish ceremonial service and meal held on the first night of Passover in Israel and on the first two nights in the Diaspora

Seudah. A meal; often used to denote a meal eaten on a special occasion

Shabbos. The Sabbath

Shacharis. The morning prayer service

Sheitel. A wig worn by a married woman

Shalom aleichem. Hebrew greeting, literally, "Peace to you"

Shema Yisrael. Prayer which affirms the Jewish belief in one God, said twice daily

sheva brachos. Literally, "seven blessings"; the seven Jewish marriage blessings. They are also the festivities that take place in honor of the new couple during the first week of marriage

shiva. The seven ritual days of mourning

shofar. Ram's horn, blown as part of the service on *Rosh Hashanah*

shul. Synagogue

siddur. Jewish prayer book

simcha. Joyous occasion

succah. Booth in which Jews live during the week of *Succos*

tallis. Prayer shawl worn by men

tamei. Impure, unholy

tefillin. Phylacteries

Tehillim. Psalms

"Tizki leMitzvos". Phrase meaning "may you merit performing further *mitzvos*"

treif. Not kosher

tumah. Impurity, unholiness

tzedokah. Charity or the act of giving charity

tzitzis. Fringes attached to a four cornered garment, commonly worn by Jewish men

yarmulka. See *kippah*

Yom Tov. The generic name for a festival day; literally, "good day"

Zeidie. Yiddish for grandfather

Zemiros. Traditional songs sung at the *Shabbos* meals

RECOMMENDED READING

*T*O *Play with Fire* is a personal story and should not be used as a halachic or philosophic reference. For detailed discussion on the differences between Judaism and Christianity, the following books are recommended:

The Real Messiah by Aryeh Kaplan, NCSY/Orthodox Union Publications, New York City

The Disputation at Barcelona and The Book of Redemption by Nachmanides, translated by Rabbi Dr. Charles B. Chavel, Shiloh Publishing House, New York City

Jews for Nothing by Dov Aharoni Fisch, Philip Feldheim, Inc., Spring Valley, New York

The Jew and the Christian Missionary by Gerald Sigal, Ktav Publishing House, New York City

You Take Jesus, I'll Take God by Samuel Levine, Hamorah Press, Los Angeles, California

ABOUT THE AUTHOR

*T*OVA Mordechai resides in Safed, Israel with her husband and four children. She holds a full-time position at the Chaya Mushka and Machon Alte seminaries as an assistant to the directors. Tova also lectures throughout the world on being Jewish in contemporary society.